P9-BJM-920

The
ILLUMINATED
LANDSCAPE

WITHDRAWN

The ILLUMINATED LANDSCAPE

A Sierra Nevada Anthology

Edited by Gary Noy and Rick Heide

Foreword by Robert Hanna

Illustrations by Joe Medeiros

Sierra College Press, Rocklin, California
Santa Clara University, Santa Clara, California
Heyday Books, Berkeley, California

© 2010 by Sierra College Press

All rights reserved. No portion of this work may be reproduced or transmitted in any form or by any means, electronic or mechanical, including photocopying and recording, or by any information storage or retrieval system, without permission in writing from Heyday Books.

"American Woman" by Jordan Fisher Smith is a work of nonfiction based on the experiences of the author. However, names, places, physical descriptions, and other particulars have been changed. For that reason, readers are cautioned that details in the text do not correspond to real people, places, or events, and any resemblance to real people is coincidental.

Library of Congress Cataloging-in-Publication Data

The illuminated landscape : a Sierra Nevada anthology / edited by Gary Noy and Rick Heide ; foreword by Robert Hanna ; illustrations by Joe Medeiros.
    p. cm. -- (A California legacy book)
  ISBN 978-1-59714-128-4 (pbk. : alk. paper)
1. Sierra Nevada (Calif. and Nev.)--Description and travel. 2. Sierra Nevada (Calif. and Nev.)--History--Anecdotes. 3. Travelers' writings, American--Sierra Nevada (Calif. and Nev.) I. Noy, Gary, 1951- II. Heide, Rick, 1943-

    F868.S5I55 2010
    917.94'4--dc22   2010000435

Cover Photograph: Lone Pine Peak, Duane Shoffner
Book Design: Lorraine Rath
Printing and Binding: Thomson-Shore, Dexter, MI

This California Legacy book was copublished by Santa Clara University, Heyday Books, and Sierra College Press. Orders, inquiries, and correspondence should be addressed to:
    Heyday Books
    P. O. Box 9145, Berkeley, CA 94709
    (510) 549-3564, Fax (510) 549-1889
    www.heydaybooks.com

Printed in the United States of America

10   9   8   7   6   5   4   3   2   1

green press INITIATIVE

Heyday Books is committed to preserving ancient forests and natural resources. We elected to print this title on 30% post consumer recycled paper, processed chlorine free. As a result, for this printing, we have saved:

26 Trees (40' tall and 6-8" diameter)
8 Million BTUs of Total Energy
2,457 Pounds of Greenhouse Gases
11,834 Gallons of Wastewater
718 Pounds of Solid Waste

Heyday Books made this paper choice because our printer, Thomson-Shore, Inc., is a member of Green Press Initiative, a nonprofit program dedicated to supporting authors, publishers, and suppliers in their efforts to reduce their use of fiber obtained from endangered forests.

For more information, visit www.greenpressinitiative.org

Environmental impact estimates were made using the Environmental Defense Paper Calculator. For more information visit: www.papercalculator.org.

CONTENTS

Chapter 3: Always Afternoon—1860–1899

Chapter 4: Shadows in the Alpenglow—1900–1950

Chapter 5: Twilight of the Dawn—1951–1990

Chapter 6: Quiet-Colored End of Evening—1991–Present

FOREWORD

Robert Hanna

In my veins courses the blood of John Muir. The famous conservationist was my great-great-grandfather. In 1906 his daughter Wanda married Thomas Hanna, my great-grandfather.

Along with the blood of the Muir family, the Hanna family, and the blood of California, the spirit of the Sierra Nevada also exists in my heart. It is part of my legacy, *our* legacy, of the mighty mountain range about which my great-great-grandfather spoke and wrote with such eloquence that his words live on—now for more than one hundred years.

In my family's possession is a crystal inkwell used by John Muir in his writing quarters. This is the inkwell he used when writing most of the words that helped shine light on his favorite place in the world—the magnificent Sierra Nevada. When I hold his inkwell in my hands and feel its glassy smoothness, its cold, inanimate contents, I can't help but think of how Muir turned lifeless ink into multidimensional stories and palpable visions of experiences in his beloved mountains. These include an encounter with a Sierra bear, windstorms while riding atop a tall Douglas fir, and glacier hikes in Alaska with the wee dog Stickeen. His words released a flood of memories and brought to life the fondness and passion that so many of us have also experienced in wilderness yet find so hard to express.

My affiliations to John Muir were downplayed in my youth, but I came to know more about Mr. Muir later in my life. I'd thought that our family's cabin, nestled in a remote glacial gorge along the Sierra's steep eastern slope, was simply an expression of domestic frugality—no modern conveniences by design, no waste of resources, and no need for contemporary contrivances. But I learned that this old cabin was an extension of Muir himself. Purposely spartan, it was to be a refuge for the family, a method for getting away from the city. My Uncle Tim encouraged me to look around. He said that here on the mountaintop we would never be closer to God than at that very moment. My visits to nearby Yosemite were filled with visions of the awe and majesty of the mountains, but I remember only peaceful, calming feelings from these childhood outings. Such intimate experiences with nature connected me with the Muir in my blood, even though I didn't know it then.

Through gatherings at various colleges and institutes, I have thoroughly enjoyed becoming reconnected to the passion that this man had for the Sierra—and for all wild things and wild places. I've attended scores of celebrations, anniversaries, and events recognizing the famous mountaineer, and over time I've endeavored to learn more about the man and his tireless efforts to promote wilderness preservation. I have begun to feel the passion and the purpose that he had for defending countless creatures and wild places that desperately needed protection and yet had no voice.

Not long ago I participated in a semester-long class at Sierra College in which Muir's "Range of Light" was the center of attention. It was an interdisciplinary course on the Sierra Nevada, led by professors Joe Medeiros and Gary Noy, and they invited us to examine, from myriad perspectives, this massive bioregion and all that it represented to the millions who used it, lived in it, worked in it, and loved it. We discussed the Sierra's natural history, its human history, how the range has been interpreted, and how it has been misused, as well as how to conserve it and keep it healthy for future generations. The Sierra College class helped me reawaken and nourish those stubborn Scottish blood cells flowing through my veins, and reconnect with a legacy that my great-great-grandfather started.

In the pages that follow are the stories and observations of writers who, like Muir, have been transfixed by the Sierra Nevada. The scope of the writings is as breathtaking as the range itself. From their voices we hear of the profound connection of customs and landscape. We consider the extraordinary transformation that occurs with the arrival of European culture and the overwhelming impact of the California Gold Rush. We read beautiful descriptions of the Sierra along with concerns about its future. We experience heart-pounding adventure and tragedy. We see how this remarkable environment can influence our perspective, both physical and emotional. We encounter the power of the written word to enhance the splendor of a spectacular geography and of our understanding of ourselves.

This varied collection, so thoroughly exploring the history, culture, natural landscape, and issues confronting the Sierra Nevada, comes at a critical moment. My great-great-grandfather's beloved Range of Light is threatened even more than in days gone by. Rapid population growth and unchecked development apply increased pressure on the limited resources. Our understanding (or, perhaps more accurately, our misunderstanding) of forests and forest health remain as contentious as ever. The specter of climate change looms large, fueling worrisome speculation for the future of the snowpack upon which many millions are dependent for our ever-growing thirst for water. It seems the very character of the Sierra Nevada is in danger. This collection reminds us of the remarkable appeal and value of the Sierra Nevada, and what can be lost if we do not act.

Just as Muir's impassioned writings inspired early efforts to use the land wisely, so too are new generations of writers inspiring, energizing, and challenging us with their words. Each of these authors has unique talents, but they share the same essence. Everyone has a voice. Everyone can make a difference. Any individual has the power to become a John Muir. The spirit is within each of us, waiting to be set free. It is a special place, as he said, where one can "climb the mountains and get their good tidings. Nature's peace will flow into you as sunshine flows into trees. The winds will blow their own freshness into you, and the storms their energy, while cares will drop off like autumn leaves."

PREFACE

Everything has a beginning.

For the Sierra Nevada, the genesis is found in the place itself—a 25,000-square-mile wondrous construction with granite cliffs as walls, wildflowers as carpet, and a star-studded sky as the ceiling.

From the largest tree to the tiniest insect, the mountain range exhibits the vast spectrum of life and the processes that influence existence. Sculpted granite, roaring cascades, towering forests, wildflower-draped meadows, thunderous storms, thousands of windswept crystalline lakes and streams, all of this inhabits the region and haunts our dreams. It is a land browsed by mule deer and bighorn sheep, roamed by the mountain lion, guarded by the golden eagle, and enchanted by the flash of a rainbow trout. Yet we can only appreciate this beauty, this complexity, this interdependence with the aid of the range's extraordinary quality of light.

This special light is unique to the Sierra Nevada. It is a light that envelops the trees, the peaks, and the creatures, bathing each subtle texture with a warm glow and creating a splendid illuminated landscape. As John Muir rhapsodized in his classic 1912 book *The Yosemite*, "It seemed to me that the Sierra should be called, not the Nevada or Snowy Range, but the Range of Light. And after ten years of wandering and wondering in the heart of it, rejoicing in its glorious floods of light, the white beams of the morning streaming through the passes, the noonday radiance on the crystal rocks, the flush of the alpenglow, and the irised spray of countless waterfalls, it still seems above all others the Range of Light." These words still ring true today, as anyone who has encountered this phenomenon can attest.

From the beginning, the Sierra Nevada has inspired artists. Whether one's discovery was eons ago or just yesterday, the remarkable diversity and breathtaking majesty of the range captivates the imagination and stirs the soul. The powerful conjunction of the ageless splendor of its landforms, the continual metamorphosis of its human agents of change, and the startling variety of the Sierra Nevada natural world are endless creative resources for the camera, the brush, and the pen. The vitality and grandeur of the Sierra Nevada offers no greater palette for the muse.

The narrative of the Sierra Nevada is a study in contrasts. Equal parts heroic effort and tragic consequence, it is a legacy of golden dreams and shattered hopes, feverish exploitation and hard-won preservation. It is an account of constant commemoration and the promise of a clean slate. It is a heritage of celebrated racial diversity and shameful discrimination.

A major theme of Sierra Nevada history is invention and re-invention in a land apart. In short, it is a story as old as the sunset and as new as the dawn—the eternal human drama enacted on a monumental stage.

In this anthology we present accounts of the remarkable Sierra Nevada experience. From the origin myths and social rituals of the first inhabitants, to the first impressions and dreams of those who would later dominate, to the breathless and frequently moving descriptions of both visitors and settlers, to the often sad transitions that mark cultural change, the Sierra Nevada story unfolds. And it is with this origin that we realize an immutable truth: the Sierra Nevada illuminates our existence. It shines a light on majestic stretches of unmatched beauty, but also on an understanding of our place in the world.

The readings collected here show remarkable range as well. Reports requiring copious scientific detail stand beside gentle poetic lyricism, and the voices of men, women, the young, the old, the outsider, the native, the victim, and the victimizer are all heard. We are honored that three authors—Joe Medeiros, Maria Melendez, and Jordan Fisher Smith—have written works especially for this anthology. There are words of inner turmoil and grandiose claims, of personal doubt and cultural exultation, of heartfelt rejoicing and bewildered resignation, of the struggle to survive and the will to understand, and of wonderment and worry. These are the thoughts of people grappling with a new reality and struggling to make sense of the situation. These are bulletins from the heart and mind, sometimes bracketed with wrenching uneasiness in the gut.

The geography presented in *The Illuminated Landscape* encompasses the entire Sierra Nevada region. The Sierra Nevada is one mountain range, 430 miles long and 40 to 80 miles wide. The anthology embraces not only the majestic granite spine of the range but its western foothills and eastern escarpment as well. California's Gold Country or Mother Lode, as part of this same bioregion, is another important part of the book. We also include neighboring areas, such as the high desert stretches of eastern California and western Nevada.

As with any anthology, the selection process was a difficult one. There are so many possibilities, and making the ultimate decision as to what should be included was daunting. As a result, one of your favorite excerpts may be missing; the good news is that it can always be added to another edition of this compilation.

It is our wish that this collection will serve as a record of the awe that this magnificent range has inspired. But we also hope that it will serve as a reminder that the Sierra Nevada is a living organism that is constantly beset by environmental and social challenges. A goal of this anthology is to raise awareness of this spectacular setting and to create an appreciation of what is at risk in the Sierra Nevada today. Since the dawn of history, the Range of Light has provided important resources and an invaluable refuge for our spirits. As the sanctuary comes under attack—whether from population pressures, climate change, or some other danger—we have a responsibility to protect this breathtaking mountain cathedral. The stakes are high and the road will require thoughtful planning and complete dedication, but if we succeed, the reward will be profound: the Sierra Nevada will remain the extraordinary illuminated landscape for generations to come.

Let's head on up the trail.

Gary Noy
Rick Heide

CHAPTER ONE

Golden Misty Dawn

To 1840

In the beginning, the Sierra Nevada was both their world and their dream.

For the Native Americans, the Sierra Nevada was home. For thousands of years, a wide diversity of tribes occupied the range, their numbers estimated at about 100,000 people in the 1830s. While the population density was significant, the impact on the land was relatively benign, as the native cultures used but did not abuse their surroundings. A deep and abiding connection to the land developed, and their perception of their environment became inseparable from their culture. They were part and parcel of the same universe.

For others, most notably Europeans, the Sierra Nevada was a new vision and a splendid opportunity. The Sierra Nevada—"snow-covered mountains" in Spanish—was already seen as a wondrous, almost mythical landscape. The Spanish and, later, European inhabitants appreciably displaced the native cultures beginning in the late eighteenth century, and continued contact with European and Euro-American societies led to substantial changes in native life patterns during this period, setting the stage for the wholesale interference of subsequent decades.

Natives suffered greatly from early contact with explorers.

1

They were introduced to European diseases, which reduced their population. Still others were forced into labor on missions or ranchos. This bred understandable mistrust of the European interlopers, and many tribes retreated farther into the protected recesses of the range. Some natives responded with armed resistance, by taking livestock, or by destroying property. In turn, this led to punitive actions by the Europeans, creating a long-term cycle of disruption for the native Sierrans.

The Yokuts, "The Origin of the Sierra Nevadas and Coast Range"

The Yokuts are Native Americans who inhabit parts of the San Joaquin Valley, the foothills of the Sierra Nevada, and the Southern Sierra. The Yokuts consisted of up to sixty ethnically and linguistically separate tribes prior to European contact, and although their population decreased more than 90 percent from 1850 to 1900, there are still a number of Yokuts in today's Sierra Nevada.

For the Yokuts, the Sierra Nevada began with an unlikely contest between two old combatants—Hawk and Crow. This ancient story was edited by Katharine Berry Judson in 1912. In this selection, references are made to Tulare Lake, a large lake, now dry, in the San Joaquin Valley; and to Ta-hi-cha-pa Pass in the southernmost Sierra Nevada, now known as Tehachapi Pass.

Once there was a time when there was nothing in the world but water. About the place where Tulare Lake is now, there was a pole standing far up out of the water, and on this pole perched a hawk and a crow. First one of them would sit on the pole a while, then the other would knock him off and sit on it himself. Thus they sat on top of the pole above the waters for many ages. At length they wearied of the lonesomeness, and they created the birds which prey on fish such as the kingfisher, eagle, pelican, and others. Among them was a very small duck, which dived down to the bottom of the water, picked its beak full of mud, came up, died, and lay floating on the water. The hawk and the crow then fell to work and gathered from the duck's beak the earth which it had brought up, and commenced making the mountains. They began at the place now known as Ta-hi-cha-pa Pass, and the hawk made the east range, while the crow made the west one. Little by little, as they dropped in the earth, these great mountains grew athwart the face of the waters, pushing north. It was a work of many years, but finally they met together at Mount Shasta, and their labors were ended. But, behold, when they compared their mountains, it was found that the crow's was a great deal the larger. Then the hawk said to the crow, "How did this happen, you rascal? I warrant you have been stealing some of the earth from my bill, and that is why your mountains are the biggest." It was a fact, and the crow laughed in his claws. Then the hawk went and got some Indian tobacco and chewed it, and it made him exceedingly wise. So he took hold of the mountains and turned them around in a circle, putting his range in place of the crow's; and that is why the Sierra Nevada is larger than the Coast Range.

The Yokuts, "Prayer for Good Fortune"

For the Yokuts, being one with the landscape is not a foreign notion; it is the essence of their character. This prayer was recorded by the distinguished University of California anthropologist Alfred Kroeber (1876–1960) from the Yawelmani Yokuts of the Kern River.

My words are tied in one
With the great mountains,
With the great rocks,
With the great trees,
In one with my body
And my heart.
Do you all help me
With supernatural power,
And you, day,
And you, night!
All of you see me
One with this world!

"A monstrous bird called the *Ong* lived in a big
nest in the middle of Lake Tahoe"

The Washo, "Weh Hai Ge Ge A"

*The Washo are a Native American people who traditionally made their
home in the region surrounding and including Lake Tahoe. Primarily
a hunting and gathering culture, the Washo had a population of about
fifteen hundred prior to contact with Euro-American settlers. Today—
although such counts can be controversial—descendants of the original
Washo probably number about two thousand.*

*"Weh Hai Ge Ge A" translates as "Washo traditions." This old caution-
ary tale was collected in 1976 by the Washo community for the Inter-
Tribal Council of Nevada.*

A long time ago, a monstrous bird called the *Ong* lived in a big nest
in the middle of Lake Tahoe. This gigantic man-eating bird picked
up unsuspecting Washo. These people, who had not heeded persistent
warnings, ventured into open areas where the monster could easily see
and capture them. The Washo greatly feared this monster, who was so
powerful that the wind from his wings could bend the trees when he
flew near shore.

One day the *Ong* snatched a Washo and took him to the huge nest in
the middle of the lake. The Washo pretended to be dead, but watched
the *Ong* carefully all the time. Luckily, the monster was not very hungry
and had another person to eat. As the Washo watched, he noticed that
the *Ong* closed his eyes to chew. This curious habit gave the Washo
an idea. Each time the monster took a bite and closed his eyes, the
Washo threw several arrowheads into his mouth. By nightfall, all these
arrowheads had made the beast very sick. As the monster moaned and
groaned with pain, a terrible storm raged. By morning the *Ong* was
dead, so the Washo pulled a feather from its tail. Using the feather as a
boat, he reached shore and returned to his home.

The Konkow, "Old Gambler's Song"

The culture of the Konkow, or Northwestern Maidu, is centered in the northern central Sierra along the branches of the Feather River, on the upper Butte and Chico Creeks, and in the Sacramento Valley along the lower courses of those streams.

This traditional song was collected in the 1870s.

I am the only one, the only one left.
An old man, I carry the gambling-board;
An old man, I sing the gambling song.
The roots I eat of the valley.
The pepper-ball is round.
The water trickles, trickles.
The water-leaves grow along the river bank.
I rub the hand, I wiggle the tail
I am a doctor, I am a doctor.

William Joseph, "Football Big-Time"

The Nisenan of the Sacramento Valley and Sierra Nevada foothills enjoyed a rough-and-tumble relay game they called "football." The idea was to carry or kick a ball to a goal and then back to the starting point, all while avoiding the opponent. Gambling on the contest was frequent, and the stakes could be high. Football games were sometimes held between men and women, which permitted, and even encouraged, the sexes to intermingle and become better acquainted.

Describing centuries-old traditions, the following two stories were collected in 1930 or 1931 from a Nisenan named William Joseph of Auburn, who was seventy-seven years old at the time.

In the early days the Indians had football "big-time." Very early in the morning the other team put up a great deal of money [i.e., many beads]. If they made goals at both ends of the field they won. Then they danced to make fun of us. When we finished we ate breakfast. After breakfast we played football again. At midday we rested, then we ate. When the sun came round to the west we were at it again; we only quit when the sun went down. We danced at night.

When it was dawn we played football again. We did that for two or three days and only quit when we had lost our money, valuables, baskets, clothes, bows. Before we parted we ate, the men of this side treating the other side. Then the men of the other side treated this side. Only then did we go each on his way. That was football "big time."

* * *

Sometimes a football game was called, the women playing the men, putting up valuables and even money to bet with each other. The men kicked the ball with the foot while the women caught it with the hand and ran with it. The men hugged the woman who carried the ball. When they tickled her belly, she threw the ball to another woman.

If that woman missed, a man kicked the ball with the foot. Another woman caught it with the hands and ran with it towards their goal. Then a man hugged her again. When he threw her on the ground and rolled her around, she threw the ball. In that way another woman caught it and brought it towards their goal.

The men played with the foot, the women played with the hand: that was their playing together so that a man could hug the woman he loved. The women on their part took every opportunity to hug the men they loved; the game was like that so that this could be done.

"Didn't my power come from the mountain upon whose back are rocks which never hurt it?"

Jack Stewart, "My Mountain"

The Owens Valley Paiute live in the eastern Sierra Nevada in the Owens Valley, which is located almost entirely in today's Inyo County. Jack Stewart, whose Paiute name was Hoavadunaki, was nearly one hundred years old when this story was collected in 1927 by anthropologist Julian Steward. Jack Stewart was already a grown man by the time the first whites arrived in Owens Valley, in 1861.

In this story, Stewart describes his childhood in the shadow of Birch Mountain, located on the great granite spine of the southern Sierra just north of Mount Whitney.

When I was still a young man, I saw Birch Mountain in a dream. It said to me: "You will always be well and strong. Nothing can hurt you and you will live to an old age." After this, Birch Mountain came and spoke to me whenever I was in trouble and told me that I would be all right. That is why nothing has happened to me and why I am so old now.

Not long after this, when I was bewitched, my power helped me out. I had been visiting one of the villages at Pitana Patu and had started back home to Tovowahamatu when I met a man who invited me to his house to have something to eat. It happened that a witch doctor lived in this vicinity, but thinking little of this, I ate a big meal of boiled meat and then went toward home. After walking a few miles, I became very ill and had a passage of blood. I went on, but became weaker and weaker, and when I reached the hot springs, a few miles north of Big Pine, I lay down under a bush. For a long time I lay there, and when it was nearly dark I got up and said to my soul, "Since my mountain has spoken and told me

that I shall not die, why should I die here?" I went on to Tovowahamatu
and made my camp just outside the village. The next day I entered the
village.

A "stick doctor," who was my cousin and lived at Pitana Patu, was
called. He arrived that night and came to my bed. He said: "How are you?
Are you still there?" I was desperately sick by now and had hardly any
strength to answer, "I am almost gone." Then the doctor began to work.
He twirled his fire drill until the end was hot and put it to my stomach
until it burned me. Then he worked over my body with his hands. This
felt good. But he did not sing; stick doctors do not do this. After a while
he said: "Soon the morning star will rise up, and after that there will be a
star brighter than the morning star. You will feel better then." It happened
as the doctor said. When the bright star arose, I felt better and soon I was
entirely well. This man, this doctor, probably helped me some, but it was
my own power, Birch Mountain, which saved me....

Once, I became so sick that I gave myself up for dead. My soul admitted
that I would have to die. I died and my soul started southward, toward
Tupusi Witu. While I was traveling, I looked down and my soul saw a
stick in the ground not quite as tall as a man. I went to the stick and dug
my foot into the ground about ankle deep. Then I turned to the stick and
said, "This is the *muguavada* ["soul stick"]." I seized the stick and looked
back toward my mountain, which was my power. I knew then that I
would be all right and live forever, for whenever a soul going south sees
the "soul stick," it knows that it will come back.

My soul then came back to Tovowahamatu, and the next day I set
about doctoring myself. I went into the mountains and gathered roots
which I boiled and put on my sores. Soon I recovered....

My power from Birch Mountain helped me just as much in hunting
as in sickness. My favorite deer-hunting ground was in the Sierra Nevada,
west of Tovowahamatu, in the vicinity of my mountain. It often happened
that after I had seen deer and tried to sneak up on them they caught wind
of me and started toward my mountain. I would say: "My mountain, I
want you to help me get some of these deer. They are yours and live
upon you." After this I always overtook one and killed him while he
was lying under a mountain mahogany tree or some other shelter on
the mountain side. This happened many times. After such a killing, I
remained overnight on the mountain and treated myself to a feast of deer
meat. The next day I returned to the valley. I distributed the meat to my
people and sold the upper part which belongs to the hunter.

Once when I started up Big Pine creek toward the foot of my mountain,

I asked my power to make it easier for me to hunt deer. I said to it: "Now, great mountain, I wish that you would give me some of your deer to eat. You have so many on you. If you would give me some, I wish you would give them at your foot, not far up." Soon I came upon a group of deer at the very foot of the mountain as I asked, and killed one. As I was packing it back to my village, I saw a herd of mountain sheep. I stopped and hid to watch them, and as I waited one came toward me. I killed it with little trouble and went on to the valley, carrying both animals. I distributed and sold them when I got home. My mountain is always good to me.

The deer and mountain sheep were a heavy load, for I had packed them both at once down to the valley. But when I was a young man nothing was too heavy for me. I enjoyed carrying a large, heavy load. Didn't my power come from the mountain upon whose back are rocks which never hurt it? It is this way with me. Once I proved my strength carrying a stump which no one had been able to move. My soul had told me that no mountain would be too high for me to climb, nor any place too far away for me to go to. That is why I have always been able to get to every place for which I have started.

I had two calls to be a doctor. In early manhood I had my first chance. My mountain spoke to me in a dream and asked me to become a doctor. It told me how I should cure. I would not have to dance, it told me. I should sit by my patient all night, holding my hands on him and singing. When the morning star should rise, I should get up and dance a few rounds, and then hold out my hand, when something like snow would appear in my palm. I should place this in my patient's mouth and blow. But my soul refused this power, for I knew that sometime in my old age it would fail me and I would die. I knew the work was dangerous. I had had another dream and saw blood on a rock, meaning that I should be killed if I were to become a doctor. I refused the power because I wished to live to be a very old man. All I had to do was refuse....

Whenever I dream, especially if it is a bad dream which means trouble, I talk to something in the darkness. I talk to my power. That is why I have lived so long. If I had not called upon my power, accident or disaster would have overtaken me long ago. Even when I have sex dreams, I talk to the night, because if I should pay no attention to them, they would continue and lead to fits....

When I die, my soul will go south to the land of the dead. It will stay there by the ocean and I will have nothing to do but enjoy myself.

The Maidu, "Mountain Lion and His Children"

The Maidu's original homeland was in the northern Sierra Nevada east and south of West Mountain, known today as Mount Lassen. Some of their stories have been collected in the 1991 book The Maidu Indian Myths and Stories of Hanc'ibyjim, *by William Shipley.*

Shipley (b. 1921)—then an ethnolinguist on the faculty of the University of California, Santa Cruz—described his "incredible good fortune" to have met Lena Thomas Benner and her family while he was a graduate student in the 1950s. Benner's daughter, Maym Benner Gallagher, "perfectly bilingual in Maidu and English," became Shipley's teacher and mentor. Three decades later, after Gallagher's death, Shipley found the linguistic keys to a richer understanding of the tales of Hanc'ibyjim— the man whom Gallagher called "the last great Maidu storyteller."
In contrast with many early translations of Native American stories, Shipley's translations were not performed by non-Native speakers alone but utilized Native speakers in the process, making his versions especially poetic and profound.

Mountain Lion went deer-hunting.
When he had packed some food on his back, he went,
and after he had gone quite a ways along,
he set up his camp for the night.
He slept, and, in the morning, he awoke and ate.
Then he strung his bow and went off to hunt.
After hunting all around a while, he shot a deer,
and, along toward dark, he carried it back to camp.
He gutted the deer, cut it into pieces and hung it up.

In the morning, when the meat was somewhat dry,
he stuffed it into a bag and set out for home.
He went along until he got there.

Now, his two children, who usually came out to meet him,
were nowhere to be seen.
The place was deserted.

"What can have happened?" he asked himself.
He threw the deer meat down; then he sat on the ground
and peered into the house.
He saw that someone was lying over alongside his wife.
They were lying there together.

"I wonder where my two children could be," he thought.
He peered into the house again, but he saw nothing.
"Where, where could they be?"

He searched around, found their tracks,
and followed them down the trail.
But then he turned back again,
and, when he got to his house,
he set fire to it.
He burned the house to the ground.

Now earlier, when the two children were playing in the house,
a man crawled in and sat down.

"Your father, where has he gone?" he asked.

But they didn't answer him. They were frightened.
They jumped over behind their mother.

Then the old woman spoke.
"He's gone deer-hunting," she said.

"Good!" said the man.

He sat there cross-legged awhile,
then he crawled over and got up close beside her.

"What are you doing?" she asked.

"What am I doing!" he exclaimed.
"I'm going to make you my woman!"

"What are you talking about?
I already have a man," she said.

"Nevertheless," he said, "I'm going to make you my woman."
And he grabbed her.

"Because you and I have done like this together,
men, talking bad and stealing women,
        will say: ·
'It's all right! Even in olden times,
they used to do bad things to women
so that they had children!'
The women will believe them,
and, even though they already have a man,
they will take another one."

So saying, the man lay down beside her,
and the woman said nothing.

Meanwhile, the two children cowered by the fire.
Then, holding each other's hand,
they crept out of the house.
After they stood around outside for awhile,
they started off.

By and by, they came to an anthill,
tore it open with their hands,
and crawled in.

Angrily, they set off, went along for awhile,
and made camp nearby.

The sister was the younger, they say,
and her brother was a little bigger.

They had already gone
when that old man, their father,
returned from hunting and burned down the house.

Then after that, the old man searched for them.
He followed their tracks, but he couldn't find them.
He circled all around to the places where they often played,
looking for traces of them.
He went weeping and crying—every day he cried.
He searched and searched for signs of them,
but he saw nothing.
Nowhere could he find any trace of them.

He went around up there in the North Country,
looking everywhere—everywhere.
Then he went southwards, going all around.
He went east and north again,
searching for their tracks.
He circled around everywhere, throughout the land,
but he still found no trace.

He went further and further away.
"To what part of the world could they have gone
so that I cannot see their trail?" he pondered.

He went on and on—toward the sunrise.
He turned and went northwards again.
"Where, oh where could they be?
Shall I never find them?" he asked himself.
Day after day he wept, but he kept on searching.

Finally, he came back to the place he had started from.
He just sat down and stayed there, crying.
"I have wandered through many a country," he said,
drying his tears.
"I must go home again!"

So he set out for home.
He went through many different places
until he got back to his house.

Then he followed the tracks
which the children had made long before.
He went along.
A little way from the house,
in a solitary place, the tracks suddenly stopped.

He didn't know how that could be.
"What am I to do?" he wondered.
After he had stood there for awhile,
he took a look around and spied the anthill.
He scraped away the sand,
and there he saw a hole going down and down.
He crawled into it.

Now, there, nearby,
was the place where the children had made camp.
He saw their tracks going away from there.
He stayed the night in that same place.
In the morning, he got up and set out again.
He went along until he came to their next campsite,
a little further on.

When his sister grew tired,
the boy had picked her up on his back, it seemed.
And, after he had carried her a little ways,
he had put her down again.
They had kept on doing that,
getting a little distance,
then stopping again for the night.

From their tracks, Mountain Lion saw what they had done.
He saw their camping place as he went along
and, a little beyond,
he, himself, spent the night.

The children had killed some birds and eaten them.
By the time they had gotten that far,
they had grown a little bigger.

It looked as if they had gone on and on,

and, a little further on, again they made camp.
There they had dug up camas bulbs
and made an evening meal of them.

Mountain Lion came to that place
and continued on his way.

And again, a little further along,
he came to their camping place.
And, when that old man got there,
he himself spent the night.

At a place further on,
the children had shot some ducks.
They had dug camas, and all kinds of things to eat,
and they had made their evening meal.
When the old man got there,
he saw what they had done,
and, when he had eaten that same kind of food,
he slept.
In the morning, he ate again and went on his way.

Going on like that, the old man ate what there was to eat.
He kept going, always camping where they had camped.

After he had travelled a far distance,
he came to one of their camping places.
They had killed a fawn there.
They had made a bow.
They had left the bow behind, along with a little seed-beater.
They gathered seeds with it, and then left it behind.
And then, they had gone on their way.

The old man came to that same place and stayed there.
He took down the deer, which was hanging up,
and roasted it. He cooked some camas in the ashes.
He ate.
In the morning, when he woke up,
he ate some more of the roasted deer meat and the camas.

Then he went, and he travelled along,
and, again, he came to a place where the children had stayed.
And *there* a *big* deer was hanging up.
A gathering basket, a digging stick and a big bow were left behind.
Well-made things were left behind.

When he got there,
he roasted meat from the deer,
he baked some camas,
and, raking it out with the gathering basket,
he served it up and,
when all was well prepared,
he ate his evening meal.
And in the morning, when he woke up,
he did the same thing again.
He roasted some deer meat,
baked some camas,
prepared everything nicely
and served it out on a willow platter.
When he had eaten, he went away.

After he had gone along for a while,
it seemed as if he might be about to catch up with the children.

He went along until he came to another of their camping places.
There, they had shot a brown bear, gutted it and hung it up.
They had nicely prepared the bear skin
and had left all this behind.
And they left behind a little burden basket,
and a willow tray,
and also some camas which they had dug.

When the old man had gotten there,
he thought: "Now I'm really about to catch up with them!"

He took down some of the bear meat which was hanging there,
and he roasted it and ate his evening meal.
Then, when he had slept, he got up and ate again.
And, afterwards, he went on his way.

Now, when the children had gone on,
they had left a little hut behind.
They had covered it over with bark and brush
and had camped there for the night.

Mountain Lion arrived there.

A burden basket and a sifting tray were left behind.
There was a quiver hanging there.
Deer meat was hanging up.
Bear meat was hanging up.

When he got there, he built a fire.
He took down some of the deer meat and roasted it
and ate it.
Then he slept,
and, in the morning, when he woke up,
he roasted some more of the deer meat
and ate it.
Then he went on his way.

He travelled and travelled
until he came to yet another place where they had camped.
And, when he got there,
he saw that there was a black bear skin hanging up.
And they had left a fisher-pelt quiver,
and a burden basket and a sifting tray.

"I think I've almost caught up with them!" he said.
And again, in the morning, when he had finished eating,
he went on his way.

Now, Mountain Lion had grown very old.
He had come so very far, travelling and travelling.
When he looked far ahead,
he saw a great winter lodge there.
He kept going along until he got there.
He was very old.

He sat down beside the lodge,

and, stretching out on the ground, he lay there.
The brother and sister looked out at that very old man.
"Who has come?" they asked.

Then the old man's daughter crawled out of the door.
"He surely looks like my father," she said.

Then her brother crawled out too.
He looked the old man over carefully,
but his father had grown so old
that his son could not quite recognize him.
He went back into the house,
brought out his bow,
and shot the old man lying there.

His father died.

Later, he picked the old man up in his arms,
and carried him down and laid him in a spring of water.

And after that, in the morning,
when the old man had become a youth again,
he came to life and rose up out of the spring.
And he went into the lodge,
and there was his daughter with her husband and children.
And when Mountain Lion came in,
they gave him food,
and when they had all eaten, they talked together.

His daughter said:
"When my brother and I saw that some strange person had grabbed
    our mother,
we became frightened and ran away"
Her brother said:
"And so, we finally got as far as this place."

So they all lived together in that country long ago.

That is all, they say.

Pedro Font, "Tuesday, April 2, 1776," from *Font's Complete Diary*

In the same year the Declaration of Independence was penned, California was still just a distant outpost of New Spain, the huge Spanish colony later known as Mexico. Although Spanish ships first visited these shores in 1542, more than two hundred years would elapse before the empire built its first permanent settlement in today's California—at San Diego in 1769. In 1775 and 1776, the viceroy of New Spain made Juan Bautista de Anza the head of two separate expeditions to Northern California—the first to explore the area, and the second to lead more than two hundred people to settle the port of San Francisco. The expedition of 1776 was difficult, featuring biting sandstorms and one of the coldest winters on record, but the party—which included many lower-class families eager to start a new life in a faraway and unknown land—eventually reached its destination.

Friar Pedro Font, a Franciscan missionary, was chosen to accompany the expedition both for his services as chaplain and for his ability to read latitudes. It was while scouting for the expedition near today's Walnut Creek that the friar observed something immense in the distance. He called it "a great Sierra Nevada," which means "snowy mountains" in Spanish. It was the first recorded use of the name to describe the mountain range.

After midday we set out from the mouth of the Puerto Dulce, and at five o'clock halted on the banks of the arroyo of Santa Angela de Fulgino, having traveled in all some seven long leagues.—Seven leagues.

The direction of the six leagues covered this afternoon was two leagues east along the top of the hills close to the water, and one east-southeast up a canyon which had some oaks and other trees, by which we again came out at the top of the hills near the water. From this height we saw that the water here makes a bend on this side and widens out to about twice the width of the mouth, and that on the other shore directly opposite this place a point of land juts out a little and near it there is a rock or farallón within the water. Looking northeast we saw an immense plain without any trees, through which the water extends for a long distance, having in it several little islands of lowland. And finally, on the other side of the immense plain, and at a distance of about forty leagues, we saw a great Sierra Nevada whose trend appeared to me to be from south-southeast to north-northwest.

CHAPTER TWO

The Opening Eyelids of Dawn

1841–1859

For thousands of years, Native Americans were the only people aware of the Sierra Nevada; while there may have been isolated, undocumented visits by non-natives, the range remained almost exclusively the domain of local tribes. That began to change in the early nineteenth century, however, when new arrivals came to explore and a few decided to stay.

In the 1820s and early 1830s, hardy adventurers such as Jedediah Smith and Zenas Leonard crossed the range and, as stories of their adventures filtered back to the East Coast, soon more Americans headed toward the Sierra Nevada. Most of these early migrants passed through the mountains on their way to the fertile fields of the Central Valley, but a handful remained in the promising mountain landscape. The journey was extremely dangerous, and some travelers never made it through the Sierra Nevada at all. The most famous of these disasters was the Donner Party, whose failed attempt to cross the range in 1846 led to tragedy. (This chapter includes an excerpt from James D. Houston's fictionalized account of the events.)

Although first Spain and then newly independent Mexico claimed nominal control of the Sierra, few of their people ventured into the range. Mexico relinquished its claim to the area in the Treaty of Guadalupe Hidalgo, which ended the war of 1846 to 1848.

Momentous change came to the region after January 24, 1848, the date when James Marshall discovered gold at Sutter's Mill, in the little foothill village of Coloma on the American River. Marshall's strike ushered in the California Gold Rush, considered by many scholars to be the single largest voluntary migration of people for a single purpose since the Crusades. Although most of the arrivals were young men from "back East," people came from every corner of the world. The impact on the Sierra Nevada was enormous, as thousands upon thousands swarmed the range to search for the elusive golden flake. In just a few years, the land was stripped of its bounty through destructive mining techniques, agricultural development, lumber harvesting, and hunting and gathering of animals and plants—in some cases to extinction.

In the blink of an eye, a way of life changed. Gone were the days of limited mining technology, relatively small Euro-American communities, and their seasonal use of the range. A new, semi-permanent, and often lawless society emerged. Native Sierran peoples became victims of organized and unorganized violence, disease, and displacement, and both their populations and their cultures suffered dramatically.

This chapter's selections represent the changes that occurred during this tumultuous time in the Sierra—the cultural collisions, the arduous experience of traversing the range, accounts of early contact between the newly arrived and the landscape, and the rapid growth of the often raucous Gold Rush communities.

"You may all think it is just a dream,—nevertheless, I feel that it will come to pass"

Chief Winnemucca, Peter Burnett, and John Bigler

The period immediately following first contact involved unprecedented cultural transition and strife between native and non-native populations. The following three excerpts dramatize the severity of this clash, which sadly fulfilled Chief Winnemucca's apocalyptic vision.

Chief Winnemucca was an important leader of the Northern Paiute, a tribe concentrated on the eastern cusp of the northern Sierra Nevada and throughout northern Nevada—the primary entryway to the Sierra and the goldfields via the California Trail. In 1883, Sarah Winnemucca, the chief's granddaughter, recalled his warning to the Paiutes in the 1840s about the coming "greatest immigration."

Peter Burnett arrived in California via the Oregon Trail during the early days of the Gold Rush, and when the Golden State was organized in 1849, Burnett was elected the first governor. In 1850, California was admitted to the Union as the thirty-first state, and Burnett continued serving as governor until 1851. The following excerpt is from his 1851 annual message.

John Bigler, the third governor of California, was in office from 1852 to 1856. Bigler was an ardent supporter of the widely held belief that the new dominant culture (i.e., European Americans) were a "civilizing influence" on the region, a belief that sometimes led to extreme measures, such as bounties offered by local California governments for dead Indians. In 1852, Governor Bigler commented on the course of the state's progress in a speech to the California State Senate.

I dreamt this same thing three nights,—the very same. I saw the greatest emigration that has yet been through our country. I looked North and South and East and West, and saw nothing but dust, and I heard a great weeping. I saw women crying, and I also saw my men shot down by white people. They were killing my people with something that made a great noise like thunder and lightning, and I saw the blood streaming from the mouths of my men that lay all around me. I saw it as if it was real. Oh, my dear children! You may all think it is just a dream,—nevertheless, I feel that it will come to pass.

CHIEF WINNEMUCCA

That a war of extermination will continue to be waged between the two races until the Indian race becomes extinct must be expected; while we cannot anticipate this result with but painful regret, the inevitable destiny of the race is beyond the power and wisdom of man to avert.

PETER BURNETT

I assure you, sir, that I deplore the unsettled question of [Indian] affairs in the North; but the settlement of new countries, and the progress of civilization have always been attended with perils. The career of civilization under the auspices of the American people, has heretofore been interrupted by no dangers, and daunted by no perils. Its progress has been an ovation—steady, august, and resistless.

JOHN BIGLER

John C. Frémont, from *Report of the Exploring Expedition to the Rocky Mountains in the year 1842, and to Oregon and California in the years 1843–'44*

John Charles Frémont (1813–1890) was a well-known and self-promoting explorer during the nineteenth century. He achieved great wealth and fame during his life but died in poverty, a victim of poor judgment and rash investments. Although court-martialed and convicted of mutiny and disobedience in 1847 for actions during the war with Mexico, he returned to Washington, D.C., as one of California's first United States senators in 1850. In 1856, the "Great Pathfinder" also became the Republican Party's first presidential candidate, shocking the political world by winning eleven states, including New York.

Frémont's 1845 report of his two most famous expeditions to the American West is part survey and part rip-roaring adventure. In this selection, Frémont describes an ultimately successful crossing of the Sierra Nevada just south of present-day Carson Pass—named after Frémont's scout, Kit Carson—in the harsh winter of 1844. It also includes Frémont's "discovery" of what came to be called Lake Tahoe.

February 1st. The snow, which had intermitted in the evening, commenced falling again in the course of the night, and it snowed steadily all day. In the morning I acquainted the men with my decision, and explained to them that necessity required us to make a great effort to clear the mountains. I reminded them of the beautiful valley of the Sacramento, with which they were familiar from the descriptions of Carson, who had been there some fifteen years ago, and who, in our late privations, had delighted us in speaking of its rich pastures and abounding game, and drew a vivid contrast between its summer climate, less than a hundred miles distant, and the falling snow around us. I informed them (and long experience had given them confidence in my observations and good instruments) that almost directly west, and only about seventy miles distant, was the great farming establishment of Captain Sutter—a gentleman who had formerly lived in Missouri, and, emigrating to this country, had become the possessor of a principality. I assured them that, from the heights of the mountain before us, we should doubtless see the valley of the Sacramento River, and with one effort place ourselves again in the midst of plenty.

The people received this decision with the cheerful obedience which had always characterized them; and the day was immediately devoted to the preparations necessary to enable us to carry it into effect. Leggings, moccasins, clothing—all were put into the best state to resist the cold. Our [Indian] guide was not neglected. Extremity of suffering might make him desert; we therefore did the best we could for him....

February 2d. It had ceased snowing, and this morning the lower air was clear and frosty; and six or seven thousand feet above, the peaks of the Sierra now and then appeared among the rolling clouds, which were rapidly dispersing before the sun. Our Indian shook his head as he pointed to the icy pinnacles shooting high up into the sky, and seeming almost immediately above us. Crossing the river on the ice, and leaving it immediately, we commenced the ascent of the mountain along the valley of a tributary stream. The people were unusually silent; for every man knew that our enterprise was hazardous, and the issue doubtful....

February 3d....During the day several Indians joined us on snowshoes. These were made of a circular hoop, about a foot in diameter, the interior space being filled with an open network of bark.

February 4th. I went ahead early with two or three men, each with a led horse, to break the road. We were obliged to abandon the hollow entirely, and work along the mountainside, which was very steep, and the snow covered with an icy crust. We cut a footing as we advanced, and trampled a road through for the animals; but occasionally one plunged outside the trail, and slid along the field to the bottom, a hundred yards below....

Tonight we had no shelter, but we made a large fire around the trunk of one of the huge pines; and covering the snow with small boughs, on which we spread our blankets, soon made ourselves comfortable. The night was very bright and clear, and though the thermometer was only at 10°, a strong wind which sprang up at sundown made it intensely cold, and this was one of the bitterest nights during the journey.

Two Indians joined our party here; and one of them, an old man, immediately began to harangue us, saying that ourselves and animals would perish in the snow, and that if we would go back, he would show us another and a better way across the mountain. He spoke in a very loud voice, and there was a singular repetition of phrases and arrangement of words which rendered his speech striking and not unmusical.

We had now begun to understand some words, and, with the aid of signs, easily comprehended the old man's simple ideas. "Rock upon rock—rock upon rock—snow upon snow—snow upon snow," said he; "even if you get over the snow, you will not be able to get down from the mountains." He made us the sign of precipices, and showed us how the feet of the horses would slip, and throw them off from the narrow trails which led along their sides.

Our Chinook [Indian], who comprehended even more readily than ourselves, and believed our situation hopeless, covered his head with his blanket, and began to weep and lament. "I wanted to see the whites," said he; "I came away from my own people to see the whites, and I wouldn't care to die among them; but here"—and he looked around into the cold night and gloomy forest, and, drawing his blanket over his head, began again to lament. Seated around the tree, the fire illuminating the rocks and the tall bolls of the pines round about, and the old Indian haranguing, we presented a group of very serious faces.

February 6th. Accompanied by Mr. Fitzpatrick, I set out today, with a reconnoitering party, on snowshoes. We marched all in single file, trampling the snow as heavily as we could. Crossing the open basin, in a march of about ten miles we reached the top of one of the peaks, to the left of the pass indicated by our guide.

Far below us, dimmed by the distance, was a large snowless valley, bounded on the western side, at the distance of about a hundred miles, by a low range of mountains, which Carson recognized with delight as the mountains bordering the coast. "There," said he, "is the little mountain—it is fifteen years since I saw it; but I am just as sure as if I had seen it yesterday." [This "little mountain" was most likely Mount Diablo.] Between us, then, and this low coast range, was the valley of the Sacramento; and no one who had not accompanied us through the incidents of our life for the last few months could realize the delight with which at last we looked down upon it. At the distance of apparently thirty miles beyond us were distinguished spots of prairie; and a dark line which could be traced with the glass, was imagined to be the course of the river; but we were evidently at a great height above the valley, and between us and the plains extended miles of snowy fields, and broken ridges of pine-covered mountains.

It was late in the day when we turned toward the camp; and it grew rapidly cold as it drew toward night. One of the men, Fallon, became fatigued, and his feet began to freeze, and building a fire in the trunk of a dry old cedar, Mr. Fitzpatrick remained with him until his clothes could be dried, and he was in a condition to come on. After a day's march of twenty miles, we straggled into camp, one after another, at nightfall, the greater number excessively fatigued, only two of the party having ever traveled on snowshoes before....

February 8th....Scenery and weather combined must render these mountains beautiful in summer; the purity and deep-blue color of the sky are singularly beautiful; the days are sunny and bright, and even warm in the noon hours; and if we could be free from the many anxieties that oppress us, even now we would be delighted here; but our provisions are getting fearfully scant....

February 10th....The elevation of the camp by the boiling-point, is eight thousand and fifty feet. We are now one thousand feet above the level of the South Pass in the Rocky Mountains; and still we are not done ascending. The top of a flat ridge near was bare of snow, and very well sprinkled with bunch grass, sufficient to pasture the animals two or three days, and this was to be their main point of support. This ridge is composed of a compact trap, or basalt, of a columnar structure; over the surface are scattered large boulders of porous trap.

The hills are in many places entirely covered with small fragments of volcanic rock.

Putting on our snowshoes, we spent the afternoon in exploring a road ahead. The glare of the snow, combined with great fatigue, had rendered many of the people nearly blind; but we were fortunate in having some black silk handkerchiefs, which, worn as veils, very much relieved the eyes....

February 13th....We continued to labor on the road.[...]A party of Indians had passed on snowshoes, who said they were going to the western side of the mountain after fish. This was an indication that the salmon were coming up the streams; and we could hardly restrain our impatience as we thought of them, and worked with increased vigor.

The meat train did not arrive this evening, and I gave Godey leave to kill our little dog (Klamath), which he prepared in Indian fashion— scorching off the hair, and washing the skin with soap and snow, and then cutting it up into pieces, which were laid on the snow. Shortly afterward the sleigh arrived with a supply of horse meat; and we had tonight an extraordinary dinner—pea soup, mule, and dog.

February 14th. With Mr. Preuss, I ascended today the highest peak near us, from which we had a beautiful view of a mountain lake at our feet [Lake Tahoe], about fifteen miles in length, and so entirely surrounded by mountains that we could not discover an outlet. We had taken with us a glass; but though we enjoyed an extended view, the valley was half hidden in mist, as when we had seen it before. Snow could be distinguished on the higher parts of the coast mountains; eastward, as far as the eye could extend, it ranged over a terrible mass of broken snowy mountains, fading off blue in the distance....

February 16th....The night was clear and very long. We heard the cries of some wild animals, which had been attracted by our fire, and a flock of geese passed over during the night. Even these strange sounds had something pleasant to our senses in this region of silence and desolation....

On the 19th, the people were occupied in making a road and bringing up the baggage; and, on the afternoon of the next day, February 20,

1844, we encamped, with the animals and all the matériel of the camp, on the summit of the pass in the dividing ridge, one thousand miles by our traveled road from the Dalles of the Columbia. The people, who had not yet been to this point, climbed the neighboring peak to enjoy a look at the valley....

Thus, at the extremity of the continent, and near the coast, the phenomenon was seen of a range of mountains still higher than the great Rocky Mountains themselves. This extraordinary fact accounts for the Great Basin, and shows that there must be a system of small lakes and rivers here scattered over a flat country, and which the extended and lofty range of the Sierra Nevada prevents from escaping to the Pacific Ocean.[...]Thus this pass in the Sierra Nevada, which so well deserves its name of Snowy Mountain, is eleven degrees west, and about four degrees south, of the South Pass....

February 23d. This was our most difficult day: we were forced off the ridges by the quantity of snow among the timber, and obliged to take to the mountainsides, where, occasionally, rocks and a southern exposure afforded us a chance to scramble along. But these were steep, and slippery with snow and ice; and the tough evergreens of the mountain impeded our way, tore our skins, and exhausted our patience. Some of us had the misfortune to wear moccasins with parfleche [rawhide] soles, so slippery that we could not keep our feet, and generally crawled across the snow beds.

Axes and mauls were necessary today to make a road through the snow. Going ahead with Carson to reconnoiter the road, we reached in the afternoon the river which made the outlet of the lake. Carson sprang over, clear across a place where the stream was compressed among rocks, but the parfleche sole of my moccasin glanced from the icy rock, and precipitated me into the river. It was some few seconds before I could recover myself in the current, and Carson, thinking me hurt, jumped in after me, and we both had an icy bath. We tried to search awhile for my gun, which had been lost in the fall, but the cold drove us out; and making a large fire on the bank, after we had partially dried ourselves we went back to meet the camp. We afterward found that the gun had been slung under the ice which lined the banks of the creek.

Using our old plan of breaking the road with alternate horses, we reached the creek in the evening, and encamped on a dry open place in the ravine. Another branch, which we had followed, here comes in on the left; and from this point the mountain wall, on which we had traveled today faces to the south along the right bank of the river, where the sun appears to have melted the snow; but the opposite ridge is entirely covered. Here, among the pines, the hillside produces but little grass—barely sufficient to keep life in the animals. We had the pleasure to be rained upon this afternoon; and grass was now our greatest solicitude. Many of the men looked badly, and some this evening were giving out.

"Well, mother," I said, "if you never see me again, you do the best you can."

James D. Houston, from *Snow Mountain Passage*

James D. Houston (1933–2009) was the author of eight novels and numerous works of nonfiction. He has been honored by organizations including the Library of Congress and the Western Literature Association, and he has received two prestigious American Book Awards. Among his most popular works is Farewell to Manzanar, *which he co-wrote with his wife, Jeanne Wakatsuki Houston, and of which an excerpt appears in Chapter 4 of this anthology.*

The following excerpt is from Houston's novel Snow Mountain Passage *(2001), which tells the story of the Donner Party's tragic trip from Springfield, Illinois, to California. This selection is told from the perspective of an elderly Patty Reed, who was a child in 1846, when more than forty of the Donner Party's members starved to death near present-day Truckee, California, and a few, cold and hungry, resorted to cannibalism. Patty's father, James, had been banished from the party and arrived in California before the snows engulfed the straggling remnants of the wagon train high in the Sierra Nevada, and his struggle to rescue his young family became one of the most poignant elements of the entire episode. Patty herself became forever linked with the event as a·symbol of hope and the loss of innocence, and her doll remains on exhibit at Sutter's Fort in Sacramento, California.*

Some people say the darkest hour comes just before the dawn. Old sayings like that are easy to quote years later when you've had some time to think back over your life. You don't quote them when you're in the middle of that darkest hour and cannot see a flicker of dawn peeping through in any direction. Nobody was quoting it at the lake camp around about the middle of February, when every one of us was wasting away, some seeing things, others going blind. Keseberg's baby boy had died, and William Eddy's wife, Eleanor. In our family all that stood between us and starvation was three hides mama had conserved, and one morning Mrs. Graves showed up saying those hides belonged to her.

She was claiming them, she said, until mama could settle her debt. She had worked herself into a fit. This time mama was not to be outshouted. They stood in the snow screaming at each other, pulling those smelly cattle hides this way and that. Mama finally tore two of them loose. Elizabeth still held on to one. She had brought along her seventeen-year-old son, who was as skinny as a stick, like the rest of us, but mama didn't have enough strength left to go after Elizabeth and her son too. They dragged that one hide back to their cabin, and mama set to work scraping at the two we had left.

After that I remember sitting still a lot. My mind would simply go away. I don't know how many days went by. It was about the time our last square of hide was boiled up that we heard a voice from somewhere far off, a voice we didn't recognize. We were down inside the Breens' cabin, with just the fireplace light. A little streak of late afternoon was leaking down the stairwell. I didn't say anything. I had been seeing angels in the darkness and hearing them sing beautiful songs. Sometimes they would call to me, and in my mind I would answer. I listened for this voice to come again. And it did.

"Hallooww!" it called.

This time mama said, "Did you hear that?"

I looked around. I knew then everyone had heard it. Mama and Peggy Breen went scrambling for the ice stairs. I was right behind them. We came up into the light and saw men spread through the trees between us and the lake, big-bundled shaggy men, still calling, "Hallooww! Hallooww!" When they saw us they stopped and stared at what must have been a horrifying sight, witches and scarecrows rising out of the snow.

Mama's voice was just a scratchy quaver. "Are you...?" She could hardly speak. "Are you men from California?"

"Yes, ma'am," one fellow shouted.

She fell onto her knees, weeping and laughing. "Thank the Lord," she said. "You've come at last."

Others were climbing out of the cabins now, my baby brothers, and Phillipine, the whole Breen clan. Patrick's prayers had been answered, it seemed, and Virginia's too. In our eyes these men were saints. Maybe they were the angels I'd been hearing in the dark, their voices floating toward me from beyond the mountains to the west. Maybe one of them was papa. I scanned their frosted eyes and craggy faces. He wasn't there. He wasn't there. I said, "Where's papa?" my voice so tiny in the hubbub of sobs and hallelujahs mama didn't hear me.

Once they slung down their loads, it didn't matter who they were or how they got there. They had packed in biscuits and jerked beef. We groveled and wept and gobbled up the morsels passed around to us, and begged for more, but they knew better than we did what can happen when you try to fill a shrunken belly.

The leader was a fellow named Glover. He had come across the plains and had camped with our party a time or two along the Platte. Mama remembered him. That night he slept with us, while the other men divided up among the cabins. We didn't know it at the time, but they were almost as bad off as we were. Our pitiful shelters were the first warm spots they'd seen in three weeks of being wet and cold and worn down with the climbing.

Since that time I've heard it said that these men in the rescue party did it for the money. It's true that they were earning wages they couldn't have made any other way. This was two years before the Gold Rush. You could buy a pound of butchered beef for two cents and a whole chicken for fifty cents. Five dollars a day was a huge amount. But something else was driving them. It wasn't family. None of them had relatives to rescue. Maybe it was some sense of kinship for the big trek we would later call the Great Migration. They had all come across to California in the past six months. I happen to think it was more than that. From time to time in this life people actually do courageous things. In my view now, looking back, it was nothing but valiant, and I cannot fault any of them for what happened next.

Those seven men needed a lot more rest. They also knew the sooner we started out, the better. They'd come through two bad storms to reach us. Now the skies were clear. The big question was, Who to take? Counting our camp and Donner's camp there were over fifty still alive. Mr. Glover made promises. Rescue teams would be going back and forth, he said, until everyone was on the other side. Some folks were too weak to walk, or too sick. Uncle George Donner, for instance. The hand he cut trying to plane a new axle had festered and the infection had spread all through him. He couldn't travel, and his wife, Tamsen, she wouldn't leave without him. They sent two of their little girls and two of Jacob Donner's children. Lewis Keseberg was bedridden, but Phillipine was still healthy and not quite so loyal. She could hike out, she said, with their little girl, Ada. The Breens sent their two oldest boys, while the rest of the family stayed put a while longer, since they had some meat in reserve. As for us, mama had nothing left, not even a scrap of hide, so we all ended up among the two dozen who set out from the lake camp behind the rescue team.

Just before we left, Keseberg emerged from the hole leading down to his buried lean-to. No one had seen him for weeks. With his son dead and his wife and daughter leaving, he didn't want to live alone. He was hobbling down to widow Murphy's. He had cut a forked branch into a homemade crutch. His tangled beard was so greasy it looked gray instead of blond. The weeks of pain had lined his face. The way his tortured eyes blinked and squinted against the light, he was like a convict released from a dungeon. He didn't look at us. He just hobbled across the snow, wincing with each tiny step. I have to confess, I hoped then I would never see him again. What a relief it was to leave that man behind, to leave those dreadful cabins behind at last, the lice, the stink, the smoky darkness. I felt that I too had been imprisoned and was finally set free.

Up ahead, someone led the way in a pair of snowshoes. The rest of us were supposed to follow along, stepping where he stepped. If you had short legs like Tommy and me, it wasn't easy. We had to climb in and out of each deep step. Tommy was four, going on five. In the whole party he was the youngest one walking, and the smallest. I called back to him a few times, "C'mon, Tommy. Papa's gonna be here pretty soon." Then my breath gave out. I couldn't do both, call to him and climb in and out of those holes everyone ahead of us made deeper and mushier.

Mama urged us on, lifting us from time to time, but we fell farther behind with each step. The party had hiked about two miles, stretched out along the side of Truckee Lake, with me and Tommy right at the end, when Mr. Glover came back and told mama we were slowing everyone else down. If we couldn't make better time we'd have to go back to the cabins.

"I'm sorry, Mrs. Reed. I got to think about the welfare of the whole party and make it across while we got the weather on our side."

Mama said if we went back she'd go with us. The whole family would go back together and wait for another rescue team. Mr. Glover, he got real stern, said he couldn't let her do that. "Every person able to walk has to walk out of here. You go back with your children, you'll only eat the others' food. Everyone that goes helps them that stays behind."

Virginia and James Junior had started to cry. Mama begged Mr. Glover not to leave us. She said it wasn't fair, it wasn't right. He said he could tell by looking at us we were too weak to walk and we were too much to carry. Two of his men were already carrying infants, and there was still the summit trail to climb.

Mama couldn't stand what he was telling her to do. She looked around at the four of us, and what I saw then was the most terrible look I've ever seen on any face before or since. It was the wild, stark, near-madness that comes into the eyes when you have eaten almost nothing for weeks and your flesh wastes away and leaves the bones and sockets showing. And it was something else. It was the mother's bottomless terror. She had already climbed the summit trail. She knew what awaited us up there. She now had to face the fact that Tommy and I would both perish if we kept on going the way we'd been going, spindly as we were, and down to nothing, with no meat on our bones. She also knew returning to the cabins was no better, maybe even worse.

When Mr. Glover saw she could not speak, he said he would come back for us. Mama turned her anguished and accusing eyes on him. She made him promise that he himself would do this, and he said he would. When they got to Bear Valley, he told her, if no other rescue team had started in, he would turn right around and come back for the two of us.

Mama dropped to her knees in the snow and pulled Tommy close and told him to stay right with me, and she would be seeing us again in a few days. Poor Tommy was so numb and cold and hungry you couldn't tell if he had any idea what was being asked of him.

She hugged me close and looked into my eyes. "Never forget that I love you, Patty. And papa loves you too."

I still do not know what possessed me to say what I said just then. Something in me had shifted. I know enough now to give words to what it was. The little girl inside me went away, as surely as if a path had opened up through the trees. She just stepped out of my body and walked down that path and into the Sierra Nevada forest, never to return. I had already seen more than you ought to see by the time you are that age. I had seen my father stab another man in the chest and watched that man bleed to death. I had heard wounded animals screaming for water in the desert night, and heard the widow Murphy crying out from her cabin like a lone wolf howling in the woods. I had watched people starving and watched my own brothers shrivel up till there was nearly nothing left and watched my mother walk away from me, out across the snow and disappear. As she prepared to do this yet again I was able for the first time to imagine my own death and to imagine that I would not see her anymore. At moments like this you are supposed to cry. I wasn't able to cry. She was the one who cried. I was the one who stood there giving motherly advice. I know now my words cut through her as surely as if a sword of ice had dropped off one of the limbs above us and speared her heart. It makes me weep to think of it. Yes, seventy-five years later my own tears come dripping down to match those she wept that day.

"Well, mother," I said, "if you never see me again, you do the best you can."

Is that too hard-hearted for an eight-year-old? Somehow I was prepared for my death and for hers too. I told as much to Mr. Glover after we turned and started back. It disturbed him, I know. In my eyes then he seemed to be an executioner. Later I would see that he was a very decent man, though rough and rugged in his looks, red-eyed from the cold and from his monumental efforts.

"Don't you talk like that," he said to me. "I give your mama my word, and I mean to keep it."…

It was like the first time mama left, but harder because Tommy didn't move much. Sometimes I had to hold a mirror to his lips to make sure he was breathing. Sometimes his eyes would open, and he would almost seem to speak. I would warm our slivers of meat and fry up some flour; then chew Tommy's portion to soften it and try to make him eat.

I don't know who was worse off then—him, because he had no idea of what was going on around us, or me, because I did. I remember hearing Patrick and Peggy say things I didn't understand. Years later I came to see that they already knew what was happening at the other cabin, where someone had gone out and uncovered Milt's body, buried in the snow, and started cutting away parts of him for food. Whether it was the widow started it, or Keseberg, no one would ever be able to say for sure.

My heart went out to widow Murphy, and still does. She was called "widow" because her husband had died on her. The fact is, she wasn't much older than mama, not yet forty. You have to give her credit for trying something most single women wouldn't have dared in that day and age. She had started west on her own, with seven children. Two of her daughters had married young and had brought their children. For a while it had been quite a clan, three wagonloads. William Foster was her son-in-law. So was William Pike, the fellow Foster shot in the back. She'd lost a boy at the lake camp. Five more of her children had already hiked out, leaving her with one small son, a boy about my age. Little by little she'd been losing her eyesight and losing her mind. By the time Keseberg moved in, she'd probably forgotten who he was. In her sad hunger she'd probably forgotten who Milt was.

I thank the Lord I had lost the will to walk more than fifty feet at a time. After Mr. Glover left I never wandered far enough in her direction to see any sign of what was going on—though I think I must have known. Deep down I must have. I must have chosen not to understand the words Patrick and Peggy whispered on the other side of the blanket.

As I think back upon those weeks it seems as if the mountains themselves had revealed an appetite, as if somewhere among the snowy crevices and windblown granite slopes there were ancient and empty places that had to be filled, laying claim to what little energy and life force remained for us. It had a pull, and it had a voice, and you couldn't resist it. When the angels came to visit I could not tell if they were heavenly angels or mountain angels, and it didn't make much difference which, their music was so sweet. They would visit me at all times of the day and night, and before long I stopped hearing much of anything but their voices. They would come from far away like the flute notes of distant birds approaching, single notes I would hear before I saw the wings. Then they'd be all around, white-winged angels singing in a forest filled with silver light. Sometimes they wouldn't sing. They would float and beckon, and start to drift away, and I would call out, "Don't go! Don't go!" And back they'd come, as if they'd just been teasing me, flirting and teasing....

One day I felt compelled to get outside. Something was calling me up into the light, whether angels with wings or the white-robed visitor again, I did not know. Something was out there. I had to know what it was.

It took a lot of effort, climbing the snow stairs. I listened for the flute notes, the tender voices coming from the lake. I remember the sky was very blue when I stepped out onto the snow. The air was quiet. The figure coming toward me through the trees this time was dark and large. No wings. No furry robes. The arms were pumping, as if punching at the air, like someone running but in slow motion, fighting through the snow. And then a call came toward me.

"Patty!"

I knew this voice. It wasn't Salvador. It wasn't Mr. Glover. My heart stopped. I had been seeing so many things, hearing so many things, I closed my eyes. Again the voice called, "Patty?" like a question.

He was closer, his huge pack thrown down behind him, and his hat thrown down. I could see his face, his beard, as he lunged toward me, calling, "Patty! Patty! Is it you?"

I tried to run, sure he would disappear before I reached him. I tried to call out, "Papa!" My voice stuck in my throat. The snow had been melting. It was soft. I couldn't lift my legs high enough to run. I fell forward. Then he was over me, lifting me. I looked into his eyes. As he held me his face filled with fear at what he saw, and that made me afraid. I threw my arms around his neck. He hugged me close against his coat, against his chest.

"It's okay, darlin'," he said, "we're okay now," his voice soothing away my confusion, his voice sweeter than all those others I'd been hearing.

I still couldn't talk. With my face pushed into the thick, scratchy wool of his coat I sobbed and sobbed. He held me until I got my breath and found my voice.

"I'm so hungry, papa. I've never been so hungry."

"I know, darlin'. I have something for you that we baked last night."

He set me down and fetched his pack, where he had a little cloth bag. He brought out a tiny biscuit about the size of a thimble. I'd never seen anything so beautiful. "Here ya go, darlin'. Just bite off a little bit. Eat it real slow."

I ate that and he gave me another one. I could see the bag was full of these biscuit morsels. My heart swelled with new love for him.

"I knew you'd come back, papa."

"You knew I wouldn't leave my little girl behind."

"Did you see James Junior and Virginia?"

"Yes, we did. By now they're safe and sound in California."

"Have you been to California, papa?"

"I sure have, darlin'."

"Is it far away?"

"Hardly any ways at all. Where's Tommy now?"

"He's down below, papa. He's sleeping. He sleeps most all the time. I tried to feed him whenever I could. But after a while…" I started to cry again. "After a while there wasn't any more…"

The days and weeks of tears I hadn't been able to feel came gushing forth. Again he picked me up and held me close and I felt his body shaking next to mine, like the day by the Humboldt when we cut away his hair. Then he put me down and gave me another biscuit and told me to sit still while he went below.

I sat there nibbling, each crumb a precious gift, until papa climbed back up the stairs carrying Tommy, so small against his coat he looked like a doll. Papa had been crying again, and he was trying not to. He didn't have time to cry.

Patrick had followed him and stood at the top of the stairs. I don't know what had passed between them in the darkness. Maybe nothing. They watched each other for quite a while.

Papa said, "I thank you, Patrick, for giving shelter to my children."

"It hasn't been easy here."

"I can see that."

"We've got our own."

"I saw your boys up past the summit. They'll be all right. Glover's a good man."

"They're good boys too."

And there they stood, meeting again, two men from Ireland who never cared much for each other in the best of days. For the first time in all these months I felt sorry for Patrick. He looked so shrunken next to papa, who'd left the company in disgrace and had now returned, weary from the climbing but in good health and vigorous after five months of constant motion, while Patrick had been mostly waiting, stiff from sitting and from nursing his kidney stones. In his eyes there was a look I now understand. His fear was that he'd be left behind, that papa bore some grudge and would rescue us but no one else. Knowing Patrick, the way his mind worked in those days, this is probably what he himself would have done, if supplies were short and there were weaker ones to contend with. The night Milt Elliott starved to death, Patrick still had meat in his cabin. Maybe he was afraid papa would find out about that.

At last papa said, "Get your family ready. We're starting back right away, with everyone who can walk."

Edwin Bryant, from *What I Saw in California*

Edwin Bryant was an early European American visitor to the Sierra Nevada region. In 1846—the same year as the Donner Party tragedy— he led a wagon train overland to California from Missouri. His journey was one of several that year that brought more than fifteen hundred immigrants westward to California and Oregon.

In 1848, Bryant published an account of his journey titled What I Saw in California: By Wagon Train from Missouri to California. *In this passage, he describes his wonderment at encountering the Sierra Nevada landscape near today's Donner Pass and Yuba Valley.*

August 26.—We did not leave our encampment until the sun, rising above the lofty mountains to the east, dispensed its warm and cheerful rays through the openings of the magnificent forest, by which we had been sheltered for the night. It is quite impossible to convey by language an adequate conception of the symmetrical beauty and stateliness of the forest trees surrounding the lake [Donner Lake], and covering the sides of the adjacent mountains. A skilful artist with his pencil and his brush, alone, can do justice to this contrast of Alpine and Elysian scenery. The sublime altitude of the mountains, their granite and barren heads piercing the sky; the umbrageous foliage of the tall pines and cedars, deepening in verdure and density as the forest approaches the more gentle and grassy slopes along the banks of the lake, the limpid and tranquil surface of which *daguerreotypes* distinctly [capture] every object, from the moss-covered rocks laved by its waves to the bald and inaccessible summits of the Sierra—these scenic objects, with the fresh incense of the forest, and the fragrant odor of the wild rose, constituted a landscape that, from associations, melted the sensibilities, blunted as they were by long exposure and privation, and brought back to our memories the endearments of home and the pleasures of civilization.

The trail leaves the shore of the lake on the right hand, ascending over some rocky hills, and after crossing some difficult ravines and swampy ground densely timbered, we reached the base of the crest of the Sierra Nevada. To mount this was our next great difficulty. Standing at the bottom and looking upwards at the perpendicular, and in some places, impending granite cliffs, the observer, without any further knowledge on the subject, would doubt if man or beast had ever made good a passage over them. But we knew that man and horse, oxen and wagon, women and children, had crossed this formidable and apparently impassable barrier erected by Nature between the desert and the fertile districts on the coast of the Pacific. What their energy had accomplished, impelled though it had been by an invincible desperation, we knew could be achieved by us.

In good heart, therefore, we commenced the steep ascent, leaping our animals from crag to crag, and climbing in places nearly perpendicular precipices of smooth granite rocks. One of our mules in this ascent, heavily packed, fell backwards twice, and rolled downwards, until her descent was interrupted by a projecting rock. We thought, each time, that her career of duty and usefulness had terminated; and that her bones would bleach among the barren rocks of the mountain. But she revived from the stunning and bruising effects of her backward somersets; and with great exertions on our own part in assisting her, she reached with us the summit of the Pass.

The view from the crest of the Sierra to the east, is inexpressibly comprehensive, grand, and picturesque. After congratulating ourselves upon the safe achievement of our morning feat, and breathing our mules a few minutes, we proceeded on our journey. A mile brought us to a small dimple on the top of the mountain, in the centre of which is a miniature lake, surrounded by green grass.

It was some time before we could determine our course down the Sierra on the western side. The emigrant wagon-trail was here entirely effaced. Around the small lake we saw the traces of encampments; but beyond it, in no direction, could we discover any signs that man had ever passed....

Descending the rocky ravine a few miles, we emerged from it and entered a beautiful level valley, some four or five miles in length from east to west, and about two miles in breadth. A narrow, sluggish stream runs through this valley, the waters of which are of considerable depth, and the banks steep and miry. A luxuriant growth of grasses, of an excellent quality, covered the entire valley with the richest verdure. Flowers were in bloom; and although late in August, the vegetation presented all the tenderness and freshness of May. This valley has been named by the emigrants "Uber Valley" [Yuba Valley]; and the stream which runs through it, and is a tributary of the Rio de los Plumas, or Feather river, has the same name. It is sometimes pronounced *Juba*; but I think Uber is the correct etymology. How the name was derived, I never could learn.

We found, after some search, a place where we could ford the stream without stalling our animals in its soft and spongy banks and bed. But it was some time before we could discover at what point the wagon-trail left the valley.

Leaving the valley we crossed a high undulating country, timbered with pines, firs, and cedars, whose symmetrical proportions and rich foliage, with the bright green moss clothing their branches, would baffle the skill and coloring of the most artistical painter, to represent them faithfully on canvass. This country is watered by a connected chain of seven small lakes, between which, and surrounded by the beautiful and fairy-like groves I have mentioned, there are several green grassy lawns and openings, which lend to the scenery a charm and a fascination more like that which the imagination ascribes to the effect of enchantment, or the creations of a beautiful dream, than the presentations of reality. The soil of this rolling country is rich and highly fertile, where there is any moisture to sustain vegetation.

Our course continued nearly south, until we reached and entered another deep ravine or gorge, down which runs a small stream of water, in a direction nearly west. After proceeding down this ravine a few miles, the elevated mountain walls on both sides of the stream, at the foot of which immense granite rocks raise their impassable forms, approach each other so nearly as to form a *cañon*, to avoid which the trail winds up and down the side of the mountain, over and under steep precipices and impending cliffs.

Our progress during the entire day, owing to the obstructions in our route, has been slow....

After we had encamped I crossed the stream, which has a very rocky bed, to ascertain if there was any convenient spot where the grazing would be better for our mules. I found, about a mile distant, two openings in the timber of the bottom, in which the grass was green and rank. Returning to camp, and assisted by McClary, (no other member of the party volunteering,) we drove the mules across the stream, and after picketing them in the tall grass, and kindling a good fire from some dead logs of fallen timber, for their protection, we bivouacked among them in the opening for the night. The timber surrounding the circular space which we occupied is very tall. The bright blaze of our fire defined indistinctly the columnar shapes of the pines, and their overarching branches. Fancy soon pictured our residence for the night a spacious gothic temple, whose walls had mouldered away, leaving the pillars and the skeleton roof, through which the bright stars were twinkling, standing, in defiance of the assaults of time and the fury of the elements. The temperature of the evening is delightful, and the sky serene and cloudless.

One of our party this morning picked up a human skull near the trail. Some unfortunate emigrant, probably, had been interred near the spot, and, being exhumed by the Indians or wolves, this was a portion of his skeleton. I saw large numbers of pheasants during our march today, and shot one with my pistol while riding along. Raspberries, and a small, bitter cherry, have been quite abundant in places. Distance 25 miles....

August 29.—The morning was clear and severely cold. The keen atmosphere, as soon as I threw off my blankets, just before daylight, produced an aguish sensation that I have not previously felt on the journey. The depth and consequent dampness of our encampment, probably, was one cause of this affection. Our physical exhaustion from incessant labor, and the want of adequate nourishment, was another....

We saw in a number of places, ladders erected by the Indians, for climbing the pine-trees to gather the nuts, and the poles used for the same purpose. An Indian was seen, but he ran from us with great speed, disappearing behind the forest-trees. Some hares and a fox were started, and a hare was killed by one of the party.

One of our pack-mules became so exhausted this afternoon, that she refused to proceed. After stripping and vainly trying various expedients to urge her along, I haltered her with a tight noose around the nose, and fastening the end of the rope to the horn of my saddle, dragged her into camp. She had performed such faithful service, that I could not leave her to perish of hunger and thirst, or to be devoured by the wolves of the wilderness. The feet of all our mules are very tender, and they move with much apparent pain. We encamped at five o'clock in a ravine, half a mile to the left of the trail, where we found some small pools of water and a little dead grass in their vicinity. A soup of the hare killed on our march to-day, constituted our supper and only meal for two days. Distance 25 miles.

Sarah Eleanor Royce, from *A Frontier Lady*

Sarah Eleanor Royce (1819–1891) traveled to California in 1849, arriving with her husband, Josiah, after a six-month journey by prairie schooner across the seemingly endless road to the land of golden dreams. Prior to their arrival in Grass Valley in 1854, the Royces had already visited many gold camps, and this town was their ninth home in five years.

On November 20, 1855, Sarah gave birth to Josiah Royce, Jr., now remembered as one of the preeminent philosophers of the nineteenth century. It was he who, in 1879, insisted Sarah revise her 1849 diary, which included her experiences of the Gold Rush and early California. Although she never intended her writing for publication, in 1932, more than forty years after his mother's death, Josiah Royce had her diary published as A Frontier Lady, *which is excerpted here.*

But the great Sierra Nevada Mountains were still all before us, and we had many miles to make, up this [Carson] River, before their ascent was fairly begun. If this sand continued many miles as looked probable, when should we ever even begin the real climbing? The men began to talk among themselves about how much easier they could get on if they left the wagon; and it was not unlikely they would try starting out without us, if we had to travel too slowly. But they could not do this to any real advantage unless they took with them their pack-mule to carry some provisions. All they had was the bacon they found on the desert, and some parched corn meal; but they felt sanguine that they could go so much faster than the cattle with the wagon, they could easily make this last them through. But the bargain had been, when we agreed to supply them with flour, that the pack mule, and the old horse if he could be of any use, should be at our service to aid in any pinch that might occur, to the end of the journey. Having shared the perils of the way thus far, it certainly seemed unwise to divide the strength of so small a party when the mountains were to be scaled.

I wished most heartily there was some more rapid way for Mary [age 2] and me to ride. But it was out of the question; for only a thoroughly trained mountain animal would do for me to ride carrying her. Besides this, all the clothing and personal conveniences we had in the world were in our wagon, and we had neither a sufficient number of sound animals nor those of the right kind, to pack them across the mountains. So the only way was to try to keep on. But it looked like rather a hopeless case when, for this whole day, we advanced but a few miles.

The next morning, Friday the 12th of October, we set out once more, hoping the sand would become lighter and the road easier to travel. But, instead of this, the wheels sank deeper than yesterday, there was more of ascent to overcome, the sun shone out decidedly hot, and, towards noon, we saw that we were approaching some pretty steep hills up which our road evidently led. It did not look as though we could ascend them but we would at least try to reach their foot. As we neared them we saw dust rising from the road at one of the turns we could distinguish high up in the hills a few miles off. Probably it was some party ahead of us. There was no hope of our overtaking anybody, so when we lost sight of the dust we did not expect to see it again. But soon another section of the road was in sight, and again the dust appeared; this time nearer, and plainly moving toward us. Conjecture now became very lively. It was probably Indians; but they could not be of the same tribes we had seen. Were they foes? How many were there? Repeatedly we saw the dust at different points, but could make out no distinct figures.

We were now so near the foot of the hills that we could distinctly see a stretch of road leading down a very steep incline to where we were moving so laboriously along. Presently at the head of this steep incline appeared two horsemen, clad in loose, flying garments that flapped, like wings on each side of them, while their broad-brimmed hats blown up from their foreheads, revealed hair and faces that belonged to no Indians. Their rapidity of motion and the steepness of the descent gave a strong impression of coming down from above, and the thought flashed into my mind, "They look heaven-sent." As they came nearer we saw that each of them led by a halter a fine mule, and the perfect ease with which all the animals cantered down that steep, was a marvel in our eyes. My husband and myself were at the heads of the lead cattle, and our little Mary was up in the front of the wagon, looking with wonder at the approaching forms.

As they came near they smiled and the forward one said "Well sir, you are the man we are after!" "How can that be?" said my husband, with surprise. "Yes, sir," continued the stranger, "you and your wife, and that little girl, are what brought us as far as this. You see we belong to the Relief Company sent out by order of the United States Government to help the late emigrants over the mountains. We were ordered only as far as Truckee Pass. When we got there we met a little company that had just got in. They'd been in a snow storm at the summit; 'most got froze to death themselves, lost some of their cattle, and just managed to get to where some of our men had fixed a relief camp. There was a woman and some children with them; and that woman set right to work at us fellows to go on over the mountains after a family she said they'd met on the desert going back for grass and water 'cause they'd missed their way. She said there was only one wagon, and there was a woman and child in it; and she knew they could never get through them cañons and over them ridges without help. We told her we had no orders to go any farther then. She said she didn't care for orders. She didn't believe anybody would blame us for doing what we were sent out to do, if we did have to go farther than ordered. And she kept at me so, I couldn't get rid of her. You see I've got a wife and little girl of my own; so I felt just how it was; and I got this man to come with me and here we are, to give you more to eat, if you want it, let you have these two mules, and tell you how to get right over the mountains the best and quickest way."

While he thus rapidly, in cheery though blunt fashion, explained their sudden presence with us, the thought of their being heaven-sent that had so lightly flashed into my mind as I at first watched their rapid descent of the hill, with flying garments—grew into a sweetly solemn conviction; and I stood in mute adoration, breathing, in my inmost heart, thanksgiving to that Providential Hand which had taken hold of the conflicting movements, the provoking blunders, the contradictory plans, of our lives and those of a dozen other people, who a few days before were utterly unknown to each other, and many miles apart, and had from those rough, broken materials wrought out for us so unlooked for a deliverance.

Having made their hasty explanation, our new friends advised us to keep on some little distance farther, to a point where there was a spring in the hills, and excellent camping, to which they would guide us. There we were to rest the remainder of the day, while they would help to select, put into proper shape and pack, everything in the wagon that could be packed. The rest we must be content to leave. As we moved leisurely on to our camping place, they explained more fully the details of our situation—which they understood so much better than we could—and told us what we were to do. There had been two nights of snow storm at the summit: had there come much more they could not have got through. But the weather had cleared, the snow was fast going off the roads as they came over; and, if no other storm occurred, the pass would be in good order when we reached it. But we must hasten with all possible despatch, for, when the storms once again set in, they were not likely at that season to give any more chance for crossing the mountains. As to keeping on with the wagon, even supposing the cattle to grow no weaker than now—it would take us two weeks at the least to ascend the Carson Valley to the cañon. That cañon could not in several places be traversed by wheels. Wagons had been taken through; but only by taking them apart and packing, at the most difficult points; which of course could only be done by strong companies with plenty of time. Our only hope, therefore, was to pack. They then went farther into details about packing. The oxen, they said, could easily be made to carry, each, two moderate sized bundles, if snugly packed and well fastened on. Then the old horse could carry something though not very much. And the mule the young men had brought along, they said must carry most of the provisions.

"And now as to these two mules we brought," continued the chief speaker, "this white one is a perfectly-trained, mountain saddle-mule. My wife has rode him for miles, over steep and slippery roads, and he'll be perfectly safe for this lady to ride, with her little girl in front of her. And this dark mule is just as good for carrying packs, and the lady is to have him for her things and the little girl's. Now," he continued, turning to me, "as soon as we stop, and have all had some dinner, you just pick out all the things you care most about, and put them by themselves—you can save out enough for two good sized packs: he's strong, and understands it—and we'll do them up snug for you, and show the men how to fasten them on safe; and you remember, now, that these two mules are yours till you get through to the gold-mines;

and all Uncle Sam asks, is, that they shall be brought safely to his boys' headquarters in Sacramento City as soon as possible after you get into California."

Thus, by the wise forethought of our good Government, and the chivalrous management of this faithful agent, I was provided for to a sufficiency that would have looked to me, two hours before, like a fairy-dream. The programme for the afternoon was successfully carried out. Every thing was arranged for an early morning start; and, at night I lay down to sleep for the last time in the wagon that had proved such a shelter for months past. I remembered well, how dreary it had seemed, on the first night of our journey (which now looked so long ago) to have *only* a *wagon* for shelter. Now we were not going to have even that. But, never mind, if we might only reach in safety the other foot of the mountains, all these privations would in their turn look small; and the same rich Providence that had led, and was still so kindly leading us, would, in that new land, perhaps, show us better things than we had seen yet.

So, when morning came, I hailed it with cheerful hope, though with some misgivings, because I had not ridden horseback for several years, and, whenever I had, it had been with side-saddle, and all the usual equipment for lady's riding, and, certainly, with no baby to carry. Now, I was to have only a common Spanish saddle, I must have Mary in front of me, and, it turned out, that several things needed for frequent use would have to be suspended from the pommel of my saddle, in a satchel on one side and a little pail on the other. At first, I was rather awkward, and so afraid Mary would get hurt, that at uneven places in the road I would ask my husband to get up and take her, while I walked. But in a few hours this awkwardness wore off; and the second day of our new style of traveling I rode twenty-five miles, only alighting once or twice for a brief time. Our friends, the government men, had left us the morning we left our wagon; taking the road to Truckee, where they felt themselves emphatically "due," considering their orders. I have more than once since wished I could see and thank them again; for, grateful as I felt then, I was able to appreciate more highly, a thousand fold, the service they had rendered us when, only ten days after we crossed the summit, the mountains were all blocked with snow, and the stormiest winter California had known for years was fully set in.

On the 24th of October at evening we reached what in our Guide Book was called "Pleasant Valley Gold Mines"; where we found two or three tents, and a few men with their gold-washing pans. We rested ourselves and animals for two or three days, and then moved into the village of "Weaverville," of which the miners had told us. This village was made up of tents, many of them very irregularly placed; though in one part, following the trend of the principal ravine, there was, already, something like a row of these primitive dwellings, though at considerable distances apart. We added one to that row, and soon began to gather about us little comforts and conveniences, which made us feel as though we once more had a home.

Bayard Taylor, from *Eldorado*

Bayard Taylor (1825–1878) was an author, reporter, and poet. Born in Pennsylvania to Quaker farmers of modest circumstances, early in his life Taylor felt driven to expand his horizons, and his restless curiosity led to the study of languages and literature. By the age of sixteen, Taylor was already published and gaining a reputation for his insightful prose and poetry, and soon he was under contract to travel the world and recount his adventures for many publications, including the Saturday Evening Post *and the* New York Tribune, *the latter of which commissioned Taylor to report on the California Gold Rush. The result of that assignment was* Eldorado: Adventures in the Path of Empire, *published in 1850.*

In this passage from Eldorado, *Taylor describes his journey through the Sierra foothills of Calaveras and Amador Counties and records his first glimpse of the majestic Sierra Nevada landscape.*

The afternoon of the second day the clouds lifted, and we saw the entire line of the Sierra Nevada, white and cold against the background of the receding storm. As the sun broke forth, near its setting, peak after peak became visible, far away to north and south, till the ridge of eternal snow was unbroken for at least a hundred and fifty miles. The peaks around the headwaters of the American Fork, highest of all, were directly in front. The pure white of their sides became gradually imbued with a rosy flame, and their cones and pinnacles burned like points of fire. In the last glow of the sun, long after it had set to us, the splendor of the whole range, deepening from gold to rose, from rose to crimson, and fading at last into an ashy violet, surpassed even the famous "Alp-glow" as I have seen it from the plains of Piedmont.

An old hunter living on the ranch came galloping up, with a fat, black-tailed doe at the end of his lariat. He had first broken the hind leg of the poor beast with a ball, and then caught her running. The pleading expression of her large eyes was almost human, but her captor coolly drew his knife across her throat, and left her to bleed to death. She lay on the ground, uttering a piteous bleat as her panting became thick and difficult, but not until the last agony was wholly over did the dull film steal across the beauty of her lustrous eyes.

On the third morning I succeeded in leaving the ranch, where I had been very hospitably entertained at four dollars a day for myself and horse. The Cosumne was very much swollen by the rains, but my gray mare swam bravely, and took me across with but a slight wetting. I passed my previous halting-place, and was advancing with difficulty through the mud of the plains, when, on climbing a small "rise," I suddenly found myself confronted by four grizzly bears—two of them half-grown cubs—who had possession of a grassy bottom on the other side. They were not more than two hundred yards distant. I halted and looked at them, and they at me, and I must say they seemed the most unconcerned of the two parties. My pistols would kill nothing bigger than a coyote, and they could easily have outrun my horse; so I went my way, keeping an eye on the most convenient tree. In case of an attack, the choice of a place of refuge would have been a delicate matter, since the bears can climb up a large tree and gnaw down a small one. It required some skill, therefore, in selecting a trunk of proper size. At Murphy's, the night previous, they told me there had been plenty of "bear-sign" along the river, and in the "pockets" of solid ground among the tule. As the rainy season sets in they always come down from the mountains.

After traveling eight or ten miles the wagon trails began to scatter, and with my imperfect knowledge of prairie hieroglyphics, I was soon at fault. The sky was by this time clear and bright; and rather than puzzle myself with wheel-tracks leading everywhere, and cattle-tracks leading nowhere, I guessed at the location of the ranch to which I was bound and took a bee-line towards it.

The knowledge of tracks and marks is a very important part of the education of a woodsman. It is only obtained by unlearning, or forgetting for the time, all one's civilized acquirements and recalling the original instincts of the animal. An observing man, fresh from the city, might with some study determine the character of a track, but it is the habit of observing them rather than the discriminating faculty which enables the genuine hunter to peruse the earth like a volume, and confidently pronounce on the number and character of all the animals and men that have lately passed over its surface. Where an inexperienced eye could discern no mark, he will note a hundred trails, and follow any particular one through the maze, with a faculty of sight as unerring as the power of scent in a dog. I was necessitated, during my journey in the interior of California, to pay some attention to this craft, but I never got beyond the rudiments.

Another necessary faculty, as I had constant occasion to notice, is that of observing and remembering the form, color, and character of animals. This may seem a simple thing; but let anyone, at the close of a ride in the country, endeavor to describe all the horses, mules, and oxen he has seen, and he will find himself at fault. A Californian will remember and give a particular description of a hundred animals which he has passed in a day's journey, and be able to recognize and identify any one of them. Horses and mules are to him what men, newspapers, books, and machinery are to us; they are the only science he need know or learn. The habit of noticing them is easily acquired, and is extremely useful in a country where there are neither pounds nor fences.

The heavy canopy of clouds was lifted from the plain almost as suddenly as the cover from a roast turkey at a hotel dinner, when the head waiter has given the wink. The snows of the Nevada shone white along the clear horizon; I could see for many a league on every side, but I was alone on the broad, warm landscape. Over wastes of loose, gravelly soil—into which my horse sank above the fetlocks—across barren ridges, alternating with marshy hollows and pools of water, I toiled for hours, and near sunset reached the first low, timbered hills on the margin of the plain. I dismounted and led my weary horse for a mile or two, but as it grew dark, was obliged to halt in a little glen—a most bearish-looking place, filled with thick chaparral. A fallen tree supplied me with fuel to hand, and I soon had a glowing fire, beside which I spread my blankets and lay down. Getting up at midnight to throw on more logs, I found my horse gone, and searched the chaparral for an hour, wondering how I should fare, trudging along on foot, with the saddle on my shoulders. At last I found her in a distant part of the wood, with the lariat wound around a tree. After this I slept no more, but lay gazing on the flickering camp-fire, and her gray figure as she moved about in the dusk. Towards dawn the tinkle of a distant mule-bell and afterwards the crowing of a cock gave me welcome signs of near habitation; and, saddling with the first streak of light, I pushed on, still in the same direction, through a thick patch of thorny chaparral, and finally reached the brow of a wooded ridge just as the sun was rising.

Oh, the cool, fresh beauty of that morning! The sky was deliciously pure and soft, and the tips of the pines on the hills were kindled with a rosy flame from the new-risen sun. Below me lay a beautiful valley, across which ran a line of timber, betraying, by its luxuriance, the watercourse it shaded. The reaches of meadow between were green and sparkling with dew; here and there, among the luxuriant foliage, peeped the white top of a tent, or rose the pale-blue threads of smoke from freshly kindled camp-fires. Cattle were grazing in places, and the tinkle of the bell I had heard sounded a blithe welcome from one of the groups. Beyond the tents, in the skirts of a splendid clump of trees stood the very ranch to which I was bound.

I rode up and asked for breakfast. My twenty-four hours' fast was broken by a huge slice of roast venison, and coffee sweetened with black Mexican sugar, which smacks not only of the juice of the cane, but of the leaves, joints, roots, and even the unctuous soil in which it grows. For this I paid a dollar and a half, but no money could procure any feed for my famishing horse. Leaving the ranch, which is owned by a settler named Hicks, my road led along the left bank of Sutter's Creek for two miles, after which it struck into the mountains. Here and there, in the gulches, I noticed signs of the gold-hunters, but their prospecting did not appear to have been successful. The timber was principally pine and oak and of the smaller growths, the red-barked madroño, and a species of *esculus*, with a fruit much larger than our Western buckeye. The hills are steep, broken, and with little apparent system. A close observation, however, shows them to have a gradual increase of elevation, to a certain point, beyond which they fall again. As in the sea the motion of the long swells is seen through all the small waves of the surface, so this broken region shows a succession of parallel ridges, regularly increasing in height till they reach the Sierra Nevada—the "tenth wave," with the white foam on its crest.

Lafayette Bunnell, from *Discovery of the Yosemite and the Indian War of 1851 Which Led to That Event*

In 1851, Lafayette Houghton Bunnell (1824–1903) was a member of the Mariposa Battalion, a local volunteer militia charged with finding Native American tribal leaders involved in recent raids on European American settlements in the region. While searching for the leaders, the Mariposa Battalion, led by James Savage, became possibly the first non-indigenous visitors to the Yosemite Valley. Bunnell later led additional expeditions into the valley and named many of its geographic features.

In 1880, Bunnell wrote Discovery of the Yosemite and the Indian War of 1851 Which Led to That Event. *This selection details the Mariposa Battalion's activities and provides valuable information about Chief Tenaya (spelled "Ten-ie-ya" by Bunnell) and the Ahwahnees, the tribe that inhabited the valley.*

As no information had been received from the camp of the Yosemites [the Ahwahnees], after an early breakfast, the order was passed to "fall in," and when the order "march" was given, we moved off in single file, Savage leading, with Ten-ie-ya as guide.

From the length of time taken by the chief to go and return from his encampment, it was supposed that with horses, and an early start, we should be able to go and return the same day, if for any cause it should be deemed desirable, although sufficient supplies were taken, in case of a longer delay.

While ascending to the divide between the South Fork and the main Merced we found but little snow, but at the divide, and beyond, it was from three to five feet in depth, and in places much deeper.

The sight of this somewhat cooled our ardor, but none asked for a "furlough."

To somewhat equalize the laborious duties of making a trail, each man was required to take his turn in front. The leader of the column was frequently changed; no horse or mule could long endure the fatigue without relief. To effect this, the tired leader dropped out of line, resigning his position to his followers, taking a place in the rear, on the beaten trail, exemplifying, that "the first shall be last, and the last shall be first." The snow packed readily, so that a very comfortable trail was left in the rear of our column.

Old Ten-ie-ya relaxed the rigidity of his bronze features, in admiration of our method of making a trail, and assured us that, notwithstanding the depth of snow, we would soon reach his village. We had in our imaginations pictured it as in some deep, rocky cañon in the mountains.

While in camp the frantic efforts of the old chief to describe the location to Major Savage had resulted in the unanimous verdict among the "boys," who were observing him, that "it must be a devil of a place." Feeling encouraged by the hope that we should soon arrive at the residences of his Satanic majesty's subjects, we wallowed on, alternately becoming the object of a joke, as we in turn were extricated from the drifts. When we had traversed a little more than half the distance, as was afterwards proved, we met the Yosemites on their way to our rendezvous on the South Fork.

As they filed past us, the major took account of their number, which was but seventy-two. As they reached our beaten trail, satisfaction was variously expressed, by grunts from the men, by the low rippling laughter from the squaws, and by the children clapping their hands in glee at the sight. On being asked where the others of his band were, the old sachem said: "This is all of my people that are willing to go with me to the plains. Many that have been with me are from other tribes. They have taken wives from my band; all have gone with their wives and children to the Tuolumne and to the Monos." Savage told Ten-ie-ya that he was telling him that which was not true. The Indians could not cross the mountains in the deep snow, neither could they go over the divide of the Tuolumne. That he knew they were still at his village or in hiding places near it. Ten-ie-ya assured the major he was telling him the truth, and in a very solemn manner declared that none of his band had been left behind—that all had gone before his people had left. His people had not started before because of the snowstorm.

With a belief that but a small part of Ten-ie-ya's band was with this party, Major Savage decided to go on to the Indian village and ascertain if any others could be found or traces of them discovered. This decision was a satisfactory one and met with a hearty approval as it was reported along the line.

This tribe had been estimated by Pon-wat-chee and Cow-chit-tee as numbering more than two hundred; as about that number usually congregated when they met together to "cache" their acorns in the valley, or for a grand annual hunt and drive of game; a custom which secured an abundant supply for the feast that followed.

At other times they were scattered in bands on the sunny slopes of the ridges, and in the mountain glens. Ten-ie-ya had been an unwilling guide thus far, and Major Savage said to him: "You may return to camp with your people, and I will take one of your young men with me. There are but few of your people here. Your tribe is large. I am going to your village to see your people, who will not come with you. They *will* come with me if I find them."

Savage then selected one of the young "braves" to accompany him. Ten-ie-ya replied, as the young Indian stepped forward by his direction, "I will go with my people; my young man shall go with you to my village. You will not find any people there. I do not know where they are. My tribe is small—not large, as the white chief has said. The Paiutes and Monos are all gone. Many of the people with my tribe are from western tribes that have come to me and do not wish to return. If they go to the plains and are seen, they will be killed by the friends of those with whom they had quarreled. I have talked with my people and told them I was going to see the white chiefs sent to make peace. I was told that I was growing old, and it was well that I should go, but that young and strong men can find plenty in the mountains; therefore why should they go? to be yarded like horses and cattle. My heart has been sore since that talk, but I am now willing to go, for it is best for my people that I do so."

The major listened to the old Indian's volubility for awhile, but interrupted him with a cheering "Forward march!" at which the impatient command moved briskly forward over the now partly broken trail, leaving the chief alone, as his people had already gone on.

We found the traveling much less laborious than before, and it seemed but a short time after we left the Indians before we suddenly came in full view of the valley in which was the village, or rather the encampments of the Yosemites. The immensity of rock I had seen in my vision on the Old Bear Valley trail from Ridley's Ferry was here presented to my astonished gaze. The mystery of that scene was here disclosed. My awe was increased by this nearer view. The face of the immense cliff was shadowed by the declining sun; its outlines only had been seen at a distance. This towering mass

"Fools our fond gaze, and greatest of the great, Defies at first our Nature's littleness, Till, growing with (to) its growth, we thus dilate Our spirits to the size of that they contemplate."

That stupendous cliff is now known as "El Capitan" (the Captain), and the plateau from which we had our first view of the valley, as Mount Beatitude.

It has been said that "it is not easy to describe in words the precise impressions which great objects make upon us." I cannot describe how completely I realized this truth. None but those who have visited this most wonderful valley can even imagine the feelings with which I looked upon the view that was there presented. The grandeur of the scene was but softened by the haze that hung over the valley—light as gossamer—and by the clouds which partially dimmed the higher cliffs and mountains. This obscurity of vision but increased the awe with which I beheld it, and as I looked, a peculiar exalted sensation seemed to fill my whole being, and I found my eyes in tears with emotion.

During many subsequent visits to this locality, this sensation was never again so fully aroused. It is probable that the shadows fast clothing all before me, and the vapory clouds at the head of the valley, leaving the view beyond still undefined, gave a weirdness to the scene, that made it so impressive; and the conviction that it was utterly indescribable added strength to the emotion. It is not possible for the same intensity of feeling to be aroused more than once by the same object, although I never looked upon these scenes except with wonder and admiration....

Mr. Richardson [author of *Beyond the Mississippi*] has expressed in graphic language the impressions produced upon nearly all who for the first time behold this wonderful valley. The public has now, to a certain degree, been prepared for these scenes.

They are educated by the descriptions, sketches, photographs and masterly paintings of Hill and Bierstadt; whereas, on our first visit, our imagination had been misled by the descriptive misrepresentations of savages, whose prime object was to keep us from their safe retreat, until we had expected to see some terrible abyss. The reality so little resembled the picture of imagination, that my astonishment was the more overpowering.

To obtain a more distinct and *quiet* view, I had left the trail and my horse and wallowed through the snow alone to a projecting granite rock. So interested was I in the scene before me, that I did not observe that my comrades had all moved on, and that I would soon be left indeed alone. My situation attracted the attention of Major Savage— who was riding in [the] rear of [the] column—who hailed me from the trail below with, "you had better wake up from that dream up there, or you may lose your hair; I have no faith in Ten-ie-ya's statement that there are no Indians about here. We had better be moving; some of the murdering devils may be lurking along this trail to pick off stragglers." I hurriedly joined the major on the descent, and as other views presented themselves, I said with some enthusiasm, "If my hair is now required, I can depart in peace, for I have here seen the power and glory of a Supreme being; the majesty of His handy-work is in that 'Testimony of the Rocks.' That mute appeal—pointing to El Capitan—illustrates it, with more convincing eloquence than can the most powerful arguments of surpliced priests." "Hold up, Doc! you are soaring too high for me; and perhaps for yourself. This is rough riding; we had better mind this devilish trail, or we shall go *soaring* over some of these slippery rocks." We, however, made the descent in safety. When we overtook the others, we found blazing fires started and preparations commenced to provide supper for the hungry command; while the light-hearted "boys" were indulging their tired horses with the abundant grass found on the meadow near by, which was but lightly covered with snow.

Hubert Howe Bancroft, from *California Inter Pocula*

Hubert Howe Bancroft (1832–1918) was California's preeminent nine-teenth-century historian. Born in Ohio, he arrived in California during the Gold Rush, and it was while managing a bookstore in San Francisco that he began to accumulate a voluminous collection of early California history. He stopped managing the bookstore in 1868, and by the 1880s he was devoting his full efforts to writing and publishing history texts. More publisher than intellectual, Bancroft developed a thriving "book factory" of California history, utilizing an army of writers and research-ers to assist his endeavors, and publishing their contributions under his own name. Bancroft produced the seven-volume History of California *that is still used by academics today, and his name lives on in the world-renowned Bancroft Library of western American history, at the Univer-sity of California, Berkeley.*

In 1888, Bancroft published his consideration of the California Gold Rush, titled California Inter Pocula. *In its pages, Bancroft sought to present the forty-niners not just as footloose adventurers but as hard-working, ingenious commercial pioneers as well.*

The California Year of 1849; what was it? An exclamation point in the history of civilization; a dash in the annals of time. This twelve-month was not so much a year as an age, not so much an episode as an era. Heart throbs, they say, rather than time tell the age of man; here then was a century of heart throbs; we could as well drop out of history a hundred of other years, as this one most notable year. Other years have been repeated, and will be many times; this one, never. Throughout the records of the race, from first to last, there will never be reproduced on this planet the California flush-times drama. It stands out in the experiences of men unique and individual, each swift day of it equal to many another year.

How vain, then, the attempt to portray this fleeting hour! Dreaming will not achieve it, nor romancing; it is neither caricature, nor burlesque, nor extravaganza. These lead the mind further from the truth. Neither will the bald facts, though plainly and fairly stated, give a perfect idea of the time; there was present much besides plain facts; there were facts running riot, and the wildest fancy turned into facts—a pandemonium of romance and reality. There were here fifty thousand active and intelligent young workers, whose experiences fully written for that year would fill fifty thousand volumes, each as large as this. And then the subject would not be fully presented, unless into each of these fifty thousand volumes the breath of inspiration might place true and living soul; for the winds of California were redolent of soul, and every morning's sun kindled new fires of energy that went not out at night. The 1849 of California, of America, of the world! It was the pivot on which the framework of human progress turned a fresh side to the sun, a side breeding maggots hitherto, but now a new and nobler race of men.

Since the days of Adam, whose eyes were opened to behold himself by his maker, there never has been a mirror held up before man which so reflected him in his true light, stripped of all the shame and conventionalities of staid societies. Leaving in their old homes every restraint, every influence that bound them to ancient forms and traditions, the latter-day Argonauts entered the mines with name and identity sunk. They were no longer their former selves; they were born and baptized anew. Hence arose a social organism at once complex and peculiar, whose growth is at every turn a new development.

Digging in the dirt, selling rum, tobacco, flour, and bacon, hammering out mining machinery, assaying gold and the like seem dull and prosaic occupations enough when compared with the tilts and tournaments of knight-errantry, the pious enthusiasm of crusaders, and the thrilling deeds on the battle-fields; nevertheless the poetry and romance are here for all who prefer reality to fantasy. Here, weather-beaten and bearded diggers are unearthing primeval treasures which shall revolutionize commerce and society; they are bringing to light brilliant gold wherewith to buy happiness; and these ministering towns and cities which spring up on every side as if by magic are the marts of their servitors who feed and clothe their occupants. Gold-getting, however, is not an end but a means; it is only an incentive or impulse in the great plan of progress. The romance of it is found in the strange developments, the wonderful events, the grand display of that force which brings order out of chaos.

Until a late day we lacked home and the home feeling in California. We began by staying here a little while, and we have remained longer than we intended. We lack the associations running back for generations, the old homestead, the grandfather, and grandmother, and uncles, and aunts, and cousins. There is nothing around us hallowed by an indistinct past. There is nothing older than ourselves; all that we see has grown up under our eyes, and for these creatures of our own creation we have no reverence. We are not yet settled, we are constantly moving to and fro like restless spirits, living in hotels and boarding houses; or if we have a home we want to sell it and go into the country, or to Europe. It is so much trouble keeping house, with these Chinamen for chambermaids!

It is true that the people of California are very greatly absorbed in making money. And this is as it should be, for what is money-making but development and progress? Culture and refinement always follow material prosperity, they never precede it. We have here lands to be put under contribution, mines to be opened, railroads and cities to be built; would it be accounted to us as wise to sit down to play when we have made no provision for our dinner? First provide for the material man, else the mental will fare poorly enough. But, say your friends at the East, "You have made money enough; it is time you should turn your attention to something better than money, if ever you intend doing so." Very true, but railway trains are not stopped at full speed, cart horses do not usually make the best racers, and ships built for the water do not sail well in the air. Money-makers are simply machines, as are philosophers and scholars; take one to pieces and remodel it, and the working of it afterward is very doubtful. I see no other way but to give the country time. The next generation will beget new inventions, experiences thus brought together propagate. Hence it is that we are more fully up to the times in everything, much more, all things put together, than almost any other community.

It is easy to understand how men and women thus thrown together, strangers to each other, strangers in ideas, speech, and traditions, without the substratum, as a social foundation, which only can coalesce as society slowly develops, fail to have that interest in each other and that intense loyalty which characterizes older and more settled communities. Society here is a malformation, or rather it is yet not society, but only materials for society; yet nowhere will the people quicker or more heartily unite for the public good; nowhere are they more free and social than here; nowhere is there less clap-trap and ridiculous apings of things traditional than here.

Strangers coming together cannot immediately embrace and become brothers. They have too little in common, see too many faults in each other, and will not mellow on the instant asperities of character. The seeds of lasting friendship are usually planted in early life, and matured in a soil of warm and tender sympathy, in order to produce a plant which will endure the storms of selfishness that beat upon it in after life. Once the social heart of California lay so imbedded in gold that it could not throb. The passions were let loose, and a moral leprosy infected the people like an epidemic. But all this passed away, as every epidemic passes after having weeded society of some of its weaknesses, and left it in fair condition for permanent growth.

To the great majority of the pioneers the Sierra was a sphinx propounding a riddle, which they must answer. Thousands laid down their lives in the attempt, for there were the lion's claws to tear the unsuccessful venture in pieces. Of rare celestial beauty was the face and bosom of the goddess as she lured men to their destruction; of dark ferocity was she as she lapped them to their final doom.

Henry David Thoreau, from *The Journal of Henry David Thoreau*

Henry David Thoreau (1817–1862) was an author, naturalist, transcendentalist philosopher, social critic, tax protestor, and prominent abolitionist in mid-nineteenth-century America. He is best known for two books: Walden, *his rumination on simple living in nature, and* Civil Disobedience, *his passionate argument for individual nonviolent resistance to injustice by civil authority. Thoreau's nature writings anticipated two pillars of modern-day environmentalism—ecological philosophy and environmental history—and his philosophy of nonviolent resistance profoundly influenced the actions of later figures, including Mohandas Gandhi, Martin Luther King, Jr., and César Chávez.*

Although Thoreau never visited the Sierra Nevada, he was well aware of the enormous cultural transformation unleashed by the California Gold Rush. In 1852, he commented in his journal on the social and environmental impact of the event.

The recent rush to California and the attitude of the world, even of its philosophers and prophets, in relation to it appears to me to reflect the greatest disgrace on mankind. That so many are ready to get their living by the lottery of gold-digging without contributing any value to society, and that the great majority who stay at home justify them in this both by precept and example! It matches the infatuation of the Hindoos who have cast themselves under the car of Juggernaut. I know of no more startling development of the morality of trade and all the modes of getting a living than the rush to California affords. Of what significance the philosophy, or poetry, or religion of a world that will rush to the lottery of California gold-digging on the receipt of the first news, to live by luck, to get the means of commanding the labor of others less lucky, *i.e.* of slaveholding, without contributing any value to society? And that is called enterprise, and the devil is only a little more enterprising! The philosophy and poetry and religion of such a mankind are not worth the dust of a puffball. The hog that *roots* his own living, and so makes manure, would be ashamed of such company. If I could command the wealth of all the worlds by lifting my finger, I would not pay such a price for it. It makes God to be a moneyed gentleman who scatters a handful of pennies in order to see mankind scramble for them. Going to California. It is only three thousand miles nearer to hell. I will resign my life sooner than live by luck. The world's raffle. A subsistence in the domains of nature a thing to be raffled for! No wonder that they gamble there. I never heard that they did anything else there. What a comment, what a satire, on our institutions! The conclusion will be that mankind will hang itself upon a tree. And who would interfere to cut it down. And have all the precepts in all the bibles taught men only this? and is the last and most admirable invention of the Yankee race only an improved muck-rake?—patented too! If one came hither to sell lottery tickets, bringing satisfactory credentials, and the prizes were seats in heaven, this world would buy them with a rush.

Did God direct us so to get our living, digging where we never planted,—and He would perchance reward us with lumps of gold? It is a text, oh! for the Jonahs of this generation, and yet the pulpits are as silent as in immortal Greece, silent, some of them, because the preacher is gone to California himself. The gold of California is a touchstone which has betrayed the rottenness, the baseness, of mankind. Satan, from one of his elevations, showed mankind the kingdom of California, and they entered into a compact with him at once.

Olive Burt, from *Jim Beckwourth, Crow Chief*

Olive Woolley Burt (1894–1981) was born in Michigan and moved with her parents to Salt Lake City in 1897. She landed her first paid, published writing gig when she was eight years old and had steady work in the business thereafter. Burt first began collecting and writing about Western themes as a schoolteacher, and in the late 1920s she changed professions and worked as a journalist, holding many positions for the Salt Lake Tribune *and the* Deseret News. *She published numerous articles and children's books and taught adult education and creative writing classes at the university level.*

In 1957, Burt published Jim Beckwourth, Crow Chief, *a biography of the African American explorer, scout, soldier, trader, and Crow Indian chief (1798–1866). The explorer's name is frequently found on the maps of California's Plumas County in the northeastern Sierra Nevada: there is the town of Beckwourth, just east of Portola; nearby Beckwourth Peak; and Beckwourth Pass, near the Nevada state line, which Jim Beckwourth himself discovered and promoted. In this excerpt, Beckwourth, having completed his army duty of taking dispatches overland from Fort Leaven-worth, Kansas, to officers in Monterey, California, is headed upriver toward the goldfields.*

At Stockton they [Jim and his fellow passenger] left the boat, laid in a supply of goods, and started for the mines. Jim was in business again, and for a couple of years he attended to it. He built the first frame building—a small store—in the Mexican camp of Sonora some fifty miles east of Stockton. But a permanent home seemed to scare Jim. No sooner was the building up than he sold out his interest to his partner, and, with a horse and a pack set out to tramp the trails of the Mother Lode country.

This was the life he loved. He wandered where he pleased; hunted when he wished; stopped at the cabin of any mountaineer to tell yarns; lived with stray bands of Indians. And so, wandering over the mountain trails one day early in 1851, Jim made a discovery. He found a beautiful, grassy valley rimmed with mountain peaks, where, he was sure, no white man had ever set foot. On one side were the headwaters of the Yuba River, flowing west, and on the other the beginnings of the Truckee, flowing east. This lush valley [today's Sierra Valley] was an easy pass between the snow-capped, granite peaks of the Sierras.

Jim was jubilant. This was his find. He could build a road here— up the eastern slope and down the western, and this road would pass through the new little town of Marysville. The community was striving to get established, while its rival to the south, Sacramento, was flourishing, largely because it was on an established emigrant road. Jim's shrewd mind grasped the possibilities. The landowners, merchants and hotelkeepers of Marysville would be glad to finance such a road. He could build a cabin here and reap the benefits of the stream of emigrants that would flow across his valley. He had given up his pueblo on Fountain Creek because of the Mexican trouble, but he was wiser now. He'd stay here and found a settlement that would carry his name down to posterity, as his father had done in Missouri.

It was a bright dream, but like so many of Jim's dreams, was doomed. He found the landowners of Marysville eager to have the new road built, but before they could do anything their entire city was burned to the ground.

Jim had the satisfaction of seeing his name in the paper. The Marysville *Herald* for June 3, 1851, proclaimed him "the discoverer and projector of this new and important route. Mr. Beckwourth states that he now has several men at work cutting a wagon road." It wasn't much, but he clipped the story and carried it with him to show to his friends.

Jim still had faith in his pass. He went up to the lovely valley in the spring of 1852 and built a sturdy house—the first to be erected in Sierra Valley. Soon emigrant trains were winding past his door, and his cabin grew into a substantial trading post.

In one emigrant train, late in 1854, there happened to be a newspaperman named T. D. Bonner. He had become ill on the road, and by the time he reached Jim's place, he was too sick to continue. He decided to stop here awhile to recuperate, but the winter snows came and he had to remain until spring. During the long evenings beside Jim's roaring fire, Bonner listened to the old mountaineer's tales of that early West when trappers and Indians ruled.

"Your life ought to be made into a book, Jim!" Bonner exclaimed more than once. "Why, man, no one knows the old days better than you do. And your life among the Crows! I'm going to write it!"

So, as Jim reminisced, Bonner took careful notes. Often he would stop his pencil's racing across the page and look up. "How can you remember so much?" he would ask in wonder. "Even the number of General Ashley's horses. And that was nearly thirty years ago!"

By spring Bonner had enough material for a book— Jim's complete biography up to the year 1855, when he was 57.

When the book was placed on sale in San Francisco, it caused no little stir. Jim was so well known all through the California mountains that many wanted to read his story. There were those who roared with laughter and remembered that Jim had a reputation as a gaudy liar. They branded every incident as a fabrication. There were others, however, who were amazed at Jim's remarkable memory. For every incident of historical record took place largely as he had described it, with the official persons he named taking the parts he ascribed to them. And, while Jim was undoubtedly the hero of every event, as he told it, those who knew of the actual happenings shrugged. "That's probably the way it seemed to him," they said tolerantly. "It's only natural!"

Jim was delighted with the book. He carried it with him in his saddlebag whenever he traveled, and on the slightest provocation would produce it to astound his companions.

"Why, even General Ashley or Tom Fitzpatrick haven't had a whole book written about them!" he often exclaimed.

The book had an unforeseen effect, however. The vigilance committees which had sprung up in many of the mining communities looked askance at Jim's tales of Indian fighting. The old stories of his inciting the Crows to attack white travelers were revived. Jim was requested to leave California. He packed up and sadly departed from the beautiful valley which had seemed like Eden to the aging wanderer. He left behind him his name for the first settlement in Sierra Valley, for an imposing butte that towered above it, and for the now important pass through the mountains.

"The pines stopped moaning, the river ceased to rush, and the fire to crackle. It seemed as if Nature had stopped to listen too."

Bret Harte, "The Luck of Roaring Camp"

Bret Harte (1836–1902) arrived in California's Gold Country from New York in the early 1850s. Many of the mining camps were disbanding by this time, and the young man found the foothills "hard, ugly, unwashed, vulgar, and lawless." Harte mined sporadically throughout the Southern Mines, moving as far north as Angels Camp, but he was more at ease in cosmopolitan San Francisco, where he embarked on a successful writing and publishing career. Some critics have noted that people of color and women have been marginalized in Harte's works, while white male miners have been overly exalted. Nevertheless, his vignettes of life in the mining camps (as well as those of his protégé Mark Twain) have largely defined the popular view of the California Gold Rush since the nineteenth century.

Although some historians and literary scholars disagree, Angels Camp or its nearby region is often considered the likely locale for one of Harte's most famous stories, "The Luck of Roaring Camp," the seriocomic yarn of a child's birth in a rough mining camp. Originally published in the August 1868 edition of The Overland Monthly, *the tale is offered here in its entirety.*

There was commotion in Roaring Camp. It could not have been a fight, for in 1850 that was not novel enough to have called together the entire settlement. The ditches and claims were not only deserted, but "Tuttle's grocery" had contributed its gamblers, who, it will be remembered, calmly continued their game the day that French Pete and Kanaka Joe shot each other to death over the bar in the front room.

The whole camp was collected before a rude cabin on the outer edge of the clearing. Conversation was carried on in a low tone, but the name of a woman was frequently repeated. It was a name familiar enough in the camp—"Cherokee Sal."

Perhaps the less said of her the better. She was a coarse and, it is to be feared, a very sinful woman. But at that time she was the only woman in Roaring Camp, and was just then lying in sore extremity, when she most needed the ministration of her own sex. Dissolute, abandoned, and irreclaimable, she was yet suffering a martyrdom hard enough to bear even when veiled by sympathizing womanhood, but now terrible in her loneliness. The primal curse had come to her in that original isolation which must have made the punishment of the first transgression so dreadful.

It was, perhaps, part of the expiation of her sin that, at a moment when she most lacked her sex's intuitive tenderness and care, she met only the half-contemptuous faces of her masculine associates. Yet a few of the spectators were, I think, touched by her sufferings. Sandy Tipton thought it was rough on Sal, and, in the contemplation of her condition, for a moment rose superior to the fact that he had an ace and two bowers in his sleeve.

It will be seen also that the situation was novel. Deaths were by no means uncommon in Roaring Camp, but a birth was a new thing. People had been dismissed from the camp effectively, finally, and with no possibility of return; but this was the first time that anybody had been introduced *ab initio*. Hence the excitement.

"You go in there, Stumpy," said a prominent citizen known as "Kentuck," addressing one of the loungers. "Go in there, and see what you kin do. You've had experience in them things."

Perhaps there was a fitness in the selection. Stumpy, in other climes, had been the putative head of two families; in fact, it was owing to some legal informality in these proceedings that Roaring Camp—a city of refuge—was indebted to his company. The crowd approved the choice, and Stumpy was wise enough to bow to the majority. The door closed on the extempore surgeon and midwife, and Roaring Camp sat down outside, smoked its pipe, and awaited the issue.

The assemblage numbered about a hundred men. One or two of these were actual fugitives from justice, some were criminal, and all were reckless. Physically they exhibited no indication of their past lives and character. The greatest scamp had a Raphael face, with a profusion of blonde hair; Oakhurst, a gambler, had the melancholy air and intellectual abstraction of a Hamlet; the coolest and most courageous man was scarcely over five feet in height, with a soft voice and an embarrassed, timid manner.

The term "roughs" applied to them was a distinction rather than a definition. Perhaps in the minor details of fingers, toes, ears, etc., the camp may have been deficient, but these slight omissions did not detract from their aggregate force. The strongest man had but three fingers on his right hand; the best shot had but one eye.

Such was the physical aspect of the men that were dispersed around the cabin. The camp lay in a triangular valley between two hills and a river. The only outlet was a steep trail over the summit of a hill that faced the cabin, now illuminated by the rising moon. The suffering woman might have seen it from the rude bunk whereon she lay—seen it winding like a silver thread until it was lost in the stars above.

A fire of withered pine boughs added sociability to the gathering. By degrees the natural levity of Roaring Camp returned. Bets were freely offered and taken regarding the result. Three to five that "Sal would get through with it"; even that the child would survive; side bets as to the sex and complexion of the coming stranger.

In the midst of an excited discussion an exclamation came from those nearest the door, and the camp stopped to listen. Above the swaying and moaning of the pines, the swift rush of the river, and the crackling of the fire rose a sharp, querulous cry—a cry unlike anything heard before in the camp. The pines stopped moaning, the river ceased to rush, and the fire to crackle. It seemed as if Nature had stopped to listen too.

The camp rose to its feet as one man! It was proposed to explode a barrel of gunpowder; but in consideration of the situation of the mother, better counsels prevailed, and only a few revolvers were discharged; for whether owing to the rude surgery of the camp, or some other reason, Cherokee Sal was sinking fast. Within an hour she had climbed, as it were, that rugged road that led to the stars, and so passed out of Roaring Camp, its sin and shame, forever.

I do not think that the announcement disturbed them much, except in speculation as to the fate of the child. "Can he live now?" was asked of Stumpy. The answer was doubtful. The only other being of Cherokee Sal's sex and maternal condition in the settlement was an ass. There was some conjecture as to fitness, but the experiment was tried. It was less problematical than the ancient treatment of Romulus and Remus, and apparently as successful.

When these details were completed, which exhausted another

hour, the door was opened, and the anxious crowd of men, who had already formed themselves into a queue, entered in single file. Beside the low bunk or shelf, on which the figure of the mother was starkly outlined below the blankets, stood a pine table. On this a candle-box was placed, and within it, swathed in staring red flannel, lay the last arrival at Roaring Camp.

Beside the candle-box was placed a hat. Its use was soon indicated. "Gentlemen," said Stumpy, with a singular mixture of authority and *ex officio* complacency—"gentlemen will please pass in at the front door, round the table, and out at the back door. Them as wishes to contribute anything toward the orphan will find a hat handy." The first man entered with his hat on; he uncovered, however, as he looked about him, and so unconsciously set an example to the next.

In such communities good and bad actions are catching. As the procession filed in comments were audible—criticisms addressed perhaps rather to Stumpy in the character of showman: "Is that him?" "Mighty small specimen"; "Hasn't more'n got the color"; "Ain't bigger nor a derringer."

The contributions were as characteristic: A silver tobacco box; a doubloon; a navy revolver, silver mounted; a gold specimen; a very beautifully embroidered lady's handkerchief, from Oakhurst the gambler; a diamond breastpin; a diamond ring, suggested by the pin, with the remark from the giver that he "saw that pin and went two diamonds better"; a slung-shot; a Bible, contributor not detected; a golden spur; a silver teaspoon, the initials, I regret to say, were not the giver's; a pair of surgeon's shears; a lancet; a Bank of England note for £5; and about $200 in loose gold and silver coin.

During these proceedings Stumpy maintained a silence as impassive as the dead on his left, a gravity as inscrutable as that of the newly born on his right. Only one incident occurred to break the monotony of the curious procession. As Kentuck bent over the candle-box half curiously, the child turned, and, in a spasm of pain, caught at his groping finger, and held it fast for a moment. Kentuck looked foolish and embarrassed. Something like a blush tried to assert itself in his weather-beaten cheek. "The d—d little cuss!" he said, as he extricated his finger, with perhaps more tenderness and care than he might have been deemed capable of showing.

He held that finger a little apart from its fellows as he went out, and examined it curiously. The examination provoked the same original remark in regard to the child. In fact, he seemed to enjoy repeating it.

"He rastled with my finger," he remarked to Tipton, holding up the member, "the d—d little cuss!"

It was four o'clock before the camp sought repose. A light burnt in the cabin where the watchers sat, for Stumpy did not go to bed that night. Nor did Kentuck. He drank quite freely, and related with great gusto his experience, invariably ending with his characteristic condemnation of the newcomer. It seemed to relieve him of any unjust implication of sentiment, and Kentuck had the weaknesses of the nobler sex.

When everybody else had gone to bed, he walked down to the river and whistled reflectingly. Then he walked up the gulch past the cabin, still whistling with demonstrative unconcern. At a large redwood tree he paused and retraced his steps, and again passed the cabin. Halfway down to the river's bank he again paused, and then returned and knocked at the door. It was opened by Stumpy.

"How goes it?" said Kentuck, looking past Stumpy toward the candle-box.

"All serene!" replied Stumpy.

"Anything up?"

"Nothing."

There was a pause—an embarrassing one—Stumpy still holding the door. Then Kentuck had recourse to his finger, which he held up to Stumpy. "Rastled with it—the d—d little cuss," he said, and retired.

The next day Cherokee Sal had such rude sepulture as Roaring Camp afforded. After her body had been committed to the hillside, there was a formal meeting of the camp to discuss what should be done with her infant. A resolution to adopt it was unanimous and enthusiastic. But an animated discussion in regard to the manner and feasibility of providing for its wants at once sprang up. It was remarkable that the argument partook of none of those fierce personalities with which discussions were usually conducted at Roaring Camp.

Tipton proposed that they should send the child to Red Dog—a distance of forty miles—where female attention could be procured. But the unlucky suggestion met with fierce and unanimous opposition. It was evident that no plan which entailed parting from their new acquisition would for a moment be entertained. "Besides," said Tom Ryder, "them fellows at Red Dog would swap it, and ring in somebody else on us." A disbelief in the honesty of other camps prevailed at Roaring Camp, as in other places.

The introduction of a female nurse in the camp also met with objection. It was argued that no decent woman could be prevailed to accept Roaring Camp as her home, and the speaker urged that "they didn't want any more of the other kind." This unkind allusion to the defunct mother, harsh as it may seem, was the first spasm of propriety—the first symptom of the camp's regeneration. Stumpy advanced nothing. Perhaps he felt a certain delicacy in interfering with the selection of a possible successor in office. But when questioned, he averred stoutly that he and "Jinny"—the mammal before alluded to—could manage to rear the child.

There was something original, independent, and heroic about the plan that pleased the camp. Stumpy was retained. Certain articles were sent for to Sacramento. "Mind," said the treasurer, as he pressed a bag of gold dust into the expressman's hand, "the best that can be got—lace, you know, and filigree-work and frills—d—n the cost!"

Strange to say, the child thrived. Perhaps the invigorating climate of the mountain camp was compensation for material deficiencies. Nature took the foundling to her broader breast. In that rare atmosphere of the Sierra foothills—that air pungent with balsamic odor, that ethereal cordial at once bracing and exhilarating—he may have found food and nourishment, or a subtle chemistry that transmuted ass's milk to lime and phosphorus. Stumpy inclined to the belief that it was the latter and good nursing. "Me and that ass," he would say, "has been father and mother to him! Don't you," he would add, apostrophizing the helpless bundle before him, "never go back on us."

By the time he was a month old the necessity of giving him a name became apparent. He had generally been known as "The Kid," "Stumpy's Boy," "The Coyote" (an allusion to his vocal powers), and even by Kentuck's endearing diminutive of "The d—d little cuss." But these were felt to be vague and unsatisfactory, and were at last dismissed under another influence. Gamblers and adventurers are generally superstitious, and Oakhurst one day declared that the baby had brought "the luck" to Roaring Camp. It was certain that of late they had been successful.

"Luck" was the name agreed upon, with the prefix of Tommy for greater convenience. No allusion was made to the mother, and the father was unknown. "It's better," said the philosophical Oakhurst, "to take a fresh deal all round. Call him Luck, and start him fair."

A day was accordingly set apart for the christening. What was meant by this ceremony the reader may imagine who has already gathered some idea of the reckless irreverence of Roaring Camp. The master of ceremonies was one "Boston," a noted wag, and the occasion seemed to promise the greatest facetiousness. This ingenious satirist had spent two days in preparing a burlesque of the Church service, with pointed local allusions. The choir was properly trained, and Sandy Tipton was to stand godfather.

But after the procession had marched to the grove with music and banners, and the child had been deposited before a mock altar, Stumpy stepped before the expectant crowd. "It ain't my style to spoil fun, boys," said the little man, stoutly eyeing the faces around him, "but it strikes me that this thing ain't exactly on the squar. It's playing it pretty low down on this yer baby to ring in fun on him that he ain't goin' to understand. And ef there's goin' to be any godfathers round, I'd like to see who's got any better rights than me."

A silence followed Stumpy's speech. To the credit of all humorists be it said that the first man to acknowledge its justice was the satirist thus stopped of his fun. "But," said Stumpy, quickly following up his advantage, "we're here for a christening, and we'll have it. I proclaim you Thomas Luck, according to the laws of the United States and the State of California, so help me God."

It was the first time that the name of the Deity had been otherwise uttered than profanely in the camp. The form of christening was perhaps even more ludicrous than the satirist had conceived; but strangely enough, nobody saw it and nobody laughed. "Tommy" was christened as seriously as he would have been under a Christian roof, and cried and was comforted in as orthodox fashion.

And so the work of regeneration began in Roaring Camp. Almost imperceptibly a change came over the settlement. The cabin assigned to "Tommy Luck"—or "The Luck," as he was more frequently called—first showed signs of improvement. It was kept scrupulously clean and whitewashed. Then it was boarded, clothed, and papered. The rosewood cradle, packed eighty miles by mule, had, in Stumpy's way of putting it, "sorter killed the rest of the furniture." So the rehabilitation of the cabin became a necessity.

The men who were in the habit of lounging in at Stumpy's to see "how 'The Luck' got on" seemed to appreciate the change, and in self-defense the rival establishment of "Tuttle's grocery" bestirred itself and imported a carpet and mirrors. The reflections of the latter on the appearance of Roaring Camp tended to produce stricter habits of personal cleanliness.

Again Stumpy imposed a kind of quarantine upon those who aspired to the honor and privilege of holding The Luck. It was a cruel mortification to Kentuck—who, in the carelessness of a large nature and the habits of frontier life, had begun to regard all garments as a second cuticle, which, like a snake's, only sloughed off through decay—to be debarred this privilege from certain prudential reasons. Yet such was the subtle influence of innovation that he thereafter appeared regularly every afternoon in a clean shirt and face still shining from his ablutions.

Nor were moral and social sanitary laws neglected. "Tommy," who was supposed to spend his whole existence in a persistent attempt to repose, must not be disturbed by noise. The shouting and yelling, which had gained the camp its infelicitous title, were not permitted within hearing distance of Stumpy's. The men conversed in whispers or smoked with Indian gravity. Profanity was tacitly given up in these sacred precincts, and throughout the camp a popular form of expletive, known as "D—n the luck!" and "Curse the luck!" was abandoned, as having a new personal bearing.

Vocal music was not interdicted, being supposed to have a soothing, tranquilizing quality; and one song, sung by "Man o' War Jack," an English sailor from her Majesty's Australian colonies, was quite popular as a lullaby. It was a lugubrious recital of the exploits of "the Arethusa, Seventy-four," in a muffled minor, ending with a prolonged dying fall at the burden of each verse, "On b-oo-o-ard of the Arethusa." It was a fine sight to see Jack holding The Luck, rocking from side to side as if with the motion of a ship, and crooning forth this naval ditty. Either through the peculiar rocking of Jack or the length of his song—it contained ninety stanzas, and was continued with conscientious deliberation to the bitter end—the lullaby generally had the desired effect.

At such times the men would lie at full length under the trees in the soft summer twilight, smoking their pipes and drinking in the melodious utterances. An indistinct idea that this was pastoral happiness pervaded the camp. "This 'ere kind o' think," said the Cockney Simmons, meditatively reclining on his elbow, "is 'evingly." It reminded him of Greenwich.

On the long summer days The Luck was usually carried to the gulch from whence the golden store of Roaring Camp was taken. There, on a blanket spread over pine boughs, he would lie while the men were working in the ditches below. Latterly there was a rude attempt to decorate this bower with flowers and sweet-smelling shrubs, and generally some one would bring him a cluster of wild honeysuckles, azaleas, or the painted blossoms of Las Mariposas.

The men had suddenly awakened to the fact that there were beauty and significance in these trifles, which they had so long trodden carelessly beneath their feet. A flake of glittering mica, a fragment of variegated quartz, a bright pebble from the bed of the creek, became beautiful to eyes thus cleared and strengthened, and were invariably put aside for The Luck. It was wonderful how many treasures the woods and hillsides yielded that "would do for Tommy." Surrounded by playthings such as never child out of fairyland had before, it is to be hoped that Tommy was content. He appeared to be serenely happy, albeit there was an infantine gravity about him, a contemplative light in his round gray eyes, that sometimes worried Stumpy.

He was always tractable and quiet, and it is recorded that once, having crept beyond his corral—a hedge of tessellated pine boughs, which surrounded his bed—he dropped over the bank on his head in the soft earth, and remained with his mottled legs in the air in that position for at least five minutes with unflinching gravity. He was extricated without a murmur. I hesitate to record the many other instances of his sagacity, which rest, unfortunately, upon the statements of prejudiced friends. Some of them were not without a tinge of superstition.

"I crep' up the bank just now," said Kentuck one day, in a breathless state of excitement "and dern my skin if he wasn't a-talking to a jay bird as was a-sittin' on his lap. There they was, just as free and sociable as anything you please, a-jawin' at each other just like two cherrybums."

Howbeit, whether creeping over the pine boughs or lying lazily on his back blinking at the leaves above him, to him the birds sang, the squirrels chattered, and the·flowers bloomed. Nature was his nurse and playfellow. For him she would let slip between the leaves golden shafts of sunlight that fell just within his grasp; she would send wandering breezes to visit him with the balm of bay and resinous gum; to him the tall redwoods nodded familiarly and sleepily, the bumblebees buzzed, and the rooks cawed a slumbrous accompaniment.

Such was the golden summer of Roaring Camp. They were "flush times," and the luck was with them. The claims had yielded enormously. The camp was jealous of its privileges and looked suspiciously on strangers. No encouragement was given to immigration, and, to make their seclusion more perfect, the land on either side of the mountain wall that surrounded the camp they duly pre-empted.

This, and a reputation for singular proficiency with the revolver, kept the reserve of Roaring Camp inviolate. The expressman—their only connecting link with the surrounding world—sometimes told wonderful stories of the camp. He would say, "They've a street up there in 'Roaring' that would lay over any street in Red Dog. They've got vines and flowers round their houses, and they wash themselves twice a day. But they're mighty rough on strangers, and they worship an Injin baby."

With the prosperity of the camp came a desire for further improvement. It was proposed to build a hotel in the following spring, and to invite one or two decent families to reside there for the sake of The Luck, who might perhaps profit by female companionship. The sacrifice that this concession to the sex cost these men, who were fiercely skeptical in regard to its general virtue and usefulness, can only be accounted for by their affection for Tommy. A few still held out. But the resolve could not be carried into effect for three months, and the minority meekly yielded in the hope that something might turn up to prevent it. And it did.

The winter of 1851 will long be remembered in the foothills. The snow lay deep on the Sierras, and every mountain creek became a river, and every river a lake. Each gorge and gulch was transformed into a tumultuous watercourse that descended the hillsides, tearing down giant trees and scattering its drift and debris along the plain. Red Dog had been twice under water, and Roaring Camp had been forewarned.

"Water put the gold into them gulches," said Stumpy. "It's been here once and will be here again!" And that night the North Fork suddenly leaped over its banks and swept up the triangular valley of Roaring Camp.

In the confusion of rushing water, crashing trees, and crackling timber, and the darkness which seemed to flow with the water and blot out the fair valley, but little could be done to collect the scattered camp.

When the morning broke, the cabin of Stumpy, nearest the riverbank, was gone. Higher up the gulch they found the body of its unlucky owner; but the pride, the hope, the joy, The Luck, of Roaring Camp had disappeared. They were returning with sad hearts when a shout from the bank recalled them.

It was a relief-boat from down the river. They had picked up, they said, a man and an infant, nearly exhausted, about two miles below. Did anybody know them, and did they belong here?

It needed but a glance to show them Kentuck lying there, cruelly crushed and bruised, but still holding The Luck of Roaring Camp in his arms. As they bent over the strangely assorted pair, they saw that the child was cold and pulseless. "He is dead," said one.

Kentuck opened his eyes. "Dead?" he repeated feebly.

"Yes, my man, and you are dying too."

A smile lit the eyes of the expiring Kentuck. "Dying!" he repeated; "he's a-taking me with him. Tell the boys I've got The Luck with me now"; and the strong man, clinging to the frail babe as a drowning man is said to cling to a straw, drifted away into the shadowy river that flows forever to the unknown sea.

"He'd give him a little punch behind, and the next minute you'd see that frog whirling in the air like a doughnut"

Mark Twain, "The Celebrated Jumping Frog of Calaveras County"

Samuel Langhorne Clemens (1835–1910) arrived in the West in 1861. After early experiences as a Mississippi riverboat pilot, a printer, a newspaper reporter, and (very briefly) a Confederate soldier, he made his way to Virginia City, Nevada, where he tried his hand at prospecting. When that didn't work out, Clemens found work as City Editor of the local paper, the Territorial Enterprise, *which is where he first used the pseudonym "Mark Twain."*

Writer and publisher Bret Harte was instrumental in furthering Twain's writing career and polishing his ragged style. In 1864, Harte mentioned his Gold Rush experiences in California's Calaveras County, and in December of 1864, Twain headed toward Angels Camp, where, in a local saloon, he heard bartender Ben Coon relate a tale about a jumping frog. Twain modified the story that by then was already a fireside classic in the mining camps, and his was the first published version of the tale, which originally appeared in New York's Saturday Press *in 1865.*

Mr. A. Ward—
Dear Sir: Well, I called on good-natured, garrulous old Simon Wheeler, and I inquired after your friend Leonidas W. Smiley, as you requested me to do, and I hereunto append the result. If you can get any information out of it you are cordially welcome to it. I have a lurking suspicion that your Leonidas W. Smiley is a myth—that you never knew such a personage, and that you only conjectured that if I asked old Wheeler about him it would remind him of his infamous *Jim* Smiley, and he would go to work and bore me nearly to death with some infernal reminiscence

of him as long and tedious as it should be useless to me. If that was your design, Mr. Ward, it will gratify you to know that it succeeded.

I found Simon Wheeler dozing comfortably by the barroom stove of the old dilapidated tavern in the ancient mining camp at Angel's, and I noticed that he was fat and bald-headed, and had an expression of winning gentleness and simplicity upon his tranquil countenance. He roused up and gave me good-day. I told him a friend of mine had commissioned me to make some inquiries about a cherished companion of his boyhood named Leonidas W. Smiley—Rev. Leonidas W. Smiley—a young minister of the Gospel, who he had heard was at one time a resident of this village of Boomerang. I added that if Mr. Wheeler could tell me any thing about this Rev. Leonidas W. Smiley, I would feel under many obligations to him.

Simon Wheeler backed me into a corner and blockaded me there with his chair—and then sat me down and reeled off the monotonous narrative which follows this paragraph. He never smiled, he never frowned, he never changed his voice from the gentle-flowing key to which he tuned the initial sentence, he never betrayed the slightest suspicion of enthusiasm—but all through the interminable narrative there ran a vein of impressive earnestness and sincerity, which showed me plainly that so far from his imagining that there was anything ridiculous or funny about his story, he regarded it as a really important matter, and admired its two heroes as men of transcendent genius in *finesse*. To me, the spectacle of a man drifting serenely along through such a queer yarn without ever smiling was exquisitely absurd. As I said before, I asked him to tell me what he knew of Rev. Leonidas W. Smiley, and he replied as follows. I let him go on in his own way, and never interrupted him once:

There was a feller here once by the name of *Jim* Smiley, in the winter of '49—or maybe it was the spring of '50—I don't recollect exactly, some how, though what makes me think it was one or the other is because I remember the big flume wasn't finished when he first came to the camp; but anyway, he was the curiosest man about always betting on anything that turned up you ever see, if he could get anybody to bet on the other side, and if he couldn't he'd change sides—any way that suited the other man would suit *him*—any way just so's he got a bet, *he* was satisfied. But still, he was lucky—uncommon lucky; he most always come out winner. He was always ready and laying for a chance; there couldn't be no solitry thing mentioned but that feller'd offer to bet on it—and take any side you please, as I was just telling you: if there was a horse race, you'd find him flush or you'd find him busted at the end of it; if there was a dog-fight, he'd bet on it; if there was a cat-fight, he'd bet on it; if there was a chicken-fight, he'd bet on it; why if there was two birds setting on a fence, he would bet you which one would fly first—or if there was a camp-meeting he would be there regular to bet on Parson Walker, which he judged to be the best exhorter about here, and so he was, too, and a good man; if he even seen a straddle-bug start to go any wheres, he would bet you how long it would take him to get wherever he was going to, and if you took him up, he would foller that straddle-bug to Mexico but what he would find out where he was bound for and how long he was on the road. Lots of the boys here has seen that Smiley and can tell you about him. Why, it never made no difference to *him*—he would bet on *anything*—the dangdest feller. Parson Walker's wife laid very sick, once, for a good while, and it seemed as if they warn't going to save her; but one morning he come in and Smiley asked him how she was, and he said she was considerable better—thank the Lord for his inf'nit mercy—and coming on so smart that with the blessing of Providence she'd get well yet—and Smiley, before he thought, says: "Well, I'll resk two-and-a-half that she don't, anyway."

Thish-yer Smiley had a mare—the boys called her the fifteen-minute nag, but that was only in fun, you know, because, of course, she was faster than that—and he used to win money on that horse, for all she was so slow and always had the asthma, or the distemper, or the consumption, or something of that kind. They used to give her two or three hundred yards' start, and then pass her under way; but always at the fag-end of the race she'd get excited and desperate like, and come cavorting and straddling up, and scattering her legs around limber, sometimes in the air, and sometimes out to one side amongst the fences, and kicking up m-o-r-e dust, and raising m-o-r-e racket with her coughing and sneezing and blowing her nose—and always fetch up at the stand just about a neck ahead, as near as you could cipher it down.

And he had a little small bull pup, that to look at him you'd think he warn't worth a cent, but to set around and look ornery, and lay for a chance to steal something. But as soon as money was up on him he was a different dog—his underjaw'd begin to stick out like the for'castle of a steamboat, and his teeth would uncover, and shine savage like the furnaces. And a dog might tackle him, and bully-rag him, and bite him, and throw him over his shoulder two or three times, and Andrew Jackson—which was the name of the pup—Andrew Jackson would never let on but what he was satisfied, and hadn't expected nothing else—and the bets being doubled and doubled on the other side all the time, till the money was all up—and then all of a sudden he would grab that other dog just by the joint of his hind leg and freeze to it—not chaw, you understand, but only just grip and hang on till they thronged up the sponge, if it was a year. Smiley always came out winner on that pup till he harnessed a dog once that didn't have no hind legs, because they'd been sawed off in a circular saw, and when the thing had gone along far enough, and the money was all up, and he come to make a snatch for his pet holt, he saw in a minute how he'd been imposed on, and how the other dog had him in the door, so to speak, and he 'peared surprised, and then he looked sorter discouraged like, and didn't try no more to win the fight, and so he got shucked out bad. He give Smiley a look as much as to say his heart was broke, and it was *his* fault, for putting up a dog that hadn't no hind legs for him to take holt of, which was his main dependence in a fight, and then he limped off a piece, and laid down and died. It was a good pup, was that Andrew Jackson, and would have made a name for hisself if he'd lived, for the stuff was in him, and he had genius—I know it, because he hadn't had no opportunities to speak of, and it don't stand to reason that a dog could make such a fight as he could under them circumstances, if he hadn't no talent. It always makes me feel sorry when I think of that last fight of his'n, and the way it turned out.

Well, thish-yer Smiley had rat-tarriers and chicken cocks, and tomcats, and all of them kind of things, till you couldn't rest, and you couldn't fetch nothing for him to bet on but he'd match you. He ketched a frog one day and took him home and said he cal'lated to educate him; and so he never done nothing for three months but set in his back yard and learn that frog to jump. And you bet you he *did* learn him, too. He'd give him a little punch behind, and the next minute you'd see that frog whirling in the air like a doughnut—see him turn one summerset, or may be a couple, if he got a good start, and come down flat-footed and all right, like a cat. He got him up so in the matter of catching flies, and kept him in practice so constant, that he'd nail a fly every time as far as he could see him. Smiley said all a frog wanted was education, and he could do most anything—and I believe him. Why, I've seen him set Dan'l Webster down here on this floor—Dan'l Webster was the name of the frog—and sing out, "Flies, Dan'l, flies," and quicker'n you could wink, he'd spring straight up, and snake a fly off'n the counter there, and flop down on the floor again as solid as a gob of mud, and fall to scratching the side of his head with his hind foot as indifferent as if he hadn't no idea he'd been doin' any more'n any frog might do. You never see a frog so modest and straightfor'ard as he was, for all he was so gifted. And when it come to fair-and-square jumping on a dead level, he could get over more ground at one straddle than any animal of his breed you ever see. Jumping on a dead level was his strong suit, you understand, and when it come to that, Smiley would ante up money on him as long as he had a red. Smiley was monstrous proud of his frog, and well he might be, for fellers that had travelled and been everywheres, all said he laid over any frog that ever *they* see.

Well, Smiley kept the beast in a little lattice box, and he used to fetch him down town sometimes and lay for a bet. One day a feller—a stranger in the camp, he was—come across him with his box, and says:

"What might it be that you've got in the box?"

And Smiley says, sorter indifferent like, "It might be a parrot, or it might be a canary, maybe, but it ain't—it's only just a frog."

And the feller took it, and looked at it careful, and turned it round this way and that, and says, "H'm—so 'tis. Well, what's *he* good for?"

"Well," Smiley says, easy and careless, "he's good enough for *one* thing, I should judge—he can out-jump any frog in Calaveras county."

The feller took the box again, and took another long, particular look, and give it back to Smiley, and says, very deliberate, "Well—I don't see no points about that frog that's any better'n any other frog."

"Maybe you don't," Smiley says. "Maybe you understand frogs, and maybe you don't understand 'em; maybe you've had experience, and maybe you ain't only a amature, as it were. Anyways, I've got *my* opinion, and I'll resk forty dollars that he can out-jump any frog in Calaveras county."

And the feller studied a minute, and then says, kinder sad, like, "Well—I'm only a stranger here, and I ain't got no frog—but if I had a frog, I'd bet you."

And then Smiley says, "That's all right—that's all right—if you'll hold my box a minute I'll go and get you a frog"; and so the feller took the box, and put up his forty dollars along with Smiley's, and set down to wait.

So he set there a good while thinking and thinking to hisself, and then he got the frog out and prized his mouth open and took a teaspoon and filled him full of quail-shot—filled him pretty near up to his chin—and set him on the floor. Smiley he went to the swamp and slopped around in the mud for a long time, and finally he ketched a frog and fetched him in and give him to this feller and says:

"Now if you're ready, set him alongside of Dan'l, with his forepaws just even with Dan'l's, and I'll give the word." Then he says, "one—two—three—jump!" and him and the feller touched up the frogs from behind, and the new frog hopped off, but Dan'l give a heave, and hysted up his shoulders—so—like a Frenchman, but it wa'nt no use—he couldn't budge; he was planted as solid as an anvil, and he couldn't no more stir than if he was anchored out. Smiley was a good deal surprised, and he was disgusted, too, but he didn't have no idea what the matter was, of course.

The feller took the money and started away, and when he was going out at the door he sorter jerked his thumb over his shoulders—this way—at Dan'l, and says again, very deliberate, "Well, I don't see no points about that frog that's any better'n any other frog."

Smiley he stood scratching his head and looking down at Dan'l a long time, and at last he says, "I do wonder what in the nation that frog throw'd off for—I wonder if there ain't something the matter with him—he 'pears to look mighty baggy, somehow"—and he ketched Dan'l by the nap of the neck, and lifted him up and says, "Why blame my cats if he don't weigh five pound," and turned him upside down, and he belched out about a double-handful of shot. And then he see how it was, and he was the maddest man—he set the frog down and took out after that feller, but he never ketchd him. And—

(Here Simon Wheeler heard his name called from the front yard, and got up to see what was wanted.) And turning to me as he moved away, he said: "Just set where you are, stranger, and rest easy—I ain't going to be gone a second."

But by your leave, I did not think that a continuation of the history of the enterprising vagabond Jim Smiley would be likely to afford me much information concerning the Rev. Leonidas W. Smiley, and so I started away.

At the door I met the sociable Wheeler returning, and he buttonholed me and recommenced:

"Well, thish-yer Smiley had a yeller one-eyed cow that didn't have no tail only jest a short stump like a bannanner, and—"

"O, curse Smiley and his afflicted cow!" I muttered, good-naturedly, and bidding the old gentleman good-day, I departed.

Yours, truly,
Mark Twain

Ramón Gil Navarro, from *Los Chilenos en California*

When the California Gold Rush began, Ramón Gil Navarro (d. 1883), a native of Argentina, was living in exile in Chile. When he heard the fantastic stories of this new El Dorado, he vowed to make the journey to California himself. In 1849, with three other investors, he raised enough capital to provide transportation to Gold Country for 120 workers and a shipload of supplies. Upon arrival, Navarro was immediately thrust into the ethnically diverse Gold Rush society and was often stunned by the racial intolerance, violence, and physical difficulty of the miners' lives. After three unsuccessful years in the area, Navarro returned to Chile and, eventually, to Argentina, where he became a journalist and a representative in the Argentine Congress. He never returned to California.

While in the United States, Navarro served as an interpreter in the California judicial system. He was witness to several instances of brutality toward Latinos, as presented in this excerpt from his 1853 memoir, Los Chilenos en California. *Navarro's account of frontier justice presents a stark contrast to the well-known, colorful tales of the era written by Bret Harte, Mark Twain, and others.*

On December 10 [1849] began the chain of events that culminated in the tragic affair at Calaveras. A group of Chileans had found a gulch full of gold on the banks of the [North Fork of the Calaveras] river; naturally it was called Chile Gulch. They were joined by others who brought supplies for a year, bought at very high prices and at great sacrifice. Each group built a house to winter in. It was hard work, but they had to do it because the weather was turning cold. It was at that point that they were told to leave the area within ten days....

[The Chileans refused, which led to confrontations. A hastily appointed judge and jury, after scaring off the actual judge, put the Chileans on trial, charging them with rebellion against the government of the United States.]

On the night of December 31, at ten o'clock, the trial ended and the following sentence was pronounced:

José del Carmen Terán, Damián Urzúa, and Francisco Cárdenas are to suffer the extreme penalty. The three named individuals are to be taken at ten o'clock the following morning to Mokelumne Hill, taken to the top, and thrown down the cliff toward the river.

Mokelumne Hill is one of the highest in the California mining area. The cliff to which the sentence referred is more than six hundred feet high, rising from inaccessible rocks. There the condemned men were to be flung from the top down the whole face of the cliff, bound hand and foot. It would truly take more than the disposition of a cannibal to devise a method of execution more cruel, and to enjoy its most gruesome details. Terán and the other two listened to their sentence being translated with stoicism. Terán wanted to make some reply, but the interpreter refused to relay his words.

Ignacio Yáñez and two companions were sentenced to receive thirty lashes, to have their heads shaved ignominiously, and then finally to have their ears cut off, to their agony and eternal disgrace. No such penalty has ever been imposed in any part of the modern world— even among the Chinese, who are notoriously cruel in the treatment of prisoners. I have before me a book, *The Mysteries of the Inquisition*, that contains one thousand or more engravings of different tortures imposed by that tribunal; and whether they are real or imaginary, I do not find in any of them the sort of torture inflicted on the wretched Chileans by the bandits of Calaveras. From four to six of the other boys were sentenced to be tied to the branches of a tree, given fifty lashes, and have their heads shaved.

Both those sentenced to lose their ears and the ones sentenced to be whipped asked, as a favor, that they be shot instead of being made to undergo a punishment applicable to robbers and criminals of a different sort. But this petition was refused. The Yankees wanted to torture and humiliate the Chileans more than they did to kill them. All of these penalties were more deserved by those who imposed them than they were by their innocent victims. The Americans wanted the mutilated Chileans to serve as a horrendous warning to all their compatriots in California, and to have the threat of such punishment carried all the way back to their mother country. The Yankees intended, when they harshly sentenced our young men to be whipped, to make them suffer shame (in addition to pain), as honorable young men would on seeing themselves subjected to such punishment as was usually applied only to the basest of criminals. The Americans' studied hatred and insatiable desire for vengeance made them determined to outrage the dignity and gentlemanly feelings that they themselves lacked, but which their captives had, and thus subject their victims to mental as well as physical suffering. Such was the condition of the Chileans in captivity on the night of December 31....

The arrival of the Americans from Mokelumne stirred up a genuine storm at [Judge] Coller's camp. If they did not succeed in saving the lives of the Chileans, at least they got the sentence passed on Terán and his comrades changed into something less cruel and barbarous. In defending the rights of the Chileans they almost came to blows. Their attitude did influence some members of the jury. "Four Eyes," for example, let Maturano live, in a show of generosity and gratitude for kindnesses he said he had been shown himself when he was a prisoner at Stockton. No one else, though, was let off and no change was made except that in the mode of execution; all else went on as planned.

The first thing they did was to administer the whippings. They lashed the Chileans with all the ferocity of savages with victims to torture. Our young men pleaded vainly to be shot rather than dishonored; the Yankees were indifferent or pretended they did not understand. One fourth of them were absolute sadists. After the victim was in position they applied the lash without caring whether they cut the flesh or shattered the skull of the poor devil. One by one the Chileans had their hands tied up to an overhanging branch so that their feet barely touched the ground, and then they were whipped so that blood spurted from their lungs....

Thus did the Americans greet the New Year, in a presentation that even they themselves would have to admit was half-tragic, half-comic. Men would have to be both wild beasts and cowards to have staged such a farcical trial and followed it by such merciless sadism. "Listen to the brave fellows," they shouted when, in the midst of the torture the Chileans were suffering, one of them let a cry of pain escape his lips. After the whippings, carried out to the very letter, Ignacio Yáñez was to undergo the third penalty, that of losing his ears; to be followed in turn by his two fellow sufferers—after they had been whipped and had their heads shaved. I still shudder, remembering the screams of those poor men as they were so barbarously mutilated. An American armed with a huge knife came to carry out the sentence. The condemned men begged on their knees as a last supreme favor that they be shot, but pleading was useless with those bandits and they did not even bother to listen. Three or four of them held the first victim and the executioner cut off his ears. The cutting was followed by a cry of pain such as one might hear in the last agony of a martyr. The ear with a part of the cheek was in the hand of the executioner who, after a moment, threw it aside and went after the other ear with the coldest insensitivity. A sea of blood inundated the face and clothing of the poor fellow, giving him a look more horrible than you can imagine. The horror of losing the second ear was not so great because the victim had fainted. But what must have been the torture and terror of those who were waiting their turn as they watched the monstrous act!

It is not possible to dwell on the account of those exquisite cruelties by the Americans. The fate that awaited Terán and his friends was even worse because they had to undergo many tortures before death, and all without the comforts of religion; religion which alone can make such sufferings bearable, and help a man rise above martyrdom and any physical or moral evils. One of the Chileans who was to die with Terán had his son with him, a boy of eight or ten; but the sobbing pleas of the innocent boy could not soften or inspire pity for his father in such men as they were. Just one glimpse of that scene of sorrow between a son and his father should have affected the most barbarous and pitiless of executioners. What would become of the boy, left an orphan among such men? Who would be a father to him, direct him away from a life of infamy and crime, when he had been exposed to the perverse example of those men and watched his own father die? This thought must have tortured the last hour of the poor father. Nevertheless the son had to be present at the execution of his own father.

The three condemned men were brought out to an open space with fifty armed riflemen standing around. The Chileans were to be shot but the firing squad had not been picked. All of them were to demonstrate their marksmanship with the chests of the Chileans as targets. It was as though the Americans intended to spare no suffering whatsoever to their victims until they were dead. The spot picked for the execution was a mile, more or less, from the house of the judge, and the prisoners were made to walk there after all the torment they had been put through during the last twelve days. Terán spoke briefly to the others during the march to encourage them; he never lost his calm, even when one of his comrades collapsed; he bent over and helped him up before anyone else could do so. Oddly the prisoners were not bound, probably so they could get through the difficult places they had to cross. Three or four of those who had been whipped had to witness the execution of their comrades so they could report on it to other Chileans in all its details.

When the execution site was reached, Terán in his own name and in that of his comrades offered money if they were let go, and promised to leave Calaveras and even California and go back to his own country. The Yankees did not believe he had any money after having been robbed twice and put no faith in his offer. The boy's father in turn said he would give thirty ounces of gold that he had if they would let him take his son out of California. The Yankees asked him whether he had that much gold. He answered, yes; he had it in a secret pocket that had escaped the searching. The Americans took it, then told him he could not be let go but they would give the gold to his son. The poor boy no more got the gold than he was ever to see his father again—except in the next world.

Terán was infuriated at seeing what was happening and said in a low voice to his companions, "Give me a knife and, by God, if I have to die I will kill three or four of those devils and die fighting." No one answered him. The other Chileans were afraid the Yankees might have heard him and would take some special vengeance on all of them because of his attitude. Terán repeated his request two or three times. He felt that even they were abandoning him. But what could they do? What he wanted was impossible; no one had any weapons. When the Americans came to tie him, Terán turned to them and said, "Give me a dagger and then you can kill me any way you choose." Some were annoyed, others paid no heed, and all went on with their work. Terán, seeing he was going to die, then asked for a pencil and paper so he could write a few words to his family. One of the Yankees dug a piece of paper out of his pack and gave it to him along with a pencil. Terán wrote on both sides of the sheet, and the Yankee promised to give the letter to the other Chileans when they were released. I am afraid the letter no more reached his family than the gold did the boy. No one knew what he had written, but his friends said he had wanted to leave his property to his brother, and earlier had told them he would like to make his will.

Finally Terán, Damián Urzúa, and Francisco Cárdenas were tied to oak trees. It is sad to write this; they had wanted to go back to their country and see their native soil, their families, and friends once more, but they had only a few minutes of life left. Death was to be their whole future. The most pathetic thing of all was the death of the boy's father. He embraced his son with tears and many words of tenderness and sorrow. But not even this most hallowed and solemn grief affected the Yankees. They separated the two and began the execution. They shot from a distance of fifty feet, not all at once but one after another. This intensified the suspense because some bullets struck and others missed, and firing successively that way only strung out the agony. But I will not prolong the harrowing of the sensibilities of their parents and fellow countrymen by dwelling upon the details of their suffering. Let me only add that the Chileans who had to bury the men found fifteen bullet holes in Terán and about the same number in the other two.

The Chilean workers were held for several weeks and made to cook for the Americans. The orphaned boy they kept permanently as a slave. The whipped and mutilated Chileans were free to leave but for several days not one of them could move.

These tragic events took place three years ago. [Judge] Coller is today a rich and respected American citizen and holds the legitimate title of a judge in Double Springs. [Jury member] Nickleson, or "Four Eyes," is a licensed doctor of medicine in Marysville. The area where it happened is populated today by farming families from New Orleans. A traveler who goes past the camp at Mokelumne toward Melones will find the ruins of the Chilean buildings in Chile Gulch on the Calaveras. A mile farther on he will see three crosses that the pious survivors erected in the names of their fallen countrymen. There is an inscription: "Say the Our Father and a Hail Mary for the souls of the Chileans who were killed here on January 1, 1850." There is no other memorial, and in years to come, when the crosses have crumbled away, these men will exist only in legend.

[Today there is a bronze California Historical Marker at Chile Gulch, on Highway 49 between Jackson and San Andreas.]

Isabel Allende, from *Daughter of Fortune*

Born in Peru, Isabel Allende (b. 1942) is the daughter of Tomás Allende—then the Chilean ambassador to Peru, and the brother of Salvador Allende, the Socialist Party leader and president of Chile from 1970 to 1973. With the fall of her uncle's government, Allende eventually went into exile in Venezuela. During a visit to California in 1988, she met her second husband and soon thereafter became a permanent resident of the state. In 2003, Allende gained United States citizenship.

Allende was working as a journalist in the 1960s when the Nobel Prize–winning poet (and fellow Chilean) Pablo Neruda encouraged her to write fiction. She then embarked upon a successful career as a novelist and short story writer that continues today. In this selection from her novel Daughter of Fortune *(1999), Allende recounts the efforts of journalist Jacob Freemont to document the story of the legendary California Gold Rush bandit Joaquín Murieta. The lynching of Josefa, mentioned in this excerpt, is also the subject of an essay by Alejandro Murguía, in Chapter 6 of this anthology.*

In the summer of 1851 Jacob Freemont decided to interview Joaquín Murieta. Outlaws and fires were the chief subjects of conversation in California; they kept citizens terrorized and the press occupied. Crime was rampant and police corruption common knowledge; most of the force was composed of crooks more interested in protecting their partners in crime than the local populace. After one more raging fire, which destroyed a large area of San Francisco, a vigilante committee had been formed by outraged citizens, headed by the ineffable Sam Brannan, the Mormon who had spread the news of the gold. Companies of firemen pulling water carts by hand ran uphill and down, but before they reached a burning building flames would be leaping from the one beside it. The fire had begun when Australian "hounds" had splashed kerosene all through the store of a merchant who had refused to pay them protection money, and then torched it. In view of the indifference of the authorities, the committee had decided to act on its own. The newspapers clamored, "How many crimes have been committed in this city this year? And who has been hanged or jailed for them? No one! How many men have been shot or stabbed, hit over the head and beat up? And who has been convicted for that? We do not condone lynching, but who can tell what an indignant public will do to protect itself?" Lynchings were precisely the public's solution. Vigilantes immediately threw themselves into the task and hanged the first suspect. The numbers of these self-appointed enforcers grew day by day, and they acted with such excessive enthusiasm that for the first time outlaws took care to move about only in the full light of day. In that climate of violence and revenge, the figure of Joaquín Murieta was on the way to becoming a symbol. Jacob Freemont took it upon himself to fan the flames of Murieta's celebrity: his sensationalist articles had created a hero for Hispanics and a devil for Americans. Murieta was believed to have a large gang and the talent of a military genius; it was said that he was fighting a war of skirmishes that authorities were powerless to combat. He attacked with cunning and speed, descending upon his victims like a curse and then disappearing without a trace, only to show up a hundred miles away with another attack of unbelievable boldness that could be explained only by magic powers. Freemont suspected that there were several "Murietas," not one, but he was careful not to write that because it would have diminished the legend. On the other hand, he had the inspired idea of labeling Murieta "the Robin Hood of California," which immediately sparked a wildfire of racial controversy. To the Yanquis [Yankees], Murieta represented what was most despicable about the greasers; and it was believed that the Mexicans hid him and provided him with weapons and supplies because he stole from the whites to help the people of his race. In the war they had lost the territories of Texas, Arizona, New Mexico, Nevada, Utah, and half of Colorado and California, and so for them any attack against the victors was an act of patriotism. The governor warned the newspaper against the rashness of making a hero of a criminal, but the name had already inflamed the public's imagination. Freemont received dozens of letters, including one from a young girl in Washington who was ready to sail halfway around the world in order to marry that "Robin Hood" and people stopped Freemont in the street to ask him details about the famous Joaquín Murieta. Without ever having seen him, the newspaperman described Murieta as a young man of virile mien, with the features of a noble Spaniard and the courage of a bullfighter. Quite by accident, Freemont had stumbled across a gold mine more productive than many in the mother lode. He decided he must interview this Joaquín, if the fellow really existed, and write his biography, and if it were all a fable he would turn it into a novel. His work as author would consist simply of writing in a heroic tone to satisfy the common man's tastes. California needed its myths and legends, Freemont maintained. To Americans, it had come into the union with a clean slate; they thought that the stroke of a pen could erase a long history of Indians, Mexicans, and Californians. For this land of empty spaces and solitary men, a land open to conquest and rape, what better hero than a bandit? Freemont packed his indispensables in a suitcase, stocked himself with a supply of notebooks and pencils, and set off in search of his character. The risks never entered his mind; having the dual arrogance of an Englishman and a journalist, he felt he was protected from any harm. In addition, traveling was by now effected with a certain ease; there were highways, and a regular stagecoach service connected the towns where he planned to make his investigations. It was not the way it had been when he had begun his work as a reporter, riding on mule back, forging a path through the uncertainty of hills and forests with no guide but insane maps that could lead one to wander in circles for all time. Along the way, he could see the changes in the region. Few men had made their fortune with gold but, thanks to adventurers who had come by the thousands, California was becoming civilized. Without gold fever, the conquest of the West would have been delayed by a couple of centuries, the journalist wrote in his notebook.

There was no dearth of subjects, such as the story of the young miner, a boy of eighteen, who after a year's backbreaking effort had gotten together the ten thousand dollars he needed to go home to Oklahoma and buy a farm for his parents. He was walking back to Sacramento through the foothills of the Sierra Nevada one radiant day, with his treasure in a sack over his shoulder, when he was surprised by a band of ruthless Mexicans or Chileans, he wasn't sure which. All he knew for sure was that they spoke Spanish, because they had the impudence to leave a sign in that language, scrawled by knife-point on a piece of wood: "Death to Yanquis." They were not content with beating and robbing him, they tied him naked to a tree and smeared him with honey. Two days later, when he was found by a patrol, he was raving. Mosquitoes had eaten away his skin.

Freemont put his talent for morbid journalism to the test with the tragic death of Josefa, a beautiful Mexican girl who worked in a dance hall. She arrived in the town of Downieville on the Fourth of July and found herself in the midst of a celebration promoted by a candidate for senator and irrigated with a river of alcohol. A drunken miner had forced his way into Josefa's room and she had fought him off, plunging her dagger deep into his heart. By the time Jacob Freemont arrived, the body was lying on a table, covered with an American flag, and a crowd of two thousand fanatics ignited by racial hatred was demanding the gallows for Josefa. Impassive, her white blouse stained with blood, smoking a cigarette as if the yelling had nothing to do with her, the woman was scanning the faces of the men with abysmal scorn, aware of the incendiary mixture of aggression and sexual desire she aroused in them. A doctor tried to take her part, explaining that she had acted in self-defense and that if they executed her they would also kill the baby in her womb, but the mob silenced him by threatening to hang him, too. Three terrified doctors were marched over to examine Josefa and all three declared that she was not pregnant, in view of which the impromptu tribunal condemned her in a matter of minutes. "Shooting these greasers is not the way to go," said one member of the jury. "We have to give them a fair trial and hang them in the full majesty of the law." Freemont had never had occasion to witness a lynching before, but this one he described in emotional sentences: how, about four in the afternoon, they had started to lead Josefa to the bridge where the ritual of execution had been prepared but she had haughtily shaken them off and walked to the gallows on her own. The beautiful woman climbed the steps without any help, bound her skirts around her ankles, placed the rope around her neck, arranged her black tresses, and bid them farewell with a courageous *"Adios, señores"* that left the journalist uncertain and the others ashamed. "Josefa did not die because she was guilty, but because she was Mexican. This is the first time a woman has been lynched in California. What a waste, when there are so few!" Freemont wrote in his article.

Following Joaquín Murieta's trail, he passed through established towns, with school, library, church, and cemetery, and others whose only signs of culture were a brothel and a jail. Saloons thrived in all of them, they were the centers of social life. Jacob Freemont would install himself there, asking questions, and so began constructing—with some truths and a mountain of lies—the life—or the legend—of Joaquín Murieta. The saloonkeepers painted him as a damned spic dressed in leather and black velvet, wearing outsize silver spurs and a dagger at his waist and riding the most spirited sorrel ever seen. They said he would ride into town, unchallenged, amid a jangle of spurs and his gang of cutthroats, slap his silver dollars on the counter and order a round of drinks for everyone in the house. No one dared refuse; even the bravest of men would down their drinks in silence under the villain's flashing gaze. For the constables, on the other hand, there was nothing splendid about him, he was nothing less than a vulgar murderer capable of the worst atrocities, who had managed to escape justice because all the greasers protected him. The Chileans thought he was one of them, born in a place called Quillota; they said he was loyal to his friends and never forgot to repay a favor, which was why it was good policy to help him, but the Mexicans swore he came from the state of Sonora and was an educated, handsome young man from an old and noble family and had turned to crime out of revenge....Jacob Freemont selected the opinions that best suited his image of the bandit, and that was how he portrayed him in his articles, always with enough ambiguity that he could print a retraction in case he should someday meet his protagonist face to face. He looked high and low during the four summer months, without finding Murieta anywhere, but from the many different versions he contrived a fanciful and heroic biography.

John Rollin Ridge, from *The Life and Adventures of Joaquín Murieta, the Celebrated California Bandit*

Born in New Echota, Georgia, John Rollin Ridge (1827–1867) was a scion of the Cherokee Nation's elite. Both his father and grandfather were prominent tribal leaders, as well as signatories to the Treaty of New Echota, which ceded to the United States all Cherokee lands east of the Mississippi River, and which ultimately led to the 1838–1839 Trail of Tears. Ridge came to California during the Gold Rush and here published what is believed to be the first novel by a Native American, as well as the first novel written in California: The Life and Adventures of Joaquín Murieta, the Celebrated California Bandit *(1854). Ridge died at age forty in his adopted hometown of Grass Valley, California.*

The Life and Adventures of Joaquín Murieta *is based on true events although compiled from stories involving many separate individuals named Joaquín. Consolidating these different characters into one heroic figure, Ridge's story is a rollicking adventure but also a powerful consideration of cultural and political loss. The novel is generally considered by folklorists to have inspired the Zorro stories.*

The first that we hear of him in the Golden State is that, in the spring of 1850, he is engaged in the honest occupation of a miner in the Stanislaus placers, then reckoned among the richest portions of the mines. He was then eighteen years of age, a little over the medium height, slenderly but gracefully built, and active as a young tiger. His complexion was neither very dark or very light, but clear and brilliant, and his countenance is pronounced to have been, at that time, exceedingly handsome and attractive. His large black eyes, mouth, his well-shaped head from which the long, glossy, black hair hung down over his shoulders, his silvery voice full of generous utterance, and the frank and cordial bearing which distinguished him made him beloved by all with whom he came in contact. He had the confidence and respect of the whole community around him, and was fast amassing a fortune from his rich mining claim. He had built himself a comfortable mining residence in which he had domiciled his heart's treasure—a beautiful Sonorian girl, who had followed the young adventurer in all his wanderings with that devotedness of passion which belongs to the dark-eyed damsels of Mexico.

It was at this moment of peace and felicity that a blight came over the young man's prospects. The country was then full of lawless and desperate men, who bore the name of Americans but failed to support the honor and dignity of that title. A feeling was prevalent among this class of contempt for any and all Mexicans, whom they looked upon as no better than conquered subjects of the United States, having no rights which could stand before a haughtier and superior race. They made no exceptions. If the proud blood of the Castilians mounted to the cheek of a partial descendant of the Mexiques, showing that he had inherited the old chivalrous spirit of his Spanish ancestry, they looked upon it as a saucy presumption in one so inferior to them. The prejudice of color, the antipathy of races, which are always stronger and bitterer with the ignorant and unlettered, they could not overcome, or if they could, would not, because it afforded them a convenient excuse for their unmanly cruelty and oppression.

A band of these lawless men, having the brute power to do as they pleased, visited Joaquín's house and peremptorily bade him leave his claim, as they would allow no Mexicans to work in that region. Upon his remonstrating against such outrageous conduct, they struck him violently over the face, and, being physically superior, compelled him to swallow his wrath. Not content with this, they tied him hand and foot and ravished his mistress before his eyes. They left him, but the soul of the young man was from that moment darkened. It was the first injury he had ever received at the hands of the Americans, whom he had always hitherto respected, and it wrung him to the soul as a deeper and deadlier wrong from that very circumstance. He departed with his weeping and almost heart-broken mistress for a more northern portion of the mines; and the next we hear of him, he is cultivating a little farm on the banks of a beautiful stream that watered a fertile valley, far out in the seclusion of the mountains. Here he might hope for peace—here he might forget the past, and again be happy.

But his dream was not destined to last. A company of unprincipled Americans—shame that there should be such bearing the name!—saw his retreat, coveted his little home surrounded by its fertile tract of land, and drove him from it, with no other excuse than that he was "an infernal Mexican intruder!" Joaquín's blood boiled in his veins, but his spirit was still unbroken, nor had the iron so far entered his soul as to sear up the innate sensitiveness to honor and right which reigned in his bosom. Twice broken up in his honest pursuit of fortune, he resolved still to labor on with unflinching brow and with that true *moral* bravery which throws its redeeming light forward upon his subsequently dark and criminal career. How deep must have been the anguish of that young heart and how strongly rooted the native honesty of his soul, none can know or imagine but they who have been tried in a like manner. He bundled up his little movable property, still accompanied by his faithful bosom-friend, and again started forth to strike once more, like a brave and honest man, for fortune and for happiness.

He arrived at "Murphy's Diggings" in Calaveras County, in the month of April, and went again to mining, but, meeting with nothing like his former success, he soon abandoned that business and devoted his time to dealing "monte," a game which is common in Mexico, and has been almost universally accepted by gamblers in California....

[One day] he had gone a short distance from Murphy's Diggings to see a half-brother, who had been located in that vicinity for several months, and returned to Murphy's upon a horse which his brother had lent him. The animal proved to have been stolen, and being recognized by a number of individuals in town, an excitement was raised on the subject. Joaquín suddenly found himself surrounded by a furious mob and charged with the crime of theft. He told them how it happened that he was riding the horse and in what manner his half-brother had come in possession of it. They listened to no explanation, but bound him to a tree, and publicly disgraced him with the lash. They then proceeded to the house of his half-brother and hung him without judge or jury. It was then that the character of Joaquín changed, suddenly and irrevocably. Wanton cruelty and the tyranny of prejudice had reached their climax. His soul swelled beyond its former boundaries, and the barrier of honor, rocked into atoms by the strong passion which shook his heart like an earthquake, crumbled around him. Then it was that he declared to a friend that he would live henceforth for revenge and that his path should be marked with blood. Fearfully did he keep his promise, as the following pages will show.

It was not long after this unfortunate affair that an American was found dead in the vicinity of Murphy's Diggings, having been cut to pieces with a knife. Though horribly mangled, he was recognized as one of the mob engaged in whipping Joaquín. A doctor, passing in the neighborhood of this murder, was met, shortly afterward, by two men on horseback, who fired revolvers at him, but, owing to his speed on foot, and the unevenness of the ground, he succeeded in escaping with no further injury than having a bullet shot through his hat within an inch of the top of his head! A panic spread among the rash individuals who had composed that mob, and they were afraid to stir out on their ordinary business. Whenever any one of them strayed out of sight of his camp or ventured on the highway, he was shot down suddenly and mysteriously. Report after report came into the villages that Americans had been found dead on the highways, having been either shot or stabbed, and it was invariably discovered, for many weeks, that the murdered men belonged to the mob who publicly whipped Joaquín. It was fearful and it was strange to see how swiftly and mysteriously those men disappeared. "Murieta's revenge was very nearly complete," said an eyewitness of these events, in reply to an inquiry which I addressed him. "I am inclined to think he *wiped out* the most of those prominently engaged in whipping him."

Thus far, who can blame him? But the iron had entered too deeply in his soul for him to stop here. He had contracted a hatred to the whole American race, and was determined to shed their blood, whenever and wherever an opportunity occurred.

Among the many thrilling instances of the daring and recklessness of spirit which belonged to Joaquín, there is one which I do not feel at liberty to omit—especially as it comes naturally and properly at this connection. Shortly after he parted from Reis and Luis Vulvia, he went up into the extreme north of the country. There, at the head of a branch of the South Fork of the Mokelumne River, in a wild and desolate region near the boundary line of Calaveras and El Dorado Counties, were located a company of miners, consisting of twenty-five men. They were at a long distance from any neighbors, having gone there well-armed on a prospecting tour which resulted in their finding diggings so rich that they were persuaded to pitch their tents and remain.

One morning while they were eating their breakfast on a flat rock—a natural table which stood in front of their tents—armed as usual with their revolvers, a young fellow with very dark hair and eyes rode up and saluted them. He spoke very good English and they could scarcely make out whether he was a Mexican or an American. They requested him to get down and eat with them, but he politely declined. He sat with one leg crossed over his horse's neck very much at his ease, conversing very freely on various subjects, until Jim Boyce, one of the partners who had been to the spring after water, appeared in sight. At first glance on him, the young horseman flung his reclining leg back over the saddle and spurred his horse.

Boyce roared out: "Boys, that fellow is *Joaquín*; d—n it, shoot him!" At the same instant, he himself fired but without effect.

Joaquín dashed down to the creek below with headlong speed and crossed with the intention, no doubt, to escape over the hills which ran parallel with the stream, but his way was blocked up by perpendicular rocks, and his only practicable path was a narrow digger-trail which led along the side of a huge mountain, directly over a ledge of rocks a hundred yards in length, which hung beatling over the rushing stream beneath in a direct line with the hill upon which the miners had pitched their tents, and not more than forty yard distant. It was a fearful gauntlet for any man to run. Not only was there danger of falling a hundred feet from the rocks, but he must run in a parallel line with his enemies, and in pistol-range, for a hundred yards. In fair view of him stood the whole company with their revolvers drawn. He dashed along that fearful trail as if he had been mounted upon a spirit-steed, shouting as he passed:

"I am Joaquín! Kill me if you can!"

Shot after shot came clanging around his head, and bullet after bullet flattened on the wall of slate at his right. In the midst of the first firing, his hat was knocked from his head, and left his long black hair streaming behind him. He had no time to use his own pistol, but, knowing that his only chance lay in the swiftness of his sure-footed animal, he drew his keenly polished bowie-knife in proud defiance of the danger and waved it in scorn as he rode on. It was perfectly sublime to see such super-human daring and recklessness. At each report, which came fast and thick, he kissed the flashing blade and waved it at his foes. He passed the ordeal, as awful and harrowing to a man's nerves as can be conceived, untouched by a ball and otherwise unharmed. In a few moments, a loud whoop rang out in the woods a quarter of a mile distant, and the bold rider was safe!

Jessie Benton Frémont, "My Grizzly Bear"

Jessie Benton Frémont (1824–1902)—the daughter of Missouri Senator Thomas Hart Benton and the wife of explorer and soldier John C. Frémont—was largely responsible for the development of her husband's reputation as the "Great Pathfinder" of the American West. She was a primary author of Colonel Frémont's expedition reports from the 1840s, and her contributions and engaging writing style, although they were largely unknown to the general public, captivated readers.

Jessie Frémont also published accounts under her own name. From 1858 to 1861, she lived in California's Mariposa County on a huge estate she called "our mining place in the Lower Sierra," and it was there that she wrote the sketches later published as Mother Lode Narratives. *These writings include the following selection, "My Grizzly Bear."*

Bear Valley was the name of the busy mining town nearest us on our mining place in the Lower Sierra. It troubled our sense of fitness to call a town a valley, but it was fixed by custom and fitness; for this had been a happy hunting-ground of the grizzlies. Acorns of the long variety, tasting like chestnuts, abounded here as well as the usual smaller varieties, while the rich oily nut of the piñon-pine made their delight. These acorns and piñones were the chief bread-supplies of the Indians also who did not give them up easily, and consequently bear-skeletons and Indian skulls remained to tell the tale to the miners, who came in to the rich "diggings" there. American rifles, then the pounding of quartz mills and strange shrieks of steam engines drove them away, and only the name remained.

To my objection of using "valley" and "town" as one and the same, I was told best let it alone or worse would follow, for there was a strong party intending to change the name of the place to "Simpkinsville," and how would I like that? The postmaster was the Simpkins—a tall, "showy" young man with an ambitious wife much older than himself; he was a London footman and she Irish, active, energetic, with a good head, and with ambition for her Simpkins. That neither of them could read or write was a trivial detail that did not seem to disturb the public. Men would swing down from horse or wagon-box, go in and select from the loose pile of letters their own and those of their neighbors, and have their drink at the bar over which Simpkins presided (they kept a tavern and the post-office was only a little detail).

But with the instinct of a man who "had seen the world" toward people of somewhat the same experience, the postmaster treated us with the largest courtesy, for everything with a capital "F" on it was laid aside for us. [This "F" was the brand on all the tools and belongings of the works—in these countries whatever else was defied, the brand had to be respected.—J.B.F.] Isaac, our part-Indian hunter, who generally rode in for the mail, did not read either, and often had to make return-trips to give back what was not ours. It was in the time of Mr. Buchanan's administration, and had Simpkins sent in a petition signed as it would have been by the *habitues* of his bar, of course so faithful a political servant would have been granted this small favor, of change of name. You may be sure I lay low in my valley to avert this cruel address on my letters.

I had never before gone up to this property, and now it was chiefly as a summer open-air and camping-out tour to be over in three months, when we were to return to Paris where all arrangements had been made for a three-years stay.

Although the bear had long disappeared from this favorite old haunt I felt nervous about horseback excursions. Mountains are grim things at best, but all those deep clefts and thickets in ravines and horrid stony hill-slopes barred me from any but the beaten stage and wagon-roads, with our cool, brave Isaac to drive me. However, there was one view Mr. Frémont wanted me to see which we could get only on horseback, with a short climb at the peak of the mountain. From the summit we could see eighty miles off the line of the San Joaquin River, defined by its broad belt of trees, running north and south parallel to our mountains; connecting the two were many mountain rivers crossing the broad plain and glittering like steel ribbons in the afternoon sun—the Merced, the Stanislaus, the Tuolumne and others; a turn of the head showed the peaks of the Yosemite thirty miles off, and lines of blue mountains back to the everlasting snow of Carson's Peak—a stretch of a hundred and fifty miles.

It was a rough ride up, and rougher climbing after the horses could go no further and had to be left tied to trees with one man to watch them—only one other was with us; our party was only myself and my daughter with her father and the two men.

We were growing more and more enthusiastic as glimpses of this rare view came to us. Mr. Frémont told us the distances, which only singularly pure mountain air could have let the eye pierce. "And the ear, too," I said. "We must be three miles from the village and yet how near sounds the barking of that dog!"

Dead silence fell on our animated people. They listened, as the rough, low bark—broader and rougher even than that of a bull-dog—rose again, sounding really close to us.

I never question any acts of some few people but I was surprised, and not too pleased, to find myself hurried back down the steep, stony peak with only, "It is too late to finish the climb—we must hurry—do not speak—keep all your breath for walking." And hurry we did. I was fairly lifted along. Mr. Burke had disappeared and was now with Lee bringing the horses to meet us—the horses refractory.

Without a word I was lifted into the saddle—Mr. Frémont gathered up my reins himself and kept close to my side—and we fairly scurried down the mountains, I shamelessly holding to the saddle as the steep grade made me dizzy. This dizziness so pre-occupied me with the fear of fainting that I felt nothing else. We gained the stage-road by the shortest cut, and then a loping gallop soon brought us home, where I was carefully lifted down and all the consideration and care which they dared not give me on the hurried ride was now lavished on me. I had been seriously ill not long before and could not understand why I was so roughly hauled along.

There was reason enough.

It was no dog, but a grizzly bear that made that warning bark, and we were very close to it.

My ignorance spared me the shock of this knowledge, but the practised mountain men knew it was not only a bear, but a she-bear with cubs. They knew she would not be likely to leave her cubs at that hour when they were settling for the night unless we came nearer or irritated her by talking and noises. Horses are terribly afraid of this powerful and dangerous animal, and one danger was that our horses would break away and run for safety leaving us to the chances of getting off on foot. There I was the weak link in the chain. My daughter was fleet of foot and so steady of nerve that she was told the truth at once, and did her part bravely in keeping me unaware of any unusual condition. Fortunately our riding horses were, each, pets and friends, and only required to be safe with their masters; Burke had got back instantly to help Lee, and once mounted we were moved by one intelligence, one will.

Very quickly our bright drawing-room filled with eager men gun in hand. Armed men rode down the glen intent on that bear—first coming to get all information of the exact locality, then to ride and raise the countryside for a general turnout against it. For everyone had kept from "the Madam" the fact that a she-bear had been prowling about for some time seeking what she could devour; and that she had devoured some and mangled more of "Quigley's hogs"—Quigley having very fine and profitable hogs at a small ranch three miles from us.

Lights frighten off wild beasts. I had no shame in illuminating the house that night. Men laughed kindly over it, but they all felt glad that I had come off so safely, and next day I was early informed that the cubs were all killed. The bear went as usual to Quigley's for her raw pork supper, the digestion of a bear making this a pleasure without drawback, but the stir about the place was evident to the keen senses of the grizzly and the men watched that night in vain. Her tracks were plain all around about, and the poor thing was tracked to her return to her cubs. She had moved them—made sure they were all dead, and her instinct sent her off into close hiding.

The watch was kept up, but she was wary and kept away.

At length one dark night the Quigley people heard sounds they were sure came from the bear though the hogs in the big pen were quiet. They were stifled sounds blown away by a high wind. There was but one man in the house, and he said his wife would not let him go after them; it was so desperately dark the odds would be all against him.

The woman said she was not sure it was a bear. She half thought it was men fighting, an equally great danger in that isolated way of living. So they shut their ears and their hearts although human groans and stifled blown-away cries made them sure it was no animal.

The sounds passed on. In the morning they went to the wagon-road which ran near their enclosure and found a trail of blood. Followed up, it led to a little creek close by with steep clay banks. Dead, his face downward in the water, lay a young man in a pool of blood— shockingly mangled across the lower part of the body. His sufferings must have been great, but his will and courage had proved greater.

He had not been torn by a bear as was first thought, but by a ball from his own pistol. This was found, a perfectly new pistol, in his trousers pocket; the scorched clothing showing it had gone off while in the pocket. The trail was followed back, leading to a brook where he must have stopped to drink when the pistol, carrying a heavy ball, went off. Yet such was his courage and determination that he crawled that long way in a state plainly told by the place where he had rolled in agony—the last was where he made his vain appeal for help at the Quigley house. Perhaps he fell face downward into the shallow streams and was mercifully drowned.

His good clothing, a geologist's hammer, and some specimens of quartz wrapped in bits of a German newspaper, told of an educated, worthy sort of man. But there was nothing to identify him, and the poor fellow was never inquired after. One of the many who came from afar with high hopes, and whose life was summed up in that most pathetic of words, "Missing."

The grizzly had disappeared and was, I am told, the last ever known in that valley, which still has as postmark for the town, "Bear Valley"; it is to be presumed the succeeding post-masters have been men who knew the whole of the alphabet as well as the letter "F."

Dame Shirley (Louise Amelia Knapp Smith Clappe), "Letter of January 27, 1852"

One of the most remarkable records to come out of the California Gold Rush was a series of letters written by a young woman, describing life in the rude mining camps of Indian Bar and Rich Bar along the Feather River. The author, who signed her pieces "Dame Shirley," was Louise Amelia Knapp Smith Clappe (1819–1906), who had accompanied her husband, Dr. Fayette Clapp (his original spelling), westward in 1850. Author Bret Harte knew of her accounts and may or may not have used them in writing his own manuscripts; Clappe generously referred to the similarities as "Unconscious Plagiarisms."

Clappe's letters, written in 1851 and 1852 to her sister Molly in Massachusetts, were first published in 1854 in the San Francisco literary magazine The Pioneer. *In this letter Dame Shirley describes a memorable Christmas celebration.*

From our Log Cabin, Indian Bar, January 27, 1852

I wish that it were possible, dear M—, to give you an idea of the perfect Saturnalia which has been held upon the river for the last three weeks, without at the same time causing you to think *too* severely of our good Mountains. In truth, it requires not only a large intellect, but a large heart, to judge with becoming charity of the peculiar temptations of riches. A more generous, hospitable, intelligent, and industrious people than the inhabitants of the half-dozen Bars—of which Rich Bar is the nucleus—never existed; for you know how proverbially wearing it is to the nerves of manhood, to be entirely without either occupation or amusement; and that has been pre-eminently the case during the present month.

Imagine a company of enterprising and excitable young men, settled upon a sandy level about as large as a poor widow's potatoe patch, walled in by sky-kissing hills, absolutely *compelled* to remain, on account of the weather, which has vetoed indefinitely their Exodus—with no place to ride or drive, even if they had the necessary vehicles and quadrupeds; with no newspapers nor politics to interest them; deprived of all books but a few dog-eared novels of the poorest class, churches, lectures, lyceums, theaters, and (most unkindest cut of all!) pretty girls having become to these unhappy men mere myths; without *one* of the thousand ways of passing time peculiar to civilization; most of them living in damp, gloomy cabins, where Heaven's dear light can enter only by the door; and, when you add to all these disagreeables the fact that, during the never-to-be-forgotten month, the most remorseless, persevering rain which ever set itself to work to drive humanity mad, has been pouring doggedly down, sweeping away bridges, lying in uncomfortable puddles about nearly all the habitations, wickedly insinuating itself beneath un-umbrella-protected shirt-collars, generously treating to a shower-bath *and* the rheumatism sleeping bipeds who did not happen to have an India-rubber blanket; and, to crown all, rendering mining utterly impossible—you cannot wonder that even the most moral should have become somewhat reckless.

The Saturnalia commenced on Christmas evening, at the Humboldt, which, on that very day, had passed into the hands of new proprietors. The most gorgeous preparations were made for celebrating the *two* events. The bar was re-trimmed with red calico, the bowling alley had a new lining of the coarsest and whitest cotton cloth, and the broken lampshades were replaced by whole ones. All day long, patient mules could be seen descending the hill, bending beneath casks of brandy and baskets of champagne, and, for the first time in the history of that celebrated building, the floor (wonderful to relate, it *has* a floor) was *washed*, at a lavish expenditure of some fifty pails of water, the using up of one entire broom, and the melting away of sundry bars of the best yellow soap, after which I am told that the enterprising and benevolent individuals who had undertaken the Herculean task succeeded in washing the boards through the hopeless load of dirt which had accumulated upon them during the summer and autumn. All these interesting particulars were communicated to me by "Ned," when he brought up dinner. That distinguished individual himself was in his element, and in a most intense state of perspiration and excitement at the same time.

About dark we were startled by the loudest hurrahs, which arose at the sight of an army of India-rubber coats (the rain was falling in riversful), each one enshrouding a Rich Barian, which was rapidly descending the hill. This troop was headed by the "General," who— lucky man that he is—waved on high, instead of a banner, a *live* lantern, actually composed of tin and window-glass, and evidently intended by its maker to act in no capacity but that *of* a lantern. The "General" is the largest and tallest and—with one exception, I think—the oldest, man upon the river. He is about fifty, I should fancy, and wears a snow-white beard of such immense dimensions, in both length and thickness, that any elderly Turk would expire with envy at the mere sight of it. Don't imagine that *he* is a reveler; by no means; the gay crowd followed *him*, for the same reason that the king followed Madam Blaize,"because he went before."

At nine o'clock in the evening, they had an oyster and champagne supper in the Humboldt, which was very gay with toasts, songs, speeches, etc. I believe that the company danced all night; at any rate, they were dancing when I went to sleep, and they were dancing when I woke the next morning. The revel was kept up in this mad way for three days, growing wilder every hour. Some never slept at all during that time. On the fourth day, they got past dancing, and, lying in drunken heaps about the bar-room, commenced a most unearthly howling— some barked like dogs, some roared like bulls, and others hissed like serpents and geese. Many were too far gone to imitate anything but their own animalized selves. The scene, from the description I have had of it, must have been a complete illustration of the fable of Circe and her fearful transformations. Some of these bacchanals were among the most respectable and respected men upon the river. Many of them had resided here for more than a year, and had never been seen intoxicated before. It seemed as if they were seized with a reckless mania for pouring down liquor, which, as I said above, everything conspired to foster and increase.

Of course, there were some who kept themselves aloof from these excesses; but they were few, and were not allowed to enjoy their sobriety in peace. The revelers formed themselves into a mock vigilance committee, and when one of these unfortunates appeared outside, a constable, followed by those who were able to keep their legs, brought him before the Court, where he was tried on some amusing charge, and *invariably* sentenced to "treat the crowd." The prisoners had generally the good sense to submit cheerfully to their fate.

Towards the latter part of the week, people were compelled to be a little more quiet from sheer exhaustion; but on New Year's day, when there was a grand dinner at Rich Bar, the excitement broke out, if possible, worse than ever. The same scenes in a more or less aggravated form, in proportion as the strength of the actors held out, were repeated at Smith's Bar and the Junction.

Nearly every day, I was dreadfully frightened by seeing a boat-load of intoxicated men fall into the river, where nothing but the fact of their *being* intoxicated saved many of them from drowning. One morning, about thirty dollars' worth of bread (it must have been "tipsy cake") which the baker was conveying to Smith's Bar fell overboard, and sailed merrily away towards Marysville. People passed the river in a boat, which was managed by a pulley and a rope that was strained across it from Indian Bar to the opposite shore.

Of the many acquaintances who had been in the habit of calling nearly every evening, three, only, appeared in the cabin during as many weeks. Now, however, the Saturnalia is about over. "Ned" and "Chock" have nearly fiddled themselves into their respective graves—the claret (a favorite wine with miners) and oysters are exhausted—brandied fruits are rarely seen, and even port wine is beginning to look scarce. Old callers occasionally drop in, looking dreadfully sheepish and subdued, and *so* sorry,—and people are evidently arousing themselves from the bacchanal madness into which they were so suddenly and so strangely drawn.

Mary Ballou, from *I Hear the Hogs in My Kitchen*

*In contrast to the early California writings by the privileged women of
the Sierra Nevada (like Jessie Frémont and Dame Shirley), Mary Ballou
(1809–1894) left records of the often hardscrabble existence of working-
class pioneers. Having left her New Hampshire home for the glittery
allure of the California Gold Rush, Ballou and her husband ran a profitable boardinghouse in Negro Bar, a mining community nestled on the
banks of the American River, near today's Folsom.*

*Mary's letters to her sons back East describe the society she encoun-
tered in California, and from a rare perspective, as women were a tiny
minority in the goldfields.*

California Negrobar
October 30, 1852

My Dear Selden,

We are about as usual in health. Well I suppose you would like to
know what I am doing in this gold region. Well I will try to tell you
what my work is here in this muddy Place. All the kitchen that I have
is four posts stuck down into the ground and covered over the top
with factory cloth—no floor but the ground. This is a Boarding House
kitchen. There is a floor in the dining room and my sleeping room
coverd with nothing but cloth. We are at work in a Boarding House.
    Oct. 27. This morning I awoke and it rained in torrents. Well I got
up and I thought of my House. I went and looket into my kitchen. The
mud and water was over my Shoes. I could not go into the kitchen

to do any work to day but kept perfectly dry in the Dining, so I got along verry well. Your Father put on his Boots and done the work in the kitchen.

I will try to tell you what my work is in this Boarding House. Well somtimes I am washing and Ironing, somtimes I am making mince pie and Apple pie and squash pies. Somtimes frying mince turnovers and Donuts. I make Buiscuit and now and then Indian jonny cake and then again I am making minute puding filled with rasons and Indian Bake pudings and then again a nice Plum Puding and then again I am Stuffing a Ham of pork that cost forty cents a pound. Somtimes I am making gruel for the sick now and then cooking oisters, somtimes making coffee for the French people strong enough for any man to walk on that has Faith as Peter had. Three times a day I set my Table which is about thirty feet in length and do all the little fixings about it such as filling pepper boxes and vinegar cruits and mustard pots and Butter cups. Somtimes I am feeding my chickens and then again I am scareing the Hogs out of my kitchen and driving the mules out of my Dining room.

Last night there a large rat came down pounce down onto our bed in the night. Somtimes I take my fan and try to fan myself but I work so hard that my Arms pain me so severely that I kneed some one to fan me so I do not find much comfort anywhere. I made a Bluberry puding to day for Dinner. Somtimes I am making soups and cramberry tarts and Baking chicken that cost four Dollars a head and cooking Eggs at three Dollars a Dozen. Somtimes boiling cabbage and Turnips and frying fritters and Broiling stake and cooking codfish and potatoes. I often cook nice Salmon trout that weigh from ten to twenty pound apiece. Somtimes I am taking care of Babies and nursing at the rate of Fifty Dollars a week but I would not advise any Lady to come out here and suffer the toil and fatigue that I have suffered for the sake of a little gold—neither do I advise any one to come. Clarks Simmon wife says if she was safe in the States she would not care if she had not one cent. She came in here last night and said, "Oh dear I am so homesick that I must die," and then again my other associate came in with tears in her eyes and said that she had cried all day. She said if she had as good a home as I had got she would not stay twenty five minutes in California. I told her that she could not pick up her duds in that time. She said she would not stop for duds nor anything else but my own heart was two sad to cheer them much.

Now I will tell you a little more about my cooking. Somtimes I am cooking rabbits and Birds that are called quails here and I cook squrrels. Occasionly I run in and have a chat with Jane and Mrs Durphy and I often have a hearty cry. No one but my maker knows my feelings. And then I run into my little cellar which is about four feet square as I have no other place to run that is cool.

I will tell you a little of my bad feelings. On the 9 of September there was a little fight took place in the store. I saw them strike each other through the window in the store. One went and got a pistol and started towards the other man. I never go into the store but your mother's tender heart could not stand that so I ran into the store and Beged and plead with him not to kill him for eight or ten minutes not to take his Life, for the sake of his wife and three little children to spare his life and then I ran through the Dining room into my sleeping room and Buried my Face in my bed so as not to hear the sound of the pistol and wept Biterly. Oh I thought if I had wings how quick I would fly to the States. That night at the supper table he told the Boarders if it had not been for what that Lady said to him Scheles would have been a dead man. After he got his pashion over he said that he was glad that he did not kill him, so you see that your mother has saved one Human being's Life. You see that I am trying to relieve all the suffering and trying to do all the good that I can.

There I hear the Hogs in my kichen turning the Pots and kettles upside down so I must drop my pen and run and drive them out. So you [see], this is the way that I have to write—jump up every five minutes for somthing and then again I washed out about a Dollars worth of gold dust the fourth of July in the cradle so you see that I am doing a little mining in this gold region but I think it harder to rock the cradle to wash out gold than it is to rock the cradle for the Babies in the States.

G. Ezra Dane, from *Ghost Town*

*G. Ezra Dane (1904–1941) was a San Francisco lawyer and a leader in
E Clampus Vitus, or "the Clampers," a social and civic organization dating back to the Gold Rush. In the early 1940s, Dane took the initiative to
commemorate the centennial of the Gold Rush, publishing articles and
editing reprints from the era. Dane's work often romanticized the period,
but his efforts nevertheless provided a significant and useful body of
literature.*

*In 1941, Dane interviewed several older residents of the goldfields and
compiled their reminiscences in his book* Ghost Town. *The setting is
Columbia, a historic mining camp in the heart of Gold Country, just north
of Sonora. Columbia is now a California State Historic Park.*

No sir, nobody has a better right than me to set on this stump. I
planted the old poplar myself on the corner here, near sixty years
ago. It got to be three foot through at the ground, as you can see, and
it must of been eighty feet high. But the roots begun to upheave the
sidewalk bricks, and when the limbs would blow they'd brush the
shakes off the awning of Mike Rehm's Pioneer Saloon, so the old tree
had to come down.

Well, they must come an end to all things, no matter how great or
how good. With men, and trees, and towns, it's all the same. And so it
is with me. I grew up with this old town and I've come down with it.

Here I set like an old owl or fox amongst the boulders and think of the
days and times that used to be. Them days and these! Them days and these!
It's like day and night, day and night. Oh, them was the days, I can tell you.
Yes, sir, them was the days of great depravitation and plenty of whisky.

A fellow didn't have to travel, in them days, to see the world. The whole world come here then with samples of all kinds of humanity. The gold, that was what they all come for, of course. They followed the track of it, in '48 and '49 and '50, like you'll see chickens follow a trail of corn, pecking and scratching away after it, up the Stanislaus River and the Tuolumne into these Sierra foothills, then along Wood's Creek, and acrost Shaw's Flat and up the main gulch here, that we called Miners' Avenue.

March 1850, that's when the first miners reached this flat—Dr. Thaddeus Hildreth and his party—and the five of them averaged fifteen pounds of gold for three days. Why, even a lazy man could do pretty well in diggins as rich as that. You take, for instance, one of these first comers, he was even too lazy to wash his drawers. To save himself the work of scrubbing them, he just tied them to a limb that overhung a little stream and let them dangle in the water. He figured, you see, that the current would wash them for him overnight. And the next morning when he come to fish them out, lo and b'God! he found his drawers gold-plated.

Well, with stories like that a-spreading, it's no wonder that Columbia's population grew from five men to six thousand in six weeks. A good many of them, of course, went out like they had come in—with the next rush to another new discovery. But others come that built, and made the camp a town, and the town a city. Yes sir, the greatest on the Mother Lode it was in its day, and they called it the Gem of the Southern Mines.

Well, that's the way it was. Columbia was born of gold; yes, and died of it. It practically ate itself up, the old town did. When the miners had scraped down to bedrock all around, then they begun to close in on the town itself. One house after another come down for the sake of the rich ground underneath. These few old buildings that still straggle along Main Street here, you see, either they've been mined under without falling down or they happened to be built in places where the bedrock come near the surface and the gold was scarce.

So that's the way the miners come in, like a swarm of locusts. They stripped the country bare, right down to its poor old limestone bones, and then they left.

To look at the old place now, you wouldn't believe that it used to be as I remember it. I can set here and look down this street and see it as it was.

Toward the end of the afternoon the men would come in from the diggins in Matelot Gulch and from Miners' Avenue, and off Gold Hill and from Gold Springs and Murphy's Defeat and Texas Flat and the diggins out Springfield way, and down from French Camp and Italian Bar and Pine Log on the South Fork of the Stanislaus, and from Yankee Hill and from Martinez and Sawmill Flat. Say, that was a sight you ought to see! The street was so packed with people that a fellow could hardly cross. He'd just be carried along with the stream of humanity. The crowd would surge back and forth, and it was made up of all sorts and conditions of people from everywhere.

You'd see all kinds of dress, from frock coats and ruffled shirts and fancy vests down to red or blue flannel shirts with no coats or vests at all and old pants tucked into heavy boots. These pants would be held up, along with a pistol and knife and other hardware, by a good stout belt; and they'd be held together by patches. Usually the patches would be made from flour sacks, each man advertising his favorite brand. Now you take, for instance, they was a fellow one time showed up with the label "Self-Rising Flour" right across the seat of his pants, and he was "Self-Rising Bill" from that day on.

Yes, and patches wasn't all they used the flour sacks for. A man didn't ever have to go without socks if he had a couple of flour sacks. He'd put his foot on the sack near one end and he'd fold the corners and the front end over the top of his foot, and then he'd bring the other end up in back over the heel and wrap it around his ankle and leg and pull his boot on over it; and that was called the "California socks."

Yes sir, and when the women begun to come in, they found the flour sack mighty useful, too. Old Mr. Bell that had the flouring mill down on Wood's Creek below Sonora—you can see his stone dam yet where the old mill stood—he used to tell how, time of the big flood at Sonora, when the creek overflowed and the women came squealing and splashing out of the houses with their skirts lifted up to their waists, of course they showed considerable of their home-made underwear, and under each lifted skirt the crowd could read: BELL'S FLOURING MILLS. Yes sir, old Mr. Bell always said that was the best advertising he ever got, and it didn't cost him a cent.

James M. Hutchings, from *Scenes of Wonder and Curiosity in California*

James Mason Hutchings (1820–1902) immigrated to the United States from his native England in 1848. In July 1855, he led the second (and first documented) tourist trip into Yosemite Valley and, soon afterward, he became one of its earliest European American settlers. Hutchings operated an inn there and was a much sought-after guide and a tireless publicist for Yosemite. Among his publications were Hutchings' Illustrated California Magazine, *which ran from 1856 to 1860;* Scenes of Wonder and Curiosity in California *(1860), which was primarily a tourist guide to Yosemite; and* In the Heart of the Sierras *(1886), a classic description of the virtues of the valley. Unfortunately, the valley that became the center of his life was also the site of his demise. In 1902, while visiting Yosemite, his horse reared and threw Hutchings from his buggy to his death.*

In this selection from Scenes of Wonder and Curiosity in California, *Hutchings describes a breathtaking outing to Yosemite Falls.*

After a substantial breakfast, made palatable by that most excellent of sauces, a good appetite, our guide announces that the horses are ready, and the saddle-bags well stored with such good things as will commend themselves acceptably, to our attention, about noon; and that the first place to visit is the Yo-Semite Fall.

Crossing a rude bridge over the main stream, which is here almost sixty feet in width, and nine in depth, we keep down the northern bank of the river for a short distance, to avoid a large portion of the valley in front of the hotel, that is probably overflowed with water. On either side of our trail, in several places, such is the luxuriant growth of the ferns, that they are above our shoulders as we ride through them.

Presently we reach one of the most beautifully picturesque scenes that eye ever saw. It is the ford. The oak, dogwood, maple, cottonwood, and other trees, form an arcade of great beauty over the sparkling, rippling, pebbly stream, and, in the back-ground, the lower fall of the Yo-Semite is dropping its sheet of snowy sheen behind a dark middle distance of pines and hemlocks.

As the snow rapidly melts beneath the fiery strength of a hot summer sun, a large body of water, most probably, is rushing past, forming several small streams—which, being comparatively shallow, are easily forded. When within about a hundred and fifty yards of the fall, as numerous large boulders begin to intercept our progress, we may as well dismount, and, after fastening our animals to some young trees, make our way up to it on foot.

Now a change of temperature soon becomes perceptible, as we advance; and the almost oppressive heat of the centre of the valley is gradually changing to that of chilliness. But up, up, we climb, over this rock, and past that tree, until we reach the foot, or as near as we can advance to it, of the great Yo-Semite Falls when a cold draught of air rushes down upon us from above, about equal in strength to an eight knot freeze; bringing with it a heavy shower of finely comminuted spray, that falls with sufficient force to saturate our clothing in a few moments. From this a beautiful phenomenon is observable—inasmuch as, after striking our hats, the diamond-like mist shoots off at an angle of about thirty-five or forty degrees, and as the sun shines upon it, a number of miniature rainbows are formed all round us.

Those who have never visited this spot, must not suppose that the cloud-like spray that descends upon us is the main fall itself, broken into infinitesimal particles, and becoming nothing but a sheet of cloud. By no means; for, although this stream shoots over the margin of the mountain, nearly seven hundred feet above, it falls almost in a solid body—not in a continuous stream exactly, but having a close resemblance to an avalanche of snowy rockets that appear to be perpetually trying to overtake each other in their descent, and mingle the one into the other; the whole composing a torrent of indescribable power and beauty.

Huge boulders, and large masses of sharp, angular rocks, are scattered here and there, forming the uneven sides of a so immense, and apparently ever-boiling cauldron; around, and in the interstices of which, numerous dwarf ferns, weeds, grasses, and flowers, are ever growing, when not actually washed by the falling stream.

It is beyond the power of language to describe the awe-inspiring majesty of the darkly-frowning and overhanging mountain walls of solid granite that here hem us in on every side, as though they would threaten us with instantaneous destruction, if not total annihilation, did we attempt for a moment to deny their power. If man ever feels his utter insignificance at any time, it is when looking upon such a scene of appalling grandeur as the one here presented.

The...lower [section of the fall], according to the measurements of Mr. Denman, superintendent of Public Schools in San Francisco; of Mr. Petersen, the engineer of the Mariposa and Yo-Semite Water Company; and of Mr. Long, county surveyor, is about seven hundred feet above the level of the valley, while the upper fall is about one thousand four hundred and forty-eight feet, and between the two, measuring about four hundred feet, is a series of rapids rather than a fall, giving the total height of the entire series fall at two thousand five hundred and forty-eight feet.

After lingering here for several hours, with inexpressible feelings of suppressed astonishment and delight, qualified and intensified by veneration, we may take a long and reluctant last upward gaze, convinced that we shall "never look upon its like again," until we pay it another visit at some future time; and, making the best of our way to where our horses are tied, proceed to endorse the truthfulness of the prognostications of our guide in the morning before starting, concerning appetites and lunch.

Horace Greeley, from *An Overland Journey from New York to San Francisco, in the Summer of 1859*

"Go West, young man, and grow up with the country." With this slogan, Horace Greeley (1811–1872) became one of the most famous promoters of the American West. Although controversy remains over who originated the phrase, Greeley's position as a leading reformer and editor of the nationally influential New York Tribune *gave his usage special clout with the public.*

In the summer of 1859, Greeley embarked on a westward journey to observe the country for himself. Traveling from New York to the Pacific Coast, Greeley visited Atchison, Denver, Salt Lake City, Sacramento, and San Francisco, publishing his impressions in his newspaper along the way. In 1860, his writings were collected and issued as An Overland Journey from New York to San Francisco, in the Summer of 1859. *While the book was primarily designed as a vehicle for one of Greeley's pet projects—the building of a transcontinental railroad—it became popular for its commentaries on the places he visited and the individuals he met on his way to the coast.*

Following is a selection from Greeley's description of the California mining regions ten years after the Gold Rush. Although his writing echoes some of the distasteful cultural stereotypes of the era, his portrayal of the Chinese was unusually sympathetic for the period. Also to his credit, his early warning of environmental devastation associated with mining was uncannily perceptive.

California Mines and Mining
Sacramento, Aug. 7, 1859

I have spent the last week mainly among the mines and miners of El
Dorado, Placer, and Nevada counties, in the heart of the gold-producing
region. There may be richer "diggings" north or south; but I believe no
other three counties lying together have yielded in the aggregate, or are
now producing, so much gold as those I have named. Of course, I have
not been within sight of more than a fraction of the mines or *placers* of
these counties, while I have not carefully studied even one of them; and
yet the little information I have been able to glean, in the intervals of
traveling, friendly greeting, and occasional speech-making, may have
some value for those whose ignorance on the subject is yet more dense
than mine.

The three counties I have named lie near the center of the state,
at the base of the Sierra Nevada, between those mountains on the
east and the valley of the Sacramento on the west. They are rugged
in formation, being composed of innumerable hills (mainly spurs of
the great chain), separated by narrow valleys, usually descending to
the west, and gradually opening out into the broad, rich valley of the
Sacramento. The three branches or "forks" of the American and those
of the Yuba River come brawling down from the Sierra Nevada through
very deep, narrow valleys or cañons, and unite respectively to run a
very short course less rapidly ere they are lost in the Sacramento—
the Yuba having previously formed a junction with the Feather. "Bear
River," "Wolf Creek," "Deer Creek," etc., are the names of still smaller
streams, taking their rise among the foot-hills, and running a short
course into some fork of the American or Yuba, their scanty waters,
with a good portion of those of the rivers aforesaid, being mainly drawn
off into canals or "ditches," as they are inaccurately termed, by which
the needful fluid is supplied to the miners.

The Canals

These canals are a striking characteristic of the entire mining region. As
you traverse a wild and broken district, perhaps miles from any human
habitation or sign of present husbandry, they intersect your dusty,
indifferent road, or are carried in flumes supported by a frame-work
of timber twenty to sixty feet over your head. Some of these flumes or
open aqueducts are carried across valleys each a mile or more in width;
I have seen two of them thus crossing side by side. The canals range

from ten to sixty or eighty miles in length, and are filled by damming the streams wherefrom they are severally fed, and taking out their water in a wide trench, which runs along the side of one bank, gradually gaining comparative altitude as the stream by its side falls lower and lower in its cañon, until it is at length on the crest of the headland or mountain promontory which projects into the plain, and may be conducted down either side of it in any direction deemed desirable. Several of these canals have cost nearly or quite half a million dollars each, having been enlarged and improved from year to year, as circumstances dictated and means could be obtained....

The Mines

Go where you will, in the mining region, you are seldom a mile distant from past or present "diggings." Speaking generally, every ravine, gully, or water-course has been prospected; each has, at some point, been dug open to the "bed-rock," and the overlaying earth or gravel run through a "rocker," "tom," or "sluice," in the hope of making it yield the shining dust. Many of these water-courses have been deeply and widely dug up for miles in extent. If any are left entirely undisturbed, the presumption is strong that the subjacent rock is so near the surface, that gold has had no chance to deposit itself thereon. In some instances, basins or depressions in the rock have been gradually filled up with earth—probably auriferous—through thousands of years, and the gold which might otherwise have been strown down the valley for miles is here collected, so that it would be sheer waste to mine throughout those miles. But the more general opinion seems to be, that gold is diffused throughout the soil of the entire mining region, especially upon, and just above the surface of, the bed-rock, though only in certain localities is it sufficiently abundant to justify efforts to extract it. I find no one seeming to cherish any apprehensions that California will cease to produce gold abundantly, at least within the next quarter of a century. On the contrary, the current belief seems to be, that the influx of population will in time so reduce the wages of labor, or the progress of invention and discovery so increase its efficiency, that extensive districts will ultimately be mined with profit, which are now necessarily avoided. If the amount of available water were doubled, with a considerable reduction of price, the gold product of California would thereupon be increased several millions per annum. At present, mining enterprises of considerable promise and indefinite magnitude remain in abeyance, simply because the price of labor, the rate of interest, and other elements of the cost of mining, are deemed too high to justify their prosecution.

Modes of Mining

In the course of a week's travel through a portion of the mining district, I did not see a single miner engaged with pick and pan in prospecting. Higher up in the mountains, or further to the north, I might have found such. Nor do I remember having seen white men, save, perhaps, in a single instance, engaged in digging and washing the gravel or earth in the bed of any water-course, whether river, creek, or dry gulch. But Chinese bands, of six to twelve, were often hard at work in these water-courses—Bear River, the south fork of the Yuba, etc.—digging, and washing with rocker, sluice, and a sort of wheel-and-flume arrangement, which I did not get the hang of.

The Chinese are hardly used [badly treated] here. In the first place, they are taxed four dollars each per month for the naked privilege of mining at all. Next, they are not allowed to mine anywhere but in diggings which white men have worked out and abandoned, or which no white man considers worth working. Thirdly, if these rejected diggings happen, in Chinese hands, to prove better than their reputation, and to begin yielding liberally, a mob of white sovereigns soon drive the Chinese out of them, neck and heels. "John" does not seem to be a very bad fellow, but he is treated worse than though he were. He is not malignant nor sanguinary, and seldom harms any but his own tribe. But he is thoroughly sensual, and intent on the fullest gratification of his carnal appetites, and on nothing else. He eats and drinks the best he can get, and as much as he can hold; but he is never so devoid of self-respect as to be seen drunk in a public place; even for an opium debauch, he secludes himself where none but a friendly eye can reach him. His "particular wanity" in the eating line is rice, whereof he will have the best only, if the best is to be had; he likes a fat chicken also, and will pay his last dollar for one, rather than go without. Lacking the dollar, it is charged that he will rob hen-roosts; at all events, hen-roosts are sometimes robbed, and "John" has to bear the blame. He is popularly held to spend nothing, but carry all his gains out of the country and home to his native land—a charge disproved by the fact that he is an inveterate gambler, an opium-smoker, a habitual rum-drinker, and a devotee of every sensual vice. But he is weak in body, and not allowed to vote, so it is safe to trample on him; he does not write English, and so cannot tell the story of his wrongs; he has no family here (the few

Chinese women brought to this country being utterly shameless and abandoned), so that he forms no domestic ties, and enjoys no social standing. Even the wretched Indians of California repel with scorn the suggestion that there is any kinship between their race and the Chinese. "John" has traits which I can neither praise nor justify; yet I suspect that, if other men's faults were punished as severely as his, a good many Californians would be less comfortable than they are.

As to quartz-mining—or the reduction to powder of the vein-stone wherein gold is contained, and the extraction of the gold from the powder, by means of water, quick-silver, etc.—I judge that the time has not even yet arrived for its profitable prosecution....

I think the most popular form of mining at present is that of sinking or drifting into hills which have a stratum of gravel at or near their base, directly overlying the bed-rock. Many of these hills would seem to have been piled, in some far-off, antediluvian period, upon a bed or basin of solid granite, which often hollows or dips toward its center like a saucer. If, then, a tunnel can be run through the "rim rock" or side of this saucer so happily as to strike the level of the bottom, thereby draining off the water, and affording the utmost facility for extracting the gold-bearing gravel, the fortune of the operator may be made by one lucky, or better than lucky, operation. In a few instances, these subterranean gravel-basins would seem to have formed parts of the beds of ancient rivers, and so to be extra-ordinarily rich in the precious dust. In some cases, the "pay dirt" is hauled by steam up an inclined plane, or even raised perpendicularly by windlass; but it is easier to extract it by a horizontal drift or tunnel, wherever possible. Many mines of this order are worked night and day on the "three-shift" plan, and are paying very handsomely.

But the newest, most efficient, most uniformly profitable mode of operation is that termed *hydraulic mining*—that is, the washing down and washing away of large deposits of auriferous earth by means of a current of water so directed as to fall on the right spot, or (better still) projected through a hose and pipe with the force generated by a heavy fall. The former of these methods is exhibited in perfection at Nevada [City], the latter at North San Juan, as, doubtless, at many other places. At North San Juan, near the middle fork of the Yuba, streams at least three inches in diameter, and probably containing twenty measured inches of water, are directed against the remaining half of a high hill, which they strike with such force that bowlders of the size of cannon-balls are started from their beds and hurled five to ten feet into the air.

By this process, one man will wash away a bank of earth sooner than a hundred men could do it by old-fashioned sluicing. I believe earth yielding a bare cent's worth of gold to the pan may be profitably washed by this process, paying a reasonable price for the water. As much as one hundred dollars per day is profitably paid for the water thrown through one pipe. The stream thus thrown will knock a man as lifeless as though it were a grape-shot. As the bank, over a hundred feet high, is undermined by this battery, it frequently caves from the top downward, reaching and burying the careless operator. Three men have been thus killed at San Juan within the last month, until at length greater caution is exercised, and the operator stands twice as far away as he formerly did. Very long sluices—as long as may be—conduct the discharged water away; and I am told that it is no matter how thick with earth the water may run, provided the sluice be long enough. It is of course so arranged as to present riffles, crevices, etc., to arrest the gold at first borne along by the turbid flood. I believe there are companies operating by this method whose gross receipts from a single sluice have reached a thousand dollars per day.

One of the novelties (to me) of this region is the presence of soft granite—putty-granite, if I may coin a name for it. Unlike most soft rocks, this seems not to harden by exposure to the atmosphere. It is found at various depths, and I know no way of accounting for it. It seems to me that one-fourth of the granite I saw at the base of recent excavations appeared soft as cheese. Is not this peculiar to California?

Mining is a necessary art, but it does not tend to beautify the face of nature. On the contrary, earth distorted into all manner of ungainly heaps and ridges, hills half torn or washed away, and the residue left in as repulsive shape as can well be conceived, roads intersected and often turned to mire by ditches, water-courses torn up and gouged out, and rivers, once pure as crystal, now dense and opaque with pulverized rock—such is the spectacle presented throughout the mining region. Not a stream of any size is allowed to escape the pollution—even the bountiful and naturally pure Sacramento is yellow with it, and flows turbid and uninviting to the Pacific. (The people of this city have to drink it, nevertheless.) Despite the intense heat and drouth always prevalent at this season, the country is full of springs, which are bright and clear as need be; but wherever three or four of these have joined to form a little rill, some gold-seeker is sharp on their track, converting them into liquid mud. California, in giving up her hoarded wealth, surrenders much of her beauty also.

Worse, still, is the general devastation of timber. The whole mining region appears to have been excellently timbered—so much of it as I have traversed was eminently so. Yellow, pitch, and sugar (white) pine (and what is here called pitch pine is a large, tall, and graceful tree), white, black, and live-oak, with stately cedars, once overspread the whole country; not densely, as in eastern forests, but with reasonable spaces between the noble trunks—the oaks often presenting the general appearance of a thrifty apple-orchard, undergrown with grass and bushes. But timber is wanted for flumes, for sluices, for drifts or tunnels, for dwellings, for running steam-engines, etc., and, as most of the land has no owner, everybody cuts and slashes as if he cared for nobody but himself, and no time but to-day. Patriarchal oaks are cut down merely to convert their limbs into fuel, leaving the trunks to rot; noble pines are pitched this way and that, merely to take a log or two from the butt for sawing or splitting, leaving the residue a cumberer of the ground; trees fit for the noblest uses are made to subserve the paltriest, merely because they are handy, and it is nobody's business to preserve them. There was timber enough here ten years ago to satisfy every legitimate need for a century; yet ten years more will not elapse before the millers will be sending far up into the mountains at a heavy cost for logs that might still have been abundant at their doors, had the timber of this region been husbanded as it ought. Remonstrance were idle, but I must be permitted to deplore.

CHAPTER THREE

Always Afternoon

1860–1899

The last four decades of the nineteenth century in the Sierra Nevada were filled with the joy of personal discovery, coupled with a troubling undercurrent of unrestricted resource development and exploitation.

Beginning in the 1860s, the state grew less isolated and more truly integrated into the American nation as rapid improvements in transportation and communication made the Sierra more readily accessible to the general public. Thousands flooded the landscape in search of individual fulfillment, spiritual union, and the possibility of daring escapades. As more and more people sojourned to the range to experience its natural phenomena, there developed a cottage industry of travel writing, which in turn brought still more visitors and greater impact on the land. In the eyes of the newcomers, the Sierra Nevada was wild, free, and dangerous—a land to be enjoyed and respected, even revered.

Conversely, there was an increasing faction for whom the range was also a place of commercial possibilities, in tune with the economic expansion of the nation. The Sierra Nevada was a splendid landscape but an equally desirable financial opportunity. These two concepts were fated to clash.

Dispatches from back East took months to reach California well into the 1850s, but as the 1860s dawned, rail expansion in the East and fast stagecoach service in the West promised coast-to-coast mail in twenty-five days. By early 1860, that time was cut to ten days by the rapid riders of the short-lived Pony Express, which was out of business by late 1861, largely a casualty of instantaneous messages sent via the transcontinental telegraph.

Wagon trains had been reaching California since the 1830s, but as travel demand increased—whether for pleasure or business—so did the need for better transportation. Rough wagon roads grew into major arteries over the years, and many of the new routes through mountain passes became toll roads. Government support for surveys and road construction further spurred expansion. Generally, roads were built where accessibility was good and where commercial enterprises, such as mining and lumbering, would be directly served.

The development of Western railroads in the 1860s and 1870s had an enormous impact on the Sierra Nevada's infrastructure. As with roads, rail construction was limited to the most advantageous areas, and often the tracks were built adjacent to or over existing trails and roads. The greatest engineering feat of the time was the building of the transcontinental railroad—particularly the construction of the Central Pacific Railroad, the western end of the line, which ran through the rugged Sierra Nevada. Utilizing the plans of the visionary Theodore Judah, the completion of this line opened the region to easier travel and greater access for commerce, settlers, and visitors. As more lines were built in the Sierra Nevada, tourism, timber harvesting, and real estate development boomed and became an important component of the economy.

A thriving lumber industry has existed in the Sierra Nevada from Gold Rush days, and in the 1870s, lumber became an even more desired commodity in light of railroad construction and the growth of underground mining. The Sierra Nevada provided this precious product in abundance, with millions upon millions of board feet of lumber annually feeding the voracious appetite of commerce, both in the region itself and in far-flung markets.

Consequences of this indiscriminate development were becoming increasingly evident, however. By the 1890s, a few voices in the wilderness were calling for a new perspective on the Sierra Nevada. The turn of the century would see these thoughts transformed into action.

Mark Twain, from *Roughing It*

*Samuel Langhorne Clemens (1835–1910), better known by his pen name
Mark Twain, was an esteemed American humorist, writer, and lecturer. A
gifted social satirist, at the peak of his career he was probably the most well-
known American around the world. His iconic characters Huckleberry Finn
and Tom Sawyer are still among the most beloved in literature.*

Mark Twain's second major work, Roughing It *(1872), records the
author's travels through the West in the 1860s. Among its most famous pas-
sages is this description of Twain's adventures at Lake Tahoe in the 1860s.*

We had heard a world of talk about the marvelous beauty of Lake
Tahoe, and finally curiosity drove us thither to see it. Three or
four members of the Brigade had been there and located some timber-
lands on its shores and stored up a quantity of provisions in their camp.
We strapped a couple of blankets on our shoulders and took an ax
apiece and started—for we intended to take up a wood ranch or so
ourselves and become wealthy. We were on foot. The reader will find
it advantageous to go horseback. We were told that the distance was
eleven miles. We tramped a long time on level ground, and then toiled
laboriously up a mountain about a thousand miles high and looked
over. No lake there. We descended on the other side, crossed the valley
and toiled up another mountain three or four thousand miles high,
apparently, and looked over again. No lake yet. We sat down tired and
perspiring, and hired a couple of Chinamen to curse those people who
had beguiled us. Thus refreshed, we presently resumed the march with
renewed vigor and determination. We plodded on, two or three hours
longer, and at last the lake burst upon us—a noble sheet of blue water

lifted six thousand three hundred feet above the level of the sea, and walled in by a rim of snow-clad mountain peaks that towered aloft full three thousand feet higher still! It was a vast oval, and one would have to use up eighty or a hundred good miles in traveling around it. As it lay there with the shadows of the mountains brilliantly photographed upon its still surface I thought it must surely be the fairest picture the whole earth affords.

We found the small skiff belonging to the Brigade boys, and without loss of time set out across a deep bend of the lake toward the landmarks that signified the locality of the camp. I got Johnny to row—not because I mind exertion myself, but because it makes me sick to ride backward when I am at work. But I steered. A three-mile pull brought us to the camp just as the night fell, and we stepped ashore very tired and wolfishly hungry. In a "cache" among the rocks we found the provisions and the cooking-utensils, and then, all fatigued as I was, I sat down on a boulder and superintended while Johnny gathered wood and cooked supper. Many a man who had gone through what I had, would have wanted to rest.

It was a delicious supper—hot bread, fried bacon, and black coffee. It was a delicious solitude we were in, too. Three miles away was a sawmill and some workmen, but there were not fifteen other human beings throughout the wide circumference of the lake. As the darkness closed down and the stars came out and spangled the great mirror with jewels, we smoked meditatively in the solemn hush and forgot our troubles and our pains. In due time we spread our blankets in the warm sand between two large boulders and soon feel asleep, careless of the procession of ants that passed in through rents in our clothing and explored our persons. Nothing could disturb the sleep that fettered us for it had been fairly earned, and if our consciences had any sins on them they had to adjourn court for that night, anyway. The wind rose just as we were losing consciousness, and we were lulled to sleep by the beating of the surf upon the shore.

It is always very cold on that lake-shore in the night, but we had plenty of blankets and were warm enough. We never moved a muscle all night, but waked at early dawn in the original positions, and got up at once, thoroughly refreshed, free from soreness, and brim full of friskiness. There is no end of wholesome medicine in such an experience. That morning we could have whipped ten such people as we were the day before—sick ones at any rate. But the world is slow, and people will go to "water cures" and "movement cures" and to foreign lands for health. Three months of camp life on Lake Tahoe would restore an Egyptian mummy to his pristine vigor, and give him an appetite like an alligator. I do not mean the oldest and driest mummies, of course, but the fresher ones. The air up there in the clouds is very pure and fine, bracing and delicious. And why shouldn't it be?—it is the same the angels breathe. I think that hardly any amount of fatigue can be gathered together that a man cannot sleep off in one night on the sand by its side. Not under a roof, but under the sky; it seldom or never rains there in the summer time. I know a man who went there to die. But he made a failure of it. He was a skeleton when he came, and could barely stand. He had no appetite, and did nothing but read tracts and reflect on the future. Three months later he was sleeping out of doors regularly, eating all he could hold, three times a day, and chasing game over mountains three thousand feet high for recreation. And he was a skeleton no longer, but weighed part of a ton. This is no fancy sketch, but the truth. His disease was consumption. I confidently commend his experience to other skeletons.

I superintended again, and as soon as we had eaten breakfast we got in the boat and skirted along the lake-shore about three miles and disembarked. We liked the appearance of the place, and so we claimed some three hundred acres of it and stuck our "notices" on a tree. It was yellow-pine timber-land—a dense forest of trees a hundred feet high and from one to five feet through at the butt. It was necessary to fence our property or we could not hold it. That is to say, it was necessary to cut down trees here and there and make them fall in such a way as to form a sort of enclosure (with pretty wide gaps in it). We cut down three trees apiece, and found it such heartbreaking work that we decided to "rest our case" on those; if they held the property, well and good; if they didn't, let the property spill out through the gaps and go; it was no use to work ourselves to death merely to save a few acres of land. Next day we came back to build a house—for a house was also necessary, in order to hold the property. We decided to build a substantial log house and excite the envy of the Brigade boys; but by the time we had cut and trimmed the first log it seemed unnecessary to be so elaborate, and so we concluded to build it of saplings. However, two saplings, duly cut and trimmed, compelled recognition of the fact that a still modester architecture would satisfy the law, and so we concluded to build a "brush" house. We devoted the next day to this work, but we did so much "sitting around" and discussing, that by the middle of the afternoon we had achieved only a half-way sort of affair which one of us had to watch while the other cut brush, lest if both turned our backs we might not be able to find it again, it had such a strong family resemblance to the surrounding vegetation. But we were satisfied with it.

We were landowners now, duly seized and possessed, and within the protection of the law. Therefore we decided to take up our residence on our own domain and enjoy that large sense of independence which only such an experience can bring. Late the next afternoon, after a good long rest, we sailed away from the Brigade camp with all the provisions and cooking-utensils we could carry off—borrow is the more accurate word—and just as the night was falling we beached the boat at our own landing.

If there is any life that is happier than the life we led on our timber ranch for the next two or three weeks, it must be a sort of life which I have not read of in books or experienced in person. We did not see a human being but ourselves during the time, or hear any sounds but those that were made by the wind and the waves, the sighing of the pines, and now and then the far-off thunder of an avalanche. The forest about us was dense and cool, the sky above us was cloudless and brilliant with sunshine, the broad lake before us was glassy and clear, or rippled and breezy, or black and storm-tossed, according to Nature's mood; and its circling border of mountain domes, clothed with forests, scarred with landslides, cloven by cañons and valleys, and helmeted with glittering snow, fitly framed and finished the noble picture. The view was always fascinating, bewitching, entrancing. The eye was never tired of gazing, night or day, in calm or storm; it suffered but one grief, and that was that it could not look always, but must close sometimes in sleep.

We slept in the sand close to the water's edge, between two protecting boulders, which took care of the stormy night-winds for us. We never took any paregoric to make us sleep. At the first break of dawn we were always up and running foot-races to tone down excess of physical vigor and exuberance of spirits. That is, Johnny was—but I held his hat. While smoking the pipe of peace after breakfast we watched the sentinel peaks put on the glory of the sun, and followed the conquering light as it swept down among the shadows, and set the captive crags and forests free. We watched the tinted pictures grow and brighten upon the water till every little detail of forest, precipice, and pinnacle was wrought in and finished, and the miracle of the enchanter complete. Then to "business."

That is, drifting around in the boat. We were on the north shore. There, the rocks on the bottom are sometimes gray, sometimes white. This gives the marvelous transparency of the water a fuller advantage than it has elsewhere on the lake. We usually pushed out a hundred yards or so from shore, and then lay down on the thwarts, in the sun, and let the boat drift by the hour whither it would. We seldom talked. It interrupted the Sabbath stillness, and marred the dreams the luxurious rest and indolence brought. The shore all along was indented with deep, curved bays and coves, bordered by narrow sand-beaches; and where the sand ended, the steep mountainsides rose right up aloft into space—rose up like a vast wall a little out of the perpendicular, and thickly wooded with tall pines.

So singularly clear was the water, that where it was only twenty or thirty feet deep the bottom was so perfectly distinct that the boat seemed floating in the air! Yes, where it was even *eighty* feet deep. Every little pebble was distinct, every speckled trout, every hand's-breadth of sand. Often, as we lay on our faces, a granite boulder, as large as a village church, would start out of the bottom apparently, and seem climbing up rapidly to the surface, till presently it threatened to touch our faces, and we could not resist the impulse to seize an oar and avert the danger. But the boat would float on, and the boulder descend again, and then we could see that when we had been exactly above it, it must still have been twenty or thirty feet below the surface. Down through the transparency of these great depths, the water was not *merely* transparent, but dazzlingly, brilliantly so. All objects seen through it had a bright, strong vividness, not only of outline, but of every minute detail, which they would not have had when seen simply through the same depth of atmosphere. So empty and airy did all spaces seem below us, and so strong was the sense of floating high aloft in mid-nothingness, that we called these boat-excursions "balloon voyages."

We fished a good deal, but we did not average one fish a week. We could see trout by the thousand winging about in the emptiness under us, or sleeping in shoals on the bottom, but they would not bite—they could see the line too plainly, perhaps. We frequently selected the trout we wanted, and rested the bait patiently and persistently on the end of his nose at a depth of eighty feet, but he would only shake it off with an annoyed manner, and shift his position.

We bathed occasionally, but the water was rather chilly, for all it looked so sunny. Sometimes we rowed out to the "blue water," a mile or two from shore. It was as dead blue as indigo there, because of the immense depth. By official measurement the lake in its center is one thousand five hundred and twenty-five feet deep!

Sometimes, on lazy afternoons, we lolled on the sand in camp, and smoked pipes and read some old well-worn novels. At night, by the camp-fire, we played euchre and seven-up to strengthen the mind— and played them with cards so greasy and defaced that only a whole summer's acquaintance with them could enable the student to tell the ace of clubs from the jack of diamonds.

We never slept in our "house." It never occurred to us, for one thing; and besides, it was built to hold the ground, and that was enough. We did not wish to strain it.

By and by our provisions began to run short, and we went back to the old camp and laid in a new supply. We were gone all day, and reached home again about nightfall, pretty tired and hungry. While Johnny was carrying the main bulk of the provisions up to our "house" for future use, I took the loaf of bread, some slices of bacon, and the coffee-pot ashore, set them down by a tree, lit a fire, and went back to the boat to get the frying-pan. While I was at this, I heard a shout from Johnny, and looking up I saw that my fire was galloping all over the premises!

Johnny was on the other side of it. He had to run through the flames to get to the lake-shore, and then we stood helpless and watched the devastation.

The ground was deeply carpeted with dry pine-needles, and the fire touched them off as if they were gunpowder. It was wonderful to see with what fierce speed the tall sheet of flame traveled! My coffee-pot was gone, and everything with it. In a minute and a half the fire seized upon a dense growth of dry manzanita chapparal six or eight feet high, and then the roaring and popping and crackling was something terrific. We were driven to the boat by the intense heat, and there we remained, spell-bound.

Within half an hour all before us was a tossing, blinding tempest of flame! It went surging up adjacent ridges—surmounted them and disappeared in the cañons beyond—burst into view upon higher and farther ridges, presently—shed a grander illumination abroad, and dove again—flamed out again, directly, higher and still higher up the mountainside—threw out skirmishing parties of fire here and there, and sent them trailing their crimson spirals away among remote ramparts and ribs and gorges, till as far as the eye could reach the lofty mountain-fronts were webbed as it were with a tangled network of red lava streams. Away across the water the crags and domes were lit with a ruddy glare, and the firmament above was a reflected hell!

Every feature of the spectacle was repeated in the glowing mirror of the lake! Both pictures were sublime, both were beautiful; but that in the lake had a bewildering richness about it that enchanted the eye and held it with the stronger fascination.

We sat absorbed and motionless through four long hours. We never thought of supper, and never felt fatigue. But at eleven o'clock the conflagration had traveled beyond our range of vision, and then darkness stole down upon the landscape again.

Hunger asserted itself now, but there was nothing to eat. The provisions were all cooked, no doubt, but we did not go to see. We were homeless wanderers again, without any property. Our fence was gone, our house burned down; no insurance. Our pine forest was well scorched, the dead trees all burned up, and our broad acres of manzanita swept away. Our blankets were on our usual sand-bed, however, and so we lay down and went to sleep. The next morning we started back to the old camp, but while out a long way from shore, so great a storm came up that we dared not try to land. So I bailed out the seas we shipped, and Johnny pulled heavily through the billows till we had reached a point three or four miles beyond the camp. The storm was increasing, and it became evident that it was better to take the hazard of beaching the boat than go down in a hundred fathoms of water; so we ran in, with tall white-caps following, and I sat down in the stern-sheets and pointed her head-on to the shore. The instant the bow struck, a wave came over the stern that washed crew and cargo ashore, and saved a deal of trouble. We shivered in the lee of a boulder all the rest of the day, and froze all the night through. In the morning the tempest had gone down, and we paddled down to the camp without any unnecessary delay. We were so starved that we ate up the rest of the Brigade's provisions, and then set out to Carson to tell them about it and ask their forgiveness. It was accorded, upon payment of damages.

We made many trips to the lake after that, and had many a hair-breadth escape and blood-curdling adventure which will never be recorded of any history.

William Brewer, from *Up and Down California in 1860–1864*

William Henry Brewer (1828–1910) started his professional career as a professor of chemistry at Washington and Jefferson College in Pennsylvania. Just two years later, in 1860, he accepted a post as chief botanist on the staff of Josiah Whitney, California's first State Geologist. Brewer was chosen to lead the field teams for the State Geologic Survey, and his 1864 book, Up and Down California in 1860–1864, *chronicles this work and provides important insights not only into Whitney's geological surveys but into the developing California society as well. After four years with Whitney's office, Brewer moved back East and became a professor of agriculture at Yale, teaching for nearly forty years.*

In the following passage, Brewer describes his adventure on what he called the south fork of the Kings River (today's Roaring River) and his ascent of the mountain peak that now bears his name. His companions were Dick Cotter, James Gardner, Charles Hoffmann, and Clarence King, the last of whom authored the piece that follows Brewer's in this anthology.

In camp on the south fork of Kings River.

Saturday, July 2, [1864,] we were up at dawn, and Hoffmann and I climbed this cone, which I had believed to be the highest of this part of the Sierra. We had a rough time, made two unsuccessful attempts to reach the summit, climbing up terribly steep rocks, and at last, after eight hours of very hard climbing, reached the top. The view was yet wilder than we have ever seen before. We were not on the highest peak, although we were a thousand feet higher than we anticipated any peaks were. We had not supposed there were any over 12,000 or 12,500 feet, while we were actually up over 13,600, and there were a dozen peaks in sight beyond as high or higher!

Such a landscape! A hundred peaks in sight over thirteen thousand feet—many very sharp—deep canyons, cliffs in every direction almost rivaling Yosemite, sharp ridges almost inaccessible to man, on which human foot has never trod—all combined to produce a view the sublimity of which is rarely equaled, one which few are privileged to behold.

There is not so much snow as in the mountains farther north, not so much falls in winter, the whole region is drier, but all the higher points above 12,000 feet are streaked with it, and patches occur as low as 10,500 feet. The last trees disappear at 11,500 feet—above this desolate bare rocks and snow. Several small lakes were in sight, some of them frozen over.

The view extended north eighty to ninety miles, south nearly as far—east we caught glimpses of the desert mountains east of Owens Valley [the White Mountains]—west to the Coast Range, 130 or more miles distant.

On our return we slid down a slope of snow perhaps eight hundred feet. We came down in two minutes the height that we had been over three hours in climbing. We got back very tired, but a cup of good tea and a fine venison soup restored us.

Sunday, July 3, we lay until late. On calculating the height of the peak, finding it so much higher than we expected, and knowing there were still higher peaks back, we were, of course, excited. Here there is the highest and grandest group of the Sierra—in fact, the grandest in the United States—not so high as Mount Shasta, but a great assemblage of high peaks. [Later expeditions would identify several Southern Sierra peaks higher than Shasta, including Mount Whitney, which at 14,494 feet is the highest point in the forty-eight contiguous states.]

King is enthusiastic, is wonderfully tough, has the greatest endurance I have ever seen, and is withal very muscular. He is a most perfect specimen of health. He begged me to let him and Dick try to reach them on foot. I feared them inaccessible, but at last gave in to their importunities and gave my consent. They made their preparations that day, anxious for a trip fraught with so much interest, hardship, and danger.

July 4 all were up at dawn. We got breakfast, and King and Dick packed their packs—six days' provisions, blankets, and instruments made packs of thirty-five or forty pounds each, to be packed into such a region! Gardner and I resolved to climb the cone again, as I had left instruments on the top, expecting someone would go up. Our way lay together for five miles, and up to thirteen thousand feet. I packed Dick's heavy pack to that point to give him a good start. I could never pack it as far as they hope to. Here we left them, and as we scaled the peak they disappeared over a steep granite ridge, the last seen of them.

Gardner and I reached the summit much easier than Hoffmann and I had two days before. The sky was cloudy and the air cold, 25°. We were on top about two hours. We planted the American flag on the top, and left a paper in a bottle with our names, the height, etc. It is not at all probable that any man was ever on the top before, or that any one will be again—for a long time at least. There is nothing but love of adventure to prompt it after we have the geography of the region described.

We were back before sundown; a hearty dinner and pleasant camp fire closed the day. We sang "Old John Brown" around the camp fire that night—we three, alone in these solitudes. Thus was spent Independence Day. The last was with Hoffmann alone, in the Sierra farther north. We heard not a gun. Would that we might know the war news—we are over a month behind.

The next morning we lay in our blankets very late, after the fatigue of the previous day—in fact were in bed eleven hours. We stayed in camp and took latitude observations. It was a most lovely day.

Clarence King, from *Mountaineering in the Sierra Nevada*

Clarence King (1842–1901) graduated from Yale at the tender age of nineteen, and soon thereafter became an assistant geologist under Josiah Whitney on the California Geological Survey. He served in that position from 1863 to 1866, and in 1867, twenty-five-year-old King was appointed director of the Geological and Geographical Exploration of the Fortieth Parallel Survey. Over the next ten years, he explored and surveyed a one-hundred-mile-wide swath from eastern Colorado to the California border, producing a seven-volume report, Geological Survey of the Fortieth Parallel, *on the latter of two expeditions. As a monument to King's career, a 12,909-foot peak in the Sierra Nevada was named in his honor.*

In his 1872 Mountaineering in the Sierra Nevada, *King melded geological scholarship with carefully crafted descriptions to present a comprehensive and occasionally moving narrative of the mountaineering experience. This selection presents his account of a steep descent from Inspiration Point to the Yosemite Valley floor during a snowstorm.*

Warmly rolled in our blankets, we suffered little from cold, but the driving sleet and hail very soon bruised our cheeks and eyelids most painfully. It required real effort of will to face the storm, and we very soon learned to take turns in breaking trail. The snow constantly balled upon our animals' feet, and they slid in every direction. Now and then, in descending a sharp slope of granite, the poor creatures would get sliding, and rush to the bottom, their legs stiffened out, and their heads thrust forward in fear. After crossing the Illilluette, which we did at our old ford, we found it very difficult to climb the long, steep hillside; for the mules were quite unable to carry us, obliging us to lead them, and to throw ourselves upon the snowdrifts to break a pathway.

This slope almost wore us out, and when at last we reached its summit, we threw ourselves upon the snow for a rest, but were in such a profuse perspiration that I deemed it unsafe to lie there for a moment, and, getting up again, we mounted the mules and rode slowly on toward open plateaus near great meadows. The snow gradually decreased in depth as we descended upon the plain directly south of Yosemite. The wind abated somewhat, and there were only occasional snow flurries, between half-hours of tolerable comfort. Constant use of the compass and reference to my little map at length brought us to the Mariposa trail, but not until after eight hours of anxious, exhaustive labor—anxious from the constant dread of losing our way in the blinding confusion of storm; exhausting, for we had more than half of the way acted as trail-breakers, dragging our frightened and tired brutes after us. The poor creatures instantly recognized the trail, and started in a brisk trot toward Inspiration Point. Suddenly an icy wind swept up the valley, carrying with it a storm of snow and hail. The wind blew with such violence that the whole freight of sleet and ice was carried horizontally with fearful swiftness, cutting the bruised faces of the mules, and giving our own eyelids exquisite torture. The brutes refused to carry us farther. We were obliged to dismount and drive them before us, beating them constantly with clubs.

Fighting our way against this bitter blast, half-blinded by hard, wind-driven snow-crystals, we at last gave up and took refuge in a dense clump of firs which crown the spur by Inspiration Point. Our poor mules cowered under shelter with us, and turned tail to the storm. The fir-trees were solid cones of snow, which now and then unloaded themselves when severely bent by a sudden gust, half burying us in dry, white powder. Wind roared below us in the Yosemite gorge; it blew from the west, rolling up in waves which smote the cliffs and surged on up the valley. While we sat still the drifts began to pile up at our backs; the mules were belly-deep, and our situation began to be serious.

Looking over the cliff-brink we saw but the hurrying snow, and only heard a confused tumult of wind. A steady increase in the severity of the gale made us fear that the trees might crash down over us; so we left the mules and crept cautiously over the edge of the cliff, and ensconced ourselves in a sheltered nook, protected by walls of rock which rose at our back.

We were on the brink of the Yosemite, and but for snow might have looked down three thousand feet. The storm eddied below us, sucking down whirlwinds of snow, and sometimes opening deep rifts,—never enough, however, to disclose more than a few hundred feet of cliffs.

We had been in this position about an hour, half frozen and soaked through, when I at length gathered conscience enough to climb back and take a look at our brutes. The forlorn pair were frosted over with a thick coating, their pitiful eyes staring eagerly at me. I had half a mind to turn them loose, but, considering that their obstinate nature might lead them back to our Obelisk camp I patted their noses, and climbed back to the shelf by Cotter, determined to try it for a quarter of an hour more, when, if the tempest did not lull, I thought we must press on and face the snow for an hour more, while we tramped down to the valley.

Suddenly there came a lull in the storm; its blinding fury of snow and wind ceased. Overhead, still hurrying eastward, the white bank drove on, unveiling, as it fled, the Yosemite walls, plateau, and every object to the eastward as far as Mount Clark. As yet the valley bottom was obscured by a layer of mist and cloud, which rose to the height of about a thousand feet, submerging cliff-foot and debris pile. Between these strata, the cloud above and the cloud below, every object was in clear, distinct view; the sharp, terrible fronts of precipices, capped with a fresh cover of white, plunged down into the still, gray river of cloud below, their stony surfaces clouded with purple, salmon-color, and bandings of brown,—all hues unnoticeable in every-day lights. Forest, and crag, and plateau, and distant mountain were snow-covered to a uniform whiteness; only the dark gorge beneath us showed the least traces of color. There all was rich, deep, gloomy. Even over the snowy surfaces above there prevailed an almost ashen gray, which reflected itself from the dull, drifting sky. A few torn locks of vapor poured over the cliff-edge at intervals, and crawled down like wreaths of smoke, floating gracefully and losing themselves at last in the bank of cloud which lay upon the bottom of the valley.

On a sudden the whole gray roof rolled away like a scroll, leaving the heavens from west to far east one expanse of pure, warm blue. Setting sunlight smote full upon the stony walls below, and shot over the plateau country, gilding here a snowy forest group, and there a wave-crest of whitened ridge. The whole air sparkled with diamond particles; red light streamed in through the open Yosemite gateway, brightening those vast, solemn faces of stone, and intensifying the deep neutral blue of shadowed alcoves.

The luminous cloud-bank in the east rolled from the last Sierra summit, leaving the whole chain of peaks in broad light, each rocky crest strongly red, the newly fallen snow marbling it over with a soft, deep rose; and wherever a cañon carved itself down the rocky fronts its course was traceable by a shadowy band of blue. The middle distance glowed with a tint of golden yellow; the broken heights along the cañon-brinks and edges of the cliff in front were of an intense, spotless white. Far below us the cloud stratum melted away, revealing the floor of the valley, whose russet and emerald and brown and red burned in the broad evening sun. It was a marvellous piece of contrasted lights,— the distance so pure, so soft in its rosy warmth, so cool in the depth of its shadowy blue; the foreground strong in fiery orange, or sparkling in absolute whiteness. I enjoyed, too, looking up at the pure, unclouded sky, which now wore an aspect of intense serenity. For half an hour nature seemed in entire repose; not a breath of wind stirred the white, snow-laden shafts of the trees; not a sound of animate creature or the most distant reverberation of waterfall reached us; no film of vapor moved across the tranquil, sapphire sky; absolute quiet reigned until a loud roar proceeding from Capitan turned our eyes in that direction. From the round, dome-like cap of its summit there moved down an avalanche, gathering volume and swiftness as it rushed to the brink, and then, leaping out two or three hundred feet into space, fell, slowly filtering down through the lighted air, like a silver cloud, until within a thousand feet of the earth it floated into the shadow of the cliff and sank to the ground as a faint blue mist. Next the Cathedral snow poured from its lighted summit in resounding avalanches; then the Three Brothers shot off their loads, and afar from the east a deep roar reached us as the whole snow-cover thundered down the flank of Cloud's Rest.

We were warned by the hour to make all haste, and, driving the poor brutes before us, worked our way down the trail as fast as possible. The light, already pale, left the distant heights in still more glorious contrast. A zone of amber sky rose behind the glowing peaks, and a cold steel-blue plain of snow skirted their bases. Mist slowly gathered again in the gorge below us and overspread the valley floor, shutting it out from our view.

We ran down the zigzag trail until we came to that shelf of bare granite immediately below the final descent into the valley. Here we paused just above the surface of the clouds, which, swept by fitful breezes, rose in swells, floating up and sinking again like waves of the sea. Intense light, more glowing than ever, streamed in upon the upper half of the cliffs, their bases sunken in the purple mist. As the cloud-waves crawled upward in the breeze they here and there touched a red-purple light and fell back again into the shadow.

We watched these effects with greatest interest, and, just as we were about moving on again, a loud burst as of heavy thunder arrested us, sounding as if the very walls were crashing in. We looked, and from the whole brow of Capitan rushed over one huge avalanche, breaking into the finest powder and floating down through orange light, disappearing in the sea of purple cloud beneath us.

Maxine Hong Kingston, from *China Men*

Maxine Hong Kingston (b. 1940) was born in Stockton, California, and attended college at the University of California, Berkeley, where she majored in engineering before switching to English. The daughter of Chinese immigrants, Kingston's writings frequently examine her cultural heritage and blend fictional elements into nonfiction narratives. Kingston has received numerous honors for her work, including a National Book Critics Circle Award, a National Book Award (for China Men*), and a National Humanities Medal. Kingston currently lives in Oakland and is a professor emeritus at U.C. Berkeley.*

Chinese labor was of crucial importance to the construction of the transcontinental railroad; an estimated 90 percent of all workers on the Central Pacific Railroad were Chinese. Kingston's China Men *(1980) examines this extraordinary task as it chronicles the experiences of her fictionalized "railroad grandfather," Ah Goong, in building the route through the Sierra.*

After tunneling into granite for about three years, Ah Goong understood the immovability of the earth. Men change, men die, weather changes, but a mountain is the same as permanence and time. This mountain would have taken no new shape for centuries, ten thousand centuries, the world a still, still place, time unmoving. He worked in the tunnel so long, he learned to see many colors in black. When he stumbled out, he tried to talk about time. "I felt time," he said. "I saw time. I saw world." He tried again, "I saw what's real. I saw time, and it doesn't move. If we break through the mountain, hollow it, time won't have moved anyway. You translators ought to tell the foreigners that."...

In the third year of pounding granite by hand, a demon invented dynamite. The railroad workers were to test it. They had stopped using gunpowder in the tunnels after avalanches, but the demons said that dynamite was more precise. They watched a scientist demon mix nitrate, sulphate, and glycerine, then flick the yellow oil, which exploded off his fingertips. Sitting in a meadow to watch the dynamite detonated in the open, Ah Goong saw the men in front of him leap impossibly high into the air; then he felt a shove as if from a giant's unseen hand—and he fell backward. The boom broke the mountain silence like fear breaking inside stomach and chest and groin. No one had gotten hurt; they stood up laughing and amazed, looking around at how they had fallen, the pattern of the explosion. Dynamite was much more powerful than gunpowder. Ah Goong had felt a nudge, as if something kind were moving him out of harm's way. "All of a sudden I was sitting next to you." "Aiya. If we had been nearer, it would have killed us." "If we were stiff, it would have gone through us." "A fist." "A hand." "We leapt like acrobats." Next time Ah Goong flattened himself on the ground, and the explosion rolled over him.

He never got used to the blasting; a blast always surprised him. Even when he himself set the fuse and watched it burn, anticipated the explosion, the bang—*bahng* in Chinese—when it came, always startled. It cleaned the crazy words, the crackling, and bingbangs out of his brain. It was like New Year's, when every problem and thought was knocked clean out of him by firecrackers, and he could begin fresh. He couldn't worry during an explosion, which jerked every head to attention. Hills flew up in rocks and dirt. Boulders turned over and over. Sparks, fires, debris, rocks, smoke burst up, not at the same time as the boom (*bum*) but before that—the sound a separate occurrence, not useful as a signal.

The terrain changed immediately. Streams were diverted, rock-scapes exposed. Ah Goong found it difficult to remember what land had looked like before an explosion. It was a good thing the dynamite was invented after the Civil War to the east was over.

The dynamite added more accidents and ways of dying, but if it were not used, the railroad would take fifty more years to finish. Nitroglycerine exploded when it was jounced on a horse or dropped. A man who fell with it in his pocket blew himself up into red pieces. Sometimes it combusted merely standing. Human bodies skipped through the air like puppets and made Ah Goong laugh crazily as if the arms and legs would come together again. The smell of burned flesh remained in rocks.

In the tunnels, the men bored holes fifteen to eighteen inches deep with a power drill, stuffed them with hay and dynamite, and imbedded the fuse in sand. Once, for extra pay, Ah Goong ran back in to see why some dynamite had not gone off and hurried back out again; it was just a slow fuse. When the explosion settled, he helped carry two-hundred-, three-hundred-, five-hundred-pound boulders out of the tunnel.

As a boy he had visited a Taoist monastery where there were nine rooms, each a replica of one of the nine hells. Lifesize sculptures of men and women were spitted on turning wheels. Eerie candles under the suffering faces emphasized eyes poked out, tongues pulled, red mouths and eyes, and real hair, eyelashes, and eyebrows. Women were split apart and men dismembered. He could have reached out and touched the sufferers and the implements. He had dug and dynamited his way into one of these hells. "Only here there are eighteen tunnels, not nine, plus all the tracks between them," he said.

One day he came out of the tunnel to find the mountains white, the evergreens and bare trees decorated, white tree sculptures and lace bushes everywhere. The men from snow country called the icicles "ice chopsticks." He sat in his basket and slid down the slopes. The snow covered the gouged land, the broken trees, the tracks, the mud, the campfire ashes, the unburied dead. Streams were stilled in mid-run, the water petrified. That winter he thought it was the task of the human race to quicken the world, blast the freeze, fire it, redden it with blood. He had to change the stupid slowness of one sunrise and one sunset per day. He had to enliven the silent world with sound. "The rock," he tried to tell the others. "The ice." "Time."

The dynamiting loosed blizzards on the men. Ears and toes fell off. Fingers stuck to the cold silver rails. Snowblind men stumbled about with bandannas over their eyes. Ah Goong helped build wood tunnels roofing the track route. Falling ice scrabbled on the roofs. The men stayed under the snow for weeks at a time. Snowslides covered the entrances to the tunnels, which they had to dig out to enter and exit, white tunnels and black tunnels. Ah Goong looked at his gang and thought, If there is an avalanche, these are the people I'll be trapped with, and wondered which ones would share food. A party of snowbound barbarians had eaten the dead. Cannibals, thought Ah Goong, and looked around. Food was not scarce; the tea man brought whiskey barrels of hot tea, and he warmed his hands and feet, held the teacup to his nose and ears. Someday, he planned, he would buy a chair with metal doors for putting hot coal inside it. The magpies did not abandon him but stayed all winter and searched the snow for food.

The men who died slowly enough to say last words said, "Don't leave me frozen under the snow. Send my body home. Burn it and put the ashes in a tin can. Take the bone jar when you come down the mountain." "When you ride the fire car back to China, tell my descendants to come for me." "Shut up," scolded the hearty men. "We don't want to hear about bone jars and dying." "You're lucky to have a body to bury, not blown to smithereens." "Stupid man to hurt yourself," they bawled out the sick and wounded. How their wives would scold if they brought back deadmen's bones. "Aiya. To be buried here, nowhere." "But this is somewhere," Ah Goong promised. "This is the Gold Mountain. We're marking the land now. The track sections are numbered, and your family will know where we leave you." But he was a crazy man, and they didn't listen to him.

Spring did come, and when the snow melted, it revealed the past year, what had happened, what they had done, where they had worked, the lost tools, the thawing bodies, some standing with tools in hand, the bright rails. "Remember Uncle Long Winded Leong?" "Remember Strong Back Wong?" "Remember Lee Brother?" "And Fong Uncle?" They lost count of the number dead; there is no record of how many died building the railroad. Or maybe it was demons doing the counting and chinamen not worth counting. Whether it was good luck or bad luck, the dead were buried or cairned next to the last section of track they had worked on. "May his ghost not have to toil," they said over graves. (In China a woodcutter ghost chops eternally; people have heard chopping in the snow and in the heat.) "Maybe his ghost will ride the train home." The scientific demons said the transcontinental railroad would connect the West to Cathay. "What if he rides back and forth from Sacramento to New York forever?" "That wouldn't be so bad. I hear the cars will be like houses on wheels." The funerals were short. "No time. No time," said both China Men and demons. The railroad was as straight as they could build it, but no ghosts sat on the tracks; no strange presences haunted the tunnels. The blasts scared ghosts away.

When the Big Dipper pointed east and the China Men detonated nitroglycerine and shot off guns for the New Year, which comes with the spring, these special bangs were not as loud as the daily bangs, not as numerous as the bangs all year. Shouldn't the New Year be the loudest day of all to obliterate the noises of the old year? But to make a bang of that magnitude, they would have to blow up at least a year's supply of dynamite in one blast. They arranged strings of chain reactions in circles and long lines, banging faster and louder to culminate in a big bang. And most importantly, there were random explosions—surprise. Surprise. SURPRISE. They had no dragon, the railroad their dragon.

The demons invented games for working faster, gold coins for miles of track laid, for the heaviest rock, a grand prize for the first team to break through a tunnel. Day shifts raced against night shifts, China Men against Welshmen, China Men against Irishmen, China Men against Injuns and black demons. The fastest races were China Men against China Men, who bet on their own teams. China Men always won because of good teamwork, smart thinking, and the need for the money. Also, they had the most workers to choose teams from. Whenever his team won anything, Ah Goong added to his gold stash.

Walt Whitman, from "Passage to India"

Walt Whitman (1819–1892) was a leading American poet, essayist, and journalist, and also a literary rebel who utilized new structures and methods in his writing. Abandoning conventions that said poetry must rhyme, he adopted a freestyle form that was characterized as irregular but rhythmic.

Whitman wrote "Passage to India" as a plea for harmony among nations. In the poem, he cites the building of the transcontinental railroad and the completion of the Suez Canal as symbols of how different cultures and geographies can be linked. Written in 1869 and first published in 1871, "Passage to India" was included in Whitman's most famous work, Leaves of Grass *(1888). The third stanza of the poem, presented here, mentions a "Genoese," referring to the explorer Christopher Columbus, who sailed for Spain but came from Genoa, Italy.*

Passage to India!
Lo soul for thee of tableaus twain,
I see in one the Suez canal initiated, open'd,
I see the procession of steamships, the Empress Eugenie's leading
    the van;
I mark from on deck the strange landscape, the pure sky, the
    level sand in the distance;
I pass swiftly the picturesque groups, the workmen gather'd,
The gigantic dredging machines.
In one again, different, (yet thine, all thine, O soul, the same,)
I see over my own continent the Pacific Railroad surmounting
    every barrier,

I see continual trains of cars winding along the Platte carrying
    freight and passengers,
I hear the locomotives rushing and roaring, and the shrill steam-
    whistle,
I hear the echoes reverberate through the grandest scenery in the
    world,
I cross the Laramie plains, I note the rocks in grotesque shapes,
    the buttes,
I see the plentiful larkspur and wild onions, the barren, colorless,
    sage-deserts,
I see in glimpses afar or towering immediately above me the
    great mountains, I see the Wind River and the Wahsatch [sic]
    mountains,
I see the Monument mountain and the Eagle's Nest, I pass the
    Promontory, I ascend the Nevadas,
I scan the noble Elk mountain and wind around its base,
I see the Humboldt range, I thread the valley and cross the river,
I see the clear waters of Lake Tahoe, I see forests of majestic
    pines,
Or crossing the great desert, the alkaline plains, I behold enchanting
    mirages of waters and meadows,
Marking through these and after all, in duplicate slender lines,
Bridging the three or four thousand miles of land travel,
Tying the Eastern to the Western sea,
The road between Europe and Asia.

(Ah Genoese thy dream! thy dream!
Centuries after thou art laid in thy grave,
The shore thou foundest verifies thy dream.)

Robert Louis Stevenson, from *Across the Plains*

The Scottish author Robert Louis Stevenson (1850–1894) is best known for his Treasure Island *and* Dr. Jekyll and Mr. Hyde. *A novelist and poet, he was also a travel writer who published several pieces about California in the late 1870s and early 1880s.*

In 1879, Stevenson—hopelessly in love with an older married woman who was divorcing her husband—traveled three thousand miles across North America to see the woman whom he would eventually wed. On the train from New York to his ultimate destination in San Francisco, as he approached the Sierra Nevada, the lovesick Stevenson's hopes were high and his senses were acute. The result was this blissful account of his passage through Donner Pass, first published in Across the Plains *in 1892.*

Of all the next day I will tell you nothing, for the best of all reasons, that I remember no more than that we continued through desolate and desert scenes, fiery hot and deadly weary. But some time after I had fallen asleep that night, I was awakened by one of my companions. It was in vain that I resisted. A fire of enthusiasm and whisky burned in his eyes; and he declared we were in a new country, and I must come forth upon the platform and see with my own eyes. The train was then, in its patient way, standing halted in a by-track. It was a clear, moonlit night; but the valley was too narrow to admit the moonshine direct, and only a diffused glimmer whitened the tall rocks and relieved the blackness of the pines. A hoarse clamour filled the air; it was the continuous plunge of a cascade somewhere near at hand among the mountains. The air struck chill, but tasted good and vigorous in the nostrils—a fine, dry, old mountain atmosphere. I was dead sleepy, but I returned to roost with a grateful mountain feeling at my heart.

When I awoke next morning, I was puzzled for a while to know if it were day or night, for the illumination was unusual. I sat up at last, and found we were grading slowly downward through a long snowshed; and suddenly we shot into an open; and before we were swallowed into the next length of wooden tunnel, I had one glimpse of a huge pine-forested ravine upon my left, a foaming river, and a sky already coloured with the fires of dawn. I am usually very calm over the displays of nature; but you will scarce believe how my heart leaped at this. It was like meeting one's wife. I had come home again—home from unsightly deserts to the green and habitable corners of the earth. Every spire of pine along the hill-top, every trouty pool along that mountain river, was more dear to me than a blood relation. Few people have praised God more happily than I did. And thenceforward, down by Blue Cañon, Alta, Dutch Flat, and all the old mining camps, through a sea of mountain forests, dropping thousands of feet toward the far sea-level as we went, not I only, but all the passengers on board, threw off their sense of dirt and heat and weariness, and bawled like school-boys and thronged with shining eyes upon the platform and became new creatures within and without. The sun no longer oppressed us with heat, it only shone laughingly along the mountain-side, until we were fain to laugh ourselves for glee. At every turn we could see farther into the land and our own happy futures. At every town the cocks were tossing their clear notes into the golden air, and crowing for the new day and the new country. For this was indeed our destination; this was "the good country" we had been going to so long.

Grace Greenwood, "Eight Days in the Yosemite"

*Born in New York as Sarah Jane Clarke, Grace Greenwood (1823–
1904) adopted her pseudonym both in print and in her personal life.
Greenwood contributed to many of the prominent journals of her day,
although her positions on contemporary social and political issues often
rankled her publishers. Taking uncompromising stances on the need
for prison reform, the abolition of capital punishment, women's rights,
and an end to war and slavery, Greenwood became a popular writer
and lecturer during the Civil War period. President Abraham Lincoln
dubbed her "Grace Greenwood the Patriot" for her fundraising efforts
for the U.S. Sanitary Commission and for her frequent appearances
before soldiers and patriotic organizations.*

By the 1870s, Greenwood wrote primarily for the New York Times,
*and many of her articles were travel pieces commenting on the wonders
and uncertainties of the American West. On July 27, 1872, the* Times
*published Greenwood's "Eight Days in the Yosemite," an account of her
adventures in the valley. The following passage's appearance in this
anthology may be its first time in print since the nineteenth century.
Greenwood's description of John Muir may also be the first reference to
the famous naturalist in a national publication.*

The Yosemite Falls proper, whose entire descent is over 2,600 feet, is
immediately in front of the Hutchings Hotel, on the north side of
the valley. Of course, from below you can see nothing of the Yosemite
Creek. It looks as though it was a cataract from the start, born of the sky
and the precipice. The roar of this king of water-falls, in his grandest

times, has a singular dual character—there is the eternal monotone, always distinct, though broken in upon by an irregular crash and boom—a sort of gusty thunder. This composite sound, so changing and unchanging, floods and shakes the air, like the roar of the deep sea and the breaking of surf on a rocky shore.

On my first night in the valley the strangeness of my surroundings, a sort of sombre delight that took possession of me, would not let me sleep for several hours. Once I rose and looked out, or tried to look out. The sky was clouded—it seemed to me the stars drew back from the abyss. It was filled with night and sound. I could not see the mighty rocks that walled us in, but a sense of their shadow was upon me. There was in the awe I felt no element of real dread or fear, but it was thrilled by fantastic terrors. I thought of [Josiah] Whitney's theory of the formation of the great pit, by subsidence. What if it should take another start in the night, and settle a mile or two with us, leaving the trail by which we descended dangling in the air, and the cataracts all spouting away, with no outlet! But in the morning the jolly sun peered down upon us, laughing, as much to say, "There you are, are you?" and the sweet, cool winds dipped down from the pines and the snows, the great fall shouted and danced all the way down his stupendous rocky stairway—the river—and overflowed meadows rippled and flashed with immortal glee. It seems to me that darkness is darker and light lighter in the Yosemite than anywhere else on earth.

Yet, in the midst of its utmost brightness and beauty you are more or less oppressed with a realization of some sudden convulsion of nature that here rent the rocks asunder, that shook the massive mountain till it shook the bottom out; or of the mighty force of drifting, driving glaciers, grinding, carving, just plowing down from the "High Sierra," leaving the stupendous furrow behind them. Somehow you feel that nature has not done with the place yet. Such a grand, abandoned workshop invites her to return. The stage of this great, tragic theatre of the elements waits, perhaps, for some terrible afterpiece. But it may be a comedy after all—horse railroads and trotting tracks, hacks and hand-organs, Saratoga trunks and croquet parties, elevators running up the face of El Capitan, the domes plastered over with circus bills and advertisements of "Plantation Bitters."

There is here at first a haunting sense of imprisonment, though on a grand scale, of course. You feel like a magnificent felon, incarcerated in the very fortress of the gods....

I found it impossible to work here, or even, to talk fluently or forcibly on what I knew about the Yosemite. The theme mastered me. I noticed that there were few singing-birds about, and was told by an old guide that they, with most animals, were afraid of the valley. Poetic thoughts and gay fancies seem struck with a like fear. You are for a time mentally unnerved; but you feel that in your powerlessness, you are gaining power; in your silence, more abundant expression....

Among our visitors in the evening was Mr. Muir, the young Scottish mountaineer, student, and enthusiast, who has taken sanctuary in the Yosemite—who stays by the variable valley with marvelous constancy—who adores her alike in the fast, gay Summer life and solemn Autumn glories, in her Winter cold and stillness, and in the passion of her Spring floods and tempests. Not profoundest snows can chill his ardor, not earthquakes can shake his allegiance. Mr. Muir talks with a quiet, quaint humor, and a simple eloquence which are quite delightful. He has a clear, blue eye, a firm, free step and marvelous nerve and endurance. He has the serious air and unconventional ways of a man who has been much with nature in her grand, solitary places. That tourist is fortunate who can have John Muir for a guide in and about the valley....

The Bridal Vail [sic] is my favorite Yosemite cataract. There is for me a tender, retrospective charm to the name. Just opposite to the Bridal Vail is the lovely little trickling cascade, called the Virgin's Tears. Had the sight of the floating, flouting Vail anything to do with that lachrymose condition? We, who reached the Vail, lingered about it for hours—read and slept, botanized, and shouted poetry in each other's ears. When the rainbows came, we went far up into the very heart of the splendor. We could have jumped through the radiant hoops like circus-performers....

Glacier Point is on the south side of the valley, 3,700 feet above the meadows. It is the point that gives you the finest comprehensive view of the valley—especially of its upper waterfalls, cañons and rocks—with vast views of the High Sierra. All the great heights were pointed out to us—Mount Hoffman, Mount Lyell, Mount Dana, Mount Clark, and Mount Starr King....

The vast view from Glacier Point is the despair of poetry and art. Certainly its grandeur can never be compassed by the grandest sweep of human language. Its divine loveliness floats forever before the mind—in smiling, radiant defiance. It is glory that *must* be seen; it is sublimity that *must* be felt; it is the "exceeding great reward" that *must* be toiled for.

Joseph LeConte, from *A Journal of Ramblings through the High Sierra of California*

Joseph LeConte (1823–1901) earned his medical degree in New York and set up a practice in his home state of Georgia, but soon discovered that his true calling was geology. LeConte went back to school, studying geology at Harvard, and upon graduation taught natural science, chemistry, and geology at numerous colleges in the South. In 1869, Joseph and his brother moved to Berkeley, California, where they joined the teaching staff of the new University of California.

In 1889, LeConte embarked on a five-week horseback trip to Yosemite Valley and the High Sierra with a party that included other University of California faculty and John Muir. The group would soon thereafter start a campaign to establish today's Yosemite National Park and to promote more recreational use of the Sierra. Many of this group's members also founded the Sierra Club in 1892, with LeConte himself serving as director for several years. A prolific author on a wide array of subjects, LeConte died during a 1901 Sierra Club excursion in Yosemite.

In this passage, LeConte recalls an 1870s "ramble" to Tuolumne Meadows with a party including John Muir.

This afternoon we went on to Lake Tenaya. The trail is very blind, in most places detectable only by the blazing of trees, and very rough. We traveled most of the way on a high ridge. When [within] about two miles of our destination, from the brow of the mountain ridge upon which we had been traveling, Lake Tenaya burst upon our delighted vision, its placid surface set like a gem amongst magnificent mountains, the most conspicuous of which are [the] Mt. Hoffman group on the left, and Cathedral Peak beyond the lake. From this point we descended to the margin of the lake, and encamped at 5 P.M. on the lower end of the lake, in a fine grove of tamaracks, near an extensive and beautiful meadow. We built an immense fire, and had a fine supper of excellent bread and delicious mutton. Our appetites were excellent; we ate up entirely one hind-quarter of mutton, and wanted more.

After supper, I went with Mr. Muir and sat on a high rock, jutting into the lake. It was full moon. I never saw a more delightful scene. This little lake, one mile long and a half mile wide, is actually embosomed in the mountains, being surrounded by rocky eminences two thousand feet high, of the most picturesque forms, which come down to the very water's edge. The deep stillness of the night; the silvery light and deep shadows of the mountains; the reflection on the water, broken into thousands of glittering points by the ruffled surface; the gentle lapping of the wavelets upon the rocky shore—all these seemed exquisitely harmonized with each other, and the grand harmony made answering music in our hearts. Gradually the lake surface became quiet and mirror-like, and the exquisite surrounding scenery was seen double. For an hour we remained sitting in silent enjoyment of this delicious scene, which we reluctantly left to go to bed. Tenaya Lake is about eight thousand feet above sea-level. The night air, therefore, is very cool.

I noticed in many places today, especially as we approached Lake Tenaya, the polishings and scorings of ancient glaciers. In many places we found broad, flat masses so polished that our horses could hardly maintain their footing in passing over them. It is wonderful that in granite so decomposable these old glacial surfaces should remain as fresh as the day they were left by the glacier. But if ever the polished surface scales off then the disintegration proceeds as usual. The destruction of these surfaces by scaling, is, in fact, continually going on. Whitney thinks the polished surface is hardened by pressure of the glacier. I cannot think so. The smoothing, I think, prevents the retention of water, and thus prevents the rotting. Like the rusting of iron, which is hastened by roughness, and still more by rust, and retarded or even prevented by cleaning and polishing, so rotting of rock is hastened by roughness, and still more by commencing to rot, and retarded or prevented by grinding down to the sound rock and then polishing.

Today, while cooking midday meal, the wind was high, and the fire furious. I singed my whiskers and mustache, and badly burned my hand with boiling-hot bacon fat.

John Muir, "A Wind Storm in the Forests of the Yuba"

Born in Scotland, John Muir (1838–1914) immigrated to the United States in 1849 and had made his way from Wisconsin to California by 1868. Enthralled by the natural beauty of the Sierra Nevada, Muir hiked throughout the range and left his indelible mark on the region, in part by founding the Sierra Club and fighting to make Yosemite a national park. He also battled (although unsuccessfully) against the damming of Hetch Hetchy Valley, located within the park's boundaries.

Muir's writings are unique among the journals of the nineteenth-century American West because, unlike narratives that emphasized "getting there" and triumphing over physical hardship, his works celebrate what he called the "spiritual affinities" of the natural experience. Mountains were not obstacles to overcome but cathedrals. Storms were not terrifying occurrences but delightful evidence of a supernatural plan. The following selection, from The Mountains of California *(1894), describes an evening Muir spent high in a Douglas fir tree (what he called a Douglas spruce) during an intense Sierra windstorm.*

One of the most beautiful and exhilarating storms I ever enjoyed in the Sierra occurred in December, 1874, when I happened to be exploring one of the tributary valleys of the Yuba River. The sky and the ground and the trees had been thoroughly rain-washed and were dry again. The day was intensely pure, one of those incomparable bits of California winter, warm and balmy and full of white sparkling sunshine, redolent of all the purest influences of the spring, and at the same time enlivened with one of the most bracing wind-storms conceivable. Instead of camping out, as I usually do, I then chanced to be stopping at the house of a friend. But when the storm began to sound, I lost no time in pushing out into the woods to enjoy it. For on such occasions Nature has always something rare to show us, and the danger to life and limb is hardly greater than one would experience crouching deprecatingly beneath a roof.

It was still early morning when I found myself fairly adrift. Delicious sunshine came pouring over the hills, lighting the tops of the pines, and setting free a steam of summery fragrance that contrasted strangely with the wild tones of the storm. The air was mottled with pine-tassels and bright green plumes, that went flashing past in the sunlight like birds pursued. But there was not the slightest dustiness, nothing less pure than leaves, and ripe pollen, and flecks of withered bracken and moss. I heard trees falling for hours at the rate of one every two or three minutes; some uprooted, partly on account of the loose, water-soaked condition of the ground; others broken straight across, where some weakness caused by fire had determined the spot. The gestures of the various trees made a delightful study. Young Sugar Pines, light and feathery as squirrel-tails, were bowing almost to the ground; while the grand old patriarchs, whose massive boles had been tried in a hundred storms, waved solemnly above them, their long, arching branches streaming fluently on the gale, and every needle thrilling and ringing and shedding off keen lances of light like a diamond. The Douglas Spruces, with long sprays drawn out in level tresses, and needles massed in a gray, shimmering glow, presented a most striking appearance as they stood in bold relief along the hilltops. The madroñas in the dells, with their red bark and large glossy leaves tilted every way, reflected the sunshine in throbbing spangles like those one so often sees on the rippled surface of a glacier lake. But the Silver Pines were now the most impressively beautiful of all. Colossal spires 200 feet in height waved like supple goldenrods chanting and bowing low as if in worship, while the whole mass of their long, tremulous foliage was kindled into one continuous blaze of white sun-fire.

The force of the gale was such that the most steadfast monarch of them all rocked down to its roots with a motion plainly perceptible when one leaned against it. Nature was holding high festival, and every fiber of the most rigid giants thrilled with glad excitement.

I drifted on through the midst of this passionate music and motion, across many a glen, from ridge to ridge; often halting in the lee of a rock for shelter, or to gaze and listen. Even when the grand anthem had swelled to its highest pitch, I could distinctly hear the varying tones of individual trees,—Spruce, and Fir, and Pine, and leafless Oak,—and even the infinitely gentle rustle of the withered grasses at my feet. Each was expressing itself in its own way,—singing its own song, and making its own peculiar gestures,—manifesting a richness of variety to be found in no other forest I have yet seen. The coniferous woods of Canada, and the Carolinas, and Florida, are made up of trees that resemble one another about as nearly as blades of grass, and grow close together in much the same way. Coniferous trees, in general, seldom possess individual character, such as is manifest among Oaks and Elms. But the California forests are made up of a greater number of distinct species than any other in the world. And in them we find, not only a marked differentiation into special groups, but also a marked individuality in almost every tree, giving rise to storm effects indescribably glorious.

Toward midday, after a long, tingling scramble through copses of hazel and ceanothus, I gained the summit of the highest ridge in the neighborhood; and then it occurred to me that it would be a fine thing to climb one of the trees to obtain a wider outlook and get my ear close to the Æolian music of its topmost needles. But under the circumstances the choice of a tree was a serious matter. One whose instep was not very strong seemed in danger of being blown down, or of being struck by others in case they should fall; another was branchless to a considerable height above the ground, and at the same time too large to be grasped with arms and legs in climbing; while others were not favorably situated for clear views. After cautiously casting about, I made choice of the tallest of a group of Douglas Spruces that were growing close together like a tuft of grass, no one of which seemed likely to fall unless all the rest fell with it. Though comparatively young, they were about 100 feet high, and their lithe, brushy tops were rocking and swirling in wild ecstasy. Being accustomed to climb trees in making botanical studies, I experienced no difficulty in reaching the top of this one, and never before did I enjoy so noble an exhilaration of motion. The slender tops fairly flapped and swished in the passionate torrent, bending and swirling backward and forward, round and round, tracing indescribable combinations of vertical and horizontal curves, while I clung with muscles firm braced, like a bobo-link on a reed.

In its widest sweeps my tree-top described an arc of from twenty to thirty degrees, but I felt sure of its elastic temper, having seen others of the same species still more severely tried—bent almost to the ground indeed, in heavy snows—without breaking a fiber. I was therefore safe, and free to take the wind into my pulses and enjoy the excited forest from my superb outlook. The view from here must be extremely beautiful in any weather. Now my eye roved over the piny hills and dales as over fields of waving grain, and felt the light running in ripples and broad swelling undulations across the valleys from ridge to ridge, as the shining foliage was stirred by corresponding waves of air. Oftentimes these waves of reflected light would break up suddenly into a kind of beaten foam, and again, after chasing one another in regular order, they would seem to bend forward in concentric curves, and disappear on some hillside, like sea-waves on a shelving shore. The quantity of light reflected from the bent needles was so great as to make whole groves appear as if covered with snow, while the black shadows beneath the trees greatly enhanced the effect of the silvery splendor.

Excepting only the shadows there was nothing somber in all this wild sea of pines. On the contrary, notwithstanding this was the winter season, the colors were remarkably beautiful. The shafts of the pine and libocedrus were brown and purple, and most of the foliage was well tinged with yellow; the laurel groves, with the pale undersides of their leaves turned upward, made masses of gray; and then there was many a dash of chocolate color from clumps of manzanita, and jet of vivid crimson from the bark of the madroños, while the ground on the hillsides, appearing here and there through openings between the groves, displayed masses of pale purple and brown.

The sounds of the storm corresponded gloriously with this wild exuberance of light and motion. The profound bass of the naked branches and boles booming like waterfalls; the quick, tense vibrations of the pine-needles, now rising to a shrill, whistling hiss, now falling to a silky murmur; the rustling of laurel groves in the dells, and the keen metallic click of leaf on leaf—all this was heard in easy analysis when the attention was calmly bent.

The varied gestures of the multitude were seen to fine advantage, so that one could recognize the different species at a distance of several miles by this means alone, as well as by their forms and colors, and the way they reflected the light. All seemed strong and comfortable, as if really enjoying the storm, while responding to its most enthusiastic greetings. We hear much nowadays concerning the universal struggle for existence, but no struggle in the common meaning of the word was manifest here; no recognition of danger by any tree; no deprecation; but rather an invincible gladness as remote from exultation as from fear.

I kept my lofty perch for hours, frequently closing my eyes to enjoy the music by itself, or to feast quietly on the delicious fragrance that was streaming past. The fragrance of the woods was less marked than that produced during warm rain, when so many balsamic buds and leaves are steeped like tea; but, from the chafing of resiny branches against each other, and the incessant attrition of myriads of needles, the gale was spiced to a very tonic degree. And besides the fragrance from these local sources there were traces of scents brought from afar. For this wind came first from the sea, rubbing against its fresh, briny waves, then distilled through the redwoods, threading rich ferny gulches, and spreading itself in broad undulating currents over many a flower-enameled ridge of the coast mountains, then across the golden plains, up the purple foot-hills, and into these piny woods with the varied incense gathered by the way.

Winds are advertisements of all they touch, however much or little we may be able to read them; telling their wanderings even by their scents alone. Mariners detect the flowery perfume of land-winds far at sea, and sea-winds carry the fragrance of dulse and tangle far inland, where it is quickly recognized, though mingled with the scents of a thousand land-flowers. As an illustration of this, I may tell here that I breathed sea-air on the Firth of Forth, in Scotland, while a boy; then was taken to Wisconsin, where I remained nineteen years; then, without in all this time having breathed one breath of the sea, I walked quietly, alone, from the middle of the Mississippi Valley to the Gulf of Mexico, on a botanical excursion, and while in Florida, far from the coast, my attention wholly bent on the splendid tropical vegetation about me, I suddenly recognized a sea-breeze, as it came sifting through the palmettos and blooming vine-tangles, which at once awakened and set free a thousand dormant associations, and made me a boy again in Scotland, as if all the intervening years had been annihilated.

Most people like to look at mountain rivers, and bear them in mind; but few care to look at the winds, though far more beautiful and sublime, and though they become at times about as visible as flowing water. When the north winds in winter are making upward sweeps over the curving summits of the High Sierra, the fact is sometimes published with flying snow-banners a mile long. Those portions of the winds thus embodied can scarce be wholly invisible, even to the darkest imagination. And when we look around over an agitated forest, we may see something of the wind that stirs it, by its effects upon the trees. Yonder it descends in a rush of water-like ripples, and sweeps over the bending pines from hill to hill. Nearer, we see detached plumes and leaves, now speeding by on level currents, now whirling in eddies, or, escaping over the edges of the whirls, soaring aloft on grand, upswelling domes of air, or tossing on flame-like crests. Smooth, deep currents, cascades, falls, and swirling eddies, sing around every tree and leaf, and over all the varied topography of the region with telling changes of form, like mountain rivers conforming to the features of their channels.

After tracing the Sierra streams from their fountains to the plains, marking where they bloom white in falls, glide in crystal plumes, surge gray and foam-filled in boulder-choked gorges, and slip through the woods in long, tranquil reaches—after thus learning their language and forms in detail, we may at length hear them chanting all together in one grand anthem, and comprehend them all in clear inner vision, covering the range like lace. But even this spectacle is far less sublime and not a whit more substantial than what we may behold of these storm-streams of air in the mountain woods.

We all travel the milky way together, trees and men; but it never occurred to me until this storm-day, while swinging in the wind, that trees are travelers, in the ordinary sense. They make many journeys, not extensive ones, it is true; but our own little journeys, away and back again, are only little more than tree-wavings—many of them not so much.

When the storm began to abate, I dismounted and sauntered down through the calming woods. The storm-tones died away, and, turning toward the east, I beheld the countless hosts of the forests hushed and tranquil, towering above one another on the slopes of the hills like a devout audience. The setting sun filled them with amber light, and seemed to say, while they listened, "My peace I give unto you."

As I gazed on the impressive scene, all the so called ruin of the storm was forgotten, and never before did these noble woods appear so fresh, so joyous, so immortal.

"American frontiers had always been hard on regional ecologies and California was no exception—except that there was more to destroy"

Kevin Starr, from *Americans and the California Dream, 1850–1915*

Kevin Starr (b. 1940) has spent decades examining the impact of California and the Sierra Nevada on our consciousness. The former California State Librarian and currently a professor of urban and regional planning at the University of Southern California, Starr is most well known for his multi-volume series Americans and the California Dream, *which focuses on the influence of California history in shaping the image of the state throughout the world.*

In this selection, Starr appraises the impact of artists, philosophers, and natural historians on the perception of the Sierra Nevada as both physical and psychic environment.

From the start, Californians were challenged by the landscape that surrounded them. It was not a subtle drama, but a bold confrontation of flatland, mountain, and valley. Topographically, California had few secrets. Two major mountain systems, the Sierra Nevada and the Coast Range, ran longitudinally down eastern and western extremes. From these, secondary chains jutted out at various angles into the interior....

Although in later years the American might lift up his eyes to the hills as he made the valleys bloom, during the Gold Rush he came to the mountains of California as a destroyer. Mining, especially in its more complex phases, devastated the foothills and stripped them of timber. By 1859 much of the Mother Lode had been left a wasteland of caved-in hillsides, heaped debris, and tree stumps. Hydraulic mining, the washing down of mountainsides by high-pressure hoses, poured thousands of tons of mud and silt into the Yuba, Feather, American, Merced, and Sacramento rivers, which ran reddish-yellow with waste. Hindering navigation and increasing the likelihood of floods as it accumulated, hydraulic sediment in its progress downstream destroyed lowland farms and ruined rich riverbanks. In certain rivers, where pollution was high, salmon no longer leaped upstream to spawn. "Nature here reminds one," wrote Bayard Taylor regarding the mining regions, "of a princess, fallen into the hands of robbers, who cut off her fingers for the sake of the jewels she wears."

In the case of California's giant trees, the Sequoia, the maiming reached demonic proportions. Centuries-old, these trees were among the natural wonders of the world. For ages they had gathered strength from the sunlight and moist earth, some of them being already 1000 years old at the dawn of the Christian era. No other living things had sojourned so long on the planet or had reached such size. [Scientists now think that the world's oldest trees are bristlecone pines, found in California's White Mountains, east of the southern Sierra.] Clustered in mountainous groves, lighted by shafts of sunlight which slanted downward from a vaulting of branches meshed at soaring heights, the big trees of California were cathedrals of nature: cool, silent, the products of a profound historicity. In them Americans might possess a symbol defiant of communal newness, a near-religious metaphor for the ancient goodness of life. In 1853, at the Calaveras grove, five Americans spent twenty-five days cutting down a 3000-year-old Sequoia, 302 feet high and 96 feet in circumference. They polished the stump into a dance floor and hollowed out the fallen trunk into a bowling alley. Another tree, called the Mother of the Forest, had its bark stripped off to the height of 116 feet for exhibit in the East and Europe. The tree died as a result, its epitaph carved into its flayed sides in the form of numerous initials, dates, graffiti and intwined hearts. In the destruction of these trees Henry David Thoreau saw at work a primal human hatred of whatever reminded men of their own insignificance. "The trees were so grand and venerable," he said of the destruction in California, "that they could not afford to let them grow a hair's breadth bigger, or live a moment longer to reproach themselves."

Contemplating the exfoliated foothills, the polluted rivers, the fallen trees, and the obscenity of a Sequoia destroyed to make a dance floor and a bowling alley, an outside observer, even one less generally hostile than Thoreau, might have little hope regarding the quality of relationship between the Californian and his environment. American frontiers had always been hard on regional ecologies and California was no exception—except that there was more to destroy. The slaughter of the animals underway since before the Gold Rush drove the sea otter from offshore and the grizzly and the elk from the Coast Range, thinned out the deer, and emptied the sky of condor and eagles. For sport, Americans walked up to sea lions basking in the sun and put a bullet between their eyes, leaving the carcasses to rot on the beach. Hunters bagged more game than they could use, and venison was often a glut on the San Francisco market. In the matter of landscape, flora and fauna, it seemed that Americans in California really did not care, that the destruction would go on until it exhausted either itself or the region.

In the late 1850's a certain sort of tourist began to argue against this ecological indifference, indeed, vehemently to upbraid it. They related in a new manner to California, in enjoyment, not exploitation or the throes of finding a living, and they brought a high degree of imagination and critical intelligence along with their delight. The literary tourism of writers like Bayard Taylor, Horace Greeley, Charles Loring Brace, Charles Nordhoff, Benjamin Taylor, and Sara Lippincott was an act of observation, selection, and judgment in which they described what California was and should be. Universally they agreed that it should mean the authentication and liberation of man through nature, since nature in California was such an overwhelming fact; hence indifference to and abuse of landscape and wildlife took on for them the significance of an especially distressing problem. Was there something in the American character, they speculated along paths already trod by Thoreau, that of itself resisted a redemptive relationship to nature, that destroyed beauty out of an uncouth rage or a maniacal urge to profit?

Over a period of time and through a variety of visits, they decided that Calvinist fears of total damnation were incorrect and even self-indulgent. Their own tourism, in fact, was part of the solution, for they came in the van of an expatriate colony which by the 1880's ensured that there resided in California at any given season a population of educated, financially secure Americans who came and stayed precisely because they liked the climate and the scenery. Helping to offset the work ethic of Gold Rush and early frontier, tourists sought out and shaped what there was to enjoy. Up and down the state, they visited geysers, hot springs, rivers, lakes, underground caverns, big trees, mountains, and beaches....

To its credit, California put the investigation of its topography on a systematic basis with the creation in 1860 of a Geological Survey.

Support from the legislature, however, was minimal and intermittent. During the active existence of the Survey, from 1861 to 1874, Josiah Dwight Whitney, Director and State Geologist, never had adequate funds. Politicians wanted the Survey to seek out new mining regions, Whitney wanted a disinterested measurement and mapping of the entire state, and so the life of this group of superb field-scientists was ill-supported and brief. It did not dissolve, however, before coming to near completion of its heroic task.

William Henry Brewer, field director of the Survey, spent four years in the open, up and down California, supervising the work....The mountains of California offered Brewer an unambiguous challenge to stamina and intellect, and he responded with clarity of scientific purpose, bravery, and lack of pretension. Brewer made an imaginative connection with the mountains as an arena of objective endeavor. Their conquest was an act of will and intelligence in the service of science— and from that act came subjective gifts of beauty, spiritual drama, and escape from sorrow.

Brewer's younger colleague on the Survey, Clarence King, pursued a more self-regarding mode of mountaineering. Like Brewer, a graduate of the Sheffield School, King had come West to avoid the Civil War. He joined the Survey in 1863 and remained until 1866, when [he was] twenty-four....

Here, suggested King, in the absence of a complex civilization, was California's one adequate reference for aesthetic endeavor. King's continual attempts to associate the Sierras with the high art of Europe— as opposed to Europe's high mountains—drove home the point. His was the preliminary connection, from the Sierras to past art. The next step, from the Sierras to future art, belonged to California.

Yosemite Valley, described by King with such force, was destined to become one of the primary symbols of California, a fixed factor of identity for all those who sought a specifically Californian aesthetic. Members of the Mariposa Battalion, a unit of mounted volunteers, discovered the Valley on 25 March 1851. [Native Californians had certainly "discovered" the Valley long before.] Yosemite scenery did inspire, as Clarence King pointed out, much lavish language, but a man of sound intelligence and imagination like Thomas Starr King was capable of putting the Valley to disciplined, effective use as a communal symbol in a theological context. And that provided a model for future appropriations. Visually so stupendous, Yosemite inspired the visual arts. Albert Bierstadt and other painters of the Hudson River

School rushed West to capture its grandeur in a series of grandiloquent canvases which even today, despite the stylization of idiom, convey the nineteenth century's first gasp of wonder. The infant art of photography felt itself especially challenged. Eadweard Muybridge, a San Francisco photographer who later did work crucial to the development of motion pictures, produced an extraordinary set of Yosemite plates between 1867 and 1872. Excluding human scale or reference, Muybridge concentrated upon the natural features of the Valley. He avoided, however, unrelieved documentation, demonstrating the impressionistic capabilities of photography in his use of weather. A drama of sunlight and shadow, shifting cloud formations, moonlight, mists, and rainbows plays across Yosemite's proscenium of granite cliffs, an evanescent dance of the hours before the Valley's eternal impassivity.

Celebrated in art, Yosemite was reverenced in life as the high shrine of California pilgrimage. Journalist, hotel-keeper, self-appointed guardian of the Valley, James Mason Hutchings, an Englishman who came during the Gold Rush, dedicated a lifetime to promoting the Yosemite in the consciousness of Californians. *Hutchings' Illustrated California Magazine*, which he founded in 1856, edited, and wrote much of singlehandedly, must take the most credit for helping to reverse the frontier relationship of Californians to their landscape. Through superb illustrations and marvelously detailed essays, *Hutchings' Magazine* encouraged Americans in California to take notice of their natural heritage and to relate to it in pleasure and informed appreciation. The Yosemite, of course, dominated Hutchings' imagination, and he settled there permanently in 1859 as a tourist-guide and hotel-keeper. His *Scenes of Wonder and Curiosity in California* (1860) provided detailed directions for an eight-day visit to the Valley.

A group of Californians and temporary Californians led by Frederick Law Olmsted, the noted traveler and landscape architect, lobbied through Congress a bill, which President Lincoln signed on 25 June 1864, setting aside under the protection of the State of California a huge tract of Sierran land which included the Yosemite Valley and the Mariposa Big Trees. The bill closed the area forever to commercial development. Nothing on such a scale and for such unselfish purposes had ever been passed by Congress, and one suspects that the distractions of the Civil War had much to do with the success of the measure. Olmstead had a comprehensive plan for the management of the preserve, but he returned to New York City in 1865 to finish the laying out of Central Park before he could put his ideas into action. It would be decades before intelligent arrangements for the supervision of Yosemite would be legislated and put into effect—but a startling fact was clear: the Yosemite had been saved. Considering the usual pattern of American behavior in such matters, considering the ravages already wrought upon the California environment by the 1860's, few could have predicted the success of this major act of preservation.

Throughout the 1860's and 1870's, in ever-increasing numbers, the tourists came to Yosemite, by train and stagecoach across the San Joaquin, by wagon into the foothills, and by horseback onto the Valley floor....

Cumulatively, from literary accounts, from paintings and photographs, from reports of all sorts, Yosemite began to assume a primary significance in the minds of Californians. Here was the one adequate symbol for all that California promised: beauty, grandeur, expansiveness, a sense of power, and a sense—this in the geological history—of titanic preparation for an assured and magnificent future. As scenery, as a physiography that was deeply symbolic, Yosemite offered Californians an objective correlative for their ideal sense of themselves: a people animated by heroic imperatives. Its configuration of mountain and valley was a grand paradigm of California's geography as a whole. From the Valley floor, standing on the banks of the Merced River and looking up to the great cliffs, one was in full possession of limits, and yet these limits were of a grandeur and an inaccessibility beyond even the suggestion of intimacy....In 1864 Americans set the Yosemite aside because it was so unutterably beautiful and because it expressed their own best hopes....

That same year John Muir was trekking through the wilds of Canada in quest of who he was and what he should do. In a sense Yosemite was being set aside for the young Scot, or at least the Valley would have to await Muir's arrival before it received its best expression and most effective conservation....

In Clarence King the mountaineer defied nature, pitting himself against rocks and gorges in a test of courage conceived of as an abstraction and reveled in psychologically. Muir despised King's elaborate self-consciousness, his risk-taking as a form of existential encounter....[M]ost especially in times of danger and decision, Muir felt himself in contact with an Other Self, a spiritual projection of his ego in mystical harmony with the mountains, telling Muir at moments of mountaineering crisis what moves were necessary and when they should be made. Near the top of Mount Ritter (which Clarence King had unsuccessfully tried to climb), Muir found himself caught on the edge of a precipice, seeing no further holds, baffled at what to do next. Suddenly his Other Self came to his rescue. "My eyes became preternaturally clear," Muir tells us, "and every rift, flaw, niche, and tablet in the cliff ahead, were seen as through a microscope. At any rate the danger was safely passed, I scarce know how, and shortly after noon I leaped with wild freedom, into the sunlight upon the highest crag of the summit. Had I been borne aloft upon wings, my deliverance could not have been more complete." Similar incidents occurred atop Mount Shasta and Mount Whitney, which Muir scaled, as usual, without equipment, wearing low-quarter shoes and living off bread and tea. Upon the heights, Clarence King conceived of himself as poised above chaos, as having defied chasms without and chasms within. On the same and even more lofty peaks Muir saw himself as soaring over a singing creation, hearing the music which the ages had prepared.

The preservation of that song so that future generations might hear it became the work of Muir's major years. His articles in *Century Magazine* were instrumental in getting a Yosemite National Park Bill through Congress in 1890. In May 1903 Muir and President Theodore Roosevelt camped out together in the Yosemite for four days—in the Mariposa Grove one night, atop Glacier Point the next, and then for two nights in Bridalveil Meadow on the Valley floor. It was one of the happiest times in Roosevelt's life, and he left the Yosemite won over to Muir's conservationist program. In 1905 California ceded the Yosemite to the federal government as part of the Department of the Interior's National Park Service. Throughout the years of struggle, as dedicated Californians sought to put conservation of their environment on an intelligent and systematic basis, John Muir led the way, prophet and warrior-priest....

On 4 June 1892, in the office of a San Francisco attorney, a group of Californians drew up and signed articles incorporating the Sierra Club, with John Muir as president. The Sierra Club gave formal expression to that distinctly Californian relationship to the outdoors which had been developing since the 1860's and which Muir best represented. The 162 charter members of the Club were in the main university-educated professional men, together with a large representation from the faculties at Palo Alto [Stanford] and Berkeley. Five professors, in fact, including David Starr Jordan, president of Stanford, sat on the founding board of directors. The Sierra Club represented the flowering of ecological stewardship on the part of California's upper middle class. The very wealthy were noticeably absent from the Club's charter ranks. Railroad kings, real estate developers, timber barons, and the like, profiting from unregulated exploitation, were naturally hostile to the conservationist core of the Sierra Club ideology. The Club gathered together those who by the 1890's were feeling themselves in the van of the California dream, people who had time, means, and taste enough to profit from what was available. They lived in beautiful homes (developing, indeed, a regional architectural style), worked just hard enough at their careers to sustain a rich and varied life, read widely, and loved the outdoors. It was they who brought to California university culture, staffing its institutions as faculty or just living in their proximity and sharing their spirit. In time, under the banner of Progressivism, they would set about the political reform of California, for they were tired of seeing their ideals mocked by corrupt corporate and union power. Meanwhile, in 1892, they rallied around unequivocal symbols of what was important about California and what they were looking for by living there. In the Sierras and John Muir and the Sierra Club they found a California already brought to redemption....

"When I was a boy in Scotland," Muir once wrote, "I was fond of everything that was wild, and all my life I've been growing fonder and fonder of wild places and wild creatures." It was this love of their land, wild and lyrical, that Californians learned from John Muir. It was the renewal of a Sierra morning which he continually asked them to regain. It was Muir's reverence for life and his joy in living that Californians found they most desperately needed when, in later years, California threatened to die before their very eyes.

Ella Sterling Cummins Mighels, "Portrait of a California Girl"

Ella Sterling Cummins Mighels (1853–1934) was a native Californian, born in the Gold Rush community of Mormon Island, on the American River near today's Folsom. Fascinated by the early days of her home state, Mighels wrote extensively about the literary and journalistic history of the era. She also wrote newspaper columns opposing women's suffrage and birth control, and supporting racial discrimination and male chauvinism. Her writings present California culture as neither glamorous nor romantic but as an often difficult, diverse social order in which people were doing their best to survive, and hopefully prosper, in a newly formed community.

This selection by Mighels is taken from a collection titled Short Stories by California Authors, *published in 1885 by the* San Francisco Golden Era. *In this excerpt, a middle-aged man, Judge Harville, has ignored storm warnings and is riding on business over the Sierra Nevada toward Mono County, on the eastern side. As he rides through the foreboding Sonora Pass, he thinks of a charming, resourceful "child-woman" named Lorena, whom he had last met in San Francisco eight years earlier.*

The road wound around the hills, and then took a line through the only natural egress or ingress—a long, dark canyon, two gloomy walls of solid rock, that once fitted evenly together in a solid mass, but in some great convulsion of nature, had separated, leaving this narrow space between—barely room enough for two teams to pass with a little stream of water running alongside.

Stories of waterspouts, very frequent in this locality, came to his mind, and he wondered if one should strike this cañon, whether the unfortunate caught between these walls could possibly escape drowning.

After a while, the walls lowered gradually, and he saw a wild horizon of jagged fantastic angles encircling him round. On the instant a picture came back to his mind of a house situated in the foreground of a wild mountain, and a group of children, and then a succession of pictures with a bright little girl figure arching in the center.

"It must be the peculiar horizon that brings back such a faint little memory as that of Lorena," said he, musingly. "It was no wonder she didn't grow up like other children, with such a horizon as that around her. What's that? Snowflakes falling? The old man was a prophet, after all. I wonder if I can't make the quartz mill before it gets too heavy." And spurring his horse, he hastened along. The weather had changed, the bracing air had given way to that strange, heavy atmosphere that precedes the snowstorm, so imperceptibly that he had not noticed it.

On leaving this uncanny place, the road verged about several small slopes, but the snow increased so suddenly and so violently, with a sudden gust of wind blowing down the canyon, that he became confused. Once he thought he had struck the trail because of the fresh horses' tracks before him in the snow, but he soon found that, in his confusion, he had been merely following in a circle upon his own trail.

To add to his distress, his horse stepped into a sudden gully and fell beneath him with a broken leg. Darkness now seemed to encompass the earth, and Judge Harville stood gazing into space utterly bewildered.

The violent efforts of his horse in attempting to rise called him back to himself, and after a moment's hesitancy, he drew out his revolver and put the beast out of his misery, performing this action of cruel kindness promptly and effectively.

He felt sure that the quartz-mill was not far away, and that he could make it within an hour. He lighted a match, and looked at his watch. It was six. He felt the need of food and shelter, and resolved to press forward.

The night was coming on fast, and it was bitter cold. He could not think of staying in this desolate spot when a place of refuge was so near.

But he soon found himself at the mercy of the pitiless elements. The snow still fell madly, the wind was beginning to throw up little drifts. Still he struggled on. Once he plunged into the creek through the shallow ice, and although wet through, and his clothes immediately stiffened, he exclaimed, "Thank God!" for it showed that the road was not far away. Bit by bit, step by step, he makes his way. In three hours he has made a mile directly forward, though five or six has been lost in retracement.

He is no longer the elegant and dignified Judge Harville. He is only a man fighting for life—a pitiable object of humanity. His clothes are torn by contact with the rocks, or stiffened with frozen water, his hands are bleeding, his feet badly frozen. Shall he give up and lie down to sweet, coaxing sleep—sleep that knows no waking, or shall he struggle on?

A sound breaking on the freezing air attracts his wandering senses.

"Help!" he cries.

The sound comes again, repeated thrice. If he was desperate before, now he was like one transfixed.

It was the bark of a coyote—a sharp, insolent bark. What an answer to a freezing man's call for help!

"What! lie down to die, and be devoured by those cowardly brutes?" And in answer he plunged along again with renewed efforts, nerved with strength born of desperation. The barks increased around him; there was a pair of them; he could see their dark shadows on the snow, waiting at a respectful distance. His hands were so cold and numb that he could not get his revolver out, and even then the water had frozen it stiff. "Great Heaven!" he cried, "was I born for this?"

His ears now told him the voices were three, he wasted no time looking for the shadowy forms on the snow. "I will keep them out of their feast as long as I can," he thought, his natural stubbornness coming to his aid. And he did, but his powers were nearly exhausted, his endurance overtried. Gradually the stiffness was creeping on him, he felt no more arms or legs, he was only a human clump struggling onward. Still the snow fell. "Heh! heh! heh!" barked the cowardly chorus. Each moment seemed a year as they gained upon him. One crept close to him; in an agony of despair he made one great effort and struck at it, the cowardly thing slunk back. It feared even the semblance of a man as long as there was a spark of life in it.

Suddenly upon his ear almost dulled in its sense of hearing, came another sound, he roused himself to listen. Could he be losing his mind already, or was it a mocking human voice imitating the coyotes? "Heh, heh, heh!" called the chorus around him. "Heh, heh, heh," called out a clear mocking voice from a distance.

"God!" said the man, and with soul swelling within him, forgetting his poor cumbersome, solid body he strove once more, with hope inspiring him. That mocking human voice was the sweetest sound he had ever heard. But his feet failed him, they would no longer do their master's bidding. Accepting this new distress, he fell upon hands and knees and crept painfully along in the direction of the voice, which seemed to take delight in mocking the voices of the night. "If it should cease!" thought the man in despair.

One more little turn of a bend, and there he saw, very near, a light; with one loud cry born of agony and despair, he cried, "Help, help!" and at that moment felt the breath of the coyotes upon his cheek.

He struggled to show there was still life in him, and in the breathing spell thus obtained, the door flung wide open and the figure of a woman rushed out, a lamp in her hand.

"Where! where are you?" she cried. "Heh, heh," cried the chorus. "Here, here," cried the man with his last strength. "Merciful Heavens!" with this ejaculation, not pausing a moment she ran directly towards them, the coyotes shrinking back out of sight at the appearance of so much life and vitality. She found a clump of frozen humanity in the snow, speechless but with grateful eyes that looked up in her face and told of life.

[Judge Harville's rescuer—now grown and married to a mining engineer—was, of course, Lorena.]

Mary Hallock Foote, from *A Victorian Gentlewoman in the Far West*

Born in New York, Mary Hallock Foote (1847–1938) came West in 1876 with her husband, Arthur DeWint Foote, a prominent mining engineer. At first, Mary was reluctant to go—"No girl ever wanted less to 'go West,'" she wrote, "or paid a man a greater compliment by doing so"—but once she arrived, the landscape and its population enchanted her. Within two years, articles she had written and illustrated began appearing in Scribner's Monthly *magazine, and from there her career as a writer grew to include novels, short stories, and more articles, many of which she also illustrated herself. The Footes moved often due to Arthur's career, but in 1895 they settled permanently in Grass Valley, California, where Arthur was superintendent of the North Star Mine, one of the richest in the region.*

In this passage from A Victorian Gentlewoman in the Far West—*a compilation of Foote's writings published in 1972—the author describes her arrival in Grass Valley, details the gold-mining lifestyle, and explains the cultural and social influence on the community of the many hard rock miners from the county of Cornwall in England.*

All the rich valley of the Sacramento was veiled in fog as we crossed it going up into the foothills. At Colfax Junction, where we boarded the little narrow gauge, we looked up as we plunged into the pinewoods and saw the great train we had left, with its two engines, rounding Cape Horn—five days now to the other side instead of seven, for that mighty shuttle between East and West. The one passenger car was stuffy and filled with that underground smell which men who have worked in the mines for years cannot wash out of the pores of their skin, it is said. We heard the gruff voices that come out of chests as big as flour barrels, and the Cornish accent again was welcome to our ears. The ends of the circle had met. Not a great harvest for a twenty years' reaping, but some experience we had gathered, besides those two faces beaming at us in the seat opposite and the eighteen-year-old son on his way east to begin his life in precisely the way we might have hoped when he was our New Almaden baby.

The Rockwell cousins had had it in mind to ask him to live with them while he was at Tech, but on second thoughts they believed it best, as they wrote us, for him to have his own rooms and keep his own hours, but they expected him regularly to Sunday night supper; and Kate wrote me as one human mother to another, after the Sunday when he first appeared in his new frock coat, to say how well he looked in it, poor child! He left it behind him in the things of the East when his four years in Boston were over; the high hat for church, and the symphony concerts, and his cousin Di's introductions to the Early Florentine painters and the fair nieces of Henry Adams—all that atmosphere of a culture which left him seemingly untouched, but we need more impressions than we can use all at once—we need a bank account to draw upon.

All the above is a look into the future. We had no future then, look as hard as we might, and economy was our watchword....Ah, but our little girls were happy in the North Star Cottage—little impoverished ones rich in imagination! The boss carpenter on the work sent them at Christmas a music box that played two tunes, a wistful air by Mozart and a gay little waltz. It might not have been a wholly disinterested offering but we took it so—all faces were kind that looked at them. When the sitting room grew dusk early on the shortening days, and their father came home and lighted the fire and set the shadows dancing in the back of the room, they wound up their music and danced themselves to the trickle of those tunes over and over—they did not know how to dance; it was a fantasy of pure happiness. They were used to not knowing where their next home would be—they were not used to their father coming home to light the fire and smoke his pipe beside it and look at them in silence.

On Christmas morning the miners' bus drove out to the cottage filled with singers and they raised a carol as they came. They gave another, grouped on the grass below the piazza—grass that was still green. Invited in, there was handshaking all around and then the room rang to their voices as they sang—not the church carols, but quaint old chapel tunes and catches, older than Methodism, which are in the Cornish blood from father to son. But the great singing was on Christmas Eve when the day shift came up and the night shift was there waiting in their underground clothes, and they sang as one family grouped around the shaft the old country carols before scattering to their work and their little new western homes....

For twenty years the mines went on under the same management, developing their double life of the Surface and the Underground.... [T]wenty years is a long lease of life for a mine which cannot reap the same field twice nor return the same rock to the crusher. The Surface has gone on spreading its boundary marks, keeping pace with the development underground; it covers now over a thousand acres of woods and pastures and old trails, with new roads crossing them and power-lines and light lines cut through the woods where they pass. An old prospector's or squatter's cabin erased here and there has left a well hole or a few foundation stones or a rose bush blossoming year after year. The miners live in town convenient to church and the shows of an evening. We see few dinner-pail men on our wood walks, but a hundred cars or more are parked in the sheds or around the works at quitting time. I once thought that when I was done writing stories I would take the stories that have been lived on the North Star Surface for a theme, but I have waited too long: I know it all too well; its roots are too deep in my own life in these thirty years we have lived here.

There are other things, not on the surface, which I shall pass over in silence; beautiful friendships we never dreamed were in store for us—these are not to be talked about as things of the past. They are too close to my daily thoughts; the perspective is lacking, and we cannot say things to the "faces" of those we hold in delicate regard, more than we could write them letters to be passed around....

These fragments of my past are presented merely as backgrounds and the figures upon them are placed by instinct in a selected light and seen from a certain point of view. To that extent I suppose I am still the artist I tried to be, and the old romancer too. And everyone knows the magic perspectives of memory—it keeps what we loved and alters the relative size and value of many things that we did not love enough—that we hated and resisted and made mountains of at the time. It turns the dust of our valleys of humiliation, now that the sun of our working hours has set, into a sad and dreamy splendor which will fade into depths beyond depths of unknown worlds of stars.

"In Placer County, California, [nature] is a vast, unconquered brute of the Pliocene epoch, savage, sullen, and magnificently indifferent to man"

Frank Norris, from *McTeague*

Benjamin Franklin Norris (1870–1902), known as Frank, was an American novelist whose short career examined Social Darwinism and the new American society developing during the Progressive Era at the turn of the twentieth century. His most famous novel was The Octopus: A California Story, *a fictionalized description of the power and corruption of the Southern Pacific Railroad.*

Norris's novel McTeague *(1899), excerpted below, tells the story of a malevolent dentist fleeing San Francisco and returning to the goldfields to escape arrest in the final years of the nineteenth century. In portraying the brute force and mind-numbing labor required to dig wealth from deep in the earth, Norris suggests its negative effects on human behavior. The novel was the basis for the first feature-length motion picture filmed in the Sierra Nevada: Erich von Stroheim's 1924 silent film* Greed.

The day was very hot, and the silence of high noon lay close and thick between the steep slopes of the cañons like an invisible, muffling fluid. At intervals the drone of an insect bored the air and trailed slowly to silence again. Everywhere were pungent, aromatic smells. The vast, moveless heat seemed to distil countless odors from the brush—odors of warm sap, of pine needles, and of tar-weed, and above all the medicinal odor of witch hazel. As far as one could look, uncounted multitudes of trees and manzanita bushes were quietly and motionlessly growing, growing, growing. A tremendous, immeasurable Life pushed steadily heavenward without a sound, without a motion. At turns of the road, on the higher points, cañons disclosed themselves far away, gigantic grooves in the landscape, deep blue in the distance, opening one into another, ocean-deep, silent, huge, and suggestive of colossal primeval forces held in reserve. At their bottoms they were solid, massive; on their crests they broke delicately into fine serrated edges where the pines and redwoods outlined their million of tops against the high white horizon. Here and there the mountains lifted themselves out of the narrow river beds in groups like giant lions rearing their heads after drinking. The entire region was untamed. In some places east of the Mississippi nature is cosey, intimate, small, and homelike, like a good-natured housewife. In Placer County, California, she is a vast, unconquered brute of the Pliocene epoch, savage, sullen, and magnificently indifferent to man.

But there were men in these mountains, like lice on mammoths' hides, fighting them stubbornly, now with hydraulic "monitors," now with drill and dynamite, boring into the vitals of them, or tearing away great yellow gravelly scars in the flanks of them, sucking their blood, extracting gold.

Here and there at long distances upon the cañon sides rose the headgear of a mine, surrounded with its few unpainted houses, and topped by its never-failing feather of black smoke. On near approach one heard the prolonged thunder of the stamp-mill, the crusher, the insatiable monster, gnashing the rocks to powder with its long iron teeth, vomiting them out again in a thin stream of wet gray mud. Its enormous maw, fed night and day with the car-boys' loads, gorged itself with gravel, and spat out the gold, grinding the rocks between its jaws, glutted, as it were, with the very entrails of the earth, and growling over its endless meal, like some savage animal, some legendary dragon, some fabulous beast, symbol of inordinate and monstrous gluttony.

McTeague had left the Overland train at Colfax, and the same afternoon had ridden some eight miles across the mountains in the stage that connects Colfax with Iowa Hill. Iowa Hill was a small one-street town, the headquarters of the mines of the district. Originally it had been built upon the summit of a mountain, but the sides of this mountain have long since been "hydraulicked" away, so that the town now clings to a mere back bone, and the rear windows of the houses on both sides of the street look down over sheer precipices, into vast pits hundreds of feet deep.

The dentist stayed over night at the Hill, and the next morning started off on foot farther into the mountains. He still wore his blue overalls and jumper; his woollen cap was pulled down over his eyes; on his feet were hob-nailed boots he had bought at the store in Colfax;

his blanket roll was over his back; in his left hand swung the bird cage wrapped in sacks.

Just outside the town he paused, as if suddenly remembering something.

"There ought to be a trail just off the road here," he muttered. "There used to be a trail—a short cut."

The next instant, without moving from his position, he saw where it opened just before him. His instinct had halted him at the exact spot. The trail zigzagged down the abrupt descent of the cañon, debauching into a gravelly river bed.

"Indian River," muttered the dentist. "I remember—I remember. I ought to hear the Morning Star's stamps from here." He cocked his head. A low, sustained roar, like a distant cataract, came to his ears from across the river. "That's right," he said, contentedly. He crossed the river and regained the road beyond. The slope rose under his feet; a little farther on he passed the Morning Star mine, smoking and thundering. McTeague pushed steadily on. The road rose with the rise of the mountain, turned at a sharp angle where a great live-oak grew, and held level for nearly a quarter of a mile. Twice again the dentist left the road and took to the trail that cut through deserted hydraulic pits. He knew exactly where to look for these trails; not once did his instinct deceive him. He recognized familiar points at once. Here was Cold Cañon, where invariably, winter and summer, a chilly wind was blowing; here was where the road to Spencer's branched off; here was Bussy's old place, where at one time there were so many dogs; here was Delmue's cabin, where unlicensed whiskey used to be sold; here was the plank bridge with its one rotten board; and here the flat overgrown with manzanita, where he once had shot three quail.

At noon, after he had been tramping for some two hours, he halted at a point where the road dipped suddenly. A little to the right of him, and flanking the road, an enormous yellow gravel-pit like an emptied lake gaped to heaven. Farther on, in the distance, a cañon zigzagged toward the horizon, rugged with pine-clad mountain crests. Nearer at hand, and directly in the line of the road, was an irregular cluster of unpainted cabins. A dull, prolonged roar vibrated in the air. McTeague nodded his head as if satisfied.

"That's the place," he muttered.

He reshouldered his blanket roll and descended the road. At last he halted again. He stood before a low one-story building, differing from the others in that it was painted. A veranda, shut in with mosquito netting, surrounded it. McTeague dropped his blanket roll on a lumber pile outside, and came up and knocked at the open door. Someone called to him to come in.

McTeague entered, rolling his eyes about him, noting the changes that had been made since he had last seen this place. A partition had been knocked down, making one big room out of the two former small ones. A counter and railing stood inside the door. There was a telephone on the wall. In one corner he also observed a stack of surveyor's instruments; a big drawing-board straddled on spindle legs across one end of the room, a mechanical drawing of some kind, no doubt the plan of the mine, unrolled upon it; a chromo representing a couple of peasants in a ploughed field (Millet's "Angelus") was nailed unframed upon the wall, and hanging from the same wire nail that secured one of its corners in place was a bullion bag and a cartridge belt with a loaded revolver in the pouch.

The dentist approached the counter and leaned his elbows upon it. Three men were in the room—a tall, lean young man, with a thick head of hair surprisingly gray, who was playing with a half-grown great Dane puppy; another fellow about as young, but with a jaw almost as salient as McTeague's, stood at the letter-press taking a copy of a letter; a third man, a little older than the other two, was pottering over a transit. This latter was massively built, and wore overalls and low boots streaked and stained and spotted in every direction with gray mud. The dentist looked slowly from one to the other; then at length, "Is the foreman about?" he asked.

The man in the muddy overalls came forward. "What you want?" He spoke with a strong German accent.

The old invariable formula came back to McTeague on the instant. "What's the show for a job?"

At once the German foreman became preoccupied, looking aimlessly out of the window. There was a silence. "You hev been miner alretty?"

"Yes, yes."

"Know how to hendle pick'n shov'le?"

"Yes, I know."

The other seemed unsatisfied. "Are you a 'cousin Jack'?"

The dentist grinned. This prejudice against Cornishmen he remembered too. "No. American."

"How long since you mine?"

"Oh, year or two."

"Show your hands." McTeague exhibited his hard, calloused palms.

"When ken you go to work? I want a chuck-tender on der night shift."

"I can tend a chuck. I'll go on to-night."

"What's your name?"

The dentist started. He had forgotten to be prepared for this. "Huh? What?"

"What's the name?"

McTeague's eye was caught by a railroad calendar hanging over the desk. There was no time to think. "Burlington," he said, loudly.

The German took a card from a file and wrote it down. "Give dis card to der boarding-boss, down at der boarding-haus, den gome find me bei der mill at sex o'clock, und I set you to work."

Straight as a homing pigeon, and following a blind and unreasoned instinct, McTeague had returned to the Big Dipper mine. Within a week's time it seemed to him as though he had never been away. He picked up his life again exactly where he had left it the day when his mother had sent him away with the travelling dentist, the charlatan who had set up his tent by the bunk house. The house McTeague had once lived in was still there, occupied by one of the shift bosses and his family. The dentist passed it on his way to and from the mine.

He himself slept in the bunk house with some thirty others of his shift. At half-past five in the evening the cook at the boarding-house sounded a prolonged alarm upon a crowbar bent in the form of a triangle that hung upon the porch of the boarding-house. McTeague rose and dressed, and with his shift had supper. Their lunch-pails were distributed to them. Then he made his way to the tunnel mouth, climbed into a car in the waiting ore train, and was hauled into the mine.

Once inside, the hot evening air turned to a cool dampness, and the forest odors gave place to the smell of stale dynamite smoke, suggestive of burning rubber. A cloud of steam came from McTeague's mouth; underneath, the water swashed and rippled around the car-wheels, while the light from the miner's candlesticks threw wavering blurs of pale yellow over the gray rotting quartz of the roof and walls. Occasionally McTeague bent down his head to avoid the lagging of the roof or the projections of an overhanging shute. From car to car all along the line the miners called to one another as the train trundled along, joshing and laughing.

A mile from the entrance the train reached the breast where McTeague's gang worked. The men clambered from the cars and took up the labor where the day shift had left it, burrowing their way steadily through a primeval river bed.

The candlesticks thrust into the crevices of the gravel strata lit up faintly the half dozen moving figures befouled with sweat and with wet gray mould. The picks struck into the loose gravel with a yielding shock. The long-handled shovels clinked amidst the piles of boulders and scraped dully in the heaps of rotten quartz. The Burly drill boring for blasts broke out from time to time in an irregular chug-chug, chug-chug, while the engine that pumped the water from the mine coughed and strangled at short intervals.

McTeague tended the chuck. In a way he was the assistant of the man who worked the Burly. It was his duty to replace the drills in the Burly, putting in longer ones as the hole got deeper and deeper. From time to time he rapped the drill with a pole-pick when it stuck fast or fitchered.

Once it even occurred to him that there was a resemblance between his present work and the profession he had been forced to abandon. In the Burly drill he saw a queer counterpart of his old-time dental engine; and what were the drills and chucks but enormous hoe excavators, hard bits, and burrs? It was the same work he had so often performed in his "Parlors," only magnified, made monstrous, distorted, and grotesqued, the caricature of dentistry.

He passed his nights thus in the midst of the play of crude and simple forces—the powerful attacks of the Burly drills; the great exertions of bared, bent backs overlaid with muscle; the brusque, resistless expansion of dynamite; and the silent, vast, Titanic force, mysterious and slow, that cracked the timbers supporting the roof of the tunnel and that gradually flattened the lagging till it was thin as paper.

The life pleased the dentist beyond words. The still, colossal mountains took him back again like a returning prodigal, and vaguely, without knowing why, he yielded to their influence—their immensity, their enormous power, crude and blind, reflecting themselves in his own nature, huge, strong, brutal in its simplicity. And this, though he only saw the mountains at night. They appeared far different then than in the daytime. At twelve o'clock he came out of the mine and lunched on the contents of his dinner-pail, sitting upon the embankment of the track, eating with both hands, and looking around him with a steady ox-like gaze.

The mountains rose sheer from every side, heaving their gigantic crests far up into the night, the black peaks crowding together, and looking now less like beasts than like a company of cowled giants. In the daytime they were silent; but at night they seemed to stir and rouse themselves. Occasionally the stamp-mill stopped, its thunder ceasing abruptly. Then one could hear the noises that the mountains made in their living. From the cañon, from the crowding crests, from the whole immense landscape, there rose a steady and prolonged sound, coming from all sides at once. It was that incessant and muffled roar which disengages itself from all vast bodies, from oceans, from cities, from forests, from sleeping armies, and which is like the breathing of an infinitely great monster, alive, palpitating.

McTeague returned to his work. At six in the morning his shift was taken off, and he went out of the mine and back to the bunk house. All day long he slept, flung at length upon the strong-smelling blankets— slept the dreamless sleep of exhaustion, crushed and overpowered with the work, flat and prone upon his belly, till again in the evening the cook sounded the alarm upon the crowbar bent into a triangle.

Jack London, "All Gold Cañon"

*Born in San Francisco and raised in various places around the Bay Area,
Jack London (1876–1916) left home at age fourteen and over the years
lived as an active Socialist, a merchant seaman, and a hobo riding the rails.
In 1894 he was arrested for vagrancy in Niagara Falls and served thirty
days in jail. Humiliated by this experience, London returned to school and
began earning his living as a full-time writer. Within a few years, his stories
started to appear in major magazines, and his later Alaska adventure novels, including* The Call of the Wild *and* White Fang, *made him perhaps
the most popular and successful writer of early-twentieth-century America.*

Jack London wrote "All Gold Cañon" for The Century Magazine *in
1905. This short story, about the travails of Bill the Prospector in the
Sierra Nevada, is a classic London offering of toil, trouble, and tragedy. It
also provides a good depiction of the technique of pocket mining.*

It was the green heart of the canyon, where the walls swerved back
from the rigid plan and relieved their harshness of line by making
a little sheltered nook and filling it to the brim with sweetness and
roundness and softness. Here all things rested. Even the narrow stream
ceased its turbulent downrush long enough to form a quiet pool. Knee-
deep in the water, with drooping head and half-shut eyes, drowsed a
red-coated, many-antlered buck.

On one side, beginning at the very lip of the pool, was a tiny
meadow, a cool, resilient surface of green that extended to the base
of the frowning wall. Beyond the pool a gentle slope of earth ran up
and up to meet the opposing wall. Fine grass covered the slope—grass
that was spangled with flowers, with here and there patches of color,

orange and purple and golden. Below, the canyon was shut in. There was no view. The walls leaned together abruptly and the canyon ended in a chaos of rocks, moss-covered and hidden by a green screen of vines and creepers and boughs of tree. Up the canyon rose far hills and peaks, the big foothills, pine-covered and remote. And far beyond, like clouds upon the border of the sky, towered minarets of white, where the Sierra's eternal snows flashed austerely the blazes of the sun.

There was no dust in the canyon. The leaves and flowers were clean and virginal. The grass was young velvet. Over the pool three cottonwoods sent their snowy fluffs fluttering down the quiet air. On the slope the blossoms of the wine-wooded manzanita filled the air with springtime odors, while the leaves, wise with experience, were already beginning their vertical twist against the coming aridity of summer. In the open spaces on the slope, beyond the farthest shadow-reach of the manzanita, poised the mariposa lilies, like so many flights of jeweled moths suddenly arrested and on the verge of trembling into flight again. Here and there that woods harlequin, the madroña, permitting itself to be caught in the act of changing its pea-green trunk to madder red, breathed its fragrance into the air from great clusters of waxen bells. Creamy white were these bells, shaped like lilies of the valley, with the sweetness of the perfume that is of the springtime.

There was not a sigh of wind. The air was drowsy with its weight of perfume. It was a sweetness that would have been cloying had the air been heavy and humid. But the air was sharp and thin. It was as starlight transmuted into atmosphere, shot through and warmed by sunshine, and flower-drenched with sweetness.

An occasional butterfly drifted in and out through the patches of light and shade. And from all about rose the low and sleepy hum of mountain bees—feasting sybarites that jostled one another good-naturedly at the board, nor found time for rough discourtesy. So quietly did the little stream drip and ripple its way through the canyon that it spoke only in faint and occasional gurgles. The voice of the stream was as a drowsy whisper, ever interrupted by dozings and silences, ever lifted again in the awakenings.

The motion of all things was a drifting in the heart of the canyon. Sunshine and butterflies drifted in and out among the trees. The hum of the bees and the whisper of the stream were a drifting of sound. And the drifting sound and drifting color seemed to weave together in the making of a delicate and intangible fabric which was the spirit of the place. It was a spirit of peace that was not of death, but of smooth-pulsing life, of quietude that was not silence, of movement that was not action, of repose that was quick with existence without being violent with struggle and travail. The spirit of the place was the spirit of the peace of the living, somnolent with the easement and content of prosperity, and undisturbed by rumors of far wars.

The red-coated, many-antlered buck acknowledged the lordship of the spirit of the place and dozed knee-deep in the cool, shaded pool. There seemed no flies to vex him and he was languid with rest. Sometimes his ears moved when the stream awoke and whispered; but they moved lazily, with foreknowledge that it was merely the stream grown garrulous at discovery that it had slept.

But there came a time when the buck's ears lifted and tensed with swift eagerness for sound. His head was turned down the canyon. His sensitive, quivering nostrils scented the air. His eyes could not pierce the green screen through which the stream rippled away, but to his ears came the voice of a man. It was a steady, monotonous, singsong voice. Once the buck heard the harsh clash of metal upon rock. At the sound he snorted with a sudden start that jerked him through the air from water to meadow, and his feet sank into the young velvet, while he pricked his ears and again scented the air. Then he stole across the tiny meadow, pausing once and again to listen, and faded away out of the cañon like a wraith, soft-footed and without sound.

The clash of steel-shod soles against the rocks began to be heard, and the man's voice grew louder. It was raised in a sort of chant and became distinct with nearness, so that the words could be heard:

"Tu'n around an' tu'n yo' face
Untoe them sweet hills of grace.
  (D' pow'rs of sin yo' am scornin'!)
Look about an' look aroun',
Fling yo' sin pack on d' groun'
  (Yo' will meet wid d' Lord in d' mornin'!)"

A sound of scrambling accompanied the song, and the spirit of the place fled away on the heels of the red-coated buck. The green screen was burst asunder, and a man peered out at the meadow and the pool and the sloping sidehill. He was a deliberate sort of man. He took in the scene with one embracing glance, then ran his eyes over the details to verify the general impression. Then, and not until then, did he open his mouth in vivid and solemn approval:

"Smoke of life an' snakes of purgatory! Will you just look at that! Wood an' water an' grass an' a sidehill! A pocket hunter's delight an' a cayuse's paradise! Cool green for tired eyes! Pink pills for pale people ain't in it. A secret pasture for prospectors and a resting place for tired burros, by damn!"

He was a sandy-complexioned man in whose face geniality and humor seemed the salient characteristics. It was a mobile face, quick-changing to inward mood and thought. Thinking was in him a visible process. Ideas chased across his face like windflaws across the surface of a lake. His hair, sparse and unkempt of growth, was as indeterminate and colorless as his complexion. It would seem that all the color of his frame had gone into his eyes, for they were startlingly blue. Also they were laughing and merry eyes, within them much of the naïveté and wonder of the child; and yet, in an unassertive way, they contained much of calm self-reliance and strength of purpose founded upon self-experience and experience of the world.

From out the screen of vines and creepers he flung ahead of him a miner's pick and shovel and gold pan. Then he crawled out himself into the open. He was clad in faded overalls and black cotton shirt, with hobnailed brogans on his feet, and on his head a hat whose shapelessness and stains advertised the rough usage of wind and rain and sun and camp smoke. He stood erect, seeing wide-eyed the secrecy of the scene and sensuously inhaling the warm, sweet breath of the canyon garden through nostrils that dilated and quivered with delight. His eyes narrowed to laughing slits of blue, his face wreathed itself in joy, and his mouth curled in a smile as he cried aloud:

"Jumping dandelions and happy hollyhocks, but that smells good to me! Talk about your attar o' roses an' cologne factories! They ain't in it!"

He had the habit of soliloquy. His quick-changing facial expressions might tell every thought and mood, but the tongue, perforce, ran hard after, repeating, like a second Boswell.

The man lay down on the lip of the pool and drank long and deep of its water. "Tastes good to me," he murmured, lifting his head and gazing across the pool at the sidehill, while he wiped his mouth with the back of his hand. The sidehill attracted his attention. Still lying on his stomach, he studied the hill formation long and carefully. It was a practiced eye that traveled up the slope to the crumbling canyon wall and back and down again to the edge of the pool. He scrambled to his feet and favored the sidehill with a second survey.

"Looks good to me," he concluded, picking up his pick and shovel and gold pan.

He crossed the stream below the pool, stepping agilely from stone to stone. Where the sidehill touched the water he dug up a shovelful of dirt and put it into the gold pan. He squatted down, holding the pan in his two hands, and partly immersing it in the stream. Then he imparted to the pan a deft circular motion that sent the water sluicing in and out through the dirt and gravel. The larger and the lighter particles worked to the surface, and these, by a skilful dipping movement of the pan, he spilled out and over the edge. Occasionally, to expedite matters, he rested the pan and with his fingers raked out the large pebbles and pieces of rock.

The contents of the pan diminished rapidly until only fine dirt and the smallest bits of gravel remained. At this stage he began to work very deliberately and carefully. It was fine washing, and he washed fine and finer, with a keen scrutiny and delicate and fastidious touch. At the last the pan seemed empty of everything but water; but with a quick semicircular flirt that sent the water flying over the shallow rim into the stream he disclosed a layer of black sand on the bottom of the pan. So thin was this layer that it was like a streak of paint. He examined it closely. In the midst of it was a tiny golden speck. He dribbled a little water in over the depressed edge of the pan. With a quick flirt he sent the water sluicing across the bottom, turning the grains of black sand over and over. A second tiny golden speck rewarded his effort.

The washing had now become very fine—fine beyond all need of ordinary placer mining. He worked the black sand, a small portion at a time, up the shallow rim of the pan. Each small portion he examined sharply, so that his eyes saw every grain of it before he allowed it to slide over the edge and away. Jealously, bit by bit, he let the black sand slip away. A golden speck, no larger than a pin point, appeared on the rim, and by his manipulation of the water it returned to the bottom of the pan. And in such fashion another speck was disclosed, and another. Great was his care of them. Like a shepherd he herded his flock of golden specks so that not one should be lost. At last, of the pan of dirt nothing remained but his golden herd. He counted it, and then, after all his labor, sent it flying out of the pan with one final swirl of water.

But his blue eyes were shining with desire as he rose to his feet. "Seven," he muttered aloud, asserting the sum of the specks for which he had toiled so hard and which he had so wantonly thrown away.

"Seven," he repeated, with the emphasis of one trying to impress a number on his memory.

He stood still a long while, surveying the hillside. In his eyes was a curiosity, new-aroused and burning. There was an exultance about his bearing and a keenness like that of a hunting animal catching the fresh scent of game.

He moved down the stream a few steps and took a second panful of dirt.

Again came the careful washing, the jealous herding of the golden specks, and the wantonness with which he sent them flying into the stream when he had counted their number.

"Five," he muttered, and repeated, "five."

He could not forbear another survey of the hill before filling the pan farther down the stream. His golden herds diminished. "Four, three, two, two, one," were his memory tabulations as he moved down the stream. When but one speck of gold rewarded his washing he stopped and built a fire of dry twigs. Into this he thrust the gold pan and burned it till it was blue-black. He held up the pan and examined it critically. Then he nodded approbation. Against such a color-background he could defy the tiniest yellow speck to elude him.

Still moving down the stream, he panned again. A single speck was his reward. A third pan contained no gold at all. Not satisfied with this, he panned three times again, taking his shovels of dirt within a foot of one another. Each pan proved empty of gold, and the fact, instead of discouraging him, seemed to give him satisfaction. His elation increased with each barren washing, until he arose, exclaiming jubilantly:

"If it ain't the real thing, may God knock off my head with sour apples!"

Returning to where he had started operations, he began to pan up the stream. At first his golden herds increased—increased prodigiously. "Fourteen, eighteen, twenty-one, twenty-six," ran his memory tabulations. Just above the pool he struck his richest pan—thirty-five colors.

"Almost enough to save," he remarked regretfully as he allowed the water to sweep them away.

The sun climbed to the top of the sky. The man worked on. Pan by pan he went up the stream, the tally of results steadily decreasing.

"It's just booful, the way it peters out," he exulted when a shovelful of dirt contained no more than a single speck of gold.

And when no specks at all were found in several pans, he straightened up and favored the hillside with a confident glance.

"Aha! Mr. Pocket!" he cried out as though to an auditor hidden somewhere above him beneath the surface of the slope. "Aha! Mr. Pocket! I'm a-comin', I'm a-comin', an' I'm shorely gwine to get yer! You heah me, Mr. Pocket? I'm gwine to get yer as shore as punkins ain't cauliflowers!"

He turned and flung a measuring glance at the sun poised above him in the azure of the cloudless sky. Then he went down the canyon, following the line of shovel holes he had made in filling the pans. He crossed the stream below the pool and disappeared through the green screen. There was little opportunity for the spirit of the place to return with its quietude and repose, for the man's voice, raised in ragtime song, still dominated the canyon with possession.

After a time, with a greater clashing of steel-shod feet on rock, he returned. The green screen was tremendously agitated. It surged back and forth in the throes of a struggle. There was a loud grating and clanging of metal. The man's voice leaped to a higher pitch and was sharp with imperativeness. A large body plunged and panted. There was a snapping and ripping and rending, and amid a shower of falling leaves a horse burst through the screen. On its back was a pack, and from this trailed broken vines and torn creepers. The animal gazed with astonished eyes at the scene into which it had been precipitated, then dropped its head to the grass and began contentedly to graze. A second horse scrambled into view, slipping once on the mossy rocks and regaining equilibrium when its hoofs sank into the yielding surface of the meadow. It was riderless, though on its back was a high-horned Mexican saddle, scarred and discolored by long usage.

The man brought up the rear. He threw off pack and saddle, with an eye to camp location, and gave the animals their freedom to graze. He unpacked his food and got out frying pan and coffeepot. He gathered an armful of dry wood, and with a few stones made a place for his fire.

"My!" he said, "but I've got an appetite! I could scoff iron filings an' horseshoe nails an' thank you kindly, ma'am, for a second helpin'."

He straightened up, and while he reached for matches in the pocket of his overalls his eyes traveled across the pool to the sidehill. His fingers had clutched the matchbox, but they relaxed their hold and the hand came out empty. The man wavered perceptibly. He looked at his preparations for cooking and he looked at the hill.

"Guess I'll take another whack at her," he concluded, starting to cross the stream.

"They ain't no sense in it, I know," he mumbled apologetically. "But keepin' grub back an hour ain't goin' to hurt none, I reckon."

A few feet back from his first line of test pans he started a second line. The sun dropped down the western sky, the shadows lengthened, but the man worked on. He began a third line of test pans. He was crosscutting the hillside, line by line, as he ascended. The center of each line produced the richest pans, while the ends came where no colors showed in the pan. And as he ascended the hillside the lines grew perceptibly shorter. The regularity with which their length diminished served to indicate that somewhere up the slope the last line would be so short as to have scarcely length at all, and that beyond could come only a point. The design was growing into an inverted V. The converging sides of this V marked the boundaries of the gold-bearing dirt.

The apex of the V was evidently the man's goal. Often he ran his eye along the converging sides and on up the hill, trying to divine the apex, the point where the gold-bearing dirt must cease. Here resided "Mr. Pocket"—for so the man familiarly addressed the imaginary point above him on the slope, crying out:

"Come down out o' that, Mr. Pocket! Be right smart an' agreeable an' come down!"

"All right," he would add later, in a voice resigned to determination. "All right, Mr. Pocket. It's plain to me I got to come right up an' snatch you out bald-headed. An' I'll do it! I'll do it!" he would threaten still later.

Each pan he carried down to the water to wash, and as he went higher up the hill the pans grew richer, until he began to save the gold in an empty baking-powder can which he carried carelessly in his hip-pocket. So engrossed was he in his toil that he did not notice the long twilight of oncoming night. It was not until he tried vainly to see the gold colors in the bottom of the pan that he realized the passage of time. He straightened up abruptly. An expression of whimsical wonderment and awe overspread his face as he drawled:

"Gosh darn my buttons, if I didn't plumb forget dinner!"

He stumbled across the stream in the darkness and lighted his long-delayed fire. Flapjacks and bacon and warmed-over beans constituted his supper. Then he smoked a pipe by the smoldering coals, listening to the night noises and watching the moonlight stream through the canyon. After that he unrolled his bed, took off his heavy shoes, and pulled the blankets up to his chin. His face showed white in the moonlight, like the face of a corpse. But it was a corpse that knew its resurrection, for the man rose suddenly on one elbow and gazed across at his hillside.

"Good night, Mr. Pocket," he called sleepily. "Good night."

He slept through the early gray of morning until the direct rays of the sun smote his closed eyelids, when he awoke with a start and looked about him until he had established the continuity of his existence and identified his present self with the days previously lived.

To dress, he had merely to buckle on his shoes. He glanced at his fireplace and at his hillside, wavered, but fought down the temptation and started the fire.

"Keep yer shirt on, Bill; keep yer shirt on," he admonished himself. "What's the good of rushin'? No use in gettin' all het up an' sweaty. Mr. Pocket'll wait for you. He ain't a-runnin' away before you can get yer breakfast. Now what you want, Bill, is something fresh in yer bill o' fare. So it's up to you to go an' get it."

He cut a short pole at the water's edge and drew from one of his pockets a bit of line and a draggled fly that had once been a royal coachman.

"Mebbe they'll bite in the early morning," he muttered, as he made his first cast into the pool. And a moment later he was gleefully crying: "What'd I tell you, eh? What'd I tell you?"

He had no reel nor any inclination to waste time, and by main strength, and swiftly, he drew out of the water a flashing ten-inch trout. Three more, caught in rapid succession, furnished his breakfast. When he came to the steppingstones on his way to his hillside, he was struck by a sudden thought, and paused.

"I'd just better take a hike downstream a ways," he said. "There's no tellin' what cuss may be snoopin' around."

But he crossed over on the stones, and with a "I really oughter take that hike" the need of the precaution passed out of his mind and he fell to work.

At nightfall he straightened up. The small of his back was stiff from stooping toil and as he put his hand behind him to soothe the protesting muscles he said:

"Now what d'ye think of that, by damn? I clean forgot my dinner again! If I don't watch out I'll sure be degeneratin' into a two-meal-a-day crank."

"Pockets is the damnedest things I ever see for makin' a man absent-minded," he communed that night as he crawled into his blankets. Nor did he forget to call up the hillside, "Good night, Mr. Pocket! Good night!"

Rising with the sun, and snatching a hasty breakfast, he was early at work. A fever seemed to be growing in him, nor did the increasing richness of the test pans allay this fever. There was a flush in his cheek other than that made by the heat of the sun, and he was oblivious to fatigue and the passage of time. When he filled a pan with dirt he ran down the hill to wash it; nor could he forbear running up the hill again, panting and stumbling profanely, to refill the pan.

He was now a hundred yards from the water, and the inverted V was assuming definite proportions. The width of the pay dirt steadily decreased, and the man extended in his mind's eye the sides of the V to their meeting place far up the hill. This was his goal, the apex of the V, and he panned many times to locate it.

"Just about two yards above that manzanita bush an' a yard to the right," he finally concluded.

Then the temptation seized him. "As plain as the nose on your face," he said as he abandoned his laborious crosscutting and climbed to the indicated apex. He filled a pan and carried it down the hill to wash. It contained no trace of gold. He dug deep, and he dug shallow, filling and washing a dozen pans, and was unrewarded even by the tiniest speck. He was enraged at having yielded to the temptation, and cursed himself blasphemously and pridelessly. Then he went down the hill and took up the crosscutting.

"Slow an' certain, Bill; slow an' certain," he crooned. "Short cuts to fortune ain't in your line, an' it's about time you know it. Get wise, Bill; get wise. Slow an' certain's the only hand you can play; so go to it, an' keep to it, too."

As the crosscuts decreased, showing that the sides of the V were converging, the depth of the V increased. The gold trace was dipping into the hill. It was only at thirty inches beneath the surface that he could get colors in his pan. The dirt he found at twenty-five inches from the surface, and at thirty-five inches, yielded barren pans. At the base of the V, by the water's edge, he had found the gold colors at the grass roots. The higher he went up the hill, the deeper the gold dipped. To dig a hole three feet deep in order to get one test pan was no mean magnitude; while between the man and the apex intervened an untold number of such holes to be dug. "An' there's no tellin' how much deeper it'll pitch," he sighed in a moment's pause, while his fingers soothed his aching back.

Feverish with desire, with aching back and stiffening muscles, with pick and shovel gouging and mauling the soft brown earth, the man toiled up the hill. Before him was the smooth slope, spangled with flowers and made sweet with their breath. Behind him was devastation. It looked like some terrible eruption breaking out on the smooth skin of the hill. His slow progress was like that of a slug, befouling beauty with a monstrous trail.

Though the dipping gold trace increased the man's work, he found consolation in the increasing richness of the pans. Twenty cents, thirty cents, fifty cents, sixty cents, were the values of the gold found in the pans, and at nightfall he washed his banner pan, which gave him a dollar's worth of gold-dust from a shovelful of dirt.

"I'll just bet it's my luck to have some inquisitive cuss come buttin' in here on my pasture," he mumbled sleepily that night as he pulled the blankets up to his chin.

Suddenly he sat upright. "Bill!" he called sharply. "Now listen to me, Bill; d'ye hear! It's up to you, tomorrow mornin', to mosey round an' see what you can see. Understand? Tomorrow morning, an' don't you forget it!"

He yawned and glanced across at his sidehill. "Good night, Mr. Pocket," he called.

In the morning he stole a march on the sun, for he had finished breakfast when its first rays caught him, and he was climbing the wall of the canyon where it crumbled away and gave footing. From the outlook at the top he found himself in the midst of loneliness. As far as he could see, chain after chain of mountains heaved themselves into his vision. To the east his eyes, leaping the miles between range and range and between many ranges, brought up at last against the white-peaked Sierras—the main crest, where the backbone of the Western world reared itself against the sky. To the north and south he could see more distinctly the cross systems that broke through the main trend of the sea of mountains. To the west the ranges fell away, one behind the other, diminishing and fading into the gentle foothills that, in turn, descended into the great valley which he could not see.

And in all that mighty sweep of earth he saw no sign of man nor of the handiwork of man—save only the torn bosom of the hillside at his feet. The man looked long and carefully. Once, far down his own canyon, he thought he saw in the air a faint hint of smoke. He looked again and decided that it was the purple haze of the hills made dark by a convolution of the canyon wall at its back.

"Hey, you, Mr. Pocket!" he called down into the canyon. "Stand out from under! I'm a-comin', Mr. Pocket! I'm a-comin'!"

The heavy brogans on the man's feet made him appear clumsy-footed, but he swung down from the giddy height as lightly and airily as a mountain goat. A rock, turning under his foot on the edge of the precipice, did not disconcert him. He seemed to know the precise time required for the turn to culminate in disaster, and in the meantime he utilized the false footing itself for the momentary earth contact necessary to carry him on into safety. Where the earth sloped so steeply that it was impossible to stand for a second upright, the man did not hesitate. His foot pressed the impossible surface for but a fraction of the fatal second and gave him the bound that carried him onward. Again, where even the fraction of a second's footing was out of the question, he would swing his body past by a moment's handgrip on a jutting knob of rock, a crevice, or a precariously rooted shrub. At last, with a wild leap and yell, he exchanged the face of the wall for an earth slide and finished the descent in the midst of several tons of sliding earth and gravel.

His first pan of the morning washed out over two dollars in coarse gold. It was from the centre of the V. To either side the diminution in the values of the pans was swift. His lines of crosscutting holes were growing very short. The converging sides of the inverted V were only a few yards apart. Their meeting point was only a few yards above him. But the pay streak was dipping deeper and deeper into the earth. By early afternoon he was sinking the test holes five feet before the pans could show the gold trace.

For that matter, the gold trace had become something more than a trace; it was a placer mine in itself, and the man resolved to come back after he had found the pocket and work over the ground. But the increasing richness of the pans began to worry him. By late afternoon the worth of the pans had grown to three and four dollars. The man scratched his head perplexedly and looked a few feet up the hill at the manzanita bush that marked approximately the apex of the V. He nodded his head and said oracularly:

"It's one o' two things, Bill; one o' two things. Either Mr. Pocket's spilled himself all out an' down the hill, or else Mr. Pocket's that damned rich you maybe won't be able to carry him all away with you. And that'd be hell, wouldn't it, now?" He chuckled at contemplation of so pleasant a dilemma.

Nightfall found him by the edge of the stream, his eyes wrestling with the gathering darkness over the washing of a five-dollar pan.

"Wisht I had an electric light to go on working," he said.

He found sleep difficult that night. Many times he composed himself and closed his eyes for slumber to overtake him; but his blood pounded with too strong desire, and as many times his eyes opened and he murmured wearily, "Wisht it was sunup."

Sleep came to him in the end, but his eyes were open with the first paling of the stars, and the gray of dawn caught him with breakfast finished and climbing the hillside in the direction of the secret abiding place of Mr. Pocket.

The first crosscut the man made, there was space for only three holes, so narrow had become the pay streak and so close was he to the fountainhead of the golden stream he had been following for four days.

"Be ca'm, Bill; be ca'm," he admonished himself as he broke ground for the final hole where the sides of the V had at last come together in a point.

"I've got the almighty cinch on you, Mr. Pocket, an' you can't lose me," he said many times as he sank the hole deeper and deeper.

Four feet, five feet, six feet, he dug his way down into the earth. The digging grew harder. His pick grated on broken rock. He examined the rock. "Rotten quartz," was his conclusion as, with the shovel, he cleared the bottom of the hole of loose dirt. He attacked the crumbling quartz with the pick, bursting the disintegrating rock asunder with every stroke.

He thrust his shovel into the loose mass. His eye caught a gleam of yellow. He dropped the shovel and squatted suddenly on his heels. As a farmer rubs the clinging earth from fresh-dug potatoes, so the man, a piece of rotten quartz held in both hands, rubbed the dirt away.

"Sufferin' Sardanopolis!" he cried. "Lumps an' chunks of it! Lumps an' chunks of it!"

It was only half rock he held in his hand. The other half was virgin gold. He dropped it into his pan and examined another piece. Little yellow was to be seen, but with his strong fingers he crumbled the rotten quartz away till both hands were filled with glowing yellow. He rubbed the dirt away from fragment after fragment, tossing them into the gold pan. It was a treasure hole. So much had the quartz rotted away that there was less of it than there was of gold. Now and again he found a piece that was all gold. A chunk, where the pick had laid open the heart of the gold, glittered like a handful of yellow jewels, and he cocked his head at it and slowly turned it around and over to observe the rich play of the light upon it.

"Talk about yer Too Much Gold diggin's!" the man snorted

contemptuously. "Why, this diggin'd make it look like thirty cents. This diggin' is all gold. An' right here an' now I name this yere canyon 'All Gold Cañon,' b'gosh!"

Still squatting on his heels, he continued examining the fragments and tossing them into the pan. Suddenly there came to him a premonition of danger. It seemed a shadow had fallen upon him. But there was no shadow. His heart had given a great jump up into his throat and was choking him. Then his blood slowly chilled and he felt the sweat of his shirt cold against his flesh.

He did not spring up nor look around. He did not move. He was considering the nature of the premonition he had received, trying to locate the source of the mysterious force that had warned him, striving to sense the imperative presence of the unseen thing that threatened him. There is an aura of things hostile, made manifest by messengers too refined for the senses to know; and this aura he felt, but knew not how he felt it. His was the feeling as when a cloud passes over the sun. It seemed that between him and life had passed something dark and smothering and menacing; a gloom, as it were, that swallowed up life and made for death—his death.

Every force of his being impelled him to spring up and confront the unseen danger, but his soul dominated the panic, and he remained squatting on his heels, in his hands a chunk of gold. He did not dare to look around, but he knew by now that there was something behind him and above him. He made believe to be interested in the gold in his hand. He examined it critically, turned it over and over, and rubbed the dirt from it. And all the time he knew that something behind him was looking at the gold over his shoulder.

Still feigning interest in the chunk of gold in his hand, he listened intently and he heard the breathing of the thing behind him. His eyes searched the ground in front of him for a weapon, but they saw only the uprooted gold, worthless to him now in his extremity. There was his pick, a handy weapon on occasion; but this was not such an occasion. The man realized his predicament. He was in a narrow hole that was seven feet deep. His head did not come to the surface of the ground. He was in a trap.

He remained squatting on his heels. He was quite cool and collected; but his mind, considering every factor, showed him only his helplessness. He continued rubbing the dirt from the quartz fragments and throwing the gold into the pan. There was nothing else for him to do. Yet he knew that he would have to rise up, sooner or later, and face the danger that breathed at his back. The minutes passed, and with the passage of each minute he knew that by so much he was nearer the time when he must stand up or else—and his wet shirt went cold against his flesh again at the thought—or else he might receive death as he stooped there over his treasure.

Still he squatted on his heels, rubbing dirt from gold and debating in just what manner he should rise up. He might rise up with a rush and claw his way out of the hole to meet whatever threatened on the even footing above ground. Or he might rise up slowly and careless, and feign casually to discover the thing that breathed at his back. His instinct and every fighting fiber of his body favored the mad, clawing rush to the surface. His intellect, and the craft thereof, favored the slow and cautious meeting with the thing that menaced and which he could not see. And while he debated, a loud, crashing noise burst on his ear. At the same instant he received a stunning blow on the left side of the back, and from the point of impact felt a rush of flame through his flesh. He sprang up in the air, but halfway to his feet collapsed. His body crumpled in like a leaf withered in sudden heat, and he came down, his chest across his pan of gold, his face in the dirt and rock, his legs tangled and twisted because of the restricted space at the bottom of the hole. His legs twitched convulsively several times. His body was shaken as with a mighty ague. There was a slow expansion of the lungs, accompanied by a deep sigh. Then the air was slowly, very slowly, exhaled, and his body as slowly flattened itself down into inertness.

Above, revolver in hand, a man was peering down over the edge of the hole. He peered for a long time at the prone and motionless body beneath him. After a while the stranger sat down on the edge of the hole so that he could see into it, and rested the revolver on his knee. Reaching his hand into a pocket, he drew out a wisp of brown paper. Into this he dropped a few crumbs of tobacco. The combination became a cigarette, brown and squat, with the ends turned in. Not once did he take his eyes from the body at the bottom of the hole. He lighted the cigarette and drew its smoke into his lungs with a caressing intake of the breath. He smoked slowly. Once the cigarette went out and he relighted it. And all the while he studied the body beneath him.

In the end he tossed the cigarette stub away and rose to his feet. He moved to the edge of the hole. Spanning it, a hand resting on each edge, and with the revolver still in the right hand, he muscled his body down into the hole. While his feet were yet a yard from the bottom he released his hands and dropped down.

At the instant his feet struck bottom he saw the pocket miner's arm leap out, and his own legs knew a swift, jerking grip that overthrew him. In the nature of the jump his revolver hand was above his head. Swiftly as the grip had flashed about his legs, just as swiftly he brought the revolver down. He was still in the air, his fall in process of completion, when he pulled the trigger. The explosion was deafening in the confined space. The smoke filled the hole so that he could see nothing. He struck the bottom on his back, and like a cat's the pocket miner's body was on top of him. Even as the miner's body passed on top, the stranger crooked in his right arm to fire; and even in that instant the miner, with a quick thrust of elbow, struck his wrist. The muzzle was thrown up and the bullet thudded into the dirt of the side of the hole.

The next instant the stranger felt the miner's hand grip his wrist. The struggle was now for the revolver. Each man strove to turn it against the other's body. The smoke in the hole was clearing. The stranger, lying on his back, was beginning to see dimly. But suddenly he was blinded by a handful of dirt deliberately flung into his eyes by his antagonist. In that moment of shock his grip on the revolver was broken. In the next moment he felt a smashing darkness descend upon his brain, and in the midst of the darkness even the darkness ceased.

But the pocket miner fired again and again, until the revolver was empty. Then he tossed it from him and, breathing heavily, sat down on the dead man's legs.

The miner was sobbing and struggling for breath. "Measly skunk!" he panted; "a-campin' on my trail an' lettin' me do the work, an' then shootin' me in the back!"

He was half crying from anger and exhaustion. He peered at the face of the dead man. It was sprinkled with loose dirt and gravel, and it was difficult to distinguish the features.

"Never laid eyes on him before," the miner concluded his scrutiny. "Just a common an' ordinary thief, damn him! An' he shot me in the back! He shot me in the back!"

He opened his shirt and felt himself, front and back, on his left side.

"Went clean through, and no harm done!" he cried jubilantly. "I'll bet he aimed all right, all right; but he drew the gun over when he pulled the trigger—the cuss! But I fixed 'm! Oh, I fixed 'm!"

His fingers were investigating the bullet hole in his side, and a shade of regret passed over his face. "It's goin' to be stiffer'n hell," he said. "An' it's up to me to get mended an' get out o' here."

He crawled out of the hole and went down the hill to his camp. Half an hour later he returned, leading his pack horse. His open shirt disclosed the rude bandages with which he had dressed his wound. He was slow and awkward with his left-hand movements, but that did not prevent his using the arm.

The bight of the pack rope under the dead man's shoulders enabled him to heave the body out of the hole. Then he set to work gathering up his gold. He worked steadily for several hours, pausing often to rest his stiffening shoulder and to exclaim:

"He shot me in the back, the measly skunk! He shot me in the back!"

When his treasure was quite cleaned up and wrapped securely into a number of blanket-covered parcels, he made an estimate of its value.

"Four hundred pounds, or I'm a Hottentot," he concluded. "Say two hundred in quartz an' dirt—that leaves two hundred pounds of gold. Bill! Wake up! Two hundred pounds of gold! Forty thousand dollars! An' it's yourn—all yourn!"

He scratched his head delightedly and his fingers blundered into an unfamiliar groove. They quested along it for several inches. It was a crease through his scalp where the second bullet had plowed.

He walked angrily over to the dead man.

"You would, would you?" he bullied. "You would, eh? Well, I fixed you good an' plenty, an' I'll give you decent burial, too. That's more'n you'd have done for me." He dragged the body to the edge of the hole and toppled it in. It struck the bottom with a dull crash, on its side, the face twisted up to the light. The miner peered down at it.

"An' you shot me in the back!" he said accusingly.

With pick and shovel he filled the hole. Then he loaded the gold on his horse. It was too great a load for the animal, and when he had gained his camp he transferred part of it to his saddle horse. Even so, he was compelled to abandon a portion of his outfit—pick and shovel and gold pan, extra food and cooking utensils, and divers odds and ends.

The sun was at the zenith when the man forced the horses at the screen of vines and creepers. To climb the huge boulders the animals were compelled to uprear and struggle blindly through the tangled mass of vegetation. Once the saddle horse fell heavily and the man removed the pack to get the animal on its feet. After it started on its way again the man thrust his head out from among the leaves and peered up at the hillside.

"The measly skunk!" he said, and disappeared.

There was a ripping and tearing of vines and boughs. The trees surged back and forth, marking the passage of the animals through the midst of them. There was a clashing of steel-shod hoofs on stone, and now and again an oath or a sharp cry of command. Then the voice of the man was raised in song:

> *"Tu'n around an' tu'n yo' face*
> *Untoe them sweet hills of grace.*
> *(D' pow'rs of sin yo' am scornin'!)*
> *Look about an' look aroun',*
> *Fling yo' sin pack on d' groun'.*
> *(Yo' will meet wid d' Lord in d' mornin'!)"*

The song grew faint and fainter, and through the silence crept back the spirit of the place. The stream once more drowsed and whispered; the hum of the mountain bees rose sleepily. Down through the perfume-weighted air fluttered the snowy fluffs of the cottonwoods. The butterflies drifted in and out among the trees, and over all blazed the quiet sunshine. Only remained the hoofmarks in the meadow and the torn hillside to mark the boisterous trail of the life that had broken the peace of the place and passed on.

CHAPTER FOUR

Shadows in the Alpenglow

1900–1950

The dawn of the twentieth century brought significant changes to the Sierra Nevada—both to its present and future.

For starters, unregulated development of the range was significantly mitigated as federal and state governments stepped forward to control most of the region during the first half of the century. The United States Forest Service, the National Parks, the United States Reclamation Service, the California Division of Forestry, various natural resource agencies of Nevada and California, and municipal water agencies all asserted their claims to jurisdiction over the resources. The changes were not without controversy or devoid of philosophical conflict, but the transformation occurred nonetheless, forever modifying the relationship between Sierra Nevada residents and their direct influence over the Range of Light.

As government struggled to characterize its relationship with the Sierra Nevada, the geography was also changed by increasing opportunities for public recreation. Largely the result of the emergence of automobiles as the preferred mode of travel (and the subsequent improvement of roads and highways), thousands of visitors flocked to the mountains to refresh their spirits. New forms of recreation provided more ways to enjoy the majesty of the range, and more-sophisticated camping equipment put the "wilderness" experience even closer at hand. A tiny ski industry emerged and gained momentum after World War II, while fearless rock climbers clung to the granite cliffs, increasing in numbers as technology and safety improved.

This expanded demand boosted tourism revenue but also placed additional pressures on the environment. Tensions developed between the conservation ethic—as exemplified by the United States Forest Service—and the preservation ethic—the standard of the National Park Service and its principal proponent, John Muir. While conservationists called for broad-based "multiple use" of the resources for the "greatest good," preservationists wanted to safeguard the natural attributes. Some saw stewardship of the land as leaving the Sierra untouched. Others viewed hydroelectric development, increased logging, supervised timber sales, grazing, and the construction of new recreation facilities as important responsibilities of the region's managers.

Some viewed government control as good, while others saw nothing but trouble, corruption, and greed. Balancing public needs against the rights of private property owners became an ongoing concern. One major point of contention in the early years of the century was construction of the O'Shaughnessy Dam and Hetch Hetchy Reservoir within the boundaries of Yosemite National Park. Controversy raged over the development of water resources at the expense of citizens' rights to enjoy an unblemished natural landscape.

Social conditions in the area also continued to be troubling during this period. The native population remained virtually invisible in the eyes of federal and state governments, and in one particularly shameful episode, Americans of Japanese ancestry were interned in military camps during World War II simply because they looked like the enemy. One of those internment camps—Manzanar—was located in the Sierra Nevada.

To some, it seemed that the old exploitive ways were merely giving way to different problems. New policies, new regulations, and new leadership provided increasingly more effective resource management, but it nevertheless failed to satisfy everyone's perceptions of the most suitable utilization of the Sierra Nevada. Battle lines were being drawn that would lead to confrontations in the future.

"Every house in the town of the vines has its garden plot, corn and brown beans and a row of peppers reddening in the sun"

Mary Austin, from *The Land of Little Rain*

A native of Illinois, Mary Austin (1868–1934) moved with her family to California in 1888 and later lived for several years in the Eastern Sierra high desert near Independence. Her "Little Brown House" in Independence is California Historic Landmark #229. While in California, Austin became a noted scholar and defender of Native American issues, authoring numerous works of fiction, poetry, drama, and criticism on those and other sociopolitical subjects, including early feminism and environmentalism. Many consider her Land of Little Rain, *an exploration of California's major deserts, a text on par with the works of John Muir and Henry David Thoreau. In 1999,* San Francisco Chronicle Book Review *readers voted it the best Western nonfiction book of the twentieth century.*

In this selection from Land of Little Rain, *the author examines El Pueblo de Las Uvas, or "The Little Town of the Grape Vines," a bustling community in transition. In the mid-nineteenth century, El Pueblo de Las Uvas was renamed Lone Pine.*

There are still some places in the west where the quails cry "*cuidado*"; where all the speech is soft, all the manners gentle; where all the dishes have *chile* in them, and they make more of the Sixteenth of September [Mexico's Independence Day] than they do of the Fourth of July. I mean in particular El Pueblo de Las Uvas. Where it lies, how to come at it, you will not get from me; rather would I show you the heron's nest in the tulares. It has a peak behind it, glinting above the tamarack pines, above a breaker of ruddy hills that have a long slope valley-wards and the shoreward steep of waves toward the Sierras.

Below the Town of the Grape Vines, which shortens to Las Uvas for common use, the land dips away to the river pastures and the tulares. It shrouds under a twilight thicket of vines, under a dome of cottonwood-trees, drowsy and murmurous as a hive. Hereabouts are some strips of tillage and the headgates that dam up the creek for the village weirs; upstream you catch the growl of the arrastra [a simple drag-stone mill for crushing ore]. Wild vines that begin among the willows lap over to the orchard rows, take the trellis and roof-tree.

There is another town above Las Uvas that merits some attention, a town of arches and airy crofts, full of linnets, blackbirds, fruit birds, small sharp hawks, and mockingbirds that sing by night. They pour out piercing, unendurably sweet cavatinas above the fragrance of bloom and musky smell of fruit. Singing is in fact the business of the night at Las Uvas as sleeping is for midday. When the moon comes over the mountain wall new-washed from the sea, and the shadows lie like lace on the stamped floors of the patios, from recess to recess of the vine tangle runs the thrum of guitars and the voice of singing.

At Las Uvas they keep up all the good customs brought out of Old Mexico or bred in a lotus-eating land; drink, and are merry and look out for something to eat afterward; have children, nine or ten to a family, have cock-fights, keep the siesta, smoke cigarettes and wait for the sun to go down. And always they dance; at dusk on the smooth adobe floors, afternoons under the trellises where the earth is damp and has a fruity smell. A betrothal, a wedding, or a christening, or the mere proximity of a guitar is sufficient occasion; and if the occasion lacks, send for the guitar and dance anyway.

All this requires explanation. Antonio Sevadra, drifting this way from Old Mexico with the flood that poured into the Tappan district after the first notable strike, discovered La Golondrina. It was a generous lode and Tony a good fellow; to work it he brought in all the Sevadras, even to the twice-removed; all the Castros who were his wife's family, all the Saises, Romeros, and Eschobars,—the relations of his relations-in-law. There you have the beginning of a pretty considerable town. To these accrued much of the Spanish California float swept out of the southwest by eastern enterprise. They slacked away again when the price of silver went down, and the ore dwindled in La Golondrina. All the hot eddy of mining life swept away from that corner of the hills, but there were always those too idle, too poor to move, or too easily content with El Pueblo de Las Uvas.

Nobody comes nowadays to the town of the grape vines except, as we say, "with the breath of crying," but of these enough. All the low sills run over with small heads. Ah, ah! There is a kind of pride in that if you did but know it, to have your baby every year or so as the time sets, and keep a full breast. So great a blessing as marriage is easily come by. It is told of Ruy Garcia that when he went for his marriage license he lacked a dollar of the clerk's fee, but borrowed it of the sheriff, who expected reëlection and exhibited thereby a commendable thrift.

Of what account is it to lack meal or meat when you may have it of any neighbor? Besides, there is sometimes a point of honor in these things. Jesus Romero, father of ten, had a job sacking ore in the Marionette which he gave up of his own accord. "Eh, why?" said Jesus, "for my fam'ly."

"It is so, señora," he said solemnly, "I go to the Marionette, I work, I eat meatpie—frijoles—good, ver' good. I come home sad'day nigh' I see my fam'ly. I play lil' game poker with the boys, have lil' drink wine, my money all gone. My fam'ly have no money, nothing eat. All time I work at mine I eat, good, ver' good grub. I think sorry for my fam'ly. No, no, señora, I no work no more that Marionette, I stay with my fam'ly." The wonder of it is, I think, that the family had the same point of view.

Every house in the town of the vines has its garden plot, corn and brown beans and a row of peppers reddening in the sun; and in damp borders of the irrigating ditches clumps of *yerba santa*, horehound, catnip, and spikenard, wholesome herbs and curative, but if no peppers then nothing at all. You will have for a holiday dinner, in Las Uvas, soup with meat balls and chile in it, chicken with chile, rice with chile, fried beans with more chile, enchilada, which is corn cake with the sauce of chile and tomatoes, onion, grated cheese, and olives, and for a relish chile *tepines* passed about in a dish, all of which is comfortable and corrective to the stomach. You will have wine which every man makes for himself, of good body and inimitable bouquet, and sweets that are not nearly so nice as they look.

There are two occasions when you may count on that kind of a meal; always on the Sixteenth of September, and on the two-yearly visits of Father Shannon. It is absurd, of course, that El Pueblo de Las Uvas should have an Irish priest, but Black Rock, Minton, Jimville, and all that country round do not find it so. Father Shannon visits them all, waits by the Red Butte to confess the shepherds who go through with their flocks, carries a blessing to small and isolated mines, and so in the course of a year or so works around to Las Uvas to bury and marry and christen. Then all the little graves in the *Campo Santo* are brave with tapers, the brown pine headboards blossom like Aaron's rod with paper roses and bright cheap prints of Our Lady of Sorrows. Then the Señora

Sevadra, who thinks herself elect of heaven for that office, gathers up the original sinners, the little Elijias, Lolas, Manuelitas, Josés, and Felipés, by dint of adjurations and sweets smuggled into small perspiring palms, to fit them for the Sacrament.

I used to peek in at them, never so softly, in Doña Ina's living-room; Raphael-eyed little imps, going sidewise on their knees to rest them from the bare floor, candles lit on the mantel to give a religious air, and a great sheaf of wild bloom before the Holy Family. Come Sunday they set out the altar in the schoolhouse, with the fine-drawn altar cloths, the beaten silver candlesticks, and the wax images, chief glory of Las Uvas, brought up mule-back from Old Mexico forty years ago. All in white the communicants go up two and two in a hushed, sweet awe to take the body of their Lord, and Tomaso, who is priest's boy, tries not to look unduly puffed up by his office. After that you have dinner and a bottle of wine that ripened on the sunny slope of Escondito. All the week Father Shannon has shriven his people, who bring clean conscience to the betterment of appetite, and the Father sets them an example. Father Shannon is rather big about the middle to accommodate the large laugh that lives in him, but a most shrewd searcher of hearts. It is reported that one derives comfort from his confessional, and I for my part believe it.

The celebration of the Sixteenth, though it comes every year, takes as long to prepare for as Holy Communion. The señoritas have each a new dress apiece, the señoras a new *rebosa*. The young gentlemen have new silver trimmings to their sombreros, unspeakable ties, silk handkerchiefs, and new leathers to their spurs. At this time when the peppers glow in the gardens and the young quail cry "*cuidado*," "have a care!" you can hear the *plump, plump* of the *metate* from the alcoves of the vines where comfortable old dames, whose experience gives them the touch of art, are pounding out corn for tamales.

School-teachers from abroad have tried before now at Las Uvas to have school begin on the first of September, but got nothing else to stir in the heads of the little Castros, Garcias, and Romeros but feasts and cock-fights until after the Sixteenth. Perhaps you need to be told that this is the anniversary of the Republic, when liberty awoke and cried in the provinces of Old Mexico. You are aroused at midnight to hear them shouting in the streets, "*Vive la Libertad!*" answered from the houses and the recesses of the vines, "*Vive la Mexico!*" At sunrise shots are fired commemorating the tragedy of unhappy Maximilian, and then music, the noblest of national hymns, as the great flag of Old Mexico floats up the flag-pole in the bare little plaza of shabby Las Uvas. The sun over Pine Mountain greets the eagle of Montezuma before it touches the vineyards and the town, and the day begins with a great shout. By and by there will be a reading of the Declaration of Independence and an address punctured by *vives;* all the town in its best dress, and some exhibits of horsemanship that make lathered bits and bloody spurs; also a cock-fight.

By night there will be dancing, and such music! old Santos to play the flute, a little lean man with a saintly countenance, young Garcia whose guitar has a soul, and Carrasco with the violin. They sit on a high platform above the dancers in the candle flare, backed by the red, white, and green of Old Mexico, and play fervently such music as you will not hear otherwise.

At midnight the flag comes down. Count yourself at a loss if you are not moved by that performance. Pine Mountain watches whitely overhead, shepherd fires glow strongly on the glooming hills. The plaza, the bare glistening pole, the dark folk, the bright dresses, are lit ruddily by a bonfire. It leaps up to the eagle flag, dies down, the music begins softly and aside. They play airs of old longing and exile; slowly out of the dark the flag drops down, bellying and falling with the midnight draught. Sometimes a hymn is sung, always there are tears. The flag is down; Tony Sevadra has received it in his arms. The music strikes a barbaric swelling tune, another flag begins a slow ascent,—it takes a breath or two to realize that they are both, flag and tune, the Star Spangled Banner,—a volley is fired, we are back, if you please, in California of America. Every youth who has the blood of patriots in him lays ahold on Tony Sevadra's flag, happiest if he can get a corner of it. The music goes before, the folk fall in two and two, singing. They sing everything, America, the Marseillaise, for the sake of the French shepherds hereabout, the hymn of Cuba, and the Chilian [sic] national air to comfort two families of that land. The flag goes to Doña Ina's, with the candlesticks and the altar cloths, then Las Uvas eats tamales and dances the sun up the slope of Pine Mountain.

You are not to suppose that they do not keep the Fourth, Washington's Birthday, and Thanksgiving at the town of the grape vines. These make excellent occasions for quitting work and dancing, but the Sixteenth is the holiday of the heart. On Memorial Day the graves have garlands and new pictures of the saints tacked to the headboards. There is great virtue in an *Ave* said in the Camp of the Saints. I like that name which the Spanish speaking people give to the garden of the dead, *Campo Santo,* as if it might be some bed of healing from which blind souls and sinners rise up whole and praising God. Sometimes the speech of simple folk hints at truth the understanding does not reach. I am persuaded only a complex soul can get any good of a plain religion. Your earthborn is a poet and a symbolist. We breed in an environment of asphalt pavements a body of people whose creeds are chiefly restrictions against other people's way of life, and have kitchens and latrines under the same roof that houses their God. Such as these go to church to be edified, but at Las Uvas they go for pure worship and to entreat their God. The logical conclusion of the faith that every good gift cometh from God is the open hand and the finer courtesy. The meal done without buys a candle for the neighbor's dead child. You do foolishly to suppose that the candle does no good.

At Las Uvas every house is a piece of earth—thick walled, white-washed adobe that keeps the even temperature of a cave; every man is an accomplished horseman and consequently bow-legged; every family keeps dogs, flea-bitten mongrels that loll on the earthen floors. They speak a purer Castilian than obtains in like villages of Mexico, and the way they count relationship everybody is more or less akin. There is not much villainy among them. What incentive to thieving or killing can there be when there is little wealth and that to be had for the borrowing! If they love too hotly, as we say "take their meat before grace," so do their betters. Eh, what! shall a man be a saint before he is dead? And besides, Holy Church takes it out of you one way or another before all is done. Come away, you who are obsessed with your own importance in the scheme of things, and have got nothing you did not sweat for, come away by the brown valleys and full-bosomed hills to the even-breathing days, to the kindliness, earthiness, ease of El Pueblo de Las Uvas.

Marie Potts, from *The Northern Maidu*

*Marie Potts (1895–1978) was a Northern Maidu from Big Meadow,
near the site of present-day Lake Almanor, in Plumas County. Originally
named Chankutpan—"one with sharp eyes"—Potts was a leader in securing rights for Native Americans. She established the American Indian Press
Association, was a founder of the Federated Indians of California Inter-
Tribal Council, and also started* Smoke Signal, *one of the oldest Indian
newspapers in the United States.*

In 1977 Potts wrote The Northern Maidu, *a memoir of her childhood
that examines the history and culture of her native community. In this
passage, Potts describes the land of her upbringing.*

Our country was beautiful, with vast open valleys or meadows—
Mountain Meadow, Hebe Meadow, Big Meadow (now covered by
Lake Almanor), and others. The surrounding mountains, their flanks
mantled with forests, were covered with snow most of the year, such
as Barter Mountain, and, looming above all, Mount Lassen, where
the snow never completely melted. Among the mountains were many
fine lakes where there was good fishing, and plenty of deer roamed
from valley to valley across ridges covered with sugar and ponderosa
pine, fir, cedar, spruce, and tamaracks. Among these grew brush—
manzanita, buck bushes, and squaw carpet, a shrub that grew close
to the ground, with leaves like holly.

There were all kinds of berry bushes on both meadows and hillsides: raspberries, strawberries, elderberries, gooseberries, sometimes
thimbleberries, and, of course, there were huckleberries. The chokecherries
we ate after mashing—then spit the seeds out. Our country was rich in
nature's food, there for the taking.

We had a good climate of the kind that makes mountain people energetic and strong, and not enervating, as in the hot summers in the Great Valley. The winter snow cover was often six to eight feet deep. "Big Meadow" might give to people now a picture of a vast hayfield, but this meadow and others was more like a swamp, with mounds and hillocks in places. It had many springs around the borders; they ran along in pools rich with fish, mostly trout. It is easy to see why we did not live down in the meadows, but on higher ground along the borders.

I also remember as a child living in the cedar bark house with my grandparents. How wonderful it was, lying awake at night sometimes, to hear the coyotes bark, and the hoot owls uttering their calls among the trees. Sometimes there would be the running clatter of squirrels on the bark slabs above us; and in spring and summer, just as it grew light before the sun rose, there came the enchantment of the bird chorus, the orchestra of the Great Spirit all around us. That clean pine smell on the morning wind—where can we find it now?

"On the giant granite castles / In the clouds and in the snow!"

Joaquin Miller, "Yosemite"

Joaquin Miller (1837 or 1841–1913) was the pen name of the American poet and eccentric Cincinnatus Heine (or Hiner) Miller. Born in Indiana, Miller moved as a young man to Oregon and then later to California, where he held a variety of occupations. A 2004 conference on Miller referred to him as "Poet of the Sierras, the founder of California's Arbor Day, prose stylist extraordinaire, horse thief, judge, Pony Express rider, newspaper editor, critic, gold miner, successful playwright, champion of Native American rights, Indian fighter, rogue and hero." After spending several years in New York and Europe, he ultimately settled in Oakland, California, where he grew fruit and published his poems. A few years after his death, the City of Oakland transformed his cottage, grounds (which he called "The Hights"), and five hundred adjoining acres into Joaquin Miller Regional Park.

Some literary critics felt that Miller was a first-class self-promoter but a second-rate poet. His love of the Sierra, however, was never in doubt, as expressed in "Yosemite."

Sound! sound! sound!
O colossal walls and crown'd
In one eternal thunder!
Sound! sound! sound!
O ye oceans overhead,
While we walk, subdued in wonder,
In the ferns and grasses, under
And beside the swift Merced!

Fret! fret! fret!
Streaming sounding banners, set
On the giant granite castles
In the clouds and in the snow!
But the foe he comes not yet,—
We are loyal, valiant vassals,
And we touch the trailing tassles
Of the banners far below.

Surge! surge! surge!
From the white Sierra's verge
To the very valley blossom.
Surge! surge! surge!
Yet the song-bird builds a home,
And the mossy branches cross them,
And the tasselled tree-tops toss them,
In the clouds of falling foam.

Sweep! sweep! sweep!
O ye heaven-born and deep,
In one dread, unbroken chorus!
We may wonder or may weep,—
We may wait on God before us;
We may shout or lift a hand,—
We may bow down and deplore us,
But we may never understand.

Beat! beat! beat!
We advance, but would retreat
From this restless, broken breast
Of the earth in a convulsion.
We would rest, but dare not rest,
For the angel of expulsion
From this Paradise below
Waves us onward and…we go.

Marc Reisner, from *A Dangerous Place*

Marc Reisner (1948–2000) was best known for his 1986 book Cadillac Desert, *a history of water management (and a call for its reform) in the American West. In addition to lecturing and writing numerous books, essays, and articles, Reisner was involved with several organizations seeking to solve California's environmental problems. His* A Dangerous Place: California's Unsettling Fate—*about the predicament the San Francisco Bay Area would face in the wake of a massive earthquake—was published posthumously in 2003.*

   Control of California's water resources—two-thirds of which come from the Sierra snowpack—has been a source of political and social conflict throughout the state's history. One of the most memorable episodes was the battle for the Owens River in the eastern Sierra during the early twentieth century, when Los Angeles officials undertook a scheme to divert the river for their own use hundreds of miles to the southwest. Reisner recounts the details in this excerpt from A Dangerous Place.

Topography was Los Angeles' implacable enemy. Completely isolated by ramrod ranges and vast, austere deserts to the north and east and south, it had three rivers within two or three hundred miles to choose from (and no city in history had ever gone that far to augment its limited water supply). One was the Colorado, emerging from the Grand Canyon on the lee side of the Mojave and Sonoran Deserts. Then there was the Kern, flowing out of the Sierra Nevada into a great marshy lake—Tulare Lake, which has since disappeared. Finally, there was the Owens River, the largest of several streams draining snowfed watersheds along the eastern slope of the Sierra Nevada.

Fred Eaton was the first southern Californian who sensed exactly how little water the basin really had. He also knew where it would have to go for more. Eaton's forebears had been early pioneers, and he had been superintendent of the privately run Los Angeles City Water Company before serving a term as mayor from 1899 to 1901. His interest in water grew out of a quintessentially southern Californian mixture of paternalism and greed; he knew that his beloved city would inevitably run out, and would pay almost anything for more water that he hoped, in some sense, to own. In the 1890s, Eaton spent several vacations roaming southern California's watersheds, surveying and measuring streamflows. His explorations had shown him that if incoming new water had to battle gravity, it would never arrive. Hydrodelectricity was still expensive and scarce, and growth was swallowing the region's oil production. Those realities ruled out any man-made river that had to be lifted over high elevations in order to reach the basin; they most emphatically ruled out the Kern River and the Colorado. Kern River water would have to surmount the Tehachapi Range, a four-thousand-foot summit to the north; Colorado River water would have to labor over San Gorgonio Pass, which was roughly as high. The alternative was tunneling. The European railroads had advanced the art of tunneling, but even the Swiss hadn't bored dozens of miles through a mountain range. Tunneling was also expensive and risky, especially in the sorts of fracture zones that surrounded Los Angeles.

The Owens River, on the other hand, was miraculously situated. It flowed through Owens Valley, a narrow finger of the high Mojave Desert between the abrupt escarpment of the eastern Sierra and the White Mountains to the east. Like all Great Basin rivers, it had no outlet; it terminated in a big lake. Owens Lake was 3,500 feet higher than Los Angeles, and no overweening topography stood between source and city. Some tunneling and siphoning would be required, but gravity could move the water all the way to the coast; at some steep elevation drops, it could even generate hydroelectricity to pay back the cost of construction. Eaton had looked at every alternative, and there were no others. Los Angeles had to capture the Owens River, or its growth had to stop.

On a fall day in 1904, Fred Eaton and William Mulholland climbed into a buckboard wagon and rode across the Mojave (hardly anyone had done it before) to look at the river. Eaton had already seen it, at high flow, and came back obsessed. It was Mulholland who needed convincing. He was a rough but literate Irish immigrant whom Eaton had groomed as his successor at the city water company, even though Mulholland had no formal training as an engineer—a lapse in learning that would someday prove as fateful as their trip.

Mulholland returned impressed but uncommitted. The distance to the Owens River was intimidating—he and Eaton had used up hogsheads of water and many bottles of whiskey as they creaked along for almost two weeks. Most of the river's flow was already appropriated by valley farmers, who had created one of the few thriving irrigated meccas in the arid West. The Reclamation Service, the new federal agency whose mission was to irrigate, or reclaim, arid terrain—a task at which most private entrepreneurs had failed—wanted to build on the valley's success; it was sketching plans for a dam that would capture the river's flood flows, which could bring thousands more acres into reliable production. Los Angeles still didn't approach New York City in size or wealth, and in Mulholland's mind the prize seemed beyond his grasp. Not only would Los Angeles have to buy up a whole river (or steal it), but it would have to shove the federal government aside and then build an aqueduct system far grander than New York's—the greatest in human history.

That is exactly what it did. By 1904, Mulholland was finally persuaded that he had no options other than, as he sometimes suggested, to murder everyone connected with the chamber of commerce. In early 1905, Eaton, who had already purchased options on some water rights, returned to the valley to buy more. Whose money he used is not exactly clear, but most everyone who counted in Los Angeles—the newspapers, the politicians and oligarchs—knew of the plot. (To help ensure success, the local newspapers swore an oath of silence, which Harrison Gray Otis [publisher of the *Los Angeles Times*] would break near the end, infuriating his rivals. Eaton's great good fortune was his friendship with Joseph Lippincott, the regional director of the Reclamation Service, and Theodore Roosevelt's warrior interest in populous cities at America's western flank. Eaton persuaded Lippincott to hire him to settle a minor water rights issue; it was a bogus cover that gave him (probably illegal) access to deeds and records in Inyo County's files that he might need to cut the necessary deals. Then Eaton—posing as a wealthy rancher who hoped to amass a big spread in the valley—began optioning water rights. Because he had learned the financial situation of many farmers and mutual water companies, his purchasing instincts were dead-on; almost everyone he approached was willing to sell, especially at the prices he offered.

Since no one suspected that his water was headed for Los Angeles, the farmers sold their rights without remorse.

The water, in so many words, was stolen fair and square, with the help of the federal government. Roosevelt's Reclamation Service abruptly bowed out of the valley. Lippincott resigned and went straight to work as Mulholland's well-paid deputy. Meanwhile, the U.S. Forest Service, under chief forester and close Roosevelt friend Gifford Pinchot, annexed a large swath of treeless Mojave Desert to the Inyo National Forest in order to clear a cheap, problem-free right-of-way for the aqueduct. Then, after the Owens River project was completed in 1913—Mulholland and the newspapers whooped the voters into such a drought panic that they approved the bond measure by a margin of fourteen to one—most of its flow never reached Los Angeles. It was diverted the moment it entered the basin and spread over the desolate San Fernando Valley, where a land syndicate comprising [Harrison Gray] Otis, [Harry] Chandler [Otis's business partner at the *Times*], the railroad magnate Henry Huntington, and other members of the city's capitalist royalty had recently bought a tract about five times the size of Manhattan. (They acquired the holding in 1902; whether that was early enough to know of the city's intentions is debatable, but in California, on the issue of water, the ravings of conspiracy buffs are too often true.) Owens River water that would, for many years, remain surplus to the city's needs let the syndicate cover their land with orange trees and other lucrative export crops. Back in the Owens Valley, roughly the same acreage, having lost its water, reverted to desert, and competition from the warmer San Fernando Valley crushed those farmers who held back some water rights and tried to hang on. In the end, San Fernando orange blossoms metamorphosed into tract homes, and the syndicate walked away with a profit that has been estimated in the hundreds of millions of World War II–era dollars.

It was a humiliation that inspired Owens Valley farmers to resort to dynamite. In the 1920s, sections of the 223-mile aqueduct were blown sky-high, again and again, until the city sent in trainloads of detectives and declared the whole region under (probably illegal) martial law. The episode earned Los Angeles eternal ill will in the rural West; most Wyoming ranchers know this history. But it did not end Los Angeles' quest for water; that had just begun....

The city's tactics were those of a junkyard dog. By the 1950s, the Metropolitan Water District was taking twice its 550,000-acre-foot entitlement from the Colorado River. Its strategy was simple: it "borrowed" much of Arizona's unused entitlement, which was unused because California's congressional delegation, ten times the size of Arizona's, sabotaged any legislation that tried to authorize the project that would let Arizona use it. At the same time, the city extended the Owens River Aqueduct northward, across the divide leading to the Mono Lake basin, and began to divert most of the streams flowing into Mono Lake, a weirdly beautiful desert apparition where—strange as it seems—most of California's seagull population breeds. The lake level was to drop by dozens of feet over the years, concentrating salinity, and causing its once astonishing wildlife to decline. The Los Angeles Department of Water and Power began hiring battalions of lawyers who did nothing but defend it against environmental lawsuits.

It still wasn't enough. Mulholland's successors grew desperate; their plans became fantastic....

The next jolt of water was to come, finally, from northern California's Feather River, via the longest aqueduct and the highest dam and the most imponderable pump lift ever engineered. The assessed valuation of greater Los Angeles guaranteed the bonds that financed the project's stratospheric cost—about $15 billion in 1999-value dollars....

The 770-foot-high dam, the 444-mile-long aqueduct, and the 3,000-foot pump lift were ultimately approved by referendum and built during the 1960s and 1970s. The project has never delivered—and may never deliver—all the water it promised, but it won southern California another thirty-year reprieve....

"Dam Hetch Hetchy! As well dam for water-tanks the people's cathedrals and churches, for no holier temple has ever been consecrated by the heart of man."

John Muir, from *The Yosemite*

At the turn of the twentieth century, San Francisco needed a reliable water source. The Tuolumne River system was considered ideal, but the project— named Hetch Hetchy after the valley where the dam would be located—was considered too expensive, and the plan was abandoned in early 1906. Then came April 18, 1906, the date of the devastating San Francisco earthquake and fire. Widespread destruction and lack of water led to a renewal of the project, and in 1913, the Raker Act officially authorized construction of the Hetch Hetchy Reservoir.

The Sierra Club—formed in 1892—and its leader, John Muir, fought the building of this reservoir deep within Yosemite National Park, but the protests were to no avail. Lawsuit followed lawsuit until building began in 1914. John Muir died soon after construction commenced—some say from a broken heart.

Hetch Hetchy Reservoir, located entirely within Yosemite National Park, is owned by the City of San Francisco and to this day provides water and power to the city. It also remains a controversial issue, with ongoing efforts to remove the dam and restore the valley.

In January 1908, Muir famously condemned the project in this scathing Sierra Club Bulletin *article that was revised and included in his 1912 book,* The Yosemite.

Yosemite is so wonderful that we are apt to regard it as an exceptional creation, the only valley of its kind in the world; but Nature is not so poor as to have only one of anything. Several other yosemites have been discovered in the Sierra that occupy the same relative positions on the Range and were formed by the same forces in the same

kind of granite. One of these, the Hetch Hetchy Valley, is in the Yosemite National Park about twenty miles from Yosemite [Valley] and is easily accessible to all sorts of travelers by a road and trail that leaves the
Big Oak Flat road at Bronson Meadows a few miles below Crane Flat,
and to mountaineers by way of Yosemite Creek basin and the head of
the middle fork of the Tuolumne.

It is said to have been discovered by Joseph Screech, a hunter, in
1850, a year before the discovery of the great Yosemite. After my first
visit to it in the autumn of 1871, I have always called it the "Tuolumne
Yosemite," for it is a wonderfully exact counterpart of the Merced
Yosemite, not only in its sublime rocks and waterfalls but in the gardens, groves and meadows of its flowery park-like floor. The floor of
Yosemite is about 4000 feet above the sea; the Hetch Hetchy floor about
3700 feet. And as the Merced River flows through Yosemite, so does the
Tuolumne through Hetch Hetchy. The walls of both are of gray granite,
rise abruptly from the floor, are sculptured in the same style and in
both every rock is a glacier monument.

Standing boldly out from the south wall is a strikingly picturesque
rock called by the Indians Kolana, the outermost of a group 2300 feet
high, corresponding with the Cathedral Rocks of Yosemite both in
relative position and form. On the opposite side of the Valley, facing
Kolana, there is a counterpart of the El Capitan that rises sheer and
plain to a height of 1800 feet, and over its massive brow flows a stream
which makes the most graceful fall I have ever seen. From the edge
of the cliff to the top of an earthquake talus it is perfectly free in the
air for a thousand feet before it is broken into cascades among talus
boulders. It is in all its glory in June, when the snow is melting fast,
but fades and vanishes toward the end of summer. The only fall I know
with which it may fairly be compared is the Yosemite Bridal Veil; but
it excels even that favorite fall both in height and airy-fairy beauty and
behavior. Lowlanders are apt to suppose that mountain streams in their
wild career over cliffs lose control of themselves and tumble in a noisy
chaos of mist and spray. On the contrary, on no part of their travels are
they more harmonious and self-controlled. Imagine yourself in Hetch
Hetchy on a sunny day in June, standing waist-deep in grass and flowers (as I have often stood), while the great pines sway dreamily with
scarcely perceptible motion. Looking northward across the Valley you
see a plain, gray granite cliff rising abruptly out of the gardens and
groves to a height of 1800 feet, and in front of it Tueeulala's silvery scarf
burning with irised sun-fire. In the first white outburst at the head

there is abundance of visible energy, but it is speedily hushed and concealed in divine repose, and its tranquil progress to the base of the cliff is like that of a downy feather in a still room. Now observe the fineness and marvelous distinctness of the various sun-illumined fabrics into which the water is woven; they sift and float from form to form down the face of that grand gray rock in so leisurely and unconfused a manner that you can examine their texture, and patterns and tones of color as you would a piece of embroidery held in the hand. Toward the top of the fall you see groups of booming, comet-like masses, their solid, white heads separate, their tails like combed silk interlacing among delicate gray and purple shadows, ever forming and dissolving, worn out by friction in their rush through the air. Most of these vanish a few hundred feet below the summit, changing to varied forms of cloud-like drapery. Near the bottom the width of the fall has increased from about twenty-five feet to a hundred feet. Here it is composed of yet finer tissues, and is still without a trace of disorder—air, water and sunlight woven into stuff that spirits might wear.

So fine a fall might well seem sufficient to glorify any valley; but here, as in Yosemite, Nature seems in nowise moderate, for a short distance to the eastward of Tueeulala booms and thunders the great Hetch Hetchy Fall, Wapama, so near that you have both of them in full view from the same standpoint. It is the counterpart of the Yosemite Fall, but has a much greater volume of water, is about 1700 feet in height, and appears to be nearly vertical, though considerably inclined, and is dashed into huge outbounding bosses of foam on projecting shelves and knobs. No two falls could be more unlike—Tueeulala out in the open sunshine descending like thistledown; Wapama in a jagged, shadowy gorge roaring and thundering, pounding its way like an earthquake avalanche.

Besides this glorious pair there is a broad, massive fall on the main river a short distance above the head of the Valley. Its position is something like that of the Vernal in Yosemite, and its roar as it plunges into a surging trout-pool may be heard a long way, though it is only about twenty feet high. On Rancheria Creek, a large stream, corresponding in position with the Yosemite Tenaya Creek, there is a chain of cascades joined here and there with swift flashing plumes like the one between the Vernal and Nevada Falls, making magnificent shows as they go their glacier-sculptured way, sliding, leaping, hurrahing, covered with crisp clashing spray made glorious with sifting sunshine. And besides all these a few small streams come over the walls at wide intervals, leaping from ledge to ledge with birdlike song and watering many a hidden cliff-garden and fernery, but they are too unshowy to be noticed in so grand a place.

The correspondence between the Hetch Hetchy walls in their trends, sculpture, physical structure, and general arrangement of the main rock-masses and those of the Yosemite Valley has excited the wondering admiration of every observer. We have seen that the El Capitan and Cathedral rocks occupy the same relative positions in both valleys; so also do their Yosemite points and North Domes. Again, that part of the Yosemite north wall immediately to the east of the Yosemite Fall has two horizontal benches, about 500 and 1500 feet above the floor, timbered with golden-cup oak. Two benches similarly situated and timbered occur on the same relative portion of the Hetch Hetchy north wall, to the east of Wapama Fall, and on no other. The Yosemite is bounded at the head by the great Half Dome. Hetch Hetchy is bounded in the same way though its head rock is incomparably less wonderful and sublime in form.

The floor of the Valley is about three and a half miles long, and from a fourth to half a mile wide. The lower portion is mostly a level meadow about a mile long, with the trees restricted to the sides and the river banks, and partially separated from the main, upper, forested portion by a low bar of glacier-polished granite across which the river breaks in rapids.

The principal trees are the yellow and sugar pines, digger pine, incense cedar, Douglas spruce, silver fir, the California and golden-cup oaks, balsam cottonwood, Nuttall's flowering dogwood, alder, maple, laurel, tumion, etc. The most abundant and influential are the great yellow or silver pines like those of Yosemite, the tallest over two hundred feet in height, and the oaks assembled in magnificent groves with massive rugged trunks four to six feet in diameter, and broad, shady, wide-spreading heads. The shrubs forming conspicuous flowery clumps and tangles are manzanita, azalea, spiraea, brier-rose, several species of ceanothus, calycanthus, philadelphus, wild cherry, etc.; with abundance of showy and fragrant herbaceous plants growing about them or out in the open in beds by themselves—lilies, Mariposa tulips, brodiaeas, orchids, iris, spraguea, draperia, collomia, collinsia, castilleja, nemophila, larkspur, columbine, goldenrods, sunflowers, mints of many species, honeysuckle, etc. Many fine ferns dwell here also, especially the beautiful and interesting rock-ferns—pellaea, and cheilanthes of several species—fringing and rosetting dry rock-piles and ledges; woodwardia and asplenium on damp spots with fronds six or seven feet high; the delicate maiden-hair in mossy nooks by the falls, and the sturdy, broad-shouldered pteris covering nearly all the dry ground beneath the oaks and pines.

It appears, therefore, that Hetch Hetchy Valley, far from being a plain, common, rock-bound meadow, as many who have not seen it seem to suppose, is a grand landscape garden, one of Nature's rarest and most precious mountain temples. As in Yosemite, the sublime rocks of its walls seem to glow with life, whether leaning back in repose or standing erect in thoughtful attitudes, giving welcome to storms and calms alike, their brows in the sky, their feet set in the groves and gay flowery meadows, while birds, bees, and butterflies help the river and waterfalls to stir all the air into music—things frail and fleeting and types of permanence meeting here and blending, just as they do in Yosemite, to draw her lovers into close and confiding communion with her.

Sad to say, this most precious and sublime feature of the Yosemite National Park, one of the greatest of all our natural resources for the uplifting joy and peace and health of the people, is in danger of being dammed and made into a reservoir to help supply San Francisco with water and light, thus flooding it from wall to wall and burying its gardens and groves one or two hundred feet deep. This grossly destructive commercial scheme has long been planned and urged (though water as pure and abundant can be got from outside of the people's park, in a dozen different places), because of the comparative cheapness of the dam and of the territory which it is sought to divert from the great uses to which it was dedicated in the Act of 1890 establishing the Yosemite National Park.

The making of gardens and parks goes on with civilization all over the world, and they increase both in size and number as their value is recognized. Everybody needs beauty as well as bread, places to play in and pray in, where Nature may heal and cheer and give strength to body and soul alike. This natural beauty-hunger is made manifest in the little window-sill gardens of the poor, though perhaps only a geranium slip in a broken cup, as well as in the carefully tended rose and lily gardens of the rich, the thousands of spacious city parks and botanical gardens, and in our magnificent National parks—the Yellowstone, Yosemite, Sequoia, etc.—Nature's sublime wonderlands, the admiration and joy of the world. Nevertheless, like anything else worth while, from the very beginning, however well guarded, they have always been subject to attack by despoiling gainseekers and mischief-makers of every degree from Satan to Senators, eagerly trying to make everything immediately and selfishly commercial, with schemes disguised in smug-smiling philanthropy, industriously, shampiously crying, "Conservation, conservation, panutilization," that man and beast may be fed and the dear Nation made great. Thus long ago a few enterprising merchants utilized the Jerusalem temple as a place of business instead of a place of prayer, changing money, buying and selling cattle and sheep and doves; and earlier still, the first forest reservation, including only one tree, was like-wise despoiled. Ever since the establishment of the Yosemite National Park, strife has been going on around its borders and I suppose this will go on as part of the universal battle between right and wrong, however much its boundaries may be shorn, or its wild beauty destroyed.

The first application to the Government by the San Francisco Supervisors for the commercial use of Lake Eleanor and the Hetch Hetchy Valley was made in 1903, and on December 22nd of that year it was denied by the Secretary of the Interior, Mr. Hitchcock, who truthfully said:

> Presumably the Yosemite National Park was created such by law because within its boundaries, inclusive alike of its beautiful small lakes, like Eleanor, and its majestic wonders, like Hetch Hetchy and Yosemite Valley. It is the aggregation of such natural scenic features that makes the Yosemite Park a wonderland which the Congress of the United States sought by law to reserve for all coming time as nearly as practicable in the condition fashioned by the hand of the Creator—a worthy object of national pride and a source of healthful pleasure and rest for the thousands of people who may annually sojourn there during the heated months.

In 1907 when Mr. Garfield became Secretary of the Interior the application was renewed and granted; but under his successor, Mr. Fisher, the matter has been referred to a Commission, which as this volume goes to press still has it under consideration.

The most delightful and wonderful camp grounds in the Park are its three great valleys—Yosemite, Hetch Hetchy, and Upper Tuolumne; and they are also the most important places with reference to their positions relative to the other great features—the Merced and Tuolumne Cañons, and the High Sierra peaks and glaciers, etc., at the head of the rivers. The main part of the Tuolumne Valley is a spacious flowery lawn four or five miles long, surrounded by magnificent snowy mountains, slightly separated from other beautiful meadows, which together make a series about twelve miles in length, the highest reaching to the feet of Mount Dana, Mount Gibbs, Mount Lyell and Mount

McClure. It is about 8500 feet above the sea, and forms the grand central High Sierra camp ground from which excursions are made to the noble mountains, domes, glaciers, etc.; across the Range to the Mono Lake and volcanoes and down the Tuolumne Cañon to Hetch Hetchy. Should Hetch Hetchy be submerged for a reservoir, as proposed, not only would it be utterly destroyed, but the sublime cañon way to the heart of the High Sierra would be hopelessly blocked and the great camping ground, as the watershed of a city drinking system, virtually would be closed to the public. So far as I have learned, few of all the thousands who have seen the park and seek rest and peace in it are in favor of this outrageous scheme.

One of my later visits to the Valley was made in the autumn of 1907 with the late William Keith, the artist. The leaf-colors were then ripe, and the great godlike rocks in repose seemed to glow with life. The artist, under their spell, wandered day after day along the river and through the groves and gardens, studying the wonderful scenery; and, after making about forty sketches, declared with enthusiasm that although its walls were less sublime in height, in picturesque beauty and charm Hetch Hetchy surpassed even Yosemite.

That any one would try to destroy such a place seems incredible; but sad experience shows that there are people good enough and bad enough for anything. The proponents of the dam scheme bring forward a lot of bad arguments to prove that the only righteous thing to do with the people's parks is to destroy them bit by bit as they are able. Their arguments are curiously like those of the devil, devised for the destruction of the first garden—so much of the very best Eden fruit going to waste; so much of the best Tuolumne water and Tuolumne scenery going to waste. Few of their statements are even partly true, and all are misleading.

Thus, Hetch Hetchy, they say, is a "low-lying meadow." On the contrary, it is a high-lying natural landscape garden, as the photographic illustrations show.

"It is a common minor feature, like thousands of others." On the contrary it is a very uncommon feature; after Yosemite, the rarest and in many ways the most important in the National Park.

"Damming and submerging it 175 feet deep would enhance its beauty by forming a crystal-clear lake." Landscape gardens, places of recreation and worship, are never made beautiful by destroying and burying them. The beautiful sham lake, forsooth, should be only an eyesore, a dismal blot on the landscape, like many others to be seen in the Sierra. For, instead of keeping it at the same level all the year, allowing Nature centuries of time to make new shores, it would, of course, be full only a month or two in the spring, when the snow is melting fast; then it would be gradually drained, exposing the slimy sides of the basin and shallower parts of the bottom, with the gathered drift and waste, death and decay of the upper basins, caught here instead of being swept on to decent natural burial along the banks of the river or in the sea. Thus the Hetch Hetchy dam-lake would be only a rough imitation of a natural lake for a few of the spring months, an open sepulcher for the others.

"Hetch Hetchy water is the purest of all to be found in the Sierra, unpolluted, and forever unpollutable." On the contrary, excepting that of the Merced below Yosemite, it is less pure than that of most of the other Sierra streams, because of the sewerage of camp grounds draining into it, especially of the Big Tuolumne Meadows camp ground, occupied by hundreds of tourists and mountaineers, with their animals, for months every summer, soon to be followed by thousands from all the world.

These temple destroyers, devotees of ravaging commercialism, seem to have a perfect contempt for Nature, and, instead of lifting their eyes to the God of the mountains, lift them to the Almighty Dollar.

Dam Hetch Hetchy! As well dam for water-tanks the people's cathedrals and churches, for no holier temple has ever been consecrated by the heart of man.

Chiura Obata, newspaper series, 1928

Chiura Obata (1885–1975) was born in Okayama Prefecture, Japan. At the age of fourteen he traveled to Tokyo, where he studied with noted artists, and a few years later, in 1903, he moved to San Francisco, where he worked as an illustrator for the city's Japanese newspapers. Obata was working as an instructor in the Art Department at the University of California, Berkeley, when, in April 1942, he was interned at the Tanforan Detention Center. While detained, he organized an art school that served more than six hundred camp residents. In September 1942, Obata was moved to the Topaz Relocation Center in Utah, where he continued creating iconic artwork of the internment experience. In 1945, when the war ended, Obata was reinstated as an instructor at U.C. Berkeley, and a year after he retired, in 1954, he became a naturalized citizen of the United States.

In the summer of 1927, Obata went on a tour of Yosemite and the Sierra Nevada high country, producing more than one hundred paintings based on the trip. In 1928, he published a series of five articles, also inspired by Yosemite, of which the following is the second.

When you climb the mountains you can find bracken and coltsfoot. In spring and autumn, after the rains, shoots of young grass and a variety of flowers grow out of the dark soil.

To catch trout, one needs only a hook and a few tools. Using pine grubs or, if you can catch them, angleworms, which live among the pebbles near the stream bank, let down your line and you will have a delicious meal for campers. (Donkeys are very fond of fried trout, so, campers, give them a treat sometimes.)

Camp life is to be found everywhere. You gather firewood with your right hand and cup clear stream water with your left. You are awakened by the chorus of chirping birds and nod off into dreamland listening to frogs and insects while gazing at the starlight through the tree branches. This is an easy, comfortable life. Moreover, in this state of California there are large plains, deserts, a mountain chain along miles of coastline, thousands of rivers and rapids, numerous hills of different shapes, cold streams, and high, famous, snowcapped mountains.

I recommend the route in the Sierra from Oakdale via Knights Ferry to see the scenery at Yosemite Junction. Visit Jacksonville where Bret Harte and Mark Twain lived. Then go over the steep incline of Priest Hill and climb Tioga Road from Big Oak Flat. Depending on the elevation, the trees, plants, flowers, birds, animals, the shape of the mountains, the condition and color of the rocks will differ even though they are the same type.

Wind, rain, thunder, snow, morning and evening views, sun rays that burn the hot sand, tranquil moonlight—all at over 10,000 feet above sea level.

Adorning the heights of the Sierra range are the wildflowers. Every three to seven days they bloom in white, red, yellow, and purple, bursting out in a kaleidoscope of beauty and giving us untold lessons and valuable experiences.

The seeds and roots of the wildflowers find a bed of ground in between the rocks. For eight or nine months of the year they patiently lie buried under several feet of snow. In the warm light of July and August they burst out toward the wide sky.

Ansel Adams, from *Sierra Club Bulletin*, February 1932

Born in San Francisco, Ansel Adams (1902–1984) was a photographer and conservationist. Although he worked as a commercial photographer for more than thirty years, he was best known for his majestic, visionary photos of western landscapes. Adams received three Guggenheim grants to photograph the national parks from 1944 to 1958, but his most famous subject, by far, was Yosemite.

In addition to his work as a photographer, Adams was a prolific writer and lecturer on photography and environmental themes, and he was involved in numerous organizations, including the Sierra Club. (He served on its board from 1934 to 1971.) He cofounded the f/64 photography group in 1932, and later helped establish the Department of Photography at the Museum of Modern Art in New York City.

In this selection from a 1932 Sierra Club Bulletin, *Adams describes the internal value of the Sierra Nevada experience.*

Mid-afternoon...a brisk wind breathed silver on the willows bordering the Tuolumne and hustled some scattered clouds beyond Kuna Crest. It was the first day of the outing—you were a little tired and dusty, but quite excited in spite of yourself. You were already aware that contact with fundamental earthy things gave a startling perspective on the high-spun unrealities of modern life. No matter how sophisticated you may be, a large granite mountain cannot be denied—it speaks in silence to the very core of your being. There are some that care not to listen but the disciples are drawn to the high altars with magnetic certainty, knowing that a great Presence hovers over the ranges. You felt all this the very first day, for you were within the portals of the temple. You were conscious of the jubilant lift of the Cathedral range, of the great choral curves of ruddy Dana, of the processional summits of Kuna Crest. You were aware of Sierra sky and stone, and of the emerald splendor of Sierra forests. Yet, at the beginning of your mountain experience, you were not impatient, for the spirit was gently all about you as some rare incense in a Gothic void. Furthermore, you were mindful of the urge of two hundred people toward fulfillment of identical experience—to enter the wilderness and seek, in the primal patterns of nature, a magical union with beauty. The secret of the strength and continuance of the Sierra Club is the unification of intricate personal differences as the foundation of composite intention and desire.

Kenneth Rexroth, "Blues"

*Kenneth Rexroth (1905–1982) was a poet, painter, union organizer,
essayist, translator, and an early participant in the Beat movement in
literature. He traveled extensively throughout the western United States,
and its landforms and society influenced and animated his verse. His
poetry was often experimental but always deeply infused with humanity
and passion.*

*Rexroth spent many days roaming the Sierra Nevada, and several
of his poems invoke that majestic panorama.*

The tops of the higher peaks
Of the Sierra Nevada
Of California are
Drenched in the perfume of
A flower which grows only there—
The blue *Polemonium*
Confertum eximium.
Soft, profound blue, like the eyes
Of impregnable innocence;
The perfume is heavy and
Clings thickly to the granite
Peaks, even in violent wind;
The leaves are clustered,
Fine, dull green, sticky, and musky.
I imagine that the scent
Of the body of Artemis
That put Endymion to sleep

Was like this and her eyes had the
Same inscrutable color.
Lawrence was lit into death
By the blue gentians of Kore.
Vanzetti had in his cell
A bowl of tall blue flowers
From a New England garden.
I hope that when I need it
My mind can always call back
This flower to its hidden senses.

*"And everywhere was the sound, which never ceased here,
of the canyon wind flowing among the crevices"*

Sally Carrighar, from *One Day on Beetle Rock*

The noted naturalist Sally Carrighar (1895–1985) studied nature on her grandparents' land in Ohio as a child. Soon she was traveling extensively, learning to track in the Canadian woods, and working as a fishing guide in the Ozarks. After coming west, she wrote for motion picture companies and radio in the 1920s and 1930s but eventually she turned back to nature writing.

For seven years, Carrighar observed the drama of animal life at Beetle Rock, an outcropping in Sequoia National Park in the southern Sierra. Her precise observations became the narrative core of her popular and critically acclaimed One Day on Beetle Rock *(1943), which chronicles one twenty-four-hour period from the individual perspectives of area wildlife, including a weasel, a black bear, a chickaree, a Stellar's jay, a coyote, a lizard, and a deer. In this passage, Carrighar describes daybreak on that June morning at Beetle Rock.*

The water of the brook reflected the sunlight up to an alder branch, where it flickered along the gray bark. On the fool's gold under the ripples lay a web of the sunlight, gently shaken. The sound of the current was subdued here, and the stir of the streamside leaves, and the Mule Deer was quiet too, as he moved slowly forward along the bank, clipping off willow buds. But the Deer was approaching a rockier channel in which the stream tumbled and splashed. When he reached the cascading water, suddenly he leapt over it, and back again, and then stood in the blowing spray, sharply white and cold, with his head flung up and excitement in his eyes.

In April all the bucks had a wild playfulness, quick to rise. Two would be sniffing for acorns among the dry leaves beneath an oak, when one would spring away—a challenge, and the second must follow. The deer's hoofs would make their clean arcs over the yuccas, over the redbuds, over the mounds of yellow fremontia blooms, arcs so high that other deer could have stood under them. At the end of the chase, the bucks would meet in a climax of vertical leaps, tossing heads, and whistling breaths. Afterwards some watching fawn might try bounding over a small yucca or redbud, but the mood of the older bucks seemed the more resilient.

Were they feeling only the exuberance of spring, or did the older deer have a memory of Beetle Rock, and were they pleased to be climbing again to the granite field in the sky?

The herd had wintered low on the ridge between the Middle and Marble Forks of the Kaweah River. They had been down in the dwarf forest, where the same storms that heaped snow on Beetle Rock fell as rain, and had brought up fescue and wild oat grass. Now the mountain's snow cover was shrinking upward. The deer stayed below the edge of it, since snow would hinder their flight from coyotes and cougars. They grazed back and forth on the side of the ridge, rising about a thousand feet every month.

The ridge became steeper the higher they climbed. In many places they had to circle sheer granite slides, polished by ancient glaciers. Beetle Rock was a similar part of the mountain's skeleton, protruding through soil and forest. But the Rock lay at the crest and its top was nearly as flat as a meadow. By summer the upper surface would be so airy and warm, with so many crannies for hiding, and such an abundance of food, that more than forty animal species, besides the insects, would be competing for homesites there. Down in the chaparral the deer had left a group of winter companions. Upon the slope they were meeting others. But nowhere in their wanderings did they find such a dense population of animals as in summer at the Rock.

By April the herd were a mile above sea level. Even there the trees were not much more than brush-high. Looking out over them the deer could see the series of mountain ranges that piled up to the Western Divide. Dropping away on the other side was the Marble Fork canyon, a vast tapering cut, spreading out at the low end upon the floor of California's great Central Valley, narrowing at the upper end between towering ridges. Beetle Rock, directly above the deer, was still covered with snow, still only a short, smooth line breaking into the treetops along the sky.

Abruptly the deer found themselves beneath firs and ponderosa pines, a few weeks later beneath sugar pines and the giant sequoias, some of the tallest trees in the world. Trees like these formed a wall around Beetle Rock's inner edge. Back among them were cabins for human beings, looking very small; six or eight of them could have been built upon one another without reaching to the lowest boughs of many of the trees. Some of the pines were twice as tall as the same trees elsewhere. Here they had a longer growing season, and perhaps the trees responded to the light on these Sierra Nevada mountains. The subtropical light, so clear on the valley below, was even more fresh and elastic at the Rock. The atmosphere seemed light more than air above the milky stone. Had the trees thrust their tips up as far as possible to reach more of it?

The deer came to Beetle Rock on a morning in May. The herd Buck, the leader, took them around the cliff's semicircular base to the west side, then back into a green-shaded gorge. Along its bottom a stream, now at flood stage, was thundering towards the canyon; before the deer started down the mountain again it would become a trickle. The herd's upward migration was over, for the meadow where all of them had been born (all but one buck) lay only a few bounds off the top of the left slope. One by one the deer leapt the water to climb to it. But the leader turned right. He would go up on Beetle Rock first....

The Buck moved from one terrace to another, browsing on the manzanita bushes, straying towards the north side of the Rock. The deer did not often go to the south side, for there they found a disturbing bear scent. It rose from a small meadow below, and from a wooded shelf on the face of the cliff where several bears stayed in the daytime. This morning the Buck caught none of their odor. The air was lightly pungent with the fragrance of new needles on the trees and new leaves on the brush. And everywhere was the sound, which never ceased here, of the canyon wind flowing among the crevices, turning between the boulders, blowing upon thin edges of stone, the wind that had given sound to the mountain before any leaves grew there to rustle, the wind that the Buck would not hear forever.

But now he has leapt to a higher ledge, is ready to bound away from the Rock, and into the forest. For a turn past a chinquapin has disclosed the Coyote, stalking granite-hoppers in a space hidden by brush. The Coyote sensed that the Buck could escape, and gave no sign that he heard the scattering gravel and the hoofs' landing upon the ledge. The Buck looked down from above. The Coyote was new

244

here; for three years no coyotes had lived in the deer's immediate range.

This summer, then, the herd leader would need even more than his usual caution. Wariness was his skill, his most significant quality. In the Buck was the best example, among all the Beetle Rock animals, of the willing tension that keeps a wilderness society stable. His was the finest alertness, but every creature had much of it. Since long before he was born, the community here had been holding together, because each of its members was ready to leap, to chase, to freeze, to threaten, to love, or to step aside—in an instant.

"As the months at Manzanar turned to years, it became a world
unto itself, with its own logic and familiar ways"

Jeanne Wakatsuki Houston and James D. Houston, from *Farewell to Manzanar*

Jeanne Wakatsuki Houston (b. 1934) was born in Inglewood, California, the daughter of Issei (first-generation) and Nisei (second-generation) Japanese American parents. During World War II, seven-year-old Jeanne and her family—along with ten thousand others—were detained for three and a half years at Manzanar, a Japanese American internment camp. Now a National Historic Site, the camp is located in the eastern Sierra Nevada, near Lone Pine, California, at the base of Mount Williamson.

In 1973, she published her memoir, Farewell to Manzanar, *which was cowritten with her husband, novelist James D. Houston. (A selection from his* Snow Mountain Passage *appears in Chapter 2 of this anthology.) Widely used in school curricula throughout the United States,* Farewell to Manzanar *was also adapted into a television movie in 1976.*

The name Manzanar meant nothing to us when we left Boyle Heights. We didn't know where it was or what it was. We went because the government ordered us to. And, in the case of my older brothers and sisters, we went with a certain amount of relief. They had all heard stories of Japanese homes being attacked, of beatings in the streets of California towns. They were as frightened of the Caucasians as Caucasians were of us. Moving, under what appeared to be government protection, to an area less directly threatened by the war seemed not such a bad idea at all. For some it actually sounded like a fine adventure.

Our pickup point was a Buddhist church in Los Angeles. It was very early, and misty, when we got there with our luggage. Mama had bought heavy coats for all of us. She grew up in eastern Washington and knew that anywhere inland in early April would be cold. I was proud of my new coat, and I remember sitting on a duffel bag trying to be friendly with the Greyhound driver. I smiled at him. He didn't smile back. He was befriending no one. Someone tied a numbered tag to my collar and to the duffel bag (each family was given a number, and that became our official designation until the camps were closed), someone else passed out box lunches for the trip, and we climbed aboard.

I had never been outside Los Angeles County, never traveled more than ten miles from the coast, had never even ridden on a bus. I was full of excitement, the way any kid would be, and wanted to look out the window. But for the first few hours the shades were drawn. Around me other people played cards, read magazines, dozed, waiting. I settled back, waiting too, and finally fell asleep. The bus felt very secure to me. Almost half its passengers were immediate relatives. Mama and my older brothers had succeeded in keeping most of us together, on the same bus, headed for the same camp. I didn't realize until much later what a job that was. The strategy had been, first, to have everyone living in the same district when the evacuation began, and then to get all of us included under the same family number, even though names had been changed by marriage. Many families weren't as lucky as ours and suffered months of anguish while trying to arrange transfers from one camp to another.

We rode all day. By the time we reached our destination, the shades were up. It was late afternoon. The first thing I saw was a yellow swirl across a blurred, reddish setting sun. The bus was being pelted by what sounded like splattering rain. It wasn't rain. This was my first look at something I would soon know very well, a billowing flurry of dust and sand churned up by the wind through Owens Valley.

We drove past a barbed-wire fence, through a gate, and into an open space where trunks and sacks and packages had been dumped from the baggage trucks that drove out ahead of us. I could see a few tents set up, the first rows of black barracks, and beyond them, blurred by sand, rows of barracks that seemed to spread for miles across this plain. People were sitting on cartons or milling around, with their backs to the wind, waiting to see which friends or relatives might be on this bus. As we approached, they turned or stood up, and some moved toward us expectantly. But inside the bus no one stirred. No one waved or spoke. They just stared out the windows, ominously silent. I didn't understand this. Hadn't we finally arrived, our whole family intact? I opened a window, leaned out, and yelled happily. "Hey! This whole bus is full of Wakatsukis!"

Outside, the greeters smiled. Inside there was an explosion of laughter, hysterical, tension-breaking laughter that left my brothers choking and whacking each other across the shoulders.

We had pulled up just in time for dinner. The mess halls weren't completed yet. An outdoor chow line snaked around a half-finished building that broke a good part of the wind. They issued us army mess kits, the round metal kind that fold over, and plopped in scoops of canned Vienna sausage, canned string beans, steamed rice that had been cooked too long, and on top of the rice a serving of canned apricots. The Caucasian servers were thinking that the fruit poured over rice would make a good dessert. Among the Japanese, of course, rice is never eaten with sweet foods, only with salty or savory foods. Few of us could eat such a mixture. But at this point no one dared protest. It would have been impolite. I was horrified when I saw the apricot syrup seeping through my little mound of rice. I opened my mouth to complain. My mother jabbed me in the back to keep quiet. We moved on through the line and joined the others squatting in the lee of half-raised walls, dabbing courteously at what was, for almost everyone there, an inedible concoction....

In Spanish, Manzanar means "apple orchard." Great stretches of Owens Valley were once green with orchards and alfalfa fields. It has been a desert ever since its water started flowing south into Los Angeles, sometime during the twenties. But a few rows of untended pear and apple trees were still growing there when the camp opened, where a shallow water table had kept them alive. In the spring of 1943 we moved to Block 28, right up next to one of the old pear orchards. That's where we stayed until the end of the war, and those trees stand in my memory for the turning of our life in camp, from the outrageous to the tolerable.

Papa pruned and cared for the nearest trees. Late that summer we picked the fruit green and stored it in a root cellar he had dug under our new barracks. At night the wind through the leaves would sound like the surf had sounded in Ocean Park, and while drifting off to sleep I could almost imagine we were still living by the beach.

Mama had set up this move. Block 28 was also close to the camp hospital. For the most part, people lived there who had to have easy access to it. Mama's connection was her job as dietician. A whole half of one barracks had fallen empty when another family relocated.

Mama hustled us in there almost before they'd snapped their suitcases shut....

Papa brought his still with him when we moved. He set it up behind the door, where he continued to brew his own sake and brandy. He wasn't drinking as much now, though. He spent a lot of time outdoors. Like many of the older Issei men, he didn't take a regular job in camp. He puttered. He had been working hard for thirty years and, bad as it was for him in some ways, camp did allow him time to dabble with hobbies he would never have found time for otherwise.

Once the first year's turmoil cooled down, the authorities started letting us outside the wire for recreation. Papa used to hike along the creeks that channeled down from the base of the Sierras. He brought back chunks of driftwood, and he would pass long hours sitting on the steps carving myrtle limbs into benches, table legs, and lamps, filling our rooms with bits of gnarled, polished furniture.

He hauled stones in off the desert and built a small rock garden outside our doorway with succulents and a patch of moss. Near it he laid flat steppingstones leading to the stairs.

He also painted watercolors. Until this time I had not known he could paint. He loved to sketch the mountains. If anything made that country habitable it was the mountains themselves, purple when the sun dropped and so sharply etched in the morning light the granite dazzled almost more than the bright snow lacing it. The nearest peaks rose ten thousand feet higher than the valley floor, with Whitney, the highest, just off to the south. They were important for all of us, but especially for the Issei. Whitney reminded Papa of Fujiyama, that is, it gave him the same kind of spiritual sustenance. The tremendous beauty of those peaks was inspirational, as so many natural forms are to the Japanese (the rocks outside our doorway could be those mountains in miniature). They also represented those forces in nature, those powerful and inevitable forces that cannot be resisted, reminding a man that sometimes he must simply endure that which cannot be changed.

Subdued, resigned, Papa's life—all our lives—took on a pattern that would hold for the duration of the war. Public shows of resentment pretty much spent themselves over the loyalty oath crises. *Shikata ga nai* ["It must be done"] again became the motto, but under altered circumstances. What had to be endured was the climate, the confinement, the steady crumbling away of family life. But the camp itself had been made livable. The government provided for our physical needs. My parents and older brothers and sisters, like most of the internees, accepted their lot and did what they could to make the best of a bad situation. "We're here," Woody would say. "We're here, and there's no use moaning about it forever."

Gardens had sprung up everywhere, in the firebreaks, between the rows of barracks—rock gardens, vegetable gardens, cactus and flower gardens. People who lived in Owens Valley during the war still remember the flowers and lush greenery they could see from the highway as they drove past the main gate. The soil around Manzanar is alluvial and very rich. With water siphoned off from the Los Angeles-bound aqueduct, a large farm was under cultivation just outside the camp, providing the mess halls with lettuce, corn, tomatoes, eggplant, string beans, horseradish, and cucumbers. Near Block 28 some of the men who had been professional gardeners built a small park, with mossy nooks, ponds, waterfalls and curved wooden bridges. Sometimes in the evenings we could walk down the raked gravel paths. You could face away from the barracks, look past a tiny rapids toward the darkening mountains, and for a while not be a prisoner at all. You could hang suspended in some odd, almost lovely land you could not escape from yet almost didn't want to leave.

As the months at Manzanar turned to years, it became a world unto itself, with its own logic and familiar ways. In time, staying there seemed far simpler than moving once again to another, unknown place. It was as if the war were forgotten, our reason for being there forgotten. The present, the little bit of busywork you had right in front of you, became the most urgent thing. In such a narrowed world, in order to survive, you learn to contain your rage and your despair, and you try to re-create, as well as you can, your normality, some sense of things continuing. The fact that America had accused us, or excluded us, or imprisoned us, or whatever it might be called, did not change the kind of world we wanted. Most of us were born in this country; we had no other models. Those parks and gardens lent it an oriental character, but in most ways it was a totally equipped American small town, complete with schools, churches, Boy Scouts, beauty parlors, neighborhood gossip, fire and police departments, glee clubs, softball leagues, Abbott and Costello movies, tennis courts, and traveling shows. (I still remember an Indian who turned up one Saturday billing himself as a Sioux chief, wearing bear claws and head feathers. In the firebreak he sang songs and danced his tribal dances while hundreds of us watched.)

In our family, while Papa puttered, Mama made her daily rounds to the mess halls, helping young mothers with their feeding, planning diets for the various ailments people suffered from. She wore a bright yellow, long-billed sun hat she had made herself and always kept stiffly starched. Afternoons I would see her coming from blocks away, heading home, her tiny figure warped by heat waves and that bonnet a yellow flower wavering in the glare.

In their disagreement over serving the country, Woody and Papa had struck a kind of compromise. Papa talked him out of volunteering; Woody waited for the army to induct him. Meanwhile he clerked in the co-op general store. Kiyo, nearly thirteen by this time, looked forward to the heavy winds. They moved the sand around and uncovered obsidian arrowheads he could sell to old men in camp for fifty cents apiece. Ray, a few years older, played in the six-man touch football league, sometimes against Caucasian teams who would come in from Lone Pine or Independence. My sister Lillian was in high school and singing with a hillbilly band called The Sierra Stars—jeans, cowboy hats, two guitars, and a tub bass. And my oldest brother, Bill, led a dance band called The Jive Bombers—brass and rhythm, with cardboard fold-out music stands lettered J. B. Dances were held every weekend in one of the recreation halls. Bill played trumpet and took vocals on Glenn Miller arrangements of such tunes as *In the Mood*, *String of Pearls*, and *Don't Fence Me In*. He didn't sing *Don't Fence Me In* out of protest, as if trying quietly to mock the authorities. It just happened to be a hit song one year, and they all wanted to be an up-to-date American swing band. They would blast it out into recreation barracks full of bobby-soxed, jitter-bugging couples:

> *Oh, give me land, lots of land*
> *Under starry skies above,*
> *Don't fence me in.*
> *Let me ride through the wide*
> *Open country that I love…*

Pictures of the band, in their bow ties and jackets, appeared in the high school yearbook for 1943–1944, along with pictures of just about everything else in camp that year. It was called *Our World*. In its pages you see school kids with armloads of books, wearing cardigan sweaters and walking past rows of tarpapered shacks. You see chubby girl yell leaders, pompons flying as they leap with glee. You read about the school play, called *Growing Pains*, "…the story of a typical American home, in this case that of the McIntyres. They see their boy and girl tossed into the normal awkward growing up stage, but can offer little assistance or direction in their turbulent course..." with Shoji Katayama as George McIntyre, Takudo Ando as Terry McIntyre, and Mrs. McIntyre played by Kazuko Nagai.

All the class pictures are in there, from the seventh grade through twelfth, with individual head shots of seniors, their names followed by the names of the high schools they would have graduated from on the outside: Theodore Roosevelt, Thomas Jefferson, Herbert Hoover, Sacred Heart. You see pretty girls on bicycles, chicken yards full of fat pullets, patients back-tilted in dental chairs, lines of laundry, and finally, two large blowups, the first of a high tower with a searchlight, against a Sierra backdrop, the next a two-page endsheet showing a wide path that curves among rows of elm trees. White stones border the path. Two dogs are following an old woman in gardening clothes as she strolls along. She is in the middle distance, small beneath the trees, beneath the snowy peaks. It is winter. All the elms are bare. The scene is both stark and comforting. This path leads toward one edge of camp, but the wire is out of sight, or out of focus. The tiny woman seems very much at ease. She and her tiny dogs seem almost swallowed by the landscape, or floating in it.

CHAPTER FIVE

Twilight of the Dawn

1951–1990

The years following World War II proved to be a turning point in Sierra Nevada history. After the struggles of the Great Depression and the bloody global conflict of the Second World War, the postwar period saw the resurgence of the national economy and renewed interest in the Sierra's resources. A more prosperous society found the means to enjoy the Sierra Nevada, and as more and more visitors experienced the splendid Range of Light, the environmental impact grew as well. The Sierra Nevada once again became a battleground for conflicting environmental values.

During this same era, people attracted by the West's promise moved here in large numbers; by 1962 California was the most populous state. Nevada experienced a burst in settlement as well, as newly developed water resources assisted the growth of former desert communities such as Las Vegas. Many of the newcomers settled in the Sierra Nevada foothills, pushing the issues of housing, recreational access, transportation, education, and infrastructure development to the fore, while promising greater demands on the Sierra Nevada in the future.

The federal and state agencies that controlled most of the range took action to address these new realities. Better access, improved roads, and upgraded facilities became a priority for the managers, and it was a widely held belief that the Sierra could provide an inexhaustible source of resources and revenue to fuel this development. The United States Forest Service, for example, even issued policies calling for additional timber harvesting to help pay for the changes.

But not everyone agreed. The postwar years spawned many progressive social movements, and environmental activism was one of the most significant. This environmental movement, however, would be different from past efforts. The modern wave, which included newborn organizations and advocacy groups, would expand upon older notions—which focused almost exclusively on resource stewardship and recreational access—and offer a more comprehensive perspective. A symbol of this evolving sensibility was the first of many annual Earth Day celebrations, in 1970. Established groups, such as the Sierra Club, also became more active in environmental issues. The movement generated legislation, regional planning agencies, task forces, lawsuits, numerous court cases, and—on a grand scale—an ever-widening awareness of the environmental challenges facing the Sierra Nevada.

A new way of thinking was emerging in the Sierra Nevada. It was a time when the boundaries and prerogatives of government agencies were giving way to a fresh concept—"ecosystem management"—that attempted to blend the often wildly varying viewpoints of landowners, residents, commercial interests, the scientific community, public policy groups, and environmentalist stakeholders. Times change, and we change with them.

Jack Kerouac, from *The Dharma Bums*

Jack Kerouac (1922–1969) was a leader in the Beat movement, which rejected the societal norms of 1950s America. Kerouac was a novelist, poet, and visual artist whose free, conversational, jazz-inspired tone challenged contemporary critics and inspired generations of writers and artists. Kerouac is sometimes considered the intellectual father of the 1960s counterculture; his work and mindset influenced artists as diverse as Bob Dylan, the Beatles, Ken Kesey, and Hunter S. Thompson. Kerouac's best known works include On the Road, Big Sur, *and* The Dharma Bums.

In this selection from The Dharma Bums *(1958), Kerouac describes his attempt to climb Matterhorn Peak in the Sierra Nevada. This fictionalized account of an actual occurrence features three characters: Ray Smith, Kerouac's alter ego; Henry Morley, the imagined version of Kerouac's librarian friend John Montgomery; and Japhy Ryder, the book's embodiment of Gary Snyder, fellow Beat writer and future Pulitzer Prize–winning poet. (Pieces by Snyder appear in Chapters 5 and 6 of this anthology.)*

"It's late so let's hurry." Japhy started up walking very rapidly and then even running sometimes where the climb had to be to the right or left along ridges of scree. Scree is long landslides of rocks and sand, very difficult to scramble through, always little avalanches going on. At every few steps we took it seemed we were going higher and higher on a terrifying elevator, I gulped when I turned around to look back and see all of the state of California it would seem stretching out in three directions under huge blue skies with frightening planetary space clouds and immense vistas of distant valleys and even plateaus and for all I knew whole Nevadas out there. It was terrifying to look down and see Morley a dreaming spot by the little lake waiting for us. "Oh why didn't I stay with old Henry?" I thought. I now began to be afraid to go any higher from sheer fear of being too high. I began to be afraid of being blown away by the wind. All the nightmares I'd ever had about falling off mountains and precipitous buildings ran through my head in perfect clarity. Also with every twenty steps we took upward we both became completely exhausted.

"That's because of the high altitude now Ray," said Japhy sitting beside me panting. "So have raisins and peanuts and you'll see what kick it gives you." And each time it gave us such a tremendous kick we both jumped up without a word and climbed another twenty, thirty steps. Then sat down again, panting, sweating in the cold wind, high on top of the world our noses sniffling like the noses of little boys playing late Saturday afternoon their final little games in winter. Now the wind began to howl like the wind in movies about the Shroud of Tibet. The steepness began to be too much for me; I was afraid now to look back any more; I peeked: I couldn't even make out Morley by the tiny lake.

"Hurry it up," yelled Japhy from a hundred feet ahead. "It's getting awfully late." I looked up to the peak. It was right there, I'd be there in five minutes. "Only a half-hour to go!" yelled Japhy. I didn't believe it. In five minutes of scrambling angrily upward I fell down and looked up and it was still just as far away. What I didn't like about that peak-top was that the clouds of all the world were blowing right through it like fog.

"Wouldn't see anything up there anyway," I muttered. "Oh why did I ever let myself into this?" Japhy was way ahead of me now, he'd left the peanuts and raisins with me, it was with a kind of lonely solemnity now he had decided to rush to the top if it killed him. He didn't sit down any more. Soon he was a whole football field, a hundred yards ahead of me, getting smaller. I looked back and like Lot's wife that did it. *This is too high!* I yelled to Japhy in a panic. He didn't hear me. I raced a few more feet up and fell exhausted on my belly, slipping back just a little. *This is too high!* I yelled. I was really scared. Supposing I'd start to slip back for good, these screes might start sliding any time anyway. That damn mountain goat Japhy, I could see him jumping through the foggy air up ahead from rock to rock, up, up, just the flash of his boot bottoms. "How can I keep up with a maniac like that?" But with nutty desperation I followed him. Finally I came to a kind of ledge where I could sit at a level angle instead of having to cling not to slip, and I nudged my whole body inside the ledge just to hold me there tight, so the wind would not dislodge me, and I looked down and around and I had had it. *"I'm stayin here!"* I yelled to Japhy.

"Come on Smith, only another five minutes. I only got a hundred feet to go!"

"I'm staying right here! It's too high!"

He said nothing and went on. I saw him collapse and pant and get up and make his run again.

I nudged myself closer into the ledge and closed my eyes and thought "Oh what a life this is, why do we have to be born in the first place, and only so we can have our poor gentle flesh laid out to such impossible horrors as huge mountains and rock and empty space," and with horror I remembered the famous Zen saying, "When you get to the top of a mountain, keep climbing." The saying made my hair stand on end; it had been such cute poetry sitting on Alvah's straw mats. Now it was enough to make my heart pound and my heart bleed for being born at all. "In fact when Japhy gets to the top of that crag he *will* keep climbing, the way the wind's blowing. Well this old philosopher is staying right here," and I closed my eyes. "Besides," I thought, "rest and be kind, you don't have to prove anything." Suddenly I heard a beautiful broken yodel of a strange musical and mystical intensity in the wind, and looked up, and it was Japhy standing on top of Matterhorn peak letting out his triumphant mountain-conquering Buddha Mountain Smashing song of joy. It was beautiful. It was funny, too, up here on the not-so-funny top of California and in all that rushing fog. But I had to hand it to him, the guts, the endurance, the sweat, and now the crazy human singing: whipped cream on top of ice cream. I didn't have enough strength to answer his yodel. He ran around up there and went out of sight to investigate the little flat top of some kind (he said) that ran a few feet west and then dropped sheer back down maybe as far as I care to the sawdust floors of Virginia City. It was insane. I could hear him yelling at me but I just nudged farther in my protective nook, trembling. I looked down at the small lake where Morley was lying on his back with a blade of grass in his mouth and said out loud "Now there's the karma of these three men here: Japhy Ryder gets to his triumphant mountaintop and makes it, I almost make it and have to give up and huddle in a bloody cave, but the smartest of them all is that poet's poet lyin down there with his knees crossed to the sky chewing on a flower dreaming by a gurgling *plage*, goddammit they'll never get me up here again."

I really was amazed by the wisdom of Morley now: "Him with all his goddamn pictures of snowcapped Swiss Alps" I thought.

Then suddenly everything was just like jazz: it happened in one insane second or so: I looked up and saw Japhy *running down the mountain* in huge twenty-foot leaps, running, leaping, landing with a great drive of his booted heels, bouncing five feet or so, running, then taking another long crazy yelling yodelaying sail down the sides of the world and in that flash I realized *it's impossible to fall off mountains you fool* and with a yodel of my own I suddenly got up and began running down the mountain after him doing exactly the same huge leaps, the same fantastic runs and jumps, and in the space of about five minutes I'd guess Japhy Ryder and I (in my sneakers, driving the heels of my sneakers right into sand, rock, boulders, I didn't care any more I was so anxious to get down out of there) came leaping and yelling like mountain goats or I'd say like Chinese lunatics of a thousand years ago, enough to raise the hair on the head of the meditating Morley by the lake, who said he looked up and saw us flying down and couldn't believe it. In fact with one of my greatest leaps and loudest screams of joy I came flying right down to the edge of the lake and dug my sneakered heels into the mud and just fell sitting there, glad. Japhy was already taking his shoes off and pouring sand and pebbles out. It was great. I took off my sneakers and poured out a couple of buckets of lava dust and said "Ah Japhy you taught me the final lesson of them all, you can't fall off a mountain."

"And that's what they mean by the saying, When you get to the top of a mountain keep climbing, Smith."

"Dammit that yodel of triumph of yours was the most beautiful thing I ever heard in my life. I wish I'd a had a tape recorder to take it down."

"Those things aren't made to be heard by the people below," says Japhy dead serious.

"By God you're right, all those sedentary bums sitting around on pillows hearing the cry of the triumphant mountain smasher, they don't deserve it. But when I looked up and saw you running down that mountain I suddenly understood everything."

"Ah a little satori for Smith today," says Morley.

"What were you doing down here?"

"Sleeping, mostly."

"Well dammit I didn't get to the top. Now I'm ashamed of myself because now that I know how to come *down* a mountain I know how to go *up* and that I can't fall off, but now it's too late."

Gary Snyder, "What Happened Here Before"

Born in San Francisco, raised in the Pacific Northwest, a frequent visitor to the Sierra Nevada, and now one of its longtime residents, Gary Snyder (b. 1930) has let his experiences in the natural world animate his work and his worldview. An early pioneer in the Beat movement of the 1950s, in the 1960s, Snyder lived and studied in a Zen monastery in Japan, and Zen Buddhism remains a powerful current flowing through all his writing. His poetry and prose have helped introduce the concepts of environmental stewardship into public and literary discourse, and this characteristic melding of literature, ecology, and policy has earned Snyder many awards and honors, including a Pulitzer Prize in 1975, as well as a Bollingen Prize for Poetry and a John Hay Award for Nature Writing, both in 1997.

Snyder resides on a mountain farm in the Yuba River watershed of the Sierra Nevada. In the following poem he takes a very long view of the range.

—300,000,000—

First a sea: soft sands, muds, and marls
   —loading, compressing, heating, crumpling,
   crushing, recrystallizing, infiltrating,
several times lifted and submerged.
intruding molten granite magma
   deep-cooled and speckling,
     gold quartz fills the cracks—

—80,000,000—

sea-bed strata raised and folded,
    granite far below.
warm quiet centuries of rains
    (make dark red tropic soils)
    wear down two miles of surface,
lay bare the veins and tumble heavy gold
    in streambeds
        slate and schist rock-riffles catch it—
volcanic ash floats down and dams the streams,
    piles up the gold and gravel—

—3,000,000—

flowing north, two rivers joined,
    to make a wide long lake.
and then it tilted and rivers fell apart
    all running west
    to cut the gorges of the Feather,
        Bear, and Yuba.

Ponderosa pine, manzanita, black oak, mountain yew.
    deer, coyote, bluejay, gray squirrel,
ground squirrel, fox, blacktail hare,
    ringtail, bobcat, bear,
        all came to live here.

—40,000—

And human people came with basket hats and nets
    winter-houses underground
    yew bows painted green,
    feasts and dances for the boys and girls
        songs and stories in the smoky dark.

—150—

Then came the white man: tossed up trees and
    boulders with big hoses,
    going after that old gravel and gold.

horses, apple-orchards, card-games,
    pistol-shooting, churches, county jail.

We asked, who the land belongs to.
    and where one pays the tax.
(two gents who never used it twenty years,
and before them the widow
    of the son of the man
    who got him a patented deed
    on a worked-out mining claim,)
laid hasty on land that was deer and acorn
    grounds of the Nisenan?
    branch of the Maidu?

(they never had a chance to speak, even,
    their name.)
(and who remembers the Treaty of Guadalupe Hidalgo.) .

    the land belongs to itself.
    "no self in self: no self in things"
    Turtle Island swims
    in the ocean-sky swirl-void
    biting its tail while the worlds go
        on-and-off
            winking

& Mr. Tobiassen, a Cousin Jack,
    assesses the county tax.
(the tax is our body-mind, guest at the banquet
    Memorial and Annual, in honor
    of sunlight grown heavy and tasty
    while moving up food-chains
in search of a body with eyes and a fairly large
    brain—
to look back at itself
    on high.)

        now,

we sit here near the diggings
in the forest, by our fire, and watch
the moon and planets and the shooting stars—

my sons ask, who are we?
drying apples picked from homestead trees
drying berries, curing meat,
shooting arrows at a bale of straw.

military jets head northeast, roaring, every dawn.
my sons ask, who are they?

WE SHALL SEE
WHO KNOWS
HOW TO BE

Bluejay screeches from a pine.

William Everson, "Bride of the Bear"

*Born in the San Joaquin Valley, William Everson (1912–1994) was
entranced by the natural landscapes of California his entire life. A poet
and scholar, Everson was influenced by the work of Robinson Jeffers
and later became an expert on Jeffers's literary legacy. In turn, Everson
himself greatly influenced members of the Beat generation of the 1950s.
A conscientious objector during World War II, it was while interned in a
federal labor camp that he began working as a fine arts printer. Following
the war, Everson underwent a religious conversion, entered a Dominican
monastery in Oakland, and renamed himself Brother Antoninus, all the
while continuing to write and produce lovingly handcrafted, hand-bound,
fine-press books. Sometimes known as the "Beat Friar," he left the Dominican Order in 1969, married, and became a long-term poet in residence at
the University of California, Santa Cruz. Everson received many awards
and honors, including a Guggenheim Fellowship and the Shelley Award
from the Poetry Society of America.*

*In this poem, Everson examines love and nature in a Sierra Nevada
setting.*

We camp by a stream among rugged stumps
In logged-over country. No tree shelters our bed.
In the year-long drought gripping the Sierras
There is no snow, and the night is warm.
After our fog-haunted coast the air at this height
Seems weightless, without substance, almost clairvoyant.
Luminous stars, low overhead, look into our lives.

At ground level the campfire
Dapples the stumps, throws fitful shadows,
Guttering the dark.

We drink late wine.
Arriving at dusk we had pitched camp quickly,
Eaten nervous supper. For a ranger going out
Warned of bear sign, and a wrangler behind him
Showed packs ripped open, bacon gorged. Seeing it
We prudently stashed our food in the jeep,
Gathered firewood, branch and root,
And built up the blaze. Fumbling through our gear
My hand touched in passing the great bearskin
Carried in from the coast, belated wedding gift
Brought along to delight you, a savage pelt to throw down by the fire,
Barbaric trophy in a mountain lair—but here,
In the actual presence, in bear country,
Furtively concealed: discreet hibernation
In the cave of the car.

When the blaze dies down
I step out of its circle to fetch more wood
Against the presences of night. Standing in the dark
I look wondering up at those luminous orbs,
Hovering like moths just out of reach, preternaturally intense.
I sense around me the ghosts of slain trees,
Nude giants, slaughtered under the axe,
Pitching down from the slopes, the prone torsos
Hauled out with engines. Listening, I hear the famished creek
Drain west, a gurgle in a gravel throat,
Gasping.

Back by the fire
You have fallen asleep, dazed with wine,
Curled by bright embers on living fern.
I lace a clutch of twigs on the coals
And in the spurt of flame see gooseflesh
Stipple your arm. Under the mellowing influence of wine
My nerves loosen, and I dismiss caution.
I fetch from the jeep the great bearskin

And draw it across you, then fondly step back to admire my care.
But what have I wrought that my own hand shaped
Yet could not forestall? Oh, most inadvertently
I have folded you in the bear's huge embrace,
A hulking lover, the brute body enveloping you,
Massively yours.

          You snuggle happily under it, sighing a bit,
The moan of a fretful satisfaction breathed from your deeps.
Is it wine on your lips that reddens them,
Or something deeper, in the bear's hug,
There, below the heart, a more elemental zone
At the body's base?

          I cannot tell.
But whatever it is it wantons your mouth,
And your mouth mocks me: inviting and denying,
The enigma of desire. I think, So be it.
Thus have I made you
Bride of the bear.

          And thinking it,
The night chill shivers me, a sudden *frisson*,
The languor of wine possessing me.
I feel surge through my veins
The madcap days of our courtship,
Crazy monk and runaway girl,
Panting in discovery, goading each other on,
Wildly in love.

          You stir in the bearskin.
Has memory touched you, two minds drenched in wine
Seeking each other through the cavern of sleep
Along the ancient line, the tendril of desire?

Drugged in dream you turn heavily. That nubile litheness
No longer is yours. But something better lives on in its place,
A mature abundance filling your flesh, the bloom of full life.

I, greybeard, nurse my drink and suck my pipe,
Watching the stars expire.

             Now you turn,
Lifting your dream-drenched face to the light,
Still sunken in sleep, the wantonness
Splashed like wine on your parted lips.
Stiffly, raised on one elbow, you fumble at your blouse,
The heat under the animal pelt
Oppressing you. When your hand succeeds,
I see the naked globes of your breasts
Flash back the fire.

             Bride of the bear.

Gazing up the dark I watch the stars
Cross the verge that shuts midnight from dawn
To walk down the west. Whatever happened to time?
When we pulled down our packs
The night lay before us. Now, in another hour,
Night is no more.

             Somewhere out there
The ubiquitous beast, gorged on raw bacon,
Sleeps off his jag.

             Raising your head
You look dazedly about, dimly comprehending,
Then sink back to sleep.

             Around the campfire
The ghosts of slain trees look over us.
Out of the eastern peaks, traced now with light,
The dawn wind whispers. The starved stream
Gropes through the stumps.

Bill Hotchkiss, "Indian Summer"

Poet, novelist, and essayist Bill Hotchkiss (b. 1937) was born in Connecticut but at an early age moved to Grass Valley—a historic gold mining community in the Sierra Nevada foothills—which he considers his hometown. A job with the United States Forest Service eventually brought him to Berkeley and the University of California, where he earned a degree, and he later earned degrees from California State University, San Francisco, and the University of Oregon. Hotchkiss was the executor of William Everson's literary estate, is an expert on California author Robinson Jeffers, and currently teaches at Sierra College, which has a campus in his adopted hometown. Hotchkiss is a prolific novelist and poet whose themes often reflect his love of the Sierra Nevada.

    The following poem was first published in Hotchkiss's 1978 collection of Sierra-related poems titled Climb to the High Country.

I awake one morning to find
That years have run on the wind:
Now autumn is here,
Yet summer refuses to die,
The heat persists, no tempering frost.

In the late morning I walk
By the pond, to the far side
Through a net of young willows,
Their leaves just starting
To yellow, and a hundred
Bullfrogs splash into the water.

Get down in the mud,
Little brothers, seasons turn fast.

Hot, dry winds leach earth,
And a touch of flame would send
Red waves through dead vegetation.

Late plums are shriveled on branches:
For all of this, the flight of the kingfisher
Suggests that winter comes sudden.

The white, drenching rains,
Then blizzard and wrenching
Of frost: the bare cirques
Of the High Sierra hunger
Snow, the rock hungers ice.

Little brothers, get down in the mud.

But I reach out now to the blast of winter,
For something within me hungers my death,
And my laughter cracks a clear, frozen air;

I race for the morning that finds
Such beautiful frost on the wind.

David Brower, from *Gentle Wilderness*

Born in Berkeley, David Brower (1912–2000) began climbing in the Sierra at an early age and is credited with first ascents of seventy routes in the range. Brower put his expertise to work during World War II as a lieutenant in the 10th Mountain Division, training soldiers in mountaineering and crosscountry skiing. His life-long love of, and experiences in, the mountains also led him to environmental activism. Brower was the first executive director of the Sierra Club (1952–1969), he served on its board three times, and he published many books with the club. He also founded Friends of the Earth in 1969 and inspired the formation of many other local and national environmental groups. One of Brower's lasting contributions was popularizing large-format books that mixed breathtaking nature photography with environmental philosophy. The following selection is from Brower's foreword to Gentle Wilderness: The Sierra Nevada, *a compilation of photos by Richard Kauffman and quotations by John Muir.*

What John Muir had to say in *My First Summer in the Sierra* led me, forty years ago, to feel I had already been in the Yosemite High Sierra he was discovering for the first time….

Is it really gentle wilderness? There is room for argument. Certainly the gentleness of this Sierra wilderness is never soft enough to be cloying. Fear can be mixed with your exhilaration. The passes come impressively high, your breath short, and your pulse rapid. Some of the deepest snows in North America fall there and nothing is gentle about the avalanches when the slopes unload, or about winter temperatures that may drop to fifty-five below. You don't feel very pampered when you are on a half-inch ledge halfway up one of the half-mile-high sheer Yosemite cliffs, or when the March wind finds you and, even though you brace against it with ski poles, flattens you on Mount Lyell's icy shoulder, or when a driving spray drenches you if you venture within a hundred yards of the foot of Vernal Fall in flood, or when a desert sun bakes you at the foot of the Sierra's eastern escarpment, two vertical miles below the summit of Mount Whitney.

Still there is always enough gentleness in the Sierra, or soon will be, when the storm clears or the rough climb ends. No other of the world's great ranges[…]that I know, or that so far as we know Muir knew, is as gentle as the Sierra.

If there is to be objection, it is that the Sierra is too gentle—too gentle to counter man's assaults against it. John Muir saw this in his first summer and in the later summers and winters when the Sierra was his address. He dedicated his life to a counterassault on man's misuse of wilderness and wildlife. He helped establish national parks, enlisted support of national leaders in a preservation movement, battled Gifford Pinchot's predominantly utilitarian interest in conservation, wrote and talked and led with exuberant energy—with the same energy that took him through his favorite forests, among the alpine gardens he loved, and on up so many of the Sierra peaks. He also founded the Sierra Club "to explore, enjoy, and render accessible" the mountain range it was named after. In 1911 he dedicated *First Summer* to the members of the club for their good work.

One of his ideas for rendering the Sierra accessible was a program of summer wilderness outings which he and William E. Colby initiated in 1901. Too many of the places he loved were being lost because too few people knew about them. There would be no hope of sparing Sierra meadows from being overgrazed and devastated by domestic sheep, for instance, unless people saw the damage firsthand and also saw unspoiled meadows so as to evaluate the loss. The giant sequoias were being logged for grape stakes. Hetch Hetchy Valley itself was to be dammed—in the last analysis to produce hydroelectric power for San Francisco. It was not enough to write about the beauty of these places and the tragedy of losing them. People must see for themselves, appraise the danger to the spot on the spot. Informed, devoted defense would ensue.

For sixty-three years since then the concept has worked, modified only slightly. Early in the game Muir had felt that accessibility should include a fairly formidable road net through the High Sierra. Late in the 'twenties the Sierra Club directors were still advocating several trans-Sierra roads they would shudder to think about today. The words "render accessible" were being misunderstood as an argument for mechanized access and were amended out of the bylaws. The emphasis shifted to getting people to know wilderness as wilderness, to travel there by foot, to leave the fewest possible marks, to spare for another generation the opportunity to discover that which they themselves had loved.

There was not yet much concern about what the foot—a man's or a mule's—might do to wilderness. The high-country was still fairly empty. As late as 1934 I myself could still spend a month in the Kings-Kern country without seeing anyone but my knapsacking companion. Before our ten-week knapsack survey of the John Muir Trail and the Sierra crest was over, we encountered only a few independent travelers—and an entire Sierra Club High Trip of nearly two hundred people and one hundred pack animals. But even then we had only to walk a mile or two to be in empty mountains again....

Today a thousand people may walk up the east-side trail to the summit of Mount Whitney over the Labor Day week end; forty thousand may hit Yosemite Valley over a Memorial Day week end. There is a new dimension in mountain use—"visitation," the National Park Service calls it. Park Service ecologists have now identified a few hot spots in the high country above Kings Canyon and Sequoia national parks, places where recreational erosion exceeds a given camping area's capability of recovering. Human erosion itself is not too noticeable, but the associated grazing, trampling, and littering by packstock is severe. What Muir had objected to in the impact of commercial sheep is now being accomplished by animals hired for pleasure. A Forest Service ranger spent a year studying what sheer numbers were doing along Bear Creek, south of Yosemite, and concluded that large groups of wilderness travelers should be eliminated: don't concentrate use in a few places, but disperse it and build primitive toilets and fireplaces in many parts of the wilderness to encourage the dispersal. Not a hundred people in one spot, but ten people in ten spots, or five in twenty. Meanwhile, back in Washington, his parent agency was arguing before Congress that there was probably already too much wilderness set aside; considering the little use it was getting, it was far more important to expedite the construction of timber-access roads and logging operations into undedicated wilderness and to make sure that dedicated wilderness was as free as possible of commercial trees. Too little use, yet so much use the land suffered; log it and end the debate!

The confusion continues. The big-trip use that Muir had advocated was the easiest target to hit, or to encourage others to hit. It also happens to be the trip that could serve the widest range of physical and financial abilities. The man too old to carry much of a pack, or the child too young to, can still walk a wilderness trail. Packstock can carry the duffel, the food, the camp equipment. Crew members (usually students who can travel fast enough to break one camp late and make the next one early) allow the wilderness visitor maximum time to enjoy the country with minimum housekeeping. If the moves aren't too far, the stock can relay loads, and half the number of stock can serve the same number of people. Four or more wilderness travelers can thus be served per head of packstock—on a moving trip, the kind that gives the visitor the feel of big, continuous wilderness.

Could wilderness be experienced in such a crowd? Could you see the mountains for the people? As a knapsacker I thought not, but changed my mind in the course of spending a year of summer days on Sierra Club High Trips, making careful notes of what happened, checking with Forest Service and National Park Service observers and ecologists, joining with trip leaders and packers in taking the dozens of steps that minimized the impact of people, whether on the wilderness itself or on other people. I was partial then, and still am eight years later, to the moving trip that can give the visitor the feel of a big, continuous wilderness—one in which you can cross pass after pass and know that on the other side you don't drop into civilization, but stay in wilderness instead. In big wilderness you learn how important size itself is to the viability of wilderness. It needs enough buffer to keep its heartland essentially free from the pervasive influences of technology. Such big wilderness is scarce, and is vanishing at the rate of about a million acres a year, chiefly to the chainsaw. People who know it can save it. No one else.

Were Muir alive today he would see the issue clearly and would keep it clear of all the conscious and unconscious confusion. He would know that the choice was not between pristine wilderness and wilderness overused in spots, but between some overuse and no wilderness at all. He would not forget irreplaceable Glen Canyon, hard-hit at some camps along the river, but still not known by enough people to be saved. The Bureau of Reclamation solved the problem of slightly overused campsites by drowning the entire length of the canyon, permanently, with an unnecessary reservoir.

Muir would see what was happening in the Sierra, and would not be fooled by the forces hostile to preservation who now point a diversionary finger at wilderness footprints. He would point out the marks far more damaging than footprints—logging roads, stumps, and trash-clogged streams—that forever killed gentle wilderness on the Kern Plateau because of too little conservationist use. He would note how the real, unbroken wilderness of the High Sierra climax, extending from the Tioga Road in Yosemite down to the Kern, is still vulnerable; a corridor for a needless trans-Sierra road is relentlessly being kept open at Mammoth Pass, and another south of Whitney Meadows. Because there had been too little use, Muir would observe, the wilderness of Vermilion Valley and of a beautiful basin in the North Fork of the Kings had been drowned by power reservoirs—in a day when hydroelectric power means less and less and unspoiled recreation places mean more and more. Muir would not have been impressed by tears about footprints in eyes that winked at mechanized scooters snorting over wilderness trails.

I am sure that John Muir would still believe that firsthand knowledge of places is vital to their survival and that their survival is vital to man. He needs places where he can be reminded that civilization is only a thin veneer over the deep evolutionary flow of things that built him. Let wilderness live, and it would always tell him truth.

For all the losses since John Muir's time, an invaluable resource still lives. Much of the Sierra wilderness is essentially what it was half a century ago, altered only by natural succession. The favorite, untouched high places are a constant that can reassure a man. So is the roll of familiar things you pass on your way up the heights—the oak savannah, the digger pines, the orderly succession of ponderosa, incense cedar, sugar pine, the firs, then the denizens of timberline. One trouble these days is that you have to call the roll of friends too fast. Speed and the wide highway have brought a deprivation, for the right reason perhaps, but in the wrong places. Speed shrinks wilderness, and there wasn't really enough in Muir's day to serve all those who followed him to California or who will one day be here to look or to live.

Even as in Muir's time, the Sierra Club's purpose is still to gather together people from all over who know how important it is that there should always be some land wild and free. They are needed to counter the rationalizations of the highway builders, and dam and logging-road builders, who would slice through and dismember the wilderness.... [N]either California nor the rest of America is rich enough to lose any more of the Gentle Wilderness or poor enough to need to.

> "Brilliant flashes of lightning split open the sky, thunder roars—
> a sound of huge rocks falling down a mountainside"

Alice Adams, "Favors"

A native of Virginia, Alice Adams (1926–1999) moved to Northern California after graduating from Radcliffe College. The author of numerous novels and short story collections, Adams received many honors for her work, including an O. Henry Award, a Best American Short Stories Award, an award from the American Academy of Arts and Letters, and grants from the Guggenheim Foundation and the National Endowment for the Arts. Her stories were regularly published in leading magazines, including The New Yorker, The Paris Review, Atlantic Monthly, *and* Cosmopolitan.

A longtime San Francisco resident and a frequent visitor to the Sierra Nevada, Adams set the following short story in the central Sierra's tranquil Truckee River Canyon.

July that year is hotter, the air heavier and more sultry than is usual in Northern California, especially up in the Sierras, near Lake Tahoe. Along the Truckee River, which emanates from that lake, mosquitoes flourish in the thick green riverside bushes and grass. Even in the early mornings—most unusual—it is already warm and damp. An absolute stillness, a brooding quiet.

"If this were Maine, there would be a thunderstorm," remarks Maria Tresca, an elderly political activist, just released from jail. By profession she is an architect. A large-boned, heavy woman, with gray-brown hair and huge very dark eyes, she is addressing the much younger couple who are with her on the terrace of her river house. The three of them have just finished a light breakfast in the dining room, inside; they now sit on old canvas deck chairs.

Having spoken, Maria closes her eyes, as though the effort involved in keeping them open were more than she could manage in the breezeless heat, the flat air.

The two young people, the couple, are Danny Michaels, a small, gray-blond young man, rather lined for someone his age, serious, bookish-looking; and thin, bright-red-haired Phoebe Knowles, Danny's very recent wife.

"That would be wonderful, a storm," says Phoebe, who seems a little short of breath.

And Danny: "We sure could use the rain."

"Actually, I'd be quite terrified," Maria opens her eyes to tell them. "I always used to be, in Maine. We had the most terrific summer storms." She recloses her eyes.

Danny has known Maria for so long (almost all the thirty-odd years of his life) that nearly all questions seem permitted; also they like and trust each other. However, so far his evident sympathetic interest in her recent experience has been balked. About Pleasanton, where the jail was, Maria has only said, not quite convincingly, "It wasn't too bad. It's minimum security, you know. I felt rather like a Watergate conspirator. The clothes they gave me were terribly uncomfortable, though. Just not fitting, and stiff."

Only Maria's posture suggests discouragement, or even age. On the old rattan sofa she slumps down in a tired way among the cushions, her large hands clasped together on the knees of old corduroys.

And goes on about Maine. "The chipmunks there were much bigger than the ones out here," she tells Phoebe and Dan. "Or maybe they only seemed bigger because I was very small. I haven't been back there since I was a child, you know."

Phoebe and Dan are in the odd position of being both Maria's hosts and her guests: it is her house—in fact, very much her house, designed by Maria for her own use. But it was lent to Danny and Phoebe by Ralph Tresca, Maria's son and a great friend of Danny's. This was to be their wedding present, two weeks alone in this extraordinary, very private house. For which they had both arranged, with some trouble, to take off from their jobs. Phoebe and her best friend, Anna, run a small restaurant on Potrero Hill; Danny works in a bookstore, also on Potrero, of which he is part owner.

Danny and Ralph have been friends since kindergarten, and thus

Danny has known Maria for all that time. He and Phoebe have known each other for less than four months; theirs was a passionate, somewhat hasty marriage, indeed precipitated by Ralph's offer of the house. Danny called Ralph in Los Angeles, where Ralph is a sometime screenwriter, to say that he had met a girl about whom he was really serious. "I think we might get married." To which Ralph responded, "Well, if you do it this summer you can have the house for two weeks at the end of July. It's rented for most of the rest."

Not the reason, surely, but an impetus. Danny has always loved the beautiful, not entirely practical house, at which he has often been a guest. A wonderfully auspicious beginning to their marriage, Danny believed those weeks would be.

But after the first week of their time at the house had passed, there was suddenly the phone call from Ralph, asking if it would be all right for Maria to come up and stay with them; Maria was about to be released, after fourteen days in jail. Danny had known about Maria's sentencing; he and Phoebe had talked about it, early on—so severe for an antinuclear protest, and for a woman of Maria's age. But they had not been entirely clear as to when Maria started to serve, nor when she was to get out. And it had certainly not occurred to Danny that Maria might want to come from jail to her house on the Truckee River. However: *Of course*, he told Ralph.

Hanging up the phone, which is in the kitchen, and walking across the long living room toward their bedroom, where he and Phoebe had been taking a semi-nap, Danny considered how he would put it to Phoebe, this quite unforeseen interruption to their time. Danny knows that he is crazy about Phoebe, but also acknowledges (to himself) some slight fear; he suspects that she is perceptibly stronger than he is. Also, it was he who insisted on marriage and finally talked her into it, mentioning their ages ("we're not exactly kids") plus the bribe of the house. But the real truth was that Danny feared losing her—he had indecisively lost a couple of other really nice women; now he wanted to settle down. In any case, although he feels himself loved by Phoebe, feels glad of their marriage, he worries perhaps unduly about her reactions.

"You see, it was such a great favor that I couldn't not do it" was one of the things he decided to say to Phoebe, approaching their room. "All that time in jail, a much longer sentence than anyone thought she would get. I think her old protest history worked against her. I know it was supposed to be our house for these two weeks, Ralph kept saying that. He really felt bad, asking me to do this," Danny meant to add.

What he did not mean to say to Phoebe, in part because he did not know quite how to phrase it, was his own sense that if Maria were to come up to them, Ralph should come too. Ralph's presence would make a better balance. Also, Ralph's frenetic nervous energy, his offbeat wit—both qualities that made Danny smile, just to think about—would have lightened the atmosphere, which so far has been more than a little heavy, what with the weather and Maria's silences, her clearly sagging spirits.

However, Dan had barely mentioned to Phoebe that Maria was getting out of jail on July 19 when Phoebe broke in, "Oh, then she must come right up. Do you think we should leave, or stay on and sort of take care of her? I could cook a lot, prison food has to be horrible. Tell Ralph not to worry, it'll be fine."

All of which led Danny to think that he does not know Phoebe well at all.

Phoebe herself has had certain odd new problems on this trip: trouble eating, for one thing; she who generally eats more than her envious friends can believe, scrawny Phoebe of the miraculous metabolism now barely manages a scant first helping of the good cold rice salads, the various special dishes she planned and made for this first leisurely time alone with Dan. And she is sometimes short of breath. Also, despite long happy nights of love, she has trouble sleeping. All these problems clearly have to do with the altitude, six thousand feet, Phoebe knows that perfectly well; still, does it possibly have something to do with being married—married in haste, as the old phrase used to go?

By far her worst problem, though, is sheer discomfort from the heat, so much heavy sun all day. Like many redheads, Phoebe does not do well in very warm weather, the affliction being an inability to perspire. Instead, out in the sun her skin seems to wither and burn, both within and without. Very likely, she thinks, if it cooled off even a little, all her troubles would disappear; she could eat and sleep again, and enjoy being married to Dan.

However, she reminds herself, there would still be the house. Danny talked about it often; he tried to describe Maria's house, and Phoebe gathered that it was beautiful—impressive, even. Still, she was unprepared for what seems to her somewhat stark: such bare structural bones, exposed textures of pine and fir, such very high, vaulted ceilings. Phoebe has never been in a house with so definite a tone, a stamp. In fact, both the house's unfamiliarity and the strength of its character have been more than a little intimidating. (Phoebe is from a small town in New Hampshire of entirely conventional, rather small-scale architecture.)

Even the bookcases have yielded up to Phoebe few clues of a personal nature, containing as they do a large, clearly much used collection of various field guides, to birds, wildflowers, trees, and rocks; some yellowed, thumbed-through Grade-B detective fiction; and a large, highly eclectic shelf of poetry—Rilke, Auden, Yeats, plus a great many small volumes of women poets. Marianne Moore, Elizabeth Bishop, Louise Bogan, Katha Pollitt, Amy Clampitt. Clues, but to Ralph or to Maria? Ralph's father, Maria's husband, died young, Dan has said; he has spoken admiringly of Maria's uncompromising professionalism, her courage—never a shopping center or a sleazy tract. The poetry, then, might belong to them both? There are no inscriptions.

Thus, occupying the house of two very strong, individualistic people, neither of whom she has met, fills Phoebe with some unease, even a sort of loneliness.

The site of the house, though, is so very beautiful—magical, even: that very private stretch of clear brown river, rushing over its smoothly rounded, wonderfully tinted rocks. And the surrounding woods of pine and fir and shimmering gray-green aspens, and the lovely sky, and clouds. The very air smells of summer, and earth, and trees. In such a place, Phoebe thinks, how can she not feel perfectly well, not be absolutely happy?

Indeed (she has admitted this to herself, though not to Dan), she welcomed Maria at least in part as a diversion.

Though since her arrival Maria has seemed neither especially diverting, as Phoebe had hoped, nor heroic—as they both had believed.

"It would be a lot better if Ralph were here too, I know that," Dan tells Phoebe, later that morning, as, barefoot, they pick their way back across the meadow to the house; they have been swimming in the river—or, rather, wading and ducking down into the water, which is disappointingly shallow, slow-moving, not the icy rush that Danny remembers from previous visits.

Phoebe, though, seems to feel considerably better; she walks along surefootedly, a little ahead of Dan, and her tone is reassuring as she says, "It's all right. I think Maria's just really tired. I'm doing a vitello tonnato for lunch, though. Remember, from the restaurant? Maybe she'll like that. God, I just wish I could eat!"

Avoiding sharp pinecones and sticks and skirting jagged rocks requires attention, and so they are quiet for a while as they walk along. But then, although he is in fact looking where he is going, Dan's foot hits something terrible and sharp, and he cries out, "Damn!"

"What's wrong?"

"My foot, I think a stone."

"Oh dear." Phoebe has stopped and turned to ask, "Shall I look?"

"No, it's okay, nothing," Dan mutters, striding on past her.

But he is thinking, Well, really, how like Ralph to saddle me with his mother on my honeymoon. And with Maria just out of jail, for God's sake. So politically correct that I couldn't possibly object. Damn Ralph, anyway.

Never having met Ralph, who has been in Los Angeles for all the time that Dan and Phoebe have known each other (the long, not long four months), Phoebe has no clear view of him, although Dan talks about him often. What has mostly come across to Phoebe is the strength of the two men's affection for each other; so rare, in her experience, such open fondness between men. She has even briefly wondered if they could have been lovers, ever, and concluded that they were not. They are simply close, as she and her friend-partner, Anna, are close. Danny would do almost anything for Ralph, including taking in his mother at a not entirely convenient time.

In fact, his strong, evident affections are among the qualities Phoebe values in Dan—and perhaps Ralph is more or less like that? His closeness to his mother has had that effect? Although so far Maria herself has not come across as an especially warm or "giving" person.

Early common ground, discovered by Dan and Phoebe on first meeting, was a firm belief in political protest. They had both taken part in demonstrations against the Nicaraguan embargo, against South African racism; both felt that there was, generally, a mood of protest in their city, San Francisco, that spring. By which they were encouraged.

And they had had serious talks about going to jail. Taking part in demonstrations is not the same as being locked up, they are agreed.

"It's hard to figure out just how much good it does. Jail."

"Especially if you're not famous. Just a person. Ellsberg going to jail is something else."

"Do famous people get lighter sentences?"

"I'd imagine. In fact, I'd bet."

"So hard to figure. Is it better to go to jail, or to stay out and do whatever your work is and send money to your cause?"

Impossible to decide, has been their conclusion.

However, someone probably has to go to jail; they think that too. So why not them?

Working in the kitchen, making lunch, Phoebe feels better than she has for several days. Good effects of the dip into the river seem to last, a lively sense of water lingers on her skin. Carefully, thinly slicing the firm moist white turkey (she is good at this, a good carver), Phoebe feels more in control of her life than she has in days just past, no longer entirely at the mercy of weather and altitude. She even feels more at peace with the house. Here in the kitchen, its bareness and extreme simplicity seem functional; the oversized butcher-block table with its long rack for knives is a great working space.

She is happily breaking an egg into the blender, reaching for oil, when she hears the sound of slow footsteps approaching the kitchen. It must be Maria, and the distress that Phoebe then experiences is both general and particular: she likes best to cook alone; in fact, she loves the solitary single-mindedness of cooking. Also, none of her conversations with Maria have been very successful, so far.

Hesitantly, distractedly, Maria comes to stand outside the kitchen doorway. Vaguely she says, "I'm sure I can't help you." She is not quite looking at Phoebe but rather out the window, to the river. "But I did wonder—you're finding everything you need?"

"Oh yes, it's a wonderful kitchen." Working there, it has become clear to Phoebe that Maria herself must be a very good cook; this is the working space of a dedicated person. "I feel bad displacing you this way," she says to Maria.

This earns the most direct and also the most humorous look from Maria yet seen. "You're good to say that. But actually I could use a little displacement, probably."

Phoebe ventures, "Do you have trouble letting people help you, the way I do?"

A wide, if fleeting, grin. "Oh, indeed I do. I seem to believe myself quite indispensable, in certain areas."

They smile, acknowledging some kinship. "Well, I won't keep you."

Maria begins to leave; then, from whatever inner depths of thought, she remarks, "I do wish Ralph were here too. It would be nice for you to meet him here."

"It would have been," agrees Phoebe. "But sometime."

Lunch, though, is no better than breakfast, conversationally, and in Phoebe's judgment even the food is not entirely successful.

They are gathered again on the terrace above the river, joined at the too large round table—scattered around it.

However, partly because he knows that Phoebe is genuinely curious, as he is himself, Danny persists in asking about Maria's time in jail. (Also, he is convinced that talking about it will help Maria.) "What does Pleasanton look like?" he asks her. "I can't even imagine it."

"Oh—" At first Maria's vague, unfocused glance goes out to the river, as though for help, but then she seems to make an effort—for her guests. "It's quite country-club-looking," she tells them. "Very clean and bland." In a tantalizing way, she adds, "It's rather like the White House."

"Really? How?" This has been a chorus, from Dan and Phoebe.

Maria sighs, and continues to try. "Well, externally it's so clean, and behind the scenes there's total corruption." Having gone so far, though, she leans back into her chair and closes her eyes.

Dan looks at Phoebe. On her face he sees both blighted curiosity and genuine if momentary helplessness. He sees too her discomfort from the increasing heat. Her skin is so bright, dry, pink. The sultry air has curled her hair so tightly that it looks uncomfortable. At that moment Danny believes that he *feels* all Phoebe's unvoiced, unspoken sensations; her feelings are his. And he further thinks, I am married to Phoebe permanently, for good.

And, looking at his wife, and at Maria, whom he has always known, Danny thinks how incredibly complex women are. How *interesting* they are.

"In Maine the air never felt exactly like this air," Maria tells them, as though Maine had been under discussion—again. "A little like it, fresh and clean, but not exactly. It's interesting. The difference, I mean. Though hard to describe," she trails off.

"I know what you mean, though," comments Phoebe. "In the same way that all the colors are different, but you can't exactly say how."

"Phoebe grew up in New Hampshire," Danny tells Maria, wondering why this fact had not emerged earlier, or did it?

"Oh, did you really." But Maria has returned to her own privacy, her thoughts. New Hampshire could be across the continent from Maine, for all of her.

The heat has gathered and intensified. Phoebe feels that she will burst, her skin rent apart, the way a tomato's skin will split in heat. What she also feels is a kind of rage, though she tries to tell herself that she is simply hot, that she feels so ill-tempered only because of the weather, the temperature. And, knowing herself, certain bad tendencies, she determines that she will not *say* how angry she is, and especially she will not take it out on Danny.

I love Dan. The weather is not his fault—nor, really, is absent Ralph. Gross, inconsiderate, totally selfish Ralph. Some friend, thinks Phoebe.

She and Dan are lying across their bed, ostensibly napping, although the turgid air seems entirely to forbid real sleep. Naked, they still do not touch, although earlier Dan has asked, "Can I douse you with some cold water, or maybe an alcohol rub?"

"No thanks, but really, thanks." (It was at that moment that Phoebe determined not to vent her ire on Dan, who is genuinely kind, well-meaning.)

They have both been whispering, although no one could conceivably hear them, the rooms being so spread apart; Maria's is several rooms away. "Maria simply clutches that prison experience to herself, doesn't she?" now whispers Phoebe. "Not that she much wants to talk about anything else either."

"Except Maine." Danny tries a small laugh. "Lots of Maine."

"And the way she eats," complains Phoebe bitterly. "Just bolting down a few bites and then a dead stop. It's not exactly flattering. Not that I really care, I mean. Did she always eat like that?"

"I sort of can't remember. Maybe not. I didn't notice, really."

"I have to say, though," announces Phoebe, "I really think this is a very selfish move on Ralph's part."

Dan very lightly sighs, just shifting in bed. "I'm afraid I agree. But people change, I think. Maybe he's pure L.A. these days. More selfish than he used to be. He's been seeing some shrink down there for years."

"That whole culture's so selfish. Crass."

"Oh, *right.*"

Feeling a little better, Phoebe reaches her fingers just to graze the top of Danny's hand. They look at each other; they smile.

Dinner that night, which again is out on the terrace, is in many ways a repeat of lunch, except of course for the menu; provident Phoebe has made a nice cold pasta, with garlicky brandied prawns. But Maria again eats very little, and that most rapidly.

And again she talks about Maine. "The soil was so rocky around our house it was hard to grow flowers," she says. "I've never even tried to plant anything out here."

The night is densely dark, pitch black; in an absolute and final way it is still. And heavy; the air seems weighted. Oppressive, stultifying.

"I do wish Ralph could have been here." It is Dan who has said this, not having at all intended to. It simply slipped out, like a sigh, and now he feels tactless. "But it's great that he has so much work down there," he feebly amends.

"I suppose so." Unhelpful Maria puts her fork down and stares out into the black.

Going about the house, as every night he has—checking door locks, turning off lights—for the first time on this visit Danny has a sad sense of spuriousness: this is not his house, he is much more guest than host. And he recalls now that this place has always been somewhat daunting; its proportions make him feel even less tall than in fact he is. And very possibly Phoebe's deepest reactions have been similar? She too has been made uncomfortable by the house, in addition to the appalling heat, her enemy? None of these facts augur poorly for their marriage, though, Danny believes. Once they are back in San Francisco, in the cool foggy summer weather, in their own newly painted rooms, then they will be fine.

He admits to himself, however, some real disappointment over what he feels as the failure of connection between Maria and Phoebe. When Ralph called about Maria's coming up, just out of jail, along with disappointment at the curtailment of their privacy, Danny experienced a small surge of happy expectation. Maria and Phoebe, despite obvious differences of age, career, could become great friends, a complement to his own friendship with Ralph. And now that this rapport seems entirely unlikely, Danny recognizes the strength of his hope—his conviction, even—that it might have taken place.

Before starting his tour of the house, Dan urged Phoebe to go and take a long cool bath. "Do you a world of good," he told her. And that presumably is where Phoebe is now, in the bathroom down the hall. (The distance between bathrooms and bedrooms in this house seems an almost deliberate inconvenience.)

As Dan gets into bed, he hears nothing, no sound from anywhere. Outside the window the air is motionless, still; the river is soundless, slow. And although he knows that in a few minutes Phoebe will be there with him, Danny experiences a solitude that seems entire, and final.

And then, around midnight, everything breaks. Brilliant flashes of lightning split open the sky, thunder roars—a sound of huge rocks falling down a mountainside. Slits of light, crashing noise.

Entirely awake, and a little scared, Phoebe abruptly remembers Maria this morning as she talked about thunderstorms in Maine. "Actually, I'd be quite terrified, I always used to be" is what Maria said.

To Dan, who is much less fully awake (he seemed to have trouble going to sleep at all), Phoebe whispers, "I'm just going down to see if Maria's all right."

Slipping into her sandals, pulling on her light cotton robe—in the new blessed cool!—Phoebe begins to feel her way down the narrow, pine-smelling hall to Maria's room at the end, the room nearest the river.

Seeing no light beneath the door, she hesitates, but then very gently she knocks, at the same time saying firmly and loudly enough to be heard across the thunder crashes, "It's Phoebe."

For a moment there is no response at all; then some faint sound comes from Maria that Phoebe chooses to interpret as assent.

Entering, she sees Maria upright in bed, sitting erect but pressed back, braced against the headboard. "Oh" is all she says to Phoebe.

Coming over to stand beside her, Phoebe asks, "Should I turn the light on?" and she reaches toward the bedside lamp, on its table.

Maria stops her, crying, "Electricity—don't!"

Recognizing true panic, Phoebe quietly tells her, "I'll just stay here for a minute, if you don't mind."

In the strange half-light between crashes, Maria reaches for her hand. She says, "Thank you," and can just be seen to smile before quickly releasing Phoebe.

Outside, a heavy pounding rain has now begun, but the thunderstorm seems suddenly to be over; there is only the hard drumbeat of rain on the shingled roof, the thud of water on windowpanes.

Phoebe pulls the small bentwood chair from Maria's desk over to the bed, and sits down.

Maria says, "It was good of you to remember."

"I was a little scared," admits Phoebe.

"The thing about prison," Maria takes this up as though prison had just then been under discussion, "is that they do everything to wreck your mind. 'Mind-fuck,' some of the younger women called it." A faint, tight smile. "But they do. Rushing you all the time. Starting you in to do something, and then right away it's over. Even eating, even that horrible food I never got to finish. And they mix up everyone's mail so you think it must be on purpose. And the noise. Radios. And people smoking."

"Jesus" is all Phoebe can manage to say.

Maria is leaning forward now, her eyes luminous, deep, immense. "At my age," she says. "I mean, I often wonder where my mind is going anyway, without all that."

"That's frightful. Terrible."

"Well, it was terrible. I didn't want to admit it to myself. I got just so plain scared. The truth is I'm still scared."

"Well, of course. Anyone is scared of jail. I'm not even sure I could do it."

Maria's gaze in the semi-dark seems to take all of Phoebe in. "I think you would if you had to, or thought you had to," she says.

"I hope so."

"But I'm worried about going back there," Maria tells her. "If for some reason I had to. Again."

At that moment, however, a new sound has begun, just audible through the steady, heavy rain. And lights can be seen to approach the house, very slowly.

Lights from a car, now visible to them both. Unnecessarily, Phoebe announces, "Someone's coming. A small sports car. Whoever—?"

"It must be Ralph," says Maria, smiling. And she exclaims, "Oh! I do think things will be better now. It's even got cool, do you feel it?" But in an anxious way her face still searches Phoebe's. "Do you want to turn on the light?"

Phoebe reaches to touch Maria's hand, very quickly, lightly—before she pushes the switch.

Standing up, then, in the sudden brightness, smiling, as Phoebe moves toward the door she turns back to Maria; she tells her, "I'll get Danny. We'll go make sandwiches—some tea? Poor Ralph, all that driving. We'll celebrate!"

"For to cook with acorn, one must create a relationship with the tree; one must understand the ground which nourishes the fruit so lovingly"

Bev Ortiz, from *It Will Live Forever*

Bev Ortiz is a naturalist and anthropologist currently pursuing a doctorate at the University of California, Berkeley. Ortiz coordinates special cultural workshops for the East Bay Regional Parks system, and for many years she has been a contributor to the quarterly magazine News from Native California.

This selection from Ortiz's It Will Live Forever: Traditional Yosemite Indian Acorn Preparation *discusses Julia Parker, an Indian woman who has dedicated her life to raising awareness and continuing the traditions of the Sierra Nevada indigenous population.*

It requires deep commitment to practice the cultural tradition of one's ancestors, especially in a world determined to crush that tradition. Julia Parker has that commitment. She has dedicated her life to continuing the ways of both her husband's ancestors and those of her own Kashia Pomo people.

Julia expressed the force behind that commitment in 1984 when she said, "My thanks and respect are to the Miwok, Paiute, Pomo and Mono elders, Mono Lake Paiute and older people who have given me the knowledge and courage to try to carry on the true story needed in today's societies, especially for our children, grandchildren and others who are yet to be born."

Julia wants the ways of the old people to never be forgotten. It is a gift they gave her, a gift she has cherished long and dear, and such gifts must be shared. They remain to touch a place deep within the spirit of the earth and the human soul; they reveal our responsibility to the earth from which they spring so kindly. For to cook with acorn, one must create a relationship with the tree; one must understand the ground which nourishes the fruit so lovingly.

These gifts brought a sense of self and the world to Julia. The road she took to receiving them was long and tough, for she has lived in that time of great change when the old ways have been difficult to continue.

Born in the redwood hill country of Graton in Sonoma County in 1929, Julia grew up moving from tent camp to tent camp with her parents as they followed the crops, picking fruit and hops for a living. Her grandmother, whom she remembers singing Indian songs and taking her out to pick clover from beneath some trees, lived with the family.

She has few recollections of these times. One vivid winter memory recalls the sound of the doorbell. When the family went to the door, they found a box of oranges left by the Salvation Army or Red Cross.

> I'll never forget that big box of oranges there sitting on that porch. And, geeee they tasted so good! Even today now I still buy boxes of oranges for my family. My grandchildren. And children.

These memories of childhood are clouded by tragedy. When Julia was only five or six, her father died. Not long after, Julia's mother, Lilly Pete, died at age 24. Lily left behind five children: Julia, the eldest; Mary Lou, a year younger; two sons, Frank and Billy; and an infant daughter, Madelaine, who was less than three months old at the time of Lilly's death.

Shortly after this, somehow or other, local social welfare authorities found the children, perhaps through their school. Separated by social welfare from their grandmother, it was unlikely the children could remain together. Children in large families usually went into different foster homes; if kept together, they ended up in orphanages.

But one of the children had tuberculosis, and a nurse was found to care for them as a foster parent. The Santa Rosa house in which this German foster mother raised them is gone now, but Julia still remembers the sleeping porch where five beds were lined up for the children. It was like sleeping out-of-doors; most of the time the porch was open, but when it was cold or rained the canvas "windows" around the porch were rolled down.

One day, Julia's foster mother loaded the children into the car and told them the first church they came to would be theirs. It turned out to be the Christian Missionary Alliance Church. Julia thought about becoming a missionary across the ocean.

The children helped earn money at odd jobs; their foster mother dropped them off at a location where a truck would pick them up and take them to work hoeing local farm fields. They also picked prunes and helped with chores at their new home, which had a family orchard, garden, and cows. In addition to milking cows, Julia cared for 50 chicks she won at the County Fair. She fed them every day, gathered their eggs, and butchered them.

Occasionally, their foster mother solicited items for the children. At Christmas time, she introduced her "poor, little orphan Indians" at various service club parties, where they received big bagfuls of oranges, nuts, and other foods. Once, as each child came to receive a gift, a club member complained that too much was going to one family. However, their foster mother stood her ground, saying they deserved a gift and were each going to get one....

It was during the eighth grade that Julia was sent to the Bureau of Indian Affairs' Stewart Indian School in Carson City, Nevada, which she came to know as Boss Indians Around School. Her sisters and brothers were also sent.

> I was just getting ready to learn the Constitution of the United States, and your rules and all that, you know. And so they took us, and when I went to the Indian school, they didn't even teach that in school. They didn't teach us our rights or anything like that...So it's been kind of a long struggle, when I think about what I do.

The years at Indian school assailed the pride Julia's foster mother had given her. The philosophy at Stewart was to teach students, "'Don't be Indian. Don't sit on the ground. Don't eat acorn.' The thought is to get you away from that so you could mix in, get by in the cities, assimilate." School days here brought the pain of being called a "dirty Indian."

At Stewart, Julia went to school with about 350 Indian students from all over, between four and twenty-three years old. Perhaps the saddest part of these years was Julia's separation from her siblings. Julia, her sisters, and brothers had been together in their foster home, but now ate and lived separately. Frank and Billy lived in the small boys' dorm, Madelaine in the small girls' dorm, Mary Lou and Julia in the same big girls' dorm area, but in different buildings. As the oldest, Julia felt a responsibility to take care of the other children. She worried about the little ones especially, afraid they were sad like her and crying from loneliness, so she visited them whenever she could.

While it was an unhappy experience, the school offered a certain security, a place to stay and something to eat. There were dances, parties, and parades to organize, and Julia liked to help. In fact, by her own admission, she was "a live wire."

After meeting the school nurse and being inspired by her foster mother's occupation, Julia thought she'd like to go into nursing and wear a tidy uniform. She even spent one session of school working in the hospital, bandaging and caring for the children that came in. Since she enjoyed working with her hands and liked to help people, Julia thought of being a surgical nurse. But it was not to be.

Although Julia excelled in her classes—she met her future husband Ralph Parker in classes for "A" students they attended together—educational opportunities at the school were limited. Julia still wonders what she and other students could have become had the classes been more rigorous.

> Had we had that higher English and Math and all that we'd be doctors, lawyers. But who knows what's going to happen.
>
> And most of the kids that graduated from that class all managed to survive in different vocations. The girls went on to get married. Some went to nursing school and some were secretaries. And a lot of them were employed by the school itself. So then, when you went back to school, there you'd see somebody as a matron or cook. The kitchen person and all that. If I had gone back there, I probably would have been a matron.

The school was oriented toward vocational training. As one of Julia's friends put it, "You were the housecleaners of the world." And as Julia herself explained, "You were a person who was just a servant."

Students attended church regularly and received four hours a day of training in the various basics—reading, writing and arithmetic. For the boys, the other time was devoted to farming, carpentry, auto mechanics, electrical, and plumbing classes. For the girls, there was home economics, and Julia found herself in the kitchen peeling potatoes or scrubbing pots, working in the bakery, sewing, or darning socks.

The children were taught to be immaculate. Matrons oversaw their work, inspecting dresser drawers for properly folded clothes and laundry sacks to make sure clothes had been washed. Hardwood floors were scrubbed with solvent on hands and knees....

Although the students were forbidden to do "Indian things," Julia was among a group of children who hid way out on campus during weekend afternoons and did "Indian things" anyway. In these small groups Julia was exposed for the first time to Paiute songs and language, as well as to traditions of other Indian people.

Unlike some of the children, Julia was poor and had no home to return to in summertime. So she stayed and worked, making what money she could, and sharing that money with her siblings. Julia also worked at various jobs throughout the school year.

She worked at the employees' club, kitchen, laundry, and office. She set tables, baked bread, cooked, sorted mail, and delivered it. She cleaned employees' houses. In the summers, she was bussed to work at farms near Reno or motels around Lake Tahoe. While working in homes, some of her shyness around strangers started to leave.

Julia bought a coat with part of her wages. Although the government issued "these old, funny coats which we'd love to have now, you know, 'cause they're all in," Julia was too proud to wear it, and went to work so she could get her own.

In 1947, the summer before her graduation, Julia came to the Yosemite home of her future husband to work in the laundry. After graduation, she returned and continued working. She sent some of the money she earned (wages were 50 to 75 cents an hour) to her siblings. She also bought them shoes and other necessities.

At Yosemite, Julia began a journey of raising a family and learning about the "old ways." At Yosemite, she had a home. Julia had been scheduled to go to a secretarial school in Oakland before moving, but her new home felt safe and secure. There were plenty of employment opportunities, and one didn't risk the chance of ending up wandering city streets. She never wanted to leave.

The years since Julia came to Yosemite have passed quickly. "I've been here 42 years," she said one day in 1990 with a laugh. "I feel like Half Dome up there! A little gray on top and a little wrinkled."

As part of the Parker family, Julia became like a granddaughter to Ralph's grandmother, Lucy Tom Parker Telles. Grandmother Lucy, or simply "Grandmother" as Julia came to call her, inspired in Julia a love for the old ways, especially a love for acorn. Julia's involvement with acorn is inseparable from Lucy, as Lucy's involvement was inseparable from her own past.

Lucy was the daughter of Bridgeport Tom (Mono Lake Paiute), who was born about 1850 and died in 1936, and Louisa Sam Tom (Yosemite

Miwok/Paiute), who also was reportedly born before 1851. Raised with strong ties to Yosemite's past, but ever a woman of the present, Lucy was a traditionalist who blended past and present with creativity.

She still made acorn the old way, with baskets, mortar, pestle, and cooking stones, but there were some changes. Cloth covered the leaching basin and metal pails replaced some of the baskets. Utilitarian baskets were made the old way, but Lucy, who was born about 1880, was among those who altered the made-for-sale basketry of her ancestors.

Among Lucy's innovations in the latter were two-color designs, "snap-in-place" lidded tops, and some completely new patterns, such as butterflies and flowers. She also made baskets of extraordinary size. One, which was three feet wide and over nineteen inches high, took four years to complete. It was exhibited at the 1939 Golden Gate International Exposition.

From the 1930s until her death in 1955, Lucy demonstrated beadwork and basketry behind the Yosemite visitor center. The money she earned by selling baskets and beadwork to tourists was an essential part of the family income. As winter approached, it helped to purchase essentials, including about 100 pounds of potatoes, 100 pounds of flour, and 100 pounds of beans. Any deer the men successfully hunted were made into jerky....

Lucy Tom Parker Telles was married twice. Her first marriage was to Jack Parker (Paiute), with whom she had two sons, David and Lloyd, who was the father of Julia's husband, Ralph. Tragically, Jack died when Lloyd was only four years old. Twelve years later Lucy married John Telles (Mexican-American from Texas), with whom she had another son, Johnny, Jr., in 1922. She also had a daughter, Hazel.

John Telles worked for Curry Company, the park concessionaire at that time, as a houseman and janitor. Because of his work, John brought home cast-off clothing and linens, from which Lucy sewed quilts and coats. Sometimes he brought acorns home.

At various times, Lucy and John shared their home with their children and grandchildren. Family members also lived in other nearby homes. The houses were in a circular cluster of thirteen three-room cabins built by the Park Service and known as the "Indian Village." The upper exterior of each house was shingle-sided, the lower vertical board and batten. The roofs were double-pitched.

Previously, the Yosemite Miwok/Paiute lived at an old village site near the present-day hospital. The housing there consisted of canvas-covered framework. The Park Service denied requests to make improvements to these houses and instead moved the people to the Indian Village. Here, Lucy chose a house above the floodplain.

A desire to segregate seems to have governed the location of the Indian Village, driven by the same prejudice that caused Indians to be buried in a separate area of Yosemite Valley's "pioneer graveyard," away from non-Indians. Built in the mid '30s and destroyed in the late '60s (one house moved to the park corporation yard still stands), the Village kept Yosemite's native people away from other residents and most tourists. Sometimes tour bus guides would point out the Indian children and announce that they might "do a little dance." After the children made the mock dance that was expected of them, the tourists would throw them money.

The new houses had two nine by twelve-foot bedrooms and a nine by sixteen-foot dining/kitchen area with cold running water. Water was heated by woodstove. A central restroom/shower facility was shared by everyone.

When Julia first came to work in Yosemite in 1947, she lived in one of these houses with her future father-in-law, Lloyd Parker, and his niece. Ralph's mother had died when he was four, so Lucy had raised him. Traditional rules dictated that a wife did not speak to her father-in-law for a while after marrying, so the newlyweds moved into John and Lucy's home for about a year.

Shortly after the birth of their first child in 1949, Julia and Ralph moved into their own Indian Village home. Every two weeks $12, a sizeable portion of their income, was taken out of Ralph's paycheck for rent, but it was manageable since there was no electricity or telephone bill, and they didn't have a car. By 1963, they would have a new, larger home made by putting two Village cabins together.

Julia never left Yosemite during her first few years in the Valley, not even to shop. She was concerned about the children, and necessities could be bought through the Montgomery Ward catalogue. Members of the Tabucco family, who had a grocery store in Mariposa, would periodically come to sell appliances. The Watkins man came with spices to sell the women for their cakes and cookies, and Lifesavers candies to give to the children.

The Kirby man even came to sell vacuums. Although there were no rugs to vacuum, Julia remembers that if one person bought a vacuum, everyone did, and these were on sale for $75. So they opened up a charge account and paid off their bill at $5 a month.

When her husband was away working, Julia would pack some sandwiches and take the children to a beach on the Merced River to practice diving off a rock and swimming. As the newest member of the Telles' extended family, she also spent much of her time helping Lucy and her granddaughter Helen with family chores. There was always a lot of work to be done providing for everyone's needs. Many a time four and five long lines of drying, laundered shirts stretched between the pine trees.

Initially, Lucy did all the laundry using a washboard propped inside a galvanized tub. Later, the boys purchased a wringer machine. Still later, a machine complete with spinner was purchased, but Lucy never liked it. Because there were so many shirts to wash, it wouldn't work half the time.

Julia and Helen helped with the ironing and, while working in the park laundry, they brought the family wash with them to clean and iron on their lunch hour, insuring that the men of the house had spic, span, and starched shirts to wear.

With so many people to feed, stew was a mainstay of everyone's diet. Once the boys encouraged Julia to ask Lucy to buy steak for them. Lucy agreed, but being a thrifty and fair-minded woman, she cut the steak into chunks to make a stew for everyone. The boys were disappointed.

There was always a pot of good, rich coffee brewing on the Telles stove in anticipation of company. From her home across the way, Julia could see company arrive. Immediately, she headed over to help, for no matter what time of day company came, Lucy would prepare a meal to feed her guests before the visiting commenced.

Except in poor weather, Lucy spent most of her time out-of-doors next to her house, by the family firepit where she heated the stones needed to cook her acorn. Next to this rock-ringed campfire circle was a grill made by mounting a flat cast-iron slab on rocks, close to the ground. Here Lucy could be found almost every day by eight in the morning, having her coffee, weaving a basket, or making stew, yeast bread, tortillas, and other food.

A community feeling permeated the Indian Village. On weekends people gathered to share big potluck meals. They sat around a bonfire and sang "49er songs" backed by guitar, banjos, and violins. On birthdays, or if there was a death, people came from all over.

When someone passed on, people were invited to a "cry." Everyone congregated at the home of a relative of the deceased to show respect.

Five men stood and sang traditional songs throughout the night. Men and women danced to the *a cappella* singing while holding dresses, shoes, and other articles that belonged to the deceased. Their feet made a step and slide motion as they danced in a circle around a bonfire, breaking every so often to rest and eat before proceeding anew.

Everyone participated. Although Julia wasn't sure what to expect at her first cry, she found out she didn't need to be taught what to do. "You just participate," she said. When the sun came up, the person's clothes and other personal belongings were thrown into the fire and burned.

The mourning songs brought Julia's mind back many years. She saw her grandmother sitting near a fire burning clothes and realized the songs she recalled her grandmother singing were songs of mourning for Julia's father.

Despite the cries, Julia's memories of the Indian Village are good. They include the sight and smell of huge sheetcakes, oatmeal cookies, and raisin cookies Lucy baked to perfection. And she remembers Lucy making acorn. Acorn was not an everyday food for Lucy, but something she made for special occasions; everyone in the community was invited to share in its goodness.

Clear memories remain of Lucy as a woman in her 70s, climbing to the top of a rock nearly 17 feet high to pound acorn—a rock from which Lucy could see everything that was going on, but not be seen herself. Today, walking past that rock brings tearful memories to Julia. Lucy died in 1955, but Julia can still recall the sound made by the rock as Lucy pounded. Every rock makes a distinctive sound, and this one resonates through Julia's mind.

Memories come flooding in at unexpected times. Helping to roll dough to make frybread for a community gathering once sparked the memory of a lesson that nothing should be wasted. The lesson came when Julia was making yeast bread:

> Lucy would never allow me to leave any flour in the pan. Once, I was rolling it and said I'm through. And she said, "No you're not. Look at all that flour. You're wasting it." So she showed me how to get all that flour off of that pot...You don't waste anything.

Lucy Telles was compassionate and devoted. She reminded Julia of her mother and served as inspiration for Julia in raising her own family and carrying on with acorn making.

> She was a busy lady, and I guess you might say I used her as a role model. That woman was up at the crack of dawn cooking, washing,

and making her own [yeast] bread.

Now Julia works in the Yosemite Indian Museum surrounded by these memories. Photographs of Lucy and other elders who have influenced Julia are mounted on the museum wall. Glass cases contain baskets made by Lucy and the women who came to visit at Lucy's house all those years ago. Behind the museum, in the same area where Lucy once demonstrated basketry and beadwork, Julia is among those who have been hired by the Park Service to make acorn for park visitors to taste.

In the museum, Julia sits on a low platform, talking to visitors while using some traditional skill or another: making a basket, a netted bag of natural fiber, a miniature doll, all following Indian tradition and the dictates of Julia's own creativity. There is an endless stream of people through the museum, but Julia is unflappable.

Today Julia's words flow easily, without self-consciousness, as she explains Yosemite Miwok/Paiute culture to museum visitors, but this was not always so. There was a time when she felt intimidated by lack of education. Now, years later, she patiently answers every question, no matter how out of context, with grace and humor....

To understand early-day methods of making acorn, one must in turn understand the baskets. While few people cook acorn with baskets today—it simply isn't practical—baskets were essential tools in earlier days, and they were an integral part of the people's daily life.

An average old-time Central California Indian household had some 20 different types of baskets which served a variety of utilitarian functions, including food gathering, storage, processing, cooking, and serving; cradling babies; general storage; animal trapping; and carrying wood and other items. They were also given as gifts.

To learn basketry, Julia first consulted library books, but they weren't of any help, so she turned to the well-known basket makers in the area. She learned in the traditional way, by quietly watching and listening to them. Just as the old ways take time and patience, so does the learning, which occurs a little at a time. The teachers know how serious their student is by how well she perseveres through the tests of learning.

Julia's path took her to Mono Lake Paiute weaver Minnie Mike, her sister Carrie Bethel, their half sister Sadie McGowan, and Lula Hess. It took her to Tina Charlie (Mono Lake Paiute), a woman in her 80s who spoke no English, so Julia's Miwok- and Paiute-speaking father-in-law acted as an interpreter. She also went to Nellie Charlie, Tina's sister, and Ida Bishop (Northfork Mono).

The "ladies" taught Julia how to know when the willow used in the baskets was right for gathering. They showed her how to split it into sewing strands for Paiute-style baskets. The willow was difficult to work with but, as Julia learned, "If you can master willow, you can master anything."...

Now, Julia can look at a rod of the right kind of willow and see baskets in it. Small willow rods become little acorn mush boilers in her mind. Big willow rods become big mush boilers. And when she looks at someone else's basket, she has respect for the hands that worked on it, a knowledge that has come from quietly listening, watching, and learning to shape her own baskets out of the basket plants.

Julia works patiently, gathering each plant in the proper season, often from the traditional places revealed to her by Lucy Telles. In the fall she travels to Mono Lake for willow shoots. She trades for sedge from the Northfork Mono. She cuts her redbud in the winter on the lower Merced River, and she finds bracken fern rhizomes in the late summer. Then she takes the plants, cleans and stores them for at least six months, resoaks and reworks them to the proper size, and begins to weave.

And always, she works with gratitude for the elders. As Julia has stated, "I owe my skill and knowledge given to me by my basket maker friends; the working, and making friends with the willow, sedge, grasses, and redbud." Her goal is to give back to the people what the grandmothers gave to her.

The lessons taught by the elders remain firm in Julia's mind: "Gather willow when the leaves turn yellow." "Scrape the willow till it sings to you." "Borrow, don't steal, the way of fellow basket maker friends." "Don't forget old way, Julia." "Take from the earth and say please." "Give back to the earth and say thank you." "Listen to the basket makers who have gone before you."

Julia's baskets have travelled to such distant places as the Smithsonian Institution in Washington, D.C., and Oslo, Norway. And on March 6, 1983, Julia had the honor of presenting England's Queen Elizabeth II with a basket which represented untold hours of her dedicated labor. The basket is now displayed in the queen's museum.

Julia made her presentation to the queen in the grand style of an ambassador, dressed in the ceremonial finery worn by Yosemite people for generations—a pale blue, late 1800s-style dress hand-stitched by

Julia, a belt decorated with abalone pendants, clamshell disk bead and trade bead necklaces, and a headband with abalone pendants. At her side, she had granddaughter Tisina, age six.

This moment was a long time coming. When Julia first started working as a demonstrator in 1960, a ranger introduced her to the public.

> And he'd always say, "Well Julia is out there in the back...She'll answer your questions, if you ask." People would come out there. And I wouldn't say too much. And then they'd ask me something. Then I'd have to talk, because it was part of my job. So the last time he came, I said to him, "Remember when I used to hide behind my basket?" And he laughed.

Initially, the job as demonstrator was two hours in the morning and two in the afternoon, so Julia also worked at the Ahwahnee Hotel gift shop.

> I was the first Native American girl to work in the Ahwahnee—of any color to work in the Ahwahnee. We had to be dressed up in suits and everything, you know. So at one time I was well suited...
>
> But anyway, you stand up there, and she [the supervisor] didn't want me to work behind the counter. And so she'd put me in the corner where all the Indian things were. So I just had to stand there... like the wooden Indian; just stand there and answer questions about baskets, and things, and all that.

One day, when an employee was absent, Julia was finally trained at the register. Because she knew the product, sales were good, and Yosemite Park and Curry Company management decided to open an Indian store, the Pohono shop, with an inventory that was half composed of park mementos. Julia agreed to manage it on the condition that her staff would be Indian.

In making this request, Julia was remembering a conversation with a young woman who was among those bussed from Sherman Institute Indian School to work in Yosemite Valley. Although qualified to do computer and secretarial work, the woman could only get work as a maid. Julia recalls telling her, "I think that they think that all you girls are just housecleaners." Now Julia could do something about it. Julia taught herself to balance the day's receipts and order inventory by studying previous ledger books. The young women needed no training in selling and keeping the shop clean. In fact, Julia learned a lot by listening to each one talk about the products of her own cultural area.

Despite the good work everyone did, Julia still could not get full-time employment at the shop, so when she was offered a full-time, summer seasonal position as a demonstrator, she took it.

> And I said, "Okay. I would rather do this over here." So I didn't work for Curry anymore. See it was—what you had in those days, you had to say, "I want to do it" or, you know, they molded you. You're a housecleaner. And there's nothing wrong with that. And if I retire, I mean that's what I'll do. I'll go clean and wash dishes or something, because I love to make things clean and neat.

Looking back on her years of becoming a demonstrator and learning basketry, Julia muses that perhaps it was her own roots she was seeking in the willows. She always loved to work with her hands, whether sewing, cooking, or cleaning. Through the baskets and her work as a cultural demonstrator, she was not only using her hands, but she was coming home to her own Indian heritage.

"At the bottom the rusty brown water exploded upward in a hellish maelstrom, filling the canyon with an unearthly rumble"

Jordan Fisher Smith, from *Nature Noir*

Jordan Fisher Smith worked as a park ranger for more than twenty years, including on the American River in the central Sierra Nevada. Nature Noir: A Park Ranger's Patrol in the Sierra (2005), Smith's first book, recounts his American River experiences. Since 1965, the river canyon has been set aside for construction of the still-unbuilt Auburn Dam, designed to protect Sacramento—the U.S. city considered most in danger of catastrophic flooding.

In this selection, Smith describes the river, swollen by a massive nine-day storm in February 1986. It was some of the heaviest rainfall in Sierra history, and other California rivers also suffered levee breaks and widespread flooding. These 1986 floods resulted in thirteen deaths, 50,000 people evacuated, and $400 million in property damage.

On Saturday, February 8, [1986,] as was their routine on winter weekend mornings, the rangers gathered at the top of the dirt road down to Mammoth Bar. Mammoth was a quarter-mile-long beach on the Middle Fork, about a mile upstream from the Confluence. In the laissez-faire regime of the Bureau prior to the rangers' arrival in 1977, it had become popular with off-road motorcyclists, and the canyon wall above it was now covered with the red gouges of hill climbs, which bled muddy water into the river whenever it rained hard. Under the relentless logic of "It'll all be underwater sometime soon anyway," State Parks could not summon the political will to close it. In fact, over the following years it was expanded. Helpless to defend their ground against this onslaught of off-road vehicles, the rangers exacted increments of revenge in a multitude of small cuts, setting up roadblocks where they stopped every pickup truckload of all-terrain vehicles coming into the area and writing whole books of tickets for offenses such as expired registration and no spark-arresting muffler.

This particular morning, two sheriff's cars came driving down the road. The deputies were looking for three all-terrain vehicles that had just been stolen in town. The rangers volunteered to check the canyon bottom. As so often happened, while looking for one thing, they found another. Down at the river they heard yells for help, and looking across the water, they saw a stranded climber hanging from a cliff on the other side. Dave Finch and his partner drove to the bridge downstream, crossed the river, and made their way up to rescue the stranded man. Later that night one of the sheriff's deputies, a young reserve by the name of Tim Ruggles, was killed when a patrol car driven by his partner skidded off the road and hit an oak tree as they were responding to back up another unit on a theft call.

The next morning the rangers were back at Mammoth Bar, running off-road vehicle license checks on the radio and eating doughnuts and cinnamon twists from Hilda's Pastries in Auburn off napkins on the hoods of their trucks. And again the comfort of their routine was disrupted, when a man named John Carta and several associates towed a trailer onto the middle of the Foresthill Bridge. On the trailer were a specially constructed ramp and a motorcycle. Carta's accomplices set up flares to stop traffic, deployed the ramp, the motorcycle, and two men with video cameras, and situated a getaway car at a trailhead in the canyon bottom. Carta donned a parachute, snugged the harness, mounted the motorcycle, and accelerated up the ramp and over the bridge railing into thin air.

Airborne, Carta pushed away from the motorcycle and pulled the ripcord. His main canopy opened with a crack and a jerk, and he drifted sideways, passing over the live oaks and gray pines as the motorcycle tumbled away from him. It landed on the canyon bottom with a distant metallic crash, a tinkle of flying parts, and a spray of oil and gasoline. The sound drifted up to Carta, mixed with the whisper of the river, as he rode his canopy and a happy wave of adrenaline, tugging the control lines toward a safe landing on the slope below him.

Someone reported the jump to the Sheriff's Department, the sheriff's dispatcher called State Parks, and two rangers were rolled from Mammoth Bar. Arriving at the big bridge at twenty minutes before noon, one of them recorded the identification numbers from the twisted wreck of the 1983 Yamaha at the bottom of the canyon. The other checked the surrounding area for clues and soon found the trailer and its ramp stashed nearby on Lake Clementine Road. The trailer was registered to Carta. Within a few hours one of the cameramen sold his tape to a television station, and there was no doubt who the daredevil was.

That Monday, on the sixteenth floor of the Resources Building, a serpentinite-green monolith in Sacramento housing the headquarters of the State Department of Water Resources, a meteorologist by the name of Bill Mork pulled the morning weather charts off the old wet-process plotter and with growing concern showed them to a fellow forecaster, Curt Schmutte.

There was something jarringly familiar to both men about the pattern, and Schmutte went looking for the old weather maps from the Christmas storm of 1964—a storm so warm it rained at ten thousand feet above sea level in the Sierra, causing flooding that killed twenty-four people—and the Christmas storm of 1955, which flooded a hundred thousand acres and killed sixty-four. When Schmutte returned, the two men spread the old weather maps out next to the new ones, and after they finished looking at them, Mork picked up the phone and called the National Weather Service's lead forecaster in Redwood City. Comparing notes, the state and federal men agreed: There was something to worry about.

By Tuesday there were high, thin clouds over the American River canyons. The upper-level charts from the National Weather Service showed that a mass of high pressure that had been blocking storms from entering California since February 5 had split into two pieces. A strong westerly flow of warm, moist air off the tropical Pacific had broken through the high in two branches. One branch took a meandering route around the northern remnant of the blocking high through the Gulf of Alaska, where it was chilled, and then flowed south again. The southern branch was charging east toward California through the breech between the two masses of high pressure. Colliding, the two branches formed a deadly pattern, because warm, moist air, when suddenly cooled, can no longer hold its moisture and drops it quickly as rain. The storm would hit the ramp of the Sierra Nevada at an almost perfect right angle, lifting it more quickly than if the storm had struck the mountains at an oblique. The quick push upward into colder regions of the higher atmosphere would increase the storm's violence, as moisture was suddenly wrung out of it over the mountains.

That morning the two rangers who'd written up Carta's jump hiked back up under the Foresthill Bridge to check on his smashed motorcycle.

The county sheriff had taken an interest in Carta and planned to remove the motorcycle as evidence. But the rangers found it gone, and when he learned of this later in the day, the sheriff was angry. There had now been at least eleven suicides from the bridge, he told a reporter from the *Auburn Journal*, and all sorts of people were making a hobby out of leaping from it on hang gliders and parachutes. He had no intention of allowing the bridge to become a destination for every crazy person who wished to risk his life, or end it. But, of course, this had already happened.

The storm set in on Wednesday, and Blue Canyon, in the mountains east of Auburn, got three and a half inches of rain. That evening a rosary was recited for Deputy Tim Ruggles, and the rain beat down on the roof of the funeral home where he was laid out, and on the mourners' umbrellas as they arrived. At ten the next morning Sheriff Nunes attended Ruggles's burial. Ruggles had been twenty-three. The grave was filled, and that afternoon the rain beat down upon the fresh mound of earth under a formless sheet of gray sky, and dusk fell early on Auburn. The town got an inch and a third that day.

By Thursday it was raining as if the world was ending. That day a request for a warrant for the arrest of John Carta made its way from the Auburn offices of Sheriff Nunes, across a wet lawn and a parking lot to the offices of District Attorney Jack Shelley, a big, red-faced man in suspenders. By this time the clay soils of the hills around the American River were saturated and every drop was running off into the river. At two-thirty that afternoon enough water was going down the North Fork alone to fill a container the size of a football field with six feet of water in less than a minute. By Friday that figure doubled; by Saturday it tripled.

By Sunday, aircraft over the Pacific Ocean were reporting jetstream winds of 210 miles per hour at thirty-five thousand feet, and airline passengers from Hawaii were arriving early at mainland airports. Satellite photos showed the normally spiral patterns of clouds coming in off the ocean straightening out into a sort of gun barrel. The gun was loaded with moisture and pointed right at the American River. That day Blue Canyon got over five inches of rain; on Monday it was eight and a half. Now enough water was going down the North Fork to fill that football-field-sized container with a foot of water in less than a second. By afternoon, every route over the Sierra Nevada was closed by weather; huge landslides covered all four lanes of Interstate 80, both lanes of State Route 50, and the main transcontinental railway tracks. For the next couple of days, the park rangers could do little but watch the water rise behind the cofferdam.

By the time of Tim Ruggles's burial, the tunnel around the foundations of the Auburn Dam had reached capacity. As the water backed up behind the cofferdam, the tunnel went under, and big slick logs began racing in crazy circles around an ugly suck hole in the brown water, like the kind that forms over a bathtub drain, but big enough to swallow a cement truck. By Saturday, February 15, one of the rangers recorded on his patrol log that the water behind the cofferdam had reached the Highway 49 Bridge and was rising toward the bridge deck. Just upstream in the Middle Fork canyon a saturated cliff face supporting the Old Foresthill Road gave way, and the road slid several hundred feet down the canyon wall into the river.

Over the weekend no one had emptied the rain gauge at the Forest Service ranger station in Foresthill. By Monday it registered eleven inches of rain. Before dawn that day the deck of the 49 Bridge went under, and at five-thirty that morning Virgil H. Morehouse of Minden, Nevada, became the last person to try—and the first to fail—to cross it.

With his three children in his two-year-old Buick sedan, Morehouse set out across the flooded bridge from the east side, but the vehicle soon stalled. He tried the doors, but the water pressure from outside would not allow him to open them. He tried to roll down the electric windows, but they weren't responding to their switches. In a growing panic, Morehouse eventually managed to break a window and, towing his children, wallowed to safety along the flooded bridge deck to the Auburn side, where he was assisted ashore by highway patrol officers who had been closing the road. Within a few hours two of the rangers drove back down Highway 49 to find the bridges at the Confluence completely submerged. Morehouse's Buick was nowhere to be seen. When the waters receded on Tuesday, the car was found sitting right side up in the river bottom about 200 feet downstream of the 49 Bridge. Missing from it was Morehouse's Ruger Single-Six .357, a big hog-leg of a single-action cowboy gun that was by far the most popular handgun in the American River canyons at that time.

During the Gold Rush, makeshift towns had appeared along the gravel bars in the bottoms of the American River canyons, providing a range of services to the thousands of men who were excavating the riverbed for gold. By the 1860s most had been washed away at least once by floods, and eventually all were abandoned. The surviving towns of that era are generally located on higher ground, mostly along smaller tributaries. The town of Auburn is one of these. Now the county seat of Placer County, it was established as a mining camp in the spring of 1848 after the discovery of gold in Auburn Ravine Creek. But by 1986 the creek had been paved over to make room for parking, and it now passed ignobly beneath the center of Auburn's historic district in a storm drain.

As the storm gathered strength, the creek got too big for its conduit. A dozen amateur actors were rehearsing a melodrama at the Opera House Dinner Theater in Auburn's Old Town when the creek burst through the back of the building and the stage exploded into the seating area. From there the water picked up tables and chairs and carried them through the front of the building into the street. Outside, one of the chairs was later found to have been propelled with such force that its leg was embedded in the asphalt. Three actors tried to save the troupe's piano by lifting it onto a pile of debris, but the water soon rose to the height of the bar and they swam to safety. Nearby, the owner of the historic Shanghai Bar and Restaurant tried to keep the creek out of his business by barricading the back door. The water soon found its way through the kitchen window, and he fled to higher ground.

The damage in Auburn was limited to the plaza along the bottom of Auburn Ravine, but where the American River flowed into the flat Central Valley, the situation was far more serious. One residential neighborhood near Sacramento State University is fifteen feet below the waterline of a major flood. In the Natomas Basin on the city's northern edges, the figure is twenty. In 1986, only two things stood between Sacramento and that water: a system of levees begun after the flood of 1850 and improved ever since—usually after they failed—and a single dam, Folsom, about twenty miles east of the city.

If much of the energy behind the construction of Folsom Dam had been generated by fear of flooding, by 1986 the dam was operated by the Bureau of Reclamation, an agency chartered to provide irrigation water, not flood control. At that time, of the reservoir's million-acre-foot capacity, only 400,000 acre-feet of space were normally kept available for flood control. But so far that winter had not been a wet one, and the Bureau had begun hoarding water to fulfill its irrigation contracts with farmers. Thus when the storm began, only three quarters of the usual flood storage capacity was available, or 300,000 acre-feet. Further, although the Bureau had its own weather forecasters, the agency based its decisions on how much water to release from the dam on changes in the lake level, not on their predictions. Thus the Bureau's responses were delayed—even to rain that had already fallen in the mountains but hadn't yet reached the lake.

Monday night the inflow to Folsom hit 200,000 cubic feet per second (CFS), but the Bureau could release only 115,000 CFS from the dam, which was the known capacity of the levees downstream, through Sacramento. And so Folsom Lake rose steadily toward the dam crest.

The deathwatch at the Auburn cofferdam began after midnight Tuesday, February 17. In the predawn hours, engineers from the Bureau set up a video camera along the canyon wall above the dam, intending to learn what they could from its destruction. By five-thirty that morning the sheet of brown water filling the canyon had reached the dam's crest. At dawn the engineers turned on the camera and stood there glumly in the drizzle to witness what would happen. The wind and rain in the canyon bottom had let up, and, looking upstream, the engineers could see a little stream of water trickling over the left side of the dam, reflecting the pale morning sky. The little creek over the dam crest looked peaceful. But the dam was made of earth, and bit by bit the creek excavated a deeper channel for itself, and as it did, its volume increased and the erosion quickened.

It took about three hours for the dam to wash out. In Skyridge, a subdivision of what had been intended to be lake-view homes on the Auburn side of the canyon, people were taking the day off from work to stand on their decks and watch their tax dollars go down the river. Six-packs and bottles of wine showed up. A partylike mood prevailed. After all, this wasn't something you saw every day—a dam failing, one man told a visiting reporter. Beneath them the little creek running down the dam face had become a horseshoe-shaped waterfall that grew steadily, 25, 50, 70, then 100 feet high as portions of the dam collapsed into it. At the bottom the rusty brown water exploded upward in a hellish maelstrom, filling the canyon with an unearthly rumble. There was something strangely beautiful about it—but not for the Bureau engineers. When the erosion finally reached upstream to the lake the dam was holding back, the whole left side of the structure melted in a heroic climax of water and mud, and a hundred thousand acre-feet of stored water roared downstream into Folsom Lake. It was a hundred thousand acre-feet the Bureau hadn't made space for.

"Somewhere, sometime, somebody taught her to question everything—though it might have been a good thing if he'd also taught her to question the act of questioning"

Wallace Stegner, from *Angle of Repose*

Wallace Stegner (1909–1993) was born in Iowa but grew up in a variety of Western mining venues. Dubbed the "Dean of Western Writers," Stegner was an instructor of creative writing at the University of Wisconsin, Harvard University, and Stanford University, and his students included prominent authors such as Larry McMurtry, Ernest Gaines, and Ken Kesey. Stegner's Western upbringing not only influenced and informed his writing but it led to a lifelong interest in the environment: he served as a special assistant to Secretary of the Interior Stewart Udall and was elected to a seat on the Sierra Club Board of Directors.

In 1971, Stegner published Angle of Repose, *which won the Pulitzer Prize for fiction the following year. The novel is based on the letters of Mary Hallock Foote, whose memoir,* A Victorian Gentlewoman in the Far West, *is excerpted in Chapter 3 of this anthology. Some critics claimed that Stegner used uncredited excerpts from Foote's letters, but in the novel's preface, he did obliquely acknowledge her contribution. The main character in* Angle of Repose *is Lyman Ward, a retired historian who is editing the papers of his grandmother Susan Burling Ward, a character based on Foote. In this passage, Ward engages in a debate with his young editorial assistant, Shelly, about communal living and what constitutes a "correct" lifestyle in the Sierra Nevada.*

For several weeks now I have had the sense of something about to come to an end—that old September feeling, left over from school days, of summer passing, vacation nearly done, obligations gathering, books and football in the air. But different now. Then, during prep school and college, and even afterward when teaching tied my life to the known patterns of the school year, there was both regret and anticipation in it. Another fall, another turned page: there was something of jubilee in that annual autumnal beginning, as if last year's mistakes and failures had been wiped clean by summer. But now it is not an ending and a beginning I can look forward to, but only an ending; and I feel that change in the air without exhilaration, with only a heaviness and unwillingness of spirit. With a little effort I could get profoundly depressed.

Part of my uneasiness comes as a direct result of living my grandmother's life for her. For the last few days I have been studying the Xeroxed newspaper stories that finally arrived from the Idaho Historical Society, and though they do straighten out for me some facts that I have never until now understood, they also raise some questions that are disturbing. There is some history that I want not to have happened. I resist the consequences of being Nemesis.

But another part of what obscurely bothers me is the probability that Shelly will be leaving very soon, with consequences to me and to. my routines that I can only contemplate with anxiety. And yet there is a sort of comic relief in Shelly, too. One result of throwing away all the maps of human experience and the guides to conduct that a tradition offers, and flying by the seat of your moral or social pants, is that you fly into situations that are absurd or pitiful, depending on how indulgently one looks at them. My own indulgence is wildly variable. Witness this afternoon.

Through most of the summer Shelly has worked seven days a week, the way I like to work, but the last two weekends she has taken off. I supposed she was getting organized to go back to college, but Ada [Hawkes, Lyman's personal assistant] tells me she has been seeing Rasmussen. "She don't tell me, but I know. Ed saw him over in Nevada City last week, purple pants and all. Honest to John, what she sees in that…What's he hanging around for? What's he want?"

"Maybe he's really fond of her."

But that only got a glare from Ada. She doesn't *want* him to be fond of her.

Nevertheless, neither Ada nor I should expect a girl of twenty to sit in this quiet place very long, working seven days a week for the Hermit of Zodiac Cottage. For reasons best known to herself, she chose to cut away from the Berkeley scene and rusticate herself here. But here she is a stranger to everybody she used to know, including her old schoolmates. They have nothing to offer her, she has nothing to give them except an occasion for a lot of lurid gossip. Probably she *was* the brightest student in Nevada City High, as Ada resentfully says. Somewhere, sometime, somebody taught her to question everything— though it might have been a good thing if he'd also taught her to question the act of questioning. Carried far enough, as far as Shelly's crowd carries it, that can dissolve the ground you stand on. I suppose wisdom could be defined as knowing what you have to accept, and I suppose by that definition she's a long way from wise.

Anyway, this afternoon when I was sitting on the porch after lunch she came in and without a word, with only a prying, challenging sort of look, puckering up her mouth into a rosebud, handed me a sheet of paper. It was mimeographed on both sides, with stick figures and drawings of flowers scattered down its margins—a sheet that might have announced the Memorial Day picnic-and-cleanup of some neighborhood improvement association. I've got it here. It says

MANIFESTO

WE HOLD THESE TRUTHS TO BE SELF EVIDENT TO EVERYBODY EXCEPT GENERALS, INDUSTRIALISTS, POLITICIANS, PROFESSORS, AND OTHER DINOSAURS:

1) That the excretions of the mass media and the obscenities of school education are forms of mind-pollution.
   We believe in meditation, discussion, communion, nature.

2) That possessions, the "my and mine" of this corrupt society, stand between us and a true, clean, liberated vision of the world and ourselves.
   We believe in communality, sharing, giving, using without using up. He is wealthiest who owns nothing and needs nothing.

3) That the acquisitive society acquires and uses women as it acquires and uses other natural resources, turning them into slaves, second-class citizens, and biological factories.
   We believe in the full equality of men and women. Proprietorship has no place in love or in any good thing of the earth.

4) That the acquisitive society begins to pollute and enslave the minds of children in infancy, turning them into dreadful replicas of their parents and thus perpetuating obscenities.

We believe that children are natural creatures close to the earth, and that they should grow up as part of the wild life.

5) That this society with its wars, waste, poisons, ugliness, and hatred of the natural and innocent must be abandoned or destroyed. To cop out is the first act in the cleansing of the spirit.

We believe in free and voluntary communities of the joyous and generous, male and female, either as garden communities in rural places or as garden enclaves in urban centers, the two working together and circulating freely back and forth—a two-way flow of experience, people, money, gentleness, love, and homegrown vegetables.

NOW THEREFORE

We have leased twenty acres of land from the Massachusetts Mining Corporation in North San Juan, California, four miles north of Nevada City on Route 49. We invite there all who believe in people and the earth, to live, study, meditate, flourish, and shed the hangups of corrupted America. We invite men, women, and children to come and begin creating the new sane healthy world within the shell of the old.

What to bring: What you have.
What to do: What you want.
What to pay: What you can.

FREEDOM   MEDITATION   LOVE   SHARING   YOGA

Address: Box 716, Nevada City, California

When I finished the front side and looked up, Shelly was watching me, moodily running a rubber band through her front teeth like dental floss. She said nothing, so I turned the sheet over. On the back were three quotations:

Let the paper remain on the desk
Unwritten, and the book on the shelf unopen'd!
Let the tools remain in the workshop!
Let the money remain unearn'd!
Let the school stand!

312

My call is the call of battle, I nourish active rebellion.
He going with me must go well arm'd,
He going with me goes often with spare diet, poverty,
angry enemies, desertions.

WHITMAN

The practice of meditation, for which one needs only the ground beneath one's feet, wipes out mountains of junk being pumped into the mind by the mass media and supermarket universities. The belief in a serene and generous fulfillment of natural desires destroys ideologies which blind, maim, and repress—and points the way to a kind of community which would amaze 'moralists' and eliminate armies of men who are fighters because they cannot be lovers.

The traditional cultures are in any case doomed, and rather than cling to their good aspects hopelessly it should be remembered that whatever is or ever was in any other culture can be reconstructed from the unconscious, through meditation. In fact, it is my own view that the coming revolution will close the circle and link us in many ways with the most creative aspects of our archaic past. If we are lucky we may eventually arrive at a totally integrated world culture with matrilineal descent, free-form marriage, natural-credit Communist economy, less industry, far less population, and lots more national parks.

GARY SNYDER

Let these be encouraged: Gnostics, hip Marxists, Teilhard de Chardin Catholics, Taoists, Biologists, Witches, Yogins, Bhikkus, Quakers, Sufis, Tibetans, Zens, Shamans, Bushmen, American Indians, Polynesians, Anarchists, Alchemists…All primitive cultures, all communal and ashram movements…Ultimately cities will exist only as joyous tribal gatherings and fairs.

BERKELEY ECOLOGY CENTER

I passed the sheet back.
"Keep it," Shelly said. "I've got more. What do you think?"
"I like the part about the home-grown vegetables."
"Come on!"
"What do you want me to say? OM?"
"Whether it makes *sense* or not."
"It's got plenty of historical precedents."
"What do you mean?"
"Plato," I said. "In his fashion. Sir Thomas More, in his way. Coleridge,

Melville, Samuel Butler, D. H. Lawrence, in their ways. Brook Farm and all the other Fourierist phalansteries. New Harmony, whether under the Rappites or the Owenites. The Icarians. Amana. Homestead. The Mennonites. The Amish. The Hutterites. The Shakers. The United Order of Zion. The Oneida Colony. Especially the Oneida Colony."

"You don't think there's anything in it."

"I didn't say that. I said it had a lot of historical precedents."

"But it makes you smile."

"That was a grimace," I said. "A historical rictus. One aspect of the precedents is that the natural tribal societies are so commonly superstition-ridden, ritual-bound, and warlike, and the utopian ones always fail. Where'd you get this?"

"It was handed to me."

"By whom? Your husband?"

"So to speak." She scowled at me, pulling her lower lip.

"Are you being asked to bring what you have to this joyous tribal gathering?"

Letting go of her lip, she smiled with a look of superiority and penetration, as if she understood my captious skepticism and made allowances for it. "I didn't say." But then the smile faded into a discontented pucker, and she burst out, "If something's wrong with it, tell me what. I've been trying to make up my mind if anything is. It's idealistic, it's for love and gentleness, it's close to nature, it hurts nobody, it's voluntary. I can't see anything wrong with any of that."

"Neither can I. The only trouble is, this commune will be inhabited by and surrounded by members of the human race."

"That sounds pretty cynical."

"Well, I wouldn't want to corrupt you with my cynicism," I said, and shut up.

But she kept after me; she was serious.

"All right," I said, "I'll tell you why I'm dubious. These will be young people in this garden commune, I assume. That means they'll be stoned half the time—one of the things you can grow in gardens is *Cannabis.* That won't go down well with the neighbors. Neither will free-form marriage or the natural-credit Communist economy. They'll be visited by the cops every week. They'll be lucky if the American Legion doesn't burn them out, or sic the dog catcher on their wild life children."

"None of that has anything to do with *them.* It only has to do with people outside."

"Sure," I said, "but those people aren't going to go away. If they won't leave the colony alone I'll give it six months. If it isn't molested it might last a year or two. By that time half the people will have drifted away in search of bigger kicks, and the rest will be quarreling about some communal woman, or who got the worst corner of the garden patch, or who ate up all the sweet corn. Satisfying natural desires is fine, but natural desires have a way of being both competitive and consequential. And women may be equal to men, but they aren't equal in attractiveness any more than men are. Affections have a way of fixing on individuals, which breeds jealousy, which breeds possessiveness, which breeds bad feeling. Q.E.D."

"You're judging by past history."

"All history is past history."

"All right. *Touché*. But it doesn't have to repeat itself."

"Doesn't it?"

She sat regarding me in a troubled way, puckering up her mouth and making fishlike, *pup-pup-pupping* noises with it. "I don't see why you're *opposed*," she said. "It's one thing to think it's sure to fail, but you sound as if you thought it was *wrong*. I suppose you think it's lunatic fringe, but why? You can't think the society we've got is so hot. I *know* you don't. Haven't you sort of copped out yourself? What's this but a rural commune, only you own it and hire the Hawkes family to run it for you?"

"Do you resent that?" I said.

"What? No. No, of course not. I was just asking something. Take marriage, say. Is that such a success story? Why not try a new way? Or look at your grandfather. Is this manifesto so different from the come-on he wrote for the Idaho Mining and Irrigation Company, except that he was doing it for profit? He was trying something that was pretty sure to fail, wasn't he? Maybe it wasn't even sound, maybe that sagebrush desert might better have been left in sagebrush, isn't that what you think? All that big dream of his was dubious ecology, and sort of greedy when you look at it, just another piece of American continent-busting. But you admire your grandfather more than anybody, even though the civilization he was trying to build was this cruddy one we've got. Here's a bunch of people willing to put their lives on the line to try to make a better one. Why put them down?"

"Look, Shelly," I said, "I didn't start this discussion. It doesn't make that much difference to me what they do. You asked me what I thought."

"I'd really like to know."

"Is that it?" I said. "I thought you were trying to convert me. That'd be hopeless. I wouldn't live in a colony like that, myself, for a thousand dollars an hour. I wouldn't want it next door. I'm not too happy it's within ten miles."

"Why?"

"Why? Because their soft-headedness irritates me. Because their beautiful thinking ignores both history and human nature. Because they'd spoil my thing with their thing. Because I don't think any of them is wise enough to play God and create a human society. Look. I like privacy, I don't like crowds, I don't like noise, I don't like anarchy, I don't even like discussion all that much. I prefer study, which is very different from meditation—not better, different. I don't like children who are part of the wild life. So are polecats and rats and other sorts of hostile and untrained vermin. I want to make a distinction between civilization and the wild life. I want a society that will protect the wild life without confusing itself with it."

"Now you're talking," Shelly said. "Tell me."

"All right. I have no faith in free-form marriage. It isn't marriage, it's promiscuity, and there's no call for civilization to encourage promiscuity. I cite you the VD statistics for California as one small piece of evidence. I'm very skeptical about the natural-credit Communist economy: how does it fare when it meets a really high-powered and ruthless economy such as ours? You can't retire to weakness—you've got to learn to control strength. As for gentleness and love, I think they're harder to come by than this sheet suggests. I think they can become as coercive a conformity as anything Mr. Hershey or Mr. Hoover ever thought up. Furthermore, I'm put off by the aggressively unfeminine and the aggressively female women that would be found in a commune like this. I'm put off by long hair, I'm put off by irresponsibility, I never liked Whitman, I can't help remembering that good old wild Thoreau wound up a tame surveyor of Concord house lots."

It was quite a harangue. About the middle of it she began to grin, I think to cover up embarrassment and anger. "Well," she said when I ran down, "I stirred up the lions. What's that supposed to mean, that about Thoreau?"

As long as I had gone that far, I thought I might as well go the rest of the way. "How would I know what it means?" I said. "I don't know what anything means. What it *suggests* to me is that the civilization he was contemptuous of—that civilization of men who lived lives of quiet desperation—was stronger than he was, and maybe righter. It out-voted him. It swallowed him, in fact, and used the nourishment he provided to alter a few cells in its corporate body. It grew richer by him, but it was bigger than he was. Civilizations grow by agreements and accommodations and accretions, not by repudiations. The rebels and the revolutionaries are only eddies, they keep the stream from getting stagnant but they get swept down and absorbed, they're a side issue. Quiet desperation is another name for the human condition. If revolutionaries would learn that they can't remodel society by day after tomorrow—haven't the wisdom to and shouldn't be permitted to—I'd have more respect for them. Revolutionaries and sociologists. God, those sociologists! They're always trying to reclaim a tropical jungle with a sprinkling can full of weed killer. Civilizations grow and change and decline—they aren't remade."

She was watching me steadily, discreetly and indulgently smiling. "But your grandfather needed the bottle."

"What does that...?" I started to say. Then, "Quiet desperation, you mean? It may be the best available alternative."

I have not had a drink for a week; Ada is upset and confused when in the evening after my bath I make her take a drink but won't take one myself. Her generosity makes her uneasy. And I don't need her daughter to remind me of the strength, maybe even the necessity, of human weakness, and the harshness of the pressures civilized living can put on a man. In the land of heart's desire, up in North San Juan, these things don't apply.

The rubber band that Shelly was running through her teeth broke, and snapped her on the lip. Wincing, she put her fingers to her mouth, but her frown didn't leave her face. Through her fingers she said, "You think Larry is a kook."

"I never met him," I said. "Sight unseen, I'd say he bites off more than I think he can chew."

"He's very bright, you know."

"I haven't the slightest doubt. So was Bronson Alcott."

"Who was he, Brook Farm?"

"Fruitlands. One I forgot to mention."

"Oh."

Probably she didn't hear what I said. She was thinking about her husband, boy friend, mate, whatever he was—the man she used to travel with—and her words came out of her thinking, not as a reply to me. "He can be so damned convincing. He could convince even you."

"I doubt that. But he seems to have convinced you."

"I don't know. He's got me all up in the air."

I had myself turned askance, as usual, and my eyes fell onto the pile of papers I'd brought down when I came to lunch. One was a letter from Rudyard Kipling, another a letter from Kipling's father. I couldn't see the dates, but I knew they were both from July 1890. Right in that time of disintegration and collapse Grandmother had finished the illustrations for something of Kipling's, and had those warm letters of thanks. How many lines an alert life has its hands on at once, even in exile! Grandmother sat like a spider with her web all around her, spun out of her insides. Probably she read those Kipling letters hastily, with a brief pleasurable surprise, while the rest of her attention went out on trembling threads to the Big Ditch, or Frank Sargent, or Agnes, or Oliver, or Ollie in his far-off school, or Bessie, or Augusta, or the odious Burns. I had left her in a disturbed state of mind, and I wanted to get back, the old werewolf craved cool historical flesh to live in and refrigerated troubles to deal with. I felt a certain irritation at Shelly Rasmussen, very brown from lying in her family's back yard, sitting in Grandmother's old wicker chair and littering my porch with her foolish young life. I thought it would serve her right to go to that nut-farm and become a den mother, head of a matrilineal line in a natural-credit Communist economy.

"I gather you've patched things up," I said.

She shrugged, a gesture at once loose and irritable. "Maybe. If I could be sure he'd stay the way he is now. He's a lot better off when he's got something to be enthusiastic about. Then he doesn't sit around and think up ways to take your skin off."

"Have you been seeing him?"

"Couple times."

"Been up to San Juan?"

"I was up this last weekend."

"And you like it."

Her gray eyes met mine, she closed them deliberately, puckered up her rosebud mouth. "Oh, you know me. I'm soft headed, I ignore history and human nature. But it was sort of nice, you know? I mean—pine woods and a clearing. Off from everything. Part of it's just a gravel pile, they worked all that country with monitors. But there are some old mine buildings they're fixing up. Eight people so far, two kids. Later, as more come in, they'll build geodesic domes. What's the matter?"

I had only made the sign of the cross. How many times lately has the future perfect been framed in geodesic domes?

"They've got chickens that roost in the trees and lay eggs under the porch," Shelly said. "None of this scientific egg culture that never lets a hen set foot to ground in her whole life. It's *obscene*, the way they keep them on chicken wire. They got there too late to plant a garden, but they're putting in berry bushes, and they're going to plow a patch for winter wheat. They'll grind their own wheat and corn. Can you see me with a *metate* between my knees?"

She laughed her hoarse laugh, rocking back and forth. *Ohne Büstenhalter.* Her breasts were very live under her thin pullover, her erect nipples made dents and dimples, appeared and disappeared again as flesh met cloth. Every now and then, in her careless unconscious (is it?) way, she makes me aware that I am only fifty-eight years old, not as old as I look, not old enough to have lost everything else when I lost my leg. I felt a hot erection rising from my mutilated lap, and fumbled my sweater over myself, though it was not cool on the porch. Maybe she noticed, maybe she understood. She stretched in her wicker chair and reached her arms over her head, yawning, with her eyes shut. The other eyes looked at me boldly from her expanded chest.

Her arms fell, she flopped back. "I don't know," she said almost crossly. "You're skeptical. But it was sort of good—no poisons, no chemicals, no gadgets. Healthy, sort of. Fun. All the time I was up there I kept thinking it was the way it must have felt to your grandmother in Boise Canyon, when they were doing everything for themselves and making something new."

"Not new," I said. "Ancient. But fun, I believe it."

Shelly threw the broken rubber band in the wastebasket by the wall. "Well, what do I do? Should I try it up there—I know what you'll say—or should I tell him no dice and go back and finish my stupid degree and enter a teaching intern program and start grinding wild life through the education machine?"

"There's another alternative," I said. "You could go on doing what you've been doing. Thousands of letters still to go, years and years of them. Don't miss tomorrow's exciting episode."

At certain times her eyes, wide and gray, get smoky and warm. They went that way then. She said, smiling, "Would you keep me on?"

"I'd like it very much."

"I'd like it too. I've really enjoyed working for you. Only..."

"Only," I said. I had subsided, that fleeting foolish dream was gone. "O.K. You know what you want to do."

"I wish to hell I did." She got up and walked, pushing chairs, adjusting things on tables. "I don't know—I think I've got to get out. There's nothing here, this is only a pause, sort of. The only lively times I have are at work, talking to you. You know—" She stopped, looking at me with her head bent. "Why couldn't I come down from San Juan—" She looked at me again. "No. You wouldn't like that."

"No," I said, "I guess I wouldn't."

She sighed, she looked at me with those wide gray smoky eyes overflowing with female, troubling warmth. "What'll you do?"

"What I'm doing now. Not so pleasantly, not so fast."

"Can you manage?"

"Of course."

"I know you don't think I should go live with Larry in his commune."

Live with half a dozen fellows in their commune, I felt like saying. Be on service to the community. No, I don't think you should. Aloud I said, "You'll have to excuse me, Shelly. All I said was that I wouldn't want to. How do I know what you should do? You'll do what you think you want to do, or what you think you ought to do. If you're very lucky, luckier than anybody I know, the two will coincide."

"Yeah," she said vaguely. "I suppose." Her smile erupted, her spread hand clawed back the hanging hair. "Tell me something."

"If I know the answer."

"You said this kind of commune will be full of aggressively unfeminine and aggressively female women. Which am I?"

But I evaded that one. "I haven't heard of you joining the Women's Liberation Front," I said.

She came up behind my chair, she bent over me and put her arms around me and hugged my rigid head against her uninhibited bosom. She loudly kissed the top of my head. "You're a gas, Mister Ward," she said. "You're O.K." She went on upstairs to work and left me there, looking out into the rose garden and across Grandfather's acres of lawn, and feeling bleak, bleak, bleak.

CHAPTER SIX

Quiet-Colored End of Evening

1991–Present

By the mid-1980s, the Sierra Nevada was appearing tired and tattered. The pressures of rapid population growth, dramatic increases in recreational use, overuse, and abuse of Sierran resources, and continuing infrastructure development had taken its toll. The condition of the range was in decline, and the future seemed grim. But it was a hidden, little-discussed concern.

That changed in 1991 when *Sacramento Bee* reporter Tom Knudson addressed the issue in his Pulitzer Prize–winning series titled *The Sierra in Peril* (excerpted in this chapter). Knudson detailed the damage inflicted upon the region's ecosystem, including polluted air, dying forests, shrinking wildlife habitat, erosion, decline in water quality, and harm caused by economic development. But the five-part series was not all gloomy: the final installment reported that there were signs of hope and positive avenues to pursue.

The impact of Knudson's report was immediate. With a spotlight shining brightly on the topic, government agencies got involved and numerous private groups took up the banner or reinvigorated their efforts. As historian David Beesley, author of *Crow's Range: An Environmental History of the Sierra Nevada*, expressed it: "In Sierra Nevada environmental history, it was as if things were to be B.K. and A.K.—before and after Knudson."

Momentum was building, but the old animosities remained between those holding different viewpoints on how the land was to be used and treated. In the early 1990s, it was clear that a baseline analysis of the region was needed before any action could be taken. Congress responded by funding what came to be known as the Sierra Nevada Ecosystem Project, or SNEP. This comprehensive study would examine the history of the Sierra ecosystem and prepare reports and recommendations on various aspects of concern. The final SNEP report, issued in 1996, identified nine priorities regarding Sierra Nevada ecosystem management. They were: consideration of climate change in planning; the impact of population growth; immediate and coordinated agency action to save endangered natural systems; a reconsideration of fire suppression policies; active response to threats to animal and plant diversity; restoring healthy forest conditions; promotion of sustainable ecological practices; improvements in water quality and repair of damaged aquatic and riparian systems; and efforts to address severe air pollution.

The SNEP report was received with both praise and derision. Commendations came from those who saw it as a necessary first step in addressing obvious problems. Anger flowed from those who thought that the report would endanger livelihoods and that it constituted inappropriate government intrusion into personal freedom and property rights. Without question, however, the report spurred action. Government agency conferences were held on Sierra Nevada ecosystem issues; President Bill Clinton and Vice President Al Gore attended a widely publicized Tahoe Summit in 1997; and many environmental organizations defined and redefined their positions on key issues.

In 2004, the California government established the Sierra Nevada Conservancy, a multimillion-dollar agency designed to coordinate efforts across 25 million acres, including all or part of 22 counties, 20 incorporated cities, 40 special districts, and 212 communities. The goals of the Conservancy are to restore the Range of Light and raise awareness about the ongoing challenges facing the region. Whether these actions would produce successful strategies and positive results was another matter, but the promise of a new day was encouraging.

Now, as never before, more people saw the Sierra Nevada not as a collection of places and aspects but as a whole—a vast, interdependent entity of great complexity. It became increasingly evident that the range requires our immediate concern and attention. More than at any time in the long history of the mountains, there are now more individuals, organizations, and interest groups involved in securing a bright future for this grand illuminated landscape.

Tom Knudson, from *The Sierra in Peril*

Tom Knudson (b. 1954) has reported for the Sacramento Bee *since 1988. In 1992, Knudson and the* Bee *won the Pulitzer Prize for public service for the previous year's five-part series* The Sierra in Peril. *Knudson had previously won a Pulitzer in 1985 for national reporting at the* Des Moines Register. *His more recent awards include a Reuters-IUCN Global Award for Excellence in Environmental Reporting (2004) and an Overseas Press Club of America Award for best web reporting of international affairs (2005).*

Knudson's eight-month investigation and subsequent reports on the Sierra focused on such concerns as polluted air, dying forests, poisoned rivers, shrinking wildlife habitat, soil erosion, and rapid population growth and development, as well as contemporary efforts to reverse the situation. The impact of the series was profound; the issues came to the forefront of national debate, spawning massive ecosystem studies, legislation, and the organization of dozens of public and private groups dedicated to Sierran improvement. A small sample of Knudson's report is excerpted here.

John Muir said it best.

The Sierra Nevada, the naturalist wrote a century ago, "seems to me above all others the Range of Light, the most divinely beautiful of all the mountain chains I have ever seen."

Remember those words. Savor them like old wine. Share them with young children.

For Muir's words no longer hold true.

Today, California's Sierra Nevada—one of the world's great mountain ranges—is suffering a slow death.

Almost everywhere there are problems: polluted air, dying forests, poisoned rivers, vanishing wildlife, eroding soil and rapid-fire development. Even Muir's holy ground, Yosemite National Park, is hurting: Much of its forest has been damaged by ozone.

Remarkably, the problems have drawn little attention, masked in part by the enormity of the range. The Sierra Nevada, after all, stretches for 430 sky-scraping miles along the eastern edge of California, spanning eighteen counties, nine national forests, a half-dozen climatic zones and three national parks.

At first glance, these mountains seem invincible. Up close, it's another story. Just as Jonathan Swift's Lilliputians subdued Gulliver, so, too, are we bringing down a giant.

The vulnerability of this majestic mountain range was the central finding in an eight-month investigation by the *Bee*, involving more than 200 interviews, 10,000 miles of travel and the examination of a small mountain of government reports, scientific studies and other documents.

There are no official estimates of overall environmental damage to the Sierra Nevada for one simple reason: No government agency, university or environmental group has taken an exhaustive look at the entire range.

The *Bee*'s investigation, though, uncovered plenty of reasons for concern. Across the range, one can find an assortment of unsettling scenes, including heavily logged forests, barren, eroding soil, silt-choked streams and scenic vistas fouled by air pollution.

The investigation also found that, in many cases, it is we Californians who are to blame.

Weary of our cities, we are spilling into the Sierra in record numbers. The mountains, already suffering from logging, mining, dam building, and other activities, must now bear new burdens: shopping malls, traffic jams, ozone, wood smoke and resort hotels.

And government, with a few exceptions, is doing little to make things better. Lack of money and manpower is a familiar refrain. That's the good news. The bad news is that federal land-management policies— particularly for logging, livestock grazing and mining—are actually hastening the destruction.

Nor is science a panacea. Scientific research in the mountains is expensive, and funding is scarce. Science, by its nature, is often selective—singling out one problem, but overlooking the larger whole. The more that scientists study the Sierra, the more questions they have. Studies beget more studies. Meanwhile, the mountains suffer.

Solutions are elusive, roadblocks numerous. The Sierra's enormous distances, convoluted geography and jigsaw pattern of land ownership make conventional land management difficult, if not impossible. Many remedies have been discussed—such as setting aside more land for wildlife, building fewer houses, cutting back on logging, creating a Sierra Nevada commission or even a new "Range of Light" national park. But change in the mountains is an uphill struggle.

Today, the Sierra is dominated by controversy. From Camp Nelson to Quincy, Lone Pine to Nevada City, people are fighting over the future of this range. At the center of the controversy stands the largest landowner in the Sierra, one that has cut vast stands of forests, caused massive soil erosion and destroyed many sparkling streams. That landowner is the U.S. Forest Service.

At risk, ultimately, is more than a mountain range. At risk is one of the world's great outdoor meccas, a citadel of stone and wind, a storehouse of wonder. "A huge granite mountain cannot be denied," photographer Ansel Adams once said. "It speaks in silence to the very core of your being."

The Sierra has long been a land of superlatives—home of the largest living things on earth, giant sequoia trees; 95 of the tallest mountains in California, including the tallest in the nation outside Alaska, Mount Whitney; and the 10th-deepest body of fresh water on the planet, Lake Tahoe.

Even the names of its places are fantastic: Sky Parlor Meadow, Pulpit Rock, Hell-for-Sure Pass, Siberian Outpost, Silver Spray Falls, Castle Rock Spire, Sawtooth Ridge, Cloud Canyon, Thousand Island Lake, Hawks Head Notch and so on.

Its enormity is daunting. Stretching from the Mojave Desert to Mount Lassen, the Sierra heaves and buckles across 15.5 million acres—enough real estate to cover more than half of Pennsylvania. But even more surprising is who owns all that territory: About 70 percent of it is public land, deeded to the citizens of the United States.

Only 10 percent of the range, though, is protected by Yosemite, Sequoia and Kings Canyon national parks. The remainder is divided up roughly along these lines: 52 percent U.S. Forest Service; 30 percent private; 7 percent U.S. Bureau of Land Management; and 1 percent state, county and municipal.

It is a land of many gifts—emerald forests, sapphire lakes, snow-clad peaks, satin sunsets and stars that swing like lanterns in the night. But its greatest gift is locked up in the dance of clouds and wind, the clash of winter storm and cold, unyielding stone—the miracle of mountain water.

Roughly six of every 10 gallons of fresh water used in California come from the Sierra Nevada. Without its cloud-stopping, moisture-wringing peaks, the most productive farmland in America—the Central Valley—would be desert. Without the Sierra, much of California would die of thirst.

The Sierra, too, is the birthplace of an idea; one put forth in 1892 to mark the formation of a small group of wilderness enthusiasts:

"To enlist the support and cooperation of the people and the government in preserving the forests and other natural features of the Sierra Nevada."

Nearly a century later, that group has become one of the most influential conservation groups in the world: the Sierra Club. But even the mighty Sierra Club has not stopped destruction of its namesake mountains. And there is controversy over that, too.

These days, the Sierra Nevada remains a magnet for accolades, a place where phrases like majestic, breathtaking and awe-inspiring are much in use, often for good reason.

But in recent years, another mountain dialect has begun to emerge, one marked not by lofty sounding adjectives, but by a tone of trouble and concern. Today, dark clouds are gathering over Muir's Range of Light—a paradise in peril.

As Douglas Bradley, editor of a recent collection of scientific articles about the Sierra, put it:

"We are wont to whittle away at our giants, such as buffaloes or elephants or the seven seas, until they are depleted. I fear often that the Sierra awaits a similar fate."...

Not since the California gold rush of 1849 has the Sierra Nevada seen such an influx of people. They are coming from Sacramento, Los Angeles, San Francisco and other places—a surge of contemporary emigrants settling into many of the same regions that lured early gold-seekers and pioneers.

Today's emigrants, though, are not looking for gold. They are searching for a commodity even more precious, something that no longer can be found in much of California: peace and quiet.

But this modern migration is also tinged with irony. For in their move to the mountains, Californians are threatening to destroy the things that make the Sierra special—its small towns, clean air, majestic forests and outdoor spirit.

Already, signs of trouble are numerous—the ribbon of headlights along Highway 49 north of Auburn, the gray curtain of wood smoke over Mammoth Lakes, the rumble of earth-moving equipment in Truckee on a Sunday afternoon.

"I love the Sierra and I want to stay here," said Jeff Schloss, a ski instructor and substitute teacher in Truckee.

"But it's so close to the Bay Area and the Valley. I'm worried the quality of life is going to deteriorate. The very things people are trying to get away from—like air pollution and traffic congestion—they're bringing up here."

Surprisingly, government has offered little protection. Often, in fact, county governments have overlooked the Sierra's natural resources in favor of economic considerations—in particular the lure of more jobs and property tax revenues.

"The basic issue becomes, 'Is there a market for the project?'" said Tom Albright, former chairman of the Nevada County Planning Commission.

"It's not, 'What is this going to do to the quality of life for the people in the area?' That's what it boils down to."

California, of course, has seen such things before. During the past half-century, the state has grown so tremendously that many of its prettiest places, from Orange County to the San Francisco Bay Area, are covered with concrete and shopping malls.

Now, as California's population nudges past 30 million, the push is on in the Sierra—a region long considered too rugged and remote to draw much development pressure.

Today, the Range of Light is looking more like the Range of Real Estate. Almost everywhere, it seems, people are pouring in. They are a diverse group: retirees fleeing urban California for wooded, foothill acreages; baby-boomers commuting to jobs in the Central Valley; business people weary of big-city pressures, and young men and women drawn to the ski slopes.

With them has come an army of builders, pavers, plumbers, mortgage bankers and real estate agents.

Together, they have wrought a remarkable change: The Sierra Nevada—known around the world for its scenic grandeur—is now one of the fastest-growing areas in the state.

Statistics help tell the story. During the 1980s, six of the state's 10 fastest growing counties were Sierra counties, U.S. Census Bureau figures show. Amador County, east of Sacramento, led the region with a population jump of 55.5 percent, third in the state behind Riverside and San Bernardino counties.

Nevada County saw its population swell from 51,645 to 78,510—a jump of 52 percent. Next door, Placer County grew from 117,246 people to 172,796—up 47.4 percent.

But statistics are dry, unfriendly things. A better gauge of change is the lens of time.

"I remember in the early days flying over the Sierra at night and finally seeing Sacramento—a discrete point of light," said David Brower, a 78-year-old veteran conservationist and former executive director of the Sierra Club.

"Now, it's just lights, lights, lights and lights."

Other changes are more subtle.

"The hierarchy of values is changing," said Chris Bowen, a spokesman for the U.S. Forest Service, the largest landowner in the Sierra.

"We're not seeing an increase in the number of ranchers, loggers and miners. We're seeing more service industries, retirees and so on.

"And that means there is more insistence on things like scenic quality. Clear cutting tends to put people off. And realistically, we can't ignore that.

"You've got more roads, more power lines and more consumers of water. And that, in turn, is having an effect on things like air quality and wildlife habitat and—over time—the ecology of the forest."

The impact of people on the central Sierra is the focus of a new research project funded by the U.S. Forest Service and the California Department of Forestry and Fire Protection.

"One of the things we're looking at is what happens when a forest is broken up by roads, shopping malls and other development," said Rowan Rowntree, a project manager with the Forest Service's Pacific Southwest Forest and Range Experiment Station in Berkeley.

"As you develop a region as large as the central Sierra, you remove pieces of its 'genetic architecture.' And we don't know what the long-term consequences of that are going to be."

Few places are feeling more pressure than Truckee.

Born a logging and railroad town in the 1860s, Truckee has long been one of California's most scenic, historical and off-beat communities: more rural than urban, more old than new, more blue-collar than button-down.

In Truckee, location is everything. For more than a century, its vital statistics—6,000 feet above sea level, second-coldest spot in the United States, except for Alaska, 100 miles from Sacramento—have kept all but the hardiest Californians at bay.

Over the years, plucky Truckee has survived forest fires, mega-snowstorms and long winters of isolation. But today, Truckee is locked in a battle it may not win—with development.

An avalanche of building is rolling through town, turning forests into shopping centers, offices and three-bedroom homes. Every month, Truckee looks a little less like Truckee—and a lot more like everyplace else in California.

And in that, it is much like scores of other Sierra towns now facing a surge of development with limited resources, inadequate roads, insufficient room to expand—and a tradition on the line.

"Truckee is a town with a character," Schloss said. "But they're making it look like Everytown USA. There's simply no reason for that to happen."

In Truckee, one project in particular stunned many townspeople recently: the Gateway shopping center.

It began in dramatic fashion. Just after Earth Day in 1990 a large stand of pine trees came crashing to the ground along Truckee's main street, Donner Pass Road.

One year later, the $12 million, 108,000-square-foot Gateway shopping center has taken root on the site.

"I was born in Orange County and remember when they tore down the first orange trees for the first tract," said Truckee resident Nancy Richards.

"When they took those trees down for Gateway, I just came unglued. It was deja vu."

But Gateway's developer sees things differently.

"If the market was not there, the shopping center would not have been built," said Mike Perry, managing partner of the Wall Street Property Co. of La Jolla.

Truckee's population of 9,225 is hardly enormous. But it is up 62 percent from 1980. And most weekends, the numbers jump dramatically as tens of thousands of tourists pour into the Lake Tahoe and Truckee area.

Traffic problems, already legendary, are growing worse. And a once brilliant blue sky is now smeared with wood smoke and automobile exhaust.

"Air quality is getting to be a serious problem," said Judd Dygert, a retired oil company engineer. "If you stand up on Rainbow Bridge and look out over town, it kind of reminds you of looking out over Los Angeles."

But if the problems are many, so, too, are the ideas for change: better traffic control, a ban on woodstoves, more bicycle trails, tougher controls on development, and so on.

Not long ago, a local group was formed to chart Truckee's future by updating the general plan for eastern Nevada County. The decisions are sure to be difficult, involving a delicate balancing of economic and quality-of-life factors. But at least they are being considered.

"Ten to 15 years ago, people weren't worried about these sorts of things," said former Planning Commissioner Albright. "But now, they're seeing the traffic increase and the trees come down. And they're starting to get concerned. The pendulum is swinging."

Wendy Rose, "Questions for a Miwok Uncle: Ahwahneechee Man"

Wendy Rose (b. 1948) is a poet, artist, teacher, anthropologist, and historian of Hopi, Miwok, and European ancestry. She is the author of numerous books of poetry (one of which was nominated for a Pulitzer Prize) and has taught Native American and ethnic studies at the University of California, Berkeley; California State University, Fresno; and Fresno City College, where she is currently coordinator of the college's American Indian Studies Program. Born and raised in the San Francisco Bay Area, Rose moved to Coarsegold, an old mining camp in the southern Sierra Nevada foothills.

In the title to this poem, Rose mentions the Ahwahneechee. This group is a band of the Miwok Nation and among the original inhabitants of Yosemite Valley.

It was before they came with their ranches,
cattle upturning and chewing our flesh.
It was before they ripped the memory from our tongues
and riddled the hills with their hungry machines.
They came from their cities, they came
from the east, they came on the water
to measure our bones
against a string of shell beads
and stolen gold, O so long ago.
Spreadeagled, uncle, preserved
against some book

you have but the ashes
of clapstick and bone flute
to color your hands as you would have them.

Is it too late to record
the monument of your movement
down and away from where you once were
parting the bear grass with a song
so quietly you came upon
the deer drinking
and put down the bow
to feel the rhythm
of her throat?

Janice Gould, "Late Summer in the Sierra"

Janice Gould (b. 1949) is a poet of Maidu/Konkow and European descent. Born in San Diego, she grew up in Berkeley and was educated at the University of California, Berkeley, and the University of New Mexico. Gould has taught creative writing at a number of academic institutions, including the University of Northern Colorado and Willamette University, and she was coeditor of Speak to Me Words: Essays on Contemporary American Indian Poetry *(2003). A prolific writer, Gould has appeared in many anthologies and is considered a leading contemporary lesbian author.*

The following poem was originally published online in 1995 by Weber State University, and the following year it was printed in Gould's collection Earthquake Weather.

I.
Our friend shows me snapshots:
late summer in the Sierra,
the river full of light, rocks
and sand the color of gold.
On the opposite shore sugar pines
sway in the hot afternoon breeze.
You stand in the water calf-deep,
naked, half-facing the camera.
You are modest.
I can see the exact shape of your breasts,
and beneath a smooth belly,
reddish hair.

You are laughing,
bending slightly towards the water.

II.
In another photo you are squatting
with the baby in your arms.
You are still by the river,
and the baby lies across your lap.
She looks to be squirming, cranky.
You look at the photographer,
laughing again. It seems to me
the camera is a little invasive.
But the one who takes the pictures teases you,
and everyone is in a good humor, except the baby
who fusses before falling asleep.

In late afternoon you pack to go home.
Everyone is quiet.
You can hear the sound of water above the swimming hole
where the river curves around a rock.
It's less hot, cool in the shadow of trees.
All day blackberries have ripened.
You pick them as you walk along,
pausing in the shade,
eating berries off the vine.
Some are sweet, some sour.
The juice is very red.
They leave a stain on your fingers
and a suggestion of invisible thorns.

III.
The burdens of the heart are these:
a declaration of love that remains inert,
a kiss that stays unbidden.
The passion of the body—
suspended—
till it can circulate through the soul
like cold pure water.

> "We came to live a permeable, porous life in our house
> set among the stands of oak and pine"

Gary Snyder, from *A Place in Space*

*In addition to his Pulitzer Prize–winning poetry, Gary Snyder (b. 1930)
has penned many essays about environmental and sustainability issues.
A resident of the Sierra Nevada foothills for decades, Snyder is intimately
attached to the land and profoundly moved by the spiritual benefits it can
provide. Excerpts of his work can be found later in this chapter and also in
Chapter 5 of this anthology.*

*The following selections are from the pieces "The Porous World" and
"Language Goes Two Ways," both from* A Place in Space: Ethics,
Aesthetics, and Watersheds *(1995), a collection of essays Snyder wrote
over the previous forty years about the environment and what we can do
to save it.*

One can choose to live in a place as a sort of visitor, or try to become
an inhabitant. My family and I decided from early on to try to be
here, in the midelevation forests of the Sierra Nevada, as fully as we
could. This brave attempt was backed by lack of resources and a lot of
dumb bravado. We figured that simplicity would of itself be beautiful,
and we had our own extravagant notions of ecological morality. But
necessity was the teacher that finally showed us how to live as part of
the natural community.

It comes down to how one thinks about screens, fences, or dogs.
These are often used for keeping the wild at bay. ("Keeping the wild
at bay" sounds like fending off hawks and bears, but it is more often a
matter of holding back carpenter ants and deer mice.) We came to live
a permeable, porous life in our house set among the stands of oak and
pine. Our buildings are entirely opened up for the long Sierra summer.

Mud daubers make their trips back and forth from inside the house to the edge of the pond like tireless little cement trucks, and pour their foundations on beams, in cracks, and (if you're not alert) in rifle-bore holes and backpack fire-pump nozzles. They dribble little spots of mud as they go. For mosquitoes, which are never much of a problem, the house is just another place to enjoy the shade. At night the bats dash around the rooms, in and out of the open skylights, swoop down past your cheek and go out an open sliding door. In the dark of the night the deer can be heard stretching for the lower leaves of the apple trees, and at dawn the wild turkeys are strolling a few yards from the bed.

The price we pay is the extra effort to put all the pantry food into jars or other mouse-proof containers. Winter bedding goes into mouse-proof chests. Then ground squirrels come right inside for fresh fruit on the table, and the deer step into the shade shelter to nibble a neglected salad. You are called to a hopeful steadiness of nerves as you lift a morsel of chicken to the mouth with four meat bees following it every inch of the way. You must sometimes (in late summer) cook and eat with the yellow jackets watching every move. This can make you peevish, but there is a kind of truce that is usually attained when one quits flailing and slapping at the wasps and bees.

"Wild" alludes to a process of self-organization that generates systems and organisms, all of which are within the constraints of—and constitute components of—larger systems that again are wild, such as major ecosystems or the water cycle in the biosphere. Wildness can be said to be the essential nature of nature. As reflected in consciousness, it can be seen as a kind of open awareness—full of imagination but also the source of alert survival intelligence. The workings of the human mind at its very richest reflect this self-organizing wildness. So language does not impose order on a chaotic universe, but reflects its own wildness back.

In doing so it goes two ways: it enables us to have a small window onto an independently existing world, but it also shapes—via its very structures and vocabularies—how we see that world. It may be argued that what language does to our seeing of reality is restrictive, narrowing, limiting, and possibly misleading. "The menu is not the meal." But rather than dismiss language from a spiritual position, speaking vaguely of Unsayable Truths, we must instead turn right back *to* language. The way to see *with* language, to be free with it and to find it a vehicle of self-transcending insight, is to know both mind and language extremely well and to play with their many possibilities without any special attachment. In doing this, a language yields up surprises and angles that amaze us and that can lead back to unmediated direct experience.

"For the first time since she'd been here, for the first time
in three long seasons, she felt naked and vulnerable"

T. Coraghessan Boyle, "Sitting on Top of the World"

*Born in Peekskill, New York, T. Coraghessan Boyle (b. 1948) is the author
of twenty books of fiction, and his work has been translated into more
than two dozen languages. Boyle's stories have appeared in many major
magazines, including* The New Yorker, Harper's, Esquire, The Atlantic
Monthly, Playboy, *and* The Paris Review. *He has received many literary
awards, including the PEN/Faulkner Award for Best Novel of the Year
(1988) for* World's End, *the Bernard Malamud Prize in Short Fiction
(1999) for the collection* T.C. Boyle Stories, *and six O. Henry Awards for
short fiction. Boyle has been a member of the English department at the
University of Southern California since 1978.*

*"Sitting on Top of the World," presented here in its entirety, is the tale
of Lainie, who staffs a lonely fire lookout post near Mount Whitney, the
tallest point in the Sierra Nevada.*

People would ask her what it was like. She'd watch them from her
tower as they weaved along the trail in their baseball caps and day
packs, their shorts, hiking boots and sneakers. The brave ones would
mount the hundred and fifty wooden steps hammered into the face of
the mountain to stand at the high-flown railing of the little glass-walled
shack she called home for seven months a year. Sweating, sucking
at canteens and bota bags, heaving for breath in the undernourished
air, they would ask her what it was like. "Beautiful," she would say.
"Peaceful."

But that didn't begin to express it. It was like floating untethered, drifting with the clouds, like being cupped in the hands of God. Nine thousand feet up, she could see the distant hazy rim of the world, she could see Mount Whitney rising up above the crenellations of the Sierra, she could see stars that haven't been discovered yet. In the morning, she was the first to watch the sun emerge from the hills to the east, and in the evening, when it was dark beneath her, the valleys and ridges gripped by the insinuating fingers of the night, she was the last to see it set. There was the wind in the trees, the murmur of the infinite needles soughing in the uncountable branches of the pines, sequoias and cedars that stretched out below her like a carpet. There was daybreak. There was the stillness of 3:00 a.m. She couldn't explain it. She was sitting on top of the world.

Don't you get lonely up here? they'd ask. Don't you get a little stir-crazy?

And how to explain that? Yes, she did, of course she did, but it didn't matter. Todd was up here with her in the summer, one week on, one week off, and then the question was meaningless. But in September he went back to the valley, to his father, to school, and the world began to drag round its tired old axis. The hikers stopped coming then too. At the height of summer, on a weekend, she'd see as many as thirty or forty in the course of a day, but now, with the fall coming on, they left her to herself—sometimes she'd go for days without seeing a soul.

But that was the point, wasn't it?

She was making breakfast—a real breakfast for a change, ham and eggs from the propane refrigerator, fresh-dripped coffee and toast—when she spotted him working his way along one of the switchbacks below. She was immediately annoyed. It wasn't even seven yet and the sign at the trailhead quite plainly stated that visitors were welcome at the lookout between the hours of ten and five *only*. What was wrong with this guy—did he think he was exempt or something? She calmed herself: maybe he was only crossing the trail. Deer season had opened—she'd been hearing the distant muted pop of gunfire all week—and maybe he was only a hunter tracking a deer.

No such luck. When she glanced down again, flipping her eggs, peering across the face of the granite peak and the steep snaking trail that clung to it, she saw that he was coming up to the tower. Damn, she thought, and then the kettle began to hoot and her stomach clenched. Breakfast was ruined. Now there'd be some stranger gawking over her shoulder and making the usual banal comments as she ate. To them it might have been like Disneyland or something up here, but this was her home, she lived here. How would they like it if she showed up on their doorstep at seven o'clock in the morning?

She was eating, her back to the glass door, hoping he'd go away, slip over the lip of the precipice and disappear, vanish in a puff of smoke, when she felt his footfall on the trembling catwalk that ran round the outside of the tower. Still, she didn't turn or look up. She was reading—she went through a truckload of books in the course of a season—and she never lifted her eyes from the page. He could gawk round the catwalk, peer through the telescope and hustle himself back on down the steps for all she cared. She wasn't a tour guide. Her job was to watch for smoke, twenty-four hours a day, and to be cordial—if she was in the mood and had the time—to the hikers who made the sweaty panting trek in from the trailhead to join her for a brief moment atop the world. There was no law that said she had to let them in the shack or show them the radio and her plotting equipment and deliver the standard lecture on how it all worked. Especially at seven in the morning. To hell with him, she thought, and she forked up egg and tried to concentrate on her book.

The problem was, she'd trained herself to look up from what she was doing and scan the horizon every thirty seconds or so, day or night, except when she was asleep, and it had become a reflex. She glanced up, and there he was. It gave her a shock. He'd gone round the catwalk to the far side and he was standing right in front of her, grinning and holding something up to the window. Flowers, wildflowers, she registered that, but then his face came into focus and she felt something go slack in her: she knew him. He'd been here before.

"Lainie," he said, tapping the glass and brandishing the flowers, "I brought you something."

Her name. He knew her name.

She tried a smile and her face froze around it. The book on the table before her upset the salt-shaker and flipped itself shut with a tiny expiring hiss. Should she thank him? Should she get up and latch the door? Should she put out an emergency call on the radio and snatch up the kitchen knife?

"Sorry to disturb you over breakfast—I didn't know the time," he said, and something happened to his grin, though his eyes—a hard metallic blue—held on to hers like pincers. He raised his voice to penetrate the glass: "I've been camping down on Long Meadow Creek and when I crossed the trail this morning I just thought you might be lonely and I'd surprise you"—he hesitated—"I mean, with some flowers."

Her whole body was frozen now. She'd had crazies up here before—it was an occupational hazard—but there was something unnerving about this one; this one she remembered. "It's too early," she said finally; miming it with her hands, as if the glass were impervious to sound, and then she got up from her untouched ham and half-eaten eggs and deliberately went to the radio. The radio was just under the window where he was standing, and when she picked up the mike and depressed the talk button she was two feet from him, the thin wall of glass all that separated them.

"Needles Lookout," she said, "this is Elaine. Zack, you there? Over."

Zack's voice came right back at her. He was a college student working on a degree in forestry, and he was her relief two days a week when she hiked out and went down the mountain to spend a day with her son, do her shopping and maybe hit a bar or movie with her best friend and soul mate, Cynthia Furman. "Elaine," he said, above the crackle of static, "what's up? See anything funny out there? Over."

She forced herself to look up then and locate the stranger's eyes—he was still grinning, but the grin was slack and unsteady and there was no joy in the deeps of those hard blue eyes—and she held the black plastic mike to her lips a moment longer than she had to before answering. "Nothing, Zack," she said, "just checking in."

His voice was tinny. "Okay," he said. "Talk to you. Over and out."

"Over and out," she said.

And now what? The guy wore a hunting knife strapped to his thigh. His cheeks were caved in as if he were sucking candy; and an old-fashioned mustache, thick and reddish, hid his upper lip. Instead of a baseball cap he wore a wide-brimmed felt hat. Wyatt Earp, she thought, and she was about to turn away from the window, prepared to ignore him till he took the hint, till he counted off the hundred and fifty wooden steps and vanished down the path and out of her life, when he rapped again on the glass and said, "You got something to put these in—the flowers, I mean?"

She didn't want his flowers. She didn't want him on her platform. She didn't want him in her thirteen-by-thirteen-foot sanctuary, touching her things, poking around, asking stupid questions, making small talk. "Look," she said finally, talking to the glass but looking through him, beyond him, scanning the infinite as she'd trained herself to do, no matter what the problem, "I've got a job to do up here and the fact is no one's allowed on the platform between the hours of five in the afternoon and ten in the morning"—now she came back to him and saw that his smile had collapsed—"you ought to know that. It says so in plain English right down there at the trailhead." She looked away; it was over, she was done with him.

She went back to her breakfast, forcing herself to stare at the page before her, though her heart was going and the words meant nothing. Todd had been with her the first time the man had come. Todd was fourteen, tall like his father, blond-headed and rangy. He was a good kid, her last and final hope, and he seemed to relish the time he spent with her up here. It was a Saturday, the middle of the afternoon, and they'd had a steady stream of visitors since the morning. Todd was in the storage room below, reading comics (in its wisdom, the Forestry Service had provided this second room, twenty-five steps down, not simply for storage but for respite too—it was a box, a womb, with only a single dull high-placed window to light it, antithesis and antidote to the naked glass box above). Elaine was at her post, chopping vegetables for soup and scanning the horizon.

She hadn't noticed him coming—there'd been so many visitors she wasn't attuned to them in the way she was in the quiet times. She was feeling hospitable, lighthearted, the hostess of an ongoing party. There'd been a professor up earlier, an ornithologist, and they'd had a long talk about the golden eagle and the red-tailed hawk. And then there was the young girl from Merced—she couldn't have been more than seventeen—with her baby strapped to her back, and two heavyset women in their sixties who'd proudly made the two-and-a-half-mile trek in from the trailhead and were giddy with the thin air and the thrill of their own accomplishment. Elaine had offered them each a cup of tea, not wanting to spoil their fun and point out that it was still two and a half miles back out.

She'd felt his weight on the platform and turned to give him a smile. He was tall and powerful across the chest and shoulders and he'd tipped his hat to her and poked his head in the open door. "Enjoying the view?" he said.

There was something in his eyes that should have warned her off, but she was feeling sociable and buoyant and she saw the generosity in his shoulders and hands. "It's nothing compared to the Ventura Freeway," she deadpanned.

He laughed out loud at that, and he was leaning in the door now, both hands on the frame. "I see the monastic life hasn't hurt your sense of humor any—" and then he paused, as if he'd gone too far. "Or that's not the word I want, 'monastic'—is there a feminine version of that?"

Pretty presumptuous. Flirtatious, too. But she was in the mood, she didn't know what it was—maybe having Todd with her, maybe just the sheer bubbling joy of living on the crest of the sky—and at least he wasn't dragging her through the same old tired conversation about loneliness and beauty and smoke on the horizon she had to endure about a hundred times a week. "Come in," she said. "Take a load off your feet."

He sat on the edge of the bed and removed his hat. He wore his hair in a modified punk style—hard irregular spikes—and that surprised her: somehow it just didn't go with the cowboy hat. His jeans were stiff and new and his tooled boots looked as if they'd just been polished. He was studying her—she was wearing khaki shorts and a T-shirt, she'd washed her hair that morning in anticipation of the crowd, and her legs were good—she knew it—tanned and shaped by her treks up and down the trail. She felt something she hadn't felt in a long time, an ice age, and she knew her cheeks were flushed. "You probably had a whole slew of visitors today, huh?" he said, and there was something incongruous in the enforced folksiness of the phrase, something that didn't go with his accent, just as the haircut didn't go with the hat.

"I've counted twenty-six since this morning." She diced a carrot and tossed it into the pan to simmer with the onions and zucchini she'd chopped a moment earlier.

He was gazing out the window, working his hands on the brim of his hat. "Hope you don't mind my saying this, but you're the best thing about this view as far as I can see. You're pretty. Really pretty."

This one she'd heard before. About a thousand times. Probably seventy percent of the day-trippers who made the hike out to the lookout were male, and if they were alone or with other males, about ninety percent of those tried to hit on her in some way. She resented it, but she couldn't blame them really. There was probably something irresistible in the formula: young woman with blond hair and good legs in a glass tower in the middle of nowhere—and all alone. Rapunzel, let down your hair. Usually she deflected the compliment—or the moves—by turning officious, standing on her authority as Forestry Service employee, government servant and the chief, queen and despot of the Needles Lookout. This time she said nothing. Just lifted her head for a quick scan of the horizon and then looked back down at the knife and the cutting board and began chopping green onion and cilantro.

He was still watching her. The bed was big, a double, one of the few creature comforts the Forestry Service provided up here. There was no headboard, of course—just a big flat hard slab of mattress attached to the wall at window level, so you could be lying in bed and still do your job. Presumably, it was designed for couples. When he spoke again, she knew what he was going to say before the words were out of his mouth. "Nice bed," he said.

What did she expect? He was no different from the rest—why would he be? All of a sudden he'd begun to get on her nerves, and when she turned her face to him her voice was cold. "Have you seen the telescope," she said, indicating the Bushnell Televar mounted on the rail of the catwalk—beyond the window and out the door.

He ignored her. He rose to his feet. Thirteen by thirteen: two's a crowd. "You must get awfully lonely up here," he said, and his voice was different now too, no attempt at folksiness or jocularity, "a pretty woman like you. A beautiful woman. You've got sexy legs, you know that?"

She flushed—he could see that, she was sure of it—and the flush made her angry. She was about to tell him off, to tell him to get the hell out of her house and stay out, when Todd came rumbling up the steps, wild-eyed and excited. "Mom!" he shouted, and he was out of breath, his voice high-pitched and hoarse, "there's water leaking all over the place out there!"

Water. It took a moment to register. The water was precious up here, irreplaceable. Once a month two bearded men with Forestry Service patches on their sleeves brought her six twenty-gallon containers of it—in the old way, on the backs of mules. She husbanded that water as if she were in the middle of the Negev, every drop of it, rarely allowing herself the luxury of a quick shampoo and rinse, as she had that morning. In the next instant she was out the door and jolting down the steps behind her son. Down below, outside the storage room where the cartons were lined up in a straight standing row, she saw that the rock face was slick with a finely spread sheen of water. She bent to the near carton. It was leaking from a thin milky stress fracture in the plastic, an inch from the bottom. "Take hold of it, Todd," she said. "We've got to turn it over so the leak's on top."

Full, the carton weighed better than a hundred and sixty pounds, and this one was nearly full. She put her weight behind it, the power of her honed and muscular legs, but the best she could do, even with

344

Todd's help, was to push the thing over on its side. She was breathing hard, sweating, she'd scraped her knee and there was a stipple of blood on the skin over the kneecap. It was then that she became aware of the stranger standing there behind her. She looked up at him framed against the vastness of the sky, the sun in his face, his big hands on his hips. "Need a hand there?" he asked.

Looking back on it, she didn't know why she'd refused—maybe it was the way Todd gaped at him in awe, maybe it was the old pretty-woman/lonely-up-here routine or the helpless-female syndrome—but before she could think she was saying "I don't need your help: I can do it myself."

And then his hands fell from his hips and he backed away a step, and suddenly he was apologetic, he was smooth and funny and winning and he was sorry for bothering her and he just wanted to help and he knew she was capable, he wasn't implying anything—and just as suddenly he caught himself, dropped his shoulders and slunk off down the steps without another word.

For a long moment she watched him receding down the trail, and then she turned back to the water container. By the time she and Todd got it upended it was half empty.

Yes. And now he was here when he had no right to be, now he was intruding and he knew it, now he was a crazy defining new levels of the affliction. She'd call in an emergency in a second—she wouldn't hesitate—and they'd have a helicopter here in less than five minutes, that's how quick these firefighters were, she'd seen them in action. Five minutes. She wouldn't hesitate. She kept her head down. She cut and chewed each piece of meat with slow deliberation and she read and reread the same paragraph until it lost all sense. When she looked up, he was gone.

After that, the day dragged on as if it would never end. He couldn't have been there more than ten minutes, slouching around with his mercenary grin and his pathetic flowers, but he'd managed to ruin her day. He'd upset her equilibrium and she found that she couldn't read, couldn't sketch or work on the sweater she was knitting for Todd. She caught herself staring at a fixed point on the horizon, drifting, her mind a blank. She ate too much. Lunch was a ceremony, dinner a ritual. There were no visitors, though for once she longed for them. Dusk lingered in the western sky and when night fell she didn't bother with her propane lantern but merely sat there on the corner of the bed, caught up in the wheeling immensity of the constellations and the dream of the Milky Way.

And then she couldn't sleep. She kept thinking of him, the stranger with the big hands and secretive eyes, kept scanning the catwalk for the sudden black shadow of him. If he came at seven in the morning, why not at three? What was to prevent him? There was no sound, nothing— the wind had died down and the night was clear and moonless. For the first time since she'd been here, for the first time in three long seasons, she felt naked and vulnerable, exposed in her glass house like a fish in a tank. The night was everything and it held her in its grip.

She thought about Mike then, about the house they'd had when he'd finished his degree and started as an assistant professor at a little state school out in the lost lush hills of Oregon. The house was an A-frame, a cabin with a loft, set down amidst the trees like a cottage in a fairy tale. It was all windows and everywhere you looked the trees bowed down and stepped into the house. The previous owner, an old widower with watery eyes and yellow hair climbing out of his ears, hadn't bothered with blinds or curtains, and Mike didn't like that—he was always after her to measure the windows and order blinds or buy the material for drapes. She'd balked. The openness, the light, the sense of connection and belonging: these were the things that had attracted her in the first place. They made love in the dark—Mike insisted on it—as if it were something to be ashamed of. After a while, it was.

Then she was thinking of a time before that, a time before Todd and graduate school, when Mike sat with her in the dormitory lounge, books spread out on the coffee table before them, the heat and murmur of a dozen other couples locking their mouths and bodies together. A study date. For hours she clung to him, the sofa like a boat pitching in a heavy sea, the tease of it, the fumbling innocence, the interminable foreplay that left her wet and itching while the wind screamed beyond the iced-over windows. That was something. The R.A. would flash the lights and it was quarter of one and they would fling themselves at each other, each step to the door drenched in hormones, sticky with them, desperate, until finally he was gone and she felt the loss like a war bride. Until the next night.

Finally—and it must have been two, three in the morning, the Big Dipper tugged down below the horizon, Orion looming overhead—she thought of the stranger who'd spoiled her breakfast. He'd sat there on the corner of the bed; he'd stood beyond the window with his sad bundle of flowers, devouring the sky. As she thought of him, in that very moment, there was a dull light thump on the steps, a faint rustle, movement, and she couldn't breathe, couldn't move. The seconds pounded in her head and the rustling—it was like the sweep of a broom—was gone, something in the night, a pack rat, the fleeting touch of an owl's wing. She thought of those hands, the eyes, the square of those shoulders, and she felt herself being drawn down into the night in relief, and finally, in gratitude.

She woke late, the sun slanting across the floor to touch her lips and mask her eyes. Zachary was on the radio with the news that Oakland had clinched the pennant and a hurricane was tearing up the East Coast. "You sound awful," he said. "I didn't wake you, did I?"

"I couldn't sleep."

"Stargazing again, huh?"

She tried out a laugh for him. "I guess," she said. There was a silence. "Jesus, you just relieved me. I've got four more days to put in before I come back down to the ground."

"Just don't get mystical on me. And leave me some granola this time, will you? And if you run out, call me. That's my breakfast we're talking about. And lunch. And sometimes, if I don't feel like cooking—"

She cut him off: "Dinner. I know. I will." She yawned. "Talk to you."

"Yeah. Over and out."

"Over and out."

When she set the kettle on the grill there was gas, but when she turned her back to dig the butter out of the refrigerator, the flame was gone. She tried another match, but there was nothing. That meant she had to switch propane tanks, a minor nuisance. The tanks, which were flown in once a year by helicopter, were located at the base of the stairway, one hundred and fifty steps down. There was a flat spot there, a gap cut into the teeth of the outcrop and overhung on one side by a sloping twenty-foot-high wall of rock. On the other side, the first step was a thousand feet down.

She shrugged into her shorts, and because it was cold despite the sun—she'd seen snow as early as the fifth of September, and the month was almost gone now—she pulled on an oversized sweater that had once belonged to Mike. After she'd moved out she'd found it in a pillowcase she'd stuffed full of clothes. He hadn't wanted it back. It was windy, and a blast knifed into her when she threw open the door and started down the steps. Big pristine tufts of cumulus hurried across the sky, swelling and attenuating and changing shape, but she didn't see anything dark enough—or big enough—to portend a storm. Still, you could never tell. The breeze was from the north and the radio had reported a storm front moving in off the Pacific—it really wouldn't surprise her to see snow on the ground by this time tomorrow. A good snowfall and the fire season would be over and she could go home. Early.

She thought about that—about the four walls of the little efficiency she rented on a dead street in a dead town to be near Todd during the winter—and hoped it wouldn't snow. Not now. Not yet. In a dry year— and this had been the third dry year in a row—she could stay through mid-November. She reached the bottom of the steps and crouched over the propane tanks, two three-hundred-gallon jobs painted Forestry Service green, feeling depressed over the thought of those four dull walls and the cold in the air and the storm that might or might not develop. There was gooseflesh on her legs and her breath crowded the air round her. She watched a ground squirrel, its shoulders bulky with patches of bright gray fur, dart up over the face of the overhang, and then she unfastened the coupling on the empty tank and switched the hose to the full one.

"Gas problems?"

The voice came from above and behind her and she jumped as if she'd been stung. Even before she whirled round she knew whose voice it was.

"Hey, hey: didn't mean to startle you. Whoa. Sorry." There he was, the happy camper, knife lashed to his thigh, standing right behind her, two steps up. This time his eyes were hidden behind a pair of reflecting sunglasses. The brim of the Stetson was pulled down low and he wore a sheepskin coat, the fleecy collar turned up in back.

She couldn't answer. Couldn't smile. Couldn't humor him. He'd caught her out of her sanctuary, caught her out in the open, one hundred and fifty steep and unforgiving steps from the radio, the kitchen knife, the hard flat soaring bed. She was crouching. He towered above her, his shoulders cut out of the sky. Todd was in school. Mike—she didn't want to think about Mike. She was all alone.

He stood there, the mustache the only thing alive in his face. It lifted from his teeth in a grin. "Those things can be a pain," he said, the folksy tone creeping into his voice, "those tanks, I mean. Dangerous. I use electricity myself."

She lifted herself cautiously from her crouch, the hard muscles swelling in her legs. She would have risked a dash up the stairs, all hundred and fifty of them, would have put her confidence in her legs, but he was blocking the stairway—almost as if he'd anticipated her. She hadn't said a word yet. She looked scared, she knew it. "Still camping?" she said, fighting to open up her face and give him his smile back, insisting on banality, normalcy, the meaningless drift of meaningless conversation.

He looked away from her, light flashing from the slick convexity of the sunglasses, and kicked at the edge of the step with the silvertipped toe of his boot. After a moment he turned back to her and removed the sunglasses. "Yeah," he said, shrugging. "I guess."

It wasn't an answer she expected. He guessed? What was that supposed to mean? He hadn't moved a muscle and he was watching her with that look in his eyes—she knew that look, knew that stance, that mustache and hat, but she didn't know his name. He knew hers but she didn't know his, not even his first name. "I'm sorry," she said, and when she put a hand up to her eyes to shade them from the sun, it was trembling, "but what was your name again? I mean, I remember you, of course, not just from yesterday but from that time a month or so ago, but…" She trailed off.

He didn't seem to have heard her. The wind sang in the trees. She just stood there, squinting into the sun—there was nothing else she could do. "I wasn't camping, not really," he said. "Not that I don't love the wilderness—and I do camp, backpack and all that—but I just—I thought that's what you'd want to hear."

What she'd want to hear? What was he talking about? She stole a glance at the tower, sun flashing the windows, clouds pricked on the peak of the roof, and it seemed as distant as the stars at night. If only she were up there she'd put out an emergency, she would, she'd have them here in five minutes.…

"Actually," and he looked away now, his shoulders slumping in that same hangdog way they had when she'd refused his help with the water carton, "actually I've got a cabin up on Cedar Slope. I just, I just thought you'd want to hear I was camping." He'd been staring down at the toe of his boots, but suddenly he looked up at her and grinned till his back fillings glinted in the light. "I think Elaine's a pretty name, did I tell you that?"

"Thank you," she said, almost against her will, and softly, so softly she could barely hear it herself. He could rape her here, he could kill her, anything. Was that what he wanted? Was that it? "Listen," she said, pushing it, she couldn't help herself, "listen, I've got to get back to work—"

"I know, I know," he said, holding up the big slab of his hand, "back to the nest, huh? I know I must be a pain in the—in the butt for you, and I'll bet I'm not the first one to say it, but you're just too good-looking a woman to be wasted out here on the squirrels and coyotes." He stepped down, stepped toward her, and she thought in that instant of trying to dart past him, a wild thought, instinctual and desperate, a thought that clawed its way into her brain and froze there before she could move. "Jesus," he said, and his voice was harsh with conviction, "don't you get lonely?"

And then she saw it, below and to the right, movement, two bobbing pink hunter's caps, coming up the trail. It was over. Just like that. She could walk away from him, mount the stairs, lock herself in the tower. But why was her heart still going, why did she feel as if it hadn't even begun? "Damn," she said, directing her gaze, "more visitors. Now I really have to get back."

He followed her eyes and looked down to where the hunters sank out of view and then bobbed back up again, working their way up the path. She could see their faces now—two men, middle-aged, wispy hair sticking out from beneath the fluorescent caps. No guns. Cameras. He studied them a moment and then looked into her eyes, looked deep, as if he'd lost something. Then he shrugged, turned his back and started down the path toward them.

She was in good shape, the best shape of her life. She'd been up the steps a thousand times, two thousand, but she'd never climbed them quicker than she did now. She flew up the stairs like something blown by the wind and she felt a kind of panic beating against her ribs and she smelled the storm coming and felt the cold to the marrow of her bones. And then she reached the door and slammed it shut behind her, fumbling for the latch. It was then, only then, that she noticed the flowers. They were in the center of the table, in a cut-glass vase, lupine, groundsel, forget-me-not.

It snowed in the night, monstrous swirling oversized flakes that clawed at the windows and filled her with despair. The lights would only have made her feel vulnerable and exposed, and for the second night running she did without them, sitting there in the dark, cradling the kitchen knife and listening for his footfall on the steps while the sky fell to pieces around her. But he wouldn't come, not in this weather, not at night—she was being foolish, childish, there was nothing to worry about. Except the snow. It meant that her season was over. And if her season was over, she had to go back down the mountain and into the real world, real time, into the smog and roar and clutter.

She thought of the four walls that awaited her, the hopeless job—waitressing or fast food or some such slow crucifixion of the spirit—and she thought of Mike before she left him, saw him there in the black glass of the window, sexless, pale, the little butterfly-wing bifocals perched on the tip of his nose, pecking at the typewriter, pecking, pecking, in love with Dryden, Swift, Pope, in love with dead poets, in love with death itself. She'd met a man at a party a month after she'd left him and he was just like Mike, only he was in love with arthropods. Arthropods. And then she came up to the tower.

She woke late again and the first thing she felt was relief. The sun was out and the snow—it was only a dusting, nothing really—had already begun to recede from the naked high crown of the rock. She put on the kettle and went to the radio. "Zack," she called, "Needle Rock. Do you copy?"

He was there, right at her fingertips. "Copy. Over."

"We had some snow up here—nothing much, just a dusting really. It's clear now."

"You're a little late—Lewis already checked in from Mule Peak with that information. Oversleep again?"

"Yeah, I guess so." She was watching the distant treetops shake off the patina of snow. A hawk sailed across the window. She held the microphone so close to her lips it could have been a part of her. "Zack—" She wanted to tell him about the crazy, about the man in the Stetson, about his hands, wanted to alert him just in case, but she hesitated. Her voice was tiny, detached, lost in the electronic crackle of time and space.

"Lainie?"

"Yes. Yes, I'm here."

"There's a cold front coming through, another storm behind it. They're saying it could drop some snow. The season's still on—Reichert says it will be until we get appreciable precipitation—but this one could be it. It's up to you. You want to come out or wait and see?"

Reichert was the boss, fifty, bald, soft as a clam. The mountains were parched—six inches of powdery duff covered the forest floor and half the creeks had run dry. The season could last till November. "Wait and see," she said.

"Okay, it's your choice. Lewis is staying too, if it makes you feel better.

I'll keep in touch if anything develops on this end."
"Yeah. Thanks."
"Over and out."
"Over and out."

It clouded up late in the afternoon and the sky closed in on her again. The temperature began to drop. It looked bad. It was early for snow yet, but they could get snow any time of the year at this altitude. The average was twenty-five feet annually, and she'd seen storms drop four and five feet at a time. She talked to Zack at four and he told her it looked pretty grim—they were calling for a seventy-percent chance of snow, with the snow level dropping to three thousand feet. "I'll take my chances," she told him. There was a pair of snowshoes in the storage room if it came to that.

The snow started an hour later. She was cooking dinner—brown rice and vegetables—and she'd opened the bottle of wine she'd brought up to commemorate the last day of the season. The flakes were tiny, pellets that sifted down with a hiss, the sort of configuration that meant serious snow. The season was over. She could drink her wine and then think about packing up and cleaning the stove and refrigerator. She put another log on the woodstove and buttoned up her jacket.

The wine was half gone and she'd sat down to eat when she noticed the smoke. At first she thought it must be a trick of the wind, the smoke from her own stove twisting back on her. But no. Below her, no more than five hundred feet, just about where the trail would be, she could see the flames. The wind blew a screen of snow across the window. There hadn't been any lightning—but there was a fire down there, she was sure of it. She got up from the table, snatched her binoculars from the hook by the door and went out on the catwalk to investigate.

The wind took her breath away. All the universe had gone pale, white above and white beneath: she was perched on the clouds, living in them, diaphanous and ghostly. She could smell the smoke on the wind now. She lifted the binoculars to her eyes and the snow screened them; she tried again and her hair beat at the lenses. It took her a moment, but there, there it was: a fire leaping up out of the swirling grip of the snow. A campfire. But no, this was bigger, fallen trees stacked up in a pyramid— this was a bonfire, deliberate, this was a sign. The snow took it away from her. Her fingers were numb. When the fire came into focus again she saw movement there, a shadow leaping round the flames, feeding them, reveling in them, and she caught her breath. And then she saw the black stabbing peak of the Stetson and she understood.

He was camping.

Camping. He could die out there—he *was* crazy, he *was*—this thing could turn into a blizzard, it could snow for days. But he was camping. And then the thought came to her: he was camping for her.

Later, when the tower floated out over the storm and the coals glowed in the stove and the darkness settled in around her like a blanket, she disconnected the radio and put the knife away in the drawer where it belonged. Then she propped herself in the corner of the bed, way out over the edge of the abyss, and watched his fire raging in the cold heart of the night. He would be back, she knew that now, and she would be ready for him.

"The wall was pretty vertical above and below, and the valley
floor was almost four thousand feet beneath my feet"

Daniel Duane, from *Lighting Out*

*Daniel Duane (b. 1967) received a Ph.D. in English from the University
of California, Santa Cruz, and wrote his dissertation on writers' views of
the American West. Inspired by thrilling climbing accounts by writers such
as Royal Robbins and Yvon Chouinard, Duane has since written many
surfing and rock climbing books. His first book,* Lighting Out: A Vision
of California and the Mountains *(1994), describes his ascents of several
dangerous peaks.*

In this excerpt from Lighting Out, *Duane tells of his climb up the
treacherous face of Half Dome.*

No sound disturbed the natural quarry below Half Dome. In predawn
light, I smeared cream cheese on a flattened onion bagel and looked
out over the whole of Yosemite Valley. A surprising view from so high
above, from a place I had until now only looked up to: the right wall
of the valley was an ordered row of forms: Washington Column, the
Royal Arches, Yosemite Falls, the Three Brothers and El Capitan; the
left—Glacier Point, Sentinel Rock and the Cathedral Group. Even at
five a.m. the air held midsummer heat; dried sweat and dust caked my
skin from the previous night's approach and my shoulders still ached
from the load. As I ate, my own stench overpowered the blandness of
the bagel. I chewed slowly and looked around at the Northwest Face—
there was something that baffled me about that wall's beauty. So out of
human scale and yet so well formed, so sculpted. A vast field of fallen
boulders lay along its base, like so many sculptor's shavings from a
work in progress.

Nick organized the haul bag quickly, and soon we had lifted off.

Half Dome wasn't so much smaller than El Cap—twenty-six pitches by comparison to thirty-two—but somehow it seemed far more manageable, less steep and less difficult. We climbed steadily and well on familiar gray granite, deep inside corners and cracks. Perhaps because the sun didn't strike the Northwest Face until noon, and the air remained still, the wall felt like a vast and empty indoor cathedral. We ran our rope systems, made moves well within our abilities, and were soon well off the ground. Sound took on a singular quality—even with Nick a hundred feet above, every little tap of metal on stone, every scuffle of shoe, his deep breaths and occasional remarks—each and every noise echoed alone like lonely footsteps in a huge stone hall.

At a ledge a few hundred feet up, light just breaking into the sky, I prepared for my first lead of the morning. Nick sat against the rock and looked blankly out over the high country; the haul bag was perched next to him, leaning against the wall. I dismantled the pulley system and clipped the haul line into my harness to take it up with me. Then the haul bag teetered back, Nick looked up and reached for it too late, and then it was gone. Well over a hundred pounds. We both grabbed reflexively for the rope; my hand caught it and instantly slammed back against the rock and split open. The rope burned skin off my thigh as coils flipped off the ledge. The bag had a hundred and sixty-five feet to fall before it would impact my harness. Nick and I stared at each other and waited for the inevitable. I wrapped my hands around the anchor webbing and held on.

The jolt slammed me down into the ledge, then stopped. My harness had held the fall. Nick's knuckles were raw. The bag was intact. My right hand bled down into my wrist. So close to blowing the whole climb. We looked at each other in disbelief: had he forgotten to clip it to the anchor? Had I unclipped the wrong knot? It didn't matter much, and we barely spoke of the incident; we just hauled the bag back in and went on with our work.

Hours and hours of quiet climbing in the still shade; hauling, belaying, jumaring, climbing, hauling, clipping and unclipping, reclipping and untying, backing up and reorganizing, rambling up across the tower toward the wall. Alternately lost in the sheer pleasure of motion and then drifting in the emptiness of waiting. Sitting on some little ledge high over the world and just staring. I never had many thoughts at belay ledges on long climbs, I didn't ruminate on what lay below or come to new clarity about my life. The task so absorbed me and the fatigue so calmed me that I really just looked, and occasionally even just saw.

We'd exchange a few words here and there about equipment or ropes or which way the route went, but I loved the feeling that very little needed saying. We'd been climbing together for a while and knew each other well. Nick had decided that cities were crowded with psychic static; he said in a pause at a ledge that high places got him above the web of noise, especially his own. And for me Half Dome, unlike El Capitan, was charted territory. My father had been here, had climbed every inch of this rock and saw it as one of his happiest experiences.

Late in the day, at pitch eight of twenty-six, Nick led out across narrow but walkable ledges and began the Robbins Traverse, where Royal Robbins had taken the first ascent team off the tower and out onto the Northwest Face. Then, with my feet in aiders I moved as fast as I could on ancient, strange-looking bolts—fat nails driven into spread-out sheaths. Only a few of the bolts had hangers, and even those were only partially bent pieces of aluminum. The last of the bolts was so bent out of the rock it was hard to imagine much was left inside.

In the early evening we reached our bivouac ledge at pitch eleven—a thirty-foot-long, three-foot-wide notch formed by a massive exfoliating flake.

"Sweet, huh?" Nick said.

After a short break, we decided to fix a line or two ahead so we could get a good start in the morning. I scrambled up to where blocks lay wedged in the opening of a chimney. Stepping across them I could hear sand and pebbles drop into the chasm. Somewhere in the darkness below, light leaked in from a crack. My pitch went well— easy aid, t.c.u.'s, fixed pieces in a beautiful white corner to the left of the chimney.

I leaned back and looked about. The crack was lined with old fixed pins; the face to either side was blank. As Nick started leading the next pitch, it became clear how tired he was—too much pro, thrashing around, stepping clumsily. At last he hung from a piece and looked back down at me with a smile.

"I'm out of here," he said.

"The whole route?" I couldn't believe my ears.

"Relax, bro. Just this pitch. Let's eat." We slid back down our skinny ropes and stumbled across blocks back to the vaguely comfortable part of the ledge. Everything came out of the bag. Feet came out of sweaty, torturous rock shoes and into clean socks. No point in so much as standing up—nowhere to walk, and everything an arm's reach away. I pulled out our dinner and started getting depressed....[W]e'd bought our food in a Berkeley health food store, and had gotten on a clean fuels kick. So we had nothing but dried this, dried that, bread, cheese, nuts, seeds—nothing that felt like a fitting meal after a hard day's work.

"Dude," Nick had his head under a rock, was reaching for something. "Check it out. Treasure!" Four full cans had been abandoned by some retreating party—blueberries, clam chowder, Spaghettios, Dinosaurs with Meatballs. Stunning good fortune—the ultimate Wall Food. I couldn't believe I hadn't thought of cans before. Nick demanded the Spaghettios, so I gladly took the Dinosaurs. The fat had congealed beautifully in the top of the can and I scooped it into my mouth with an old piton. The blueberries occupied nearly an hour as we sucked them down one by one.

A red glow rose out of the horizon and Yosemite Valley three thousand feet below softened and seemed of a piece, a valley proper. The distinct monoliths fell into a pattern of overlapping slopes and walls. Darkness filled the valley from below as the harsh white of sun on granite faded into soft, deep grays. Lights appeared, marking Curry and Yosemite Villages. Faint car headlights crawling through the trees actually looked homey and pleasant.

I'd always though that bivies up that high should be wild, dangerous, somehow violent and disorderly. Nothing could have been farther from the truth. The wind stopped and the valley's warm air rose as a soft breeze. No Valley tour busses roared, no traffic honked and smoked. No sound, no wind. Just warm air. Darkness obscured the wild exposure of our perch; it seemed a natural, even exquisite place to be.

I flaked ropes between blocks to make a bed, grinning like an idiot, almost crying with pleasure at the thought of sleep. My back, legs, arms, neck and chest burned sore; my hands were swollen, raw and scabbed. My extra clothing filled another spot, and the tent fly filled another. When at last I lay down I felt so heavy that rolling over and dangling in the void never occurred to me as a danger. I sank into the crevice in the rocks, comfortably lodged. But for a full hour after dark, I couldn't sleep. There was too much beauty to see, too striking and unique a view, so much precious sky. A perfect place attained by perfect means, by adequate struggle. Each time I began to fade, I wanted a last look; I whispered the whole scene out loud to myself, panting lightly as I spoke, mouthing the colors, the feeling of the warmth, the unbelievable quiet and stillness and my own attendant tiredness. I told myself the whole scene again and again to remember everything.

I opened my eyes in the middle of the night, that vast wild wall just a quiet, immobile place. The full moon, out of sight behind Half Dome, washed the sweeping granite apron of Glacier Point in cold white light. And then I realized what was before me: a moonshadow of Half Dome framed in the middle of the glow, a perfect projection of its curves on the apron. It occurred to me that these mountains always etched themselves across one another by sun and by moon, by shadow, dawn and dusk, and that for that moment on that night I lay with a blessed point of view between. Soon the shadow blurred and merged with the wider brushing of moonlight; before the moon itself rose into sight from behind the dome, I had fallen asleep.

When Nick's watch alarm beeped, the sky had iced over with light and the full moon had faded. I sat up in my sleeping bag and turned so my back was against the wall and my feet off the edge. We looked about for a while, faced once again where we were. Nick fished out our ration of bagels. I drank a whole liter of water mixed with electrolyte supplements. We were slow getting moving, but when we were both well awake, stretched, and warmed, we packed the terrific mess back into the haul bag and started climbing.

I felt like a fish on a line as I thrashed up our fixed ropes in a flaring chimney. For the first lead of the day, I groveled into a miserable fissure and lost confidence—aiding behind an expanding flake at the back of another chimney, I could barely turn my head around because of my helmet. Loose rock threatened to fall and kill Nick. I asked him to lower me down to clean a piece because the rope drag was stopping my upward motion.

"You can't just haul enough up?" Nick asked. "Come on, just try to haul it. It'll take forever to lower you." I looked around, already drained, worn out, tried to pull some more rope and couldn't. I got planted on a small ledge and did a full leg-press—a foot of rope came. Another press, another foot, and then I could build the anchor and relax. The day went as smoothly as the one before, and Nick and I began to talk and yell at each other, to laugh at what an absurdity it was.

We reached our bivouac—Big Sandy Ledge—at 3:30 with a storm gathering in the high mountains. We'd just dropped our gear on the ledge and sat down when three climbers popped up and hooted with delight at the sight of the approaching clouds—without bivy gear, rain gear, or food. They'd left the car at Curry Village at 9:00 a.m. that same day and had walked eight miles and climbed seventeen pitches since: bearded, sweating, psychotic super-hardmen having the time of their lives.

I admitted to one of them that I thought Nick and I might be in for a wild night on the ledge—looked like a big storm coming in; lightning flashed in the distance.

"But you'll have the greatest story to tell," he said, looking around at the sky, "and the bettys'll just be like 'give me your throbbing member!'" He was gone. Up the cracks called the zigzags. For a few hours later we could hear them yelling at each other.

With hours to kill till dark we sat on the ledge and stared, peed on different terraces, looked off into the sun for hours, watched a slow changing of the day, took turns shitting into paper bags and hurling them into space. Nick didn't even clear the ledge. Quite a mess. The storm moved overhead and deep booms and cracks sent us scampering for rain gear. Lightning charged into peaks; a black curtain of rain deluged Tenaya Canyon only a half-mile away. Nick giggled with nervous anticipation, apparently hoping for the thrill. We were well anchored down, had plenty of warm clothing and rain gear, and these storms rarely lasted more than a few hours. So let us have it. Blow us off the mountain.

And then the storm pulled back, just like that, and left us with a long beautiful afternoon. Sleep was again difficult because of the beauty of the night. I watched meteors, picked out constellations, leaned over to look at the valley again and again, thinking about my dad sleeping here. We woke up late, had a slow breakfast, and mosied up the zigzags. After an hour and a half, we reached Thank God Ledge, which ran left for fifty feet. I'd seen pictures of my dad on Thank God Ledge, crawling like a lowly rat. Rather undignified. I'd bet him ten dollars I'd walk the whole thing. Nick got out the camera.

I walked right out there, no sweat. Shuffling along like a man. I could swear the ledge started narrowing a bit, but I kept walking just the same. The wall was pretty vertical above and below, and the valley floor was almost four thousand feet beneath my feet, but I just put one foot in front of the other. After ten feet or so, I turned to face the wall—spread my arms out flat against it and shuffled sideways with my cheek pressed flat—just to be safe. I mean, after all, at least I was still behaving like a biped. Five feet later, I sank right down to my knees and never looked back. The hell with it. Nick shot three frames of my retreating behind.

As we approached the summit, a few tourists looked down and waved. Unlike great Alpine peaks—snowy pinnacles in the stratosphere—the tops of Yosemite walls feel more like endings than goals, they remind you that the great part was being on the route, not, as [my friend] Aaron [Lehrman] would say, having done it. At last I scrambled up a rather mundane series of ramps and stood on top. Hikers who'd come up the cable staircase milled about. A startled teenage girl in cutoff Levis and a bikini top looked at my haggard face and said,

"Did you just come up that way?"

Great question. God, what a good question. Thank you so much for asking that question. "Well, ah, yes. Now that you mention it, I did."

She looked at me, then off the edge.

"Rad," she said. She spun on her heels and walked away, apparently having changed the channel.

On that high mesa of exfoliating granite, overweight marmots scavenged in unattended backpacks and the twenty or thirty people sitting around spoke quietly as if in a museum. A wind blew across the summit and out into the air over the valley. Kids had their pictures taken on the diving board—a thin block that stuck straight out over the abyss. Nick lay on his belly and looked over the edge back down on the route. He yelled at me to join him, but I couldn't do it—too acute a sense of gravity.

The eight miles home were all downhill, and we ran almost the whole way, fast and stumbling, trying to make the showers before closing. Down the mist trail—steep riprapping, pounding on the knees, the fabulous torrent of Nevada Falls and the green meadow at its base—utterly unlike the surrounding plants. Vernal Falls was a wild column of water framed by moss and ferns, and its staircase trail, absolutely paved, suggested an Inca trail. At last, into the human zoo of Curry Village for showers. After washing off the whole experience, we went to the Loft Restaurant, where a Dutch milkmaiden of a girl served us hamburgers.

"Why you guys so thirsty?" she asked. "Half Dome? The Regular Route? Oh yeah, my boyfriend and I did a one-day winter ascent. It was so great."

We slept in our clean cotton T-shirts and jeans in the back of the truck. Coffee milkshakes at ten a.m., and then back to Berkeley. A Big Wall.

"Wisps of clouds radiate outward from Sawtooth Ridge
like the gold rays in a baroque sculpture"

Ann Zwinger, from *Yosemite*

*Ann Haymond Zwinger (b. 1925) was born in Indiana and grew up along
the banks of the White River, gaining a lifelong love of the natural world.
After completing her education at Wellesley and Indiana University, Zwinger
moved to Colorado Springs, Colorado, where, along with raising her family
and teaching Southwest studies and English at Colorado College, she authored
the first of her many naturalist books. She has since written more than a dozen
other books and has appeared in numerous anthologies. In 1976, Zwinger
received the prestigious John Burroughs Memorial Association Gold Medal for
distinguished contribution to natural history for her book* Run, River, Run: A
Naturalist's Journey Down One of the Great Rivers of the West.*

In this selection from her* Yosemite: Valley of Thunder *(1996),
Zwinger recounts an excursion with her daughter Susan in the granite-
walled expanses of Yosemite.*

This July morning a light breeze streaks the otherwise calm surface
of an alpine tarn, then dies, leaving a polished, stainless-steel skin.
Yesterday my elder daughter, Susan, and I hiked eight miles into the
Sierra, and twenty-five hundred feet up, into the northeast corner of the
Yosemite backcountry wilderness, which brought us to this charming
tarn nestled into a granite bowl at around ten thousand feet.

The sky brightens but does not heat; I enjoy earth's staging time,
getting everything adjusted, ordered, before turning on the sun. By six,
full sunlight stains a ridge ruddy at the far edge of the lake, reflecting in
the water like warp-dyed silk. Then this July day begins with blazing
trumpets of light. I've never been averse to a little glory before breakfast,
and watching sunrise bestir this pond does it for me.

I suspect the real glories of Yosemite belong to the backpackers, the trudgers and trekkers, those who finish a strenuous climb and wait for their psyches to catch up, suffer a thunderstorm on an alpine fell, and most of all, let the night spirits seep into their sleep. The real glories of Yosemite belong to those who are comfortable with being uncomfortable, who know it's all right to be afraid, to be cold, wet, tired, and hungry, to be euphoric and, on occasion, ecstatic.

More than 706,000 acres, over 94 percent of the park, is managed as wilderness and can never be developed. A permit system applies to hikers and groups on horseback who plan to remain overnight, thus guaranteeing that hikers are not falling over one another or overusing one area. The park instituted a permit system because rangers counted almost five thousand campfire rings in the backcountry in 1972. The wilderness areas cope well so far with the 30 percent of the visitors who go there, perhaps because they are of a different outlook than the three million who jam into the valley and spend their time commuting between the stores at the Visitor Center and Curry Village.

Kerrick Meadow lies a little above nine thousand feet, depending on a knob here or a depression there. Laid between granite walls, the valley looks quilted in all shades of green. In this wet soil, wildflowers abound, and little apricot-colored day moths flutter up against my legs as I walk. A grasshopper with dark brown wings alights at right angles to the sun, then ratchets off again.

Like better-known Tuolumne Meadows, Kerrick Meadow has seasonally saturated soils that maintain a water table too high for trees to grow. The meadow bears the name of James D. Kerrick, who trailed sheep here around 1880. Most of its yearly precipitation, between thirty and fifty inches, falls as snow, and the growing season seldom lasts more than nine weeks.

In the middle of Kerrick Meadow, Rancheria Creek (also probably a name used by sheepmen) flutters its way downhill on a gradual gradient. A tinsel-ribbon of water, it pauses occasionally to spread into small pools at the outside of a meander or to nibble at a bank, in no hurry to get anywhere. According to the sandy, gravelly flats alongside, its channel at high runoff sometimes widens to fifty feet. Frost heaves that make the ground expand disturb plant roots and leave bare, gravelly patches that resemble shaven spots in the lush sedge meadow that bounds the stream. These active, top layers of soil discourage plant growth and allow only the most sturdy pioneer plants, those that can withstand the thaws and freezes that unceremoniously assault their roots. These plants, like tiny daisies and lupines and bright pink pussy-paws, have many of the same adaptations as those that occupy alpine heights. They are small, close to the ground, and often densely furred with hairs.

Following the creek, Susan and I sometimes walk in a horse pack trail incised six to twelve inches below the surface. One horse concentrates more pounds per square inch and causes as much damage as twenty-five or more people. Vegetation and soil at camps where horses are tethered is impacted ten times as much as at other camps, and meadows are grazed into mud. But horse use continues because it provides easier and longer access to the backcountry.

An ominous, dark cloud to the north sits astride the valley upstream. From my perch I watch the virga, filmy veils of rain, shred down out of it. The storm crawls like a tank, filling the breadth of the canyon, scraping the granite, dragging against the ground, marching toward us with an overweening arrogance. It formed from heated air rising from the Central Valley, cooling as it rose and capturing enough moisture to form thunderheads. A grumbling muttering-in-its-beard thunder beats on the granite as if it were a tympanum, an unmistakable announcement of intent. One minute the rocks are dry, then suddenly the downpour rushes off their flanks. It rains the rest of the afternoon. It rains all night.

In the morning, watching a tent fly dry is in the same category as watching a pot boil, and the need to wait legitimizes some morning lethargy. I return to yesterday's storm-watching perch. Handfuls of moisture hang in the air, swathing everything in lingering dampness. Tiny yellow monkey flowers that would fit into a shirt button, plants maybe less than half an inch high, interweave in familial mats. The lip of each flower carries a drop of water that magnifies the red specks of its throat.

Spiny gooseberry bushes sprawl across the slope behind me, double thorns on the stems. Indians used to burn Yosemite Valley just to encourage such berry bushes to sprout, for gooseberry and other berry plants come in quicker after a burn. In more recent times, however, gooseberry and currant, shrubs of the genus *Ribes*, have been indicted as being an alternate host to white pine blister rust. Blister rust infections come in waves, usually when cool and moist conditions encourage spores to form in the gooseberry phase. For decades foresters killed gooseberries and currants to stop the spread until, in the 1960s, the rust infection was judged not to be such a threat after all. Scattered plants that escaped execution remain at higher altitudes.

While I lodgepole- and monkey-flower-watch, the sun levitates seven inches above the rock rim across the valley, and as it rises above the mists it paints sharp, clear shadows. With it comes a light breeze. I check my sleeping bag. Contrary to my pessimistic expectation of a soggy sleeping bag forever, it is dry.

Another afternoon, Susan and I hike to a higher tarn. The gravel apron around it scrunches underfoot. The water is so cold and lacking in minerals, so "pure," that no algae grow in it, no plankton, no fish.

A path crosses behind the tarn beneath its source of supply, a snowbank plastered on the scooped-out slope of granite wall a quarter mile away. Thick sedges hide threads of water that don't show up until you step into them ankle deep. At the edge of one rivulet, I spy a little half-inch tan frog with a black stripe through its eye. It hops off through skyscraper sedge—a Pacific tree frog.

After crossing the meadow, the path starts up to a divide. When it runs down again, I leave it to scramble up a bare talus slope. I intend to go only partway to a dark rocky ridge on the horizon, but it's a Pied Piper landscape, calling me through one more rock doorway, up one more rise to one more interesting plant, one more different kind of rock. I follow meekly, hypnotized, into the severe, sculptural spaces of one of my favorite places, the alpine zone.

The dark rock outcropping is so splintered into silver-dollar pieces that it clinks as I walk through it. The metamorphic hornfels shatters into smaller chips than granite, contains more minerals, and is darker and more heat absorbent than the granites, an assist to plants at cold altitudes. The outcrop is a leftover from the metamorphics that once completely covered the mountains. Surrounded above, below, and alongside by pearly gray granite, the dark rock stands out as powerfully as the clenched fist in a Rodin sculpture.

Sun shines 354 days (almost 97 percent) of the year up here, but at the same time, it can freeze any night. Wind shaves the ground like a straight razor. Precipitation drops to less than half an inch in July, with August even drier. What little moisture there is comes from melting snow.

Plants up here tend to be low cushions and mats, white phlox and pink moss campion, tiny buckwheats and little lupines, all of which withstand freezing and can photosynthesize at lower temperatures than plants of lower altitude. Lupine is heavily furred, an adaptation that lessens water loss and insulates the plant against evaporation, solar radiation, and cold. Like most alpine plants, lupines are perennials. Most annuals do not have time enough to sprout, grow, flower, and set seed in the abbreviated growing season. Many species grow for a decade or more before they store up enough energy to flower. Some reproduce by vegetative means, which gives new plants a better start and an assured source of nourishment.

Plants here take root in nearly sterile, pulverized granite, chips of feldspar, quartz bits, and sparkly flecks of mica, with not enough organic matter in it to deserve the designation of "soil." With cold temperatures and few plants, humus neither forms nor stays put on steep alpine talus slopes. Red heather, full of pink blossoms, espaliers across a rock face, preferring the acids provided by disintegrating granites. White heather nestles against a pegmatite dike full of big handsome feldspar crystals. By growing on a slight incline facing the sun, the heather receives half again more heat and light than if it grew on the flat. Creeping mats of magenta penstemons and alpine sorrel always grow along the downhill edge of rocks, capturing the runoff moisture. A dainty sandwort raises little starlike blooms with five rosy stamens hovering above five starched white petals.

Downhill, puffy patches of flake lichen tint the ground an odd and distinctive bluish-gray. Flake lichen thrives within a growing season of seven to twelve weeks and signals that this area holds snow late into the summer. Snow is more protector than growth-stopper at high altitude. On days when the wind-chill factor may drop to minus forty degrees, snow shields alpine plants from a brutal buffeting.

Upslope, narrow rivulets weep out from under a raggedy patch of snow shining like tinsel. How does a snowfield die? Rather ignominiously, I'm afraid. A beautiful expanse of pristine white snow becomes crusted with dirt and dust, its surface porous and granulated from freezing over each night, melting each day, looking like Japanese rice paper with pine needles, willow leaves, and other plant bits encased in it. These absorb enough heat to sink in a quarter inch, blackening and embedding themselves in a bezel of snow. Pink algae color teacup-sized hollows. No longer big enough to sluice a stream of icy water downhill, the snowfield drips like a dozen leaky faucets. It languishes, passing away from sun disease, a fragile Camille, a wan Traviata, a doomed Mimi, dying with operatic slowness. It goes out with neither a bang nor a whimper—just a tiny liquid tinkling, it requires the soprano of a mosquito.

As I start down, a muted clucking comes from nearby, stops, resumes.

As quietly as possible, I slip out binoculars and wait. About ten feet away, close enough to see the red line above the eye, I spot a handsome male ptarmigan. About the size of a chicken, ptarmigan are an instance of Bergmann's Rule in action: creatures of cold climates tend to be larger than tropical animals, since size gives a better relationship of volume to exposed area and makes it easier to retain body heat. The bird proceeds with considerable dignity up a boulder face, snapping at flower heads, ambling up the rock to a small shady overhang. Speckled brown and white on back and wings, he blends into the dappled light under the overhang. In winter, ptarmigan turn totally white, with extravagant white pantaloons, a heavy feathering that gives extra insulation to legs and feet. Males winter above timberline, the only birds to do so in this stringent climate.

Later, after loping down a rain-greased talus slope with nothing taller in sight than I, lightning flashing and thunder banging simultaneously, a hastily donned poncho flapping, boots and pants soaked and hands stiff with cold, I finally reach a lower flat and hunker down. Just when I don't think I can get any wetter or any colder comes the hail. Stinging *petit-pois*-sized pellets insinuate themselves into every crease of my poncho, fill the puddles around my feet, and leave windrows around the rocks. What isn't already wet gets wet—soaking, irrevocably, irretrievably wet, wet from the outside and through to the other side.

At the far edge of misery a pale sun appears, not a moment too soon for this huddled mass of dripping, dirty laundry, with runny nose and squishy boots. As the last BBs of hail clear the valley, a rainbow, an incredible swatch of color, materializes against the gloomy clouds. Not your same old arch, but a rectangular banner broadcasting its blazing spectrum of color, it flutters out from under a mass of clouds in the southwest sky, undulating like northern lights.

That evening, tent pitched and trenched, clothes dry, and the comforts reestablished, I pull out the obligatory "ice-cream-and-cake-and-candle," a day-late birthday celebration for Susan: two small, slightly squashed cupcakes, one pink candle, and a packet of freeze-dried ice cream that tastes like ice cream even if it isn't cold. What's a mother for? We raise a toast of freshly filtered, very cold stream water to the pleasures of wilderness. My cup runneth over.

* * *

Waning sun, shuttered behind a pure white cloud, traces its rim with eye-blinding incandescence. Wisps of clouds radiate outward from Sawtooth Ridge like the gold rays in a baroque sculpture. Tall, dark green, narrow triangles of trees rise against a backdrop of white granite beneath a deep blue Sierran sky: unmistakably Yosemite. The sky chills to an aquamarine of limpid clarity and transparency, a cut-crystal atmosphere, before it deepens to navy blue in which stars begin to glint.

Shadows inch up the last sunlit face. With my sketchbook in my lap, I recall James D. Smillie, who published *Yellowstone to Yosemite: Early Adventures in the Mountain West* in 1872. Smillie wrote and illustrated his summer in Yosemite and with an artist's eye noted that Yosemite's granites, being so pale, are exceptionally responsive to changes in atmosphere. At sunset, he wrote that "they glow with a ruddy light, that is slowly extinguished by the upcreeping shadows of night, until the highest point flames for one moment, then dies, ashy pale, under the glory that is lifted to the sky above. Then the cold moon tips with silver those giant, sleeping forms, and by its growing light I cleared my palette, and closed the box upon my last study of the Yosemite and Sierras."

I unfold my map for the last time to check our route out tomorrow. Now its folds are worn, its edges shredded. Well used indeed. Miles calculated, elevation lines counted, meadows walked, streams crossed, heights climbed. Now, when I trace with my finger where we've been on this trip, the map lines segue into images of clumps of pines or shining tarns or mellifluous meadows. That green spot here was full of flowers and butterflies, and that blue line there was a booming waterfall, sweetened with birdsong. Those concentric ruffled circles describe the top of a dome on which I stood, those dotted blue lines the beginning of a stream that wiggled downslope.

No longer is the map two-dimensional. It is composed of height of ponderosa, breadth of valley, depth of stream, wintertime, summertime, springtime, autumntime, the vanilla smell of Jeffrey pine, the gritty feel of granite, the puckery taste of alpine sorrel, the unexpected song of a canyon wren, the senses of time, the waterfalls of the mind.

"Californios have always, by a quirk of fate, occupied land rich in gold deposits, but we have never looked upon this metal with the obsessive avarice of Europeans"

Alejandro Murguía, "Josefa of Downieville: The Obscure Life and Notable Death of a Chicana in Gold Rush California"

Few people in California—and virtually nobody who is not descended from California's native tribes—can claim deeper ancestral roots to this region than Alejandro Murguía (b. 1949). One of his ancestors, for instance, marched with a Spanish expedition from Baja to Alta California in 1773 and led the construction of Mission Santa Clara. An important figure in the cultural, social, and political movements centered in San Francisco's Mission District for more than thirty-five years, Murguía is a professor in the College of Ethnic Studies at San Francisco State University. An acclaimed writer of short stories, he received a 2003 American Book Award for his collection Southern Front.

In this excerpt from his wide-ranging, biographically based Medicine of Memory: A Mexica Clan in California, *Murguía reexamines a lynching— and the cultural atmosphere surrounding it—in the Sierra County village of Downieville in 1851. The victim here is Josefa, a Mexican woman arrested for defending herself against, and killing, a white man. This true story is also mentioned in the selection from Isabel Allende's* Daughter of Fortune, *in Chapter 2 of this anthology.*

> I told the deceased that was no place to call me bad names, come in and call me so, and as he was coming in I stabbed him.
> —Josefa, in her own defense, Downieville, July 5, 1851

These words spoken by a Mexican woman on trial for murder at the height of the California Gold Rush jumped out at me when I first read them in a newspaper dated 1851. Who was this woman who spoke in public so calmly yet forcefully, and for whom the only name we have is Josefa? The tragic circumstances of her death obsessed me for weeks, till finally, one summer day I drove out from San Francisco to visit the Mother Lode country, La Veta Madre [in Spanish, "the mother vein" or "Mother Lode"], as the *mexicanos* called it, the site of this story. I crossed over the San Mateo Bridge and over the Altamont pass, then through Tracy, headed for Stockton. But way before driving out of San Francisco, I too, in my own way, had become obsessed with gold. What role does it play in my memory? All the history books praise the forty-niners, but I don't like them or their history (I don't even like the football team named after them). I am a victim of their arrival: the forty-niners displaced and murdered those who were already here—the Native Americans and the Californios. My Gold Rush heritage is that Chicanos are now foreigners in their own land. Yet at the start of the Gold Rush we claimed the land with our names: Hornitos, Sonora, Mariposa—names that still survive, especially in the heart of gold country.

As I drive east, I think of the events of that day in 1851, in a now insignificant town at the end of Highway 49. Of all the stories of the Gold Rush, of incredible fortunes made and lost overnight, of violent deaths that occurred in the goldfields with boring repetition, Josefa's is the one that matters most to me, the one I choose to recover from the dustbins of history. It is a story of drunken vigilantes and ignoble patriots, and of men who stood by while a woman was lynched, and those stories are never pretty. I often ask myself what I might have done that day in Downieville. I sometimes imagine myself the hero, rushing to Josefa's rescue wielding a shotgun, and then taking her away on my horse. But I don't know for sure; I might have just closed my eyes, not wanting to see. Her violent death is an open wound in my memory, and yet I cannot right the wrong done to her. Perhaps the only thing I can do is recover her story, restore to her a sense of human dignity. And by telling the story, vindicate all good women and men, including myself, because if good people allow evil to go unchallenged, even if it's an incident a hundred and fifty years old, our perceptions and attitudes of race and gender, of right and wrong, become entrenched, sometimes forever....

Native Americans didn't care for gold. It had no value to them. None. They valued gypsum and amethyst for jewelry, serpentine for charm stones. They adored abalone shell, polishing it to a bright mother of pearl, and feathers of different types of birds: condors, eagles, hawks, and hummingbirds. Once the forty-niners invaded the region, Native Americans did work in the goldfields, sometimes for wages; other times they bartered the gold for needed supplies. The Californios blew hot and cold about gold. It's an old story in Chicano history that in 1841, in a canyon behind Mission San Fernando, Francisco López sat down to eat his lunch, pulled out a wild onion growing alongside the creek, and discovered clinging to the roots—¡Oro! Gold, *compadre!* His lucky find inspired some miners to trek north from Sonora, Mexico. They worked for a while around the area where López had found gold, now named Placerita Canyon, and then lost interest in the project and moved on, south to Los Angeles or north to Monterey. Another Mexicano, Pablo Gutiérrez, found gold in the Bear River of Northern California in March 1844, but he was unable to procure a *batea* for panning, so nothing came of it. The Californios who came to the goldfields in 1848 were casual miners; many were established rancheros, like Antonio Franco Coronel, who left as the troubles escalated, disgusted with the violence and the murders.

The forty-niners, on the other hand, hungered for gold with a sickness. They even described it as "gold fever." They would do anything for it. They left families, homes, everything behind; they sailed for eight months aboard leaky, smelly ships to reach California; others, captains and sailors, jumped ship at San Francisco, leaving a fleet of abandoned brigs, barks, and schooners to rot by the piers. They slaughtered all the game they could find and so muddied the rivers and creeks with silt that the once plentiful salmon couldn't survive. The herds of elk and deer, the food source for Native Americans, were practically wiped out in one summer. The miners cheated and killed each other in the goldfields. The newspaper accounts of the day are filled with their bloody deeds and grizzly frontier justice, or maybe it should be called injustice. And in 1851, after an all-day celebration for the Fourth of July, a mob of forty-niners unleashed all their venom and hatred on a Mexican woman.

Several things disturbed me about this incident when I first read about it: the misogynist and racial implications, as well as the absence of a last name for Josefa. I, who was obsessed with names, who could spend days in sterile archives searching for even a minute reference to a Lugo, Olivas, or Murguía, suddenly found myself faced with one specific person who had no full name. In general, when writing about violence toward Amerindians or Mexicans, Western historiographers tend to use incomplete names, usually just the first name or a generic one, like "José," as if the individual didn't matter. It made me realize that it is not names and bloodlines that hold clans together, but rather their shared experience.

The eyewitness account published in *The Steamer Pacific Star* dated July 15, 1851, lists the full names of the judge, the jury, the witnesses—all of them white males—and four names for the victim, also white, a first name, a middle name, and two last names. Yet with Josefa, not even the reporter who was present records her last name, nor does it appear in any of the forty-niner journals that describe the event. Sure, no one takes notes at a lynching, but there was a pretense of a trial, with a judge and jury sworn in. All the accounts state that she testified in her own defense, and, therefore, must have been sworn in too. So what happened that her last name was never recorded, an important detail in any judicial hearing, even at a kangaroo court? Didn't anyone ask "What's your full name?"

Without a doubt, the California Gold Rush is the most written about event in the West. Yet not a single historian has questioned why Josefa has no last name. It seems that a Mexican woman in the goldfields was insignificant, not even worthy of a last name, just another "greaser." And then, over the course of many decades, historians like Hubert Howe Bancroft changed her name to fit the stereotypical Mexican image: she is now referred to as "Juanita of Downieville," which just adds insult to injury. In some accounts she's even called "Juanita, the Spanish woman." So even her single name and her nationality have been distorted.

At other times, Josefa is portrayed in all sorts of romantic images, including the ridiculous, such as she "cheerfully passed away." But no one has ever stood up for her. No one has ever asked why she was given such a harsh sentence, carried out so brutally, or where she learned the poise to defend herself before a kangaroo court and a frenzied mob. Where did she find the *corazón* to stand on the gallows and show more bravery than any man that day?

These questions were what set me on the road to Downieville.

* * *

In the history of Mexico and Latin America, gold has always been a double-edged sword. The Europeans, the Spaniards, and the North Americans invaded our lands, driven by their desire to acquire the precious metal. Latin Americans, Mexicans, and Californios have always, by a quirk of fate, occupied land rich in gold deposits, but we have never looked upon this metal with the obsessive avarice of Europeans. Gold might be decorative and beautiful, but in pre-Columbian America it was never the coin of the realm, and never something worth killing for.

As a young boy, I'd heard the stories of gold-crazed Spaniards: Cortés melting to ingots the intricate gifts Moctezuma had offered him, completely disregarding their beauty; his only concern was their monetary value. Or the story of the Inca, Atahualpa, who offered to fill one room with gold and one with silver if Pizarro would release him; but when the ransom was paid, Atahualpa was hung. And somewhere I have seen an old engraving of Indians pouring molten gold down a Spaniard's throat in the belief that only that remedy would cure them of their gold sickness.

So for me, gold has always been suspicious. And in spite of its allure, within my lifetime, I've seen gold lose much of its luster. As I write this, an ounce of gold on the London market is worth much less than an ounce of Humboldt green [marijuana] on any barrio street. So gold has an arbitrary value that is relative, depending on the importance you put on it, much like the value of a human life in the Gold Rush. But how can we compare a human life to a fistful of gold dust? I can't. I suspect few of us can. For the ancient Mexicans and Peruvians, gold was precious, but with no monetary value. For others, it's the engine that drives the wheel. And that wheel has always crushed us....

At the beginning of the Gold Rush, in 1848, the gold was literally lying about in the creeks and streams. A person didn't even have to pan for it. You could walk along a stream and maybe pick up several nuggets wedged between the rocks. The biggest nugget found was the size of a cantaloupe, cubic in form, and nearly pure—a twenty-three-pound gold nugget just sitting in the riverbed waiting to be picked up.

At first, it was mostly locals who were in the goldfields, but by 1849 the word had spread and thousands started arriving from all over the world, from Chile and Peru, China, even Malaysia and points east. Soon, approximately one hundred thousand miners were roaming the Sierra foothills, and 7 million dollars' worth of gold was coming out every month. The totals are staggering: in 1851, the year of this story,

75 million dollars' worth of gold flowed out of California. By the end of the decade, 594 million dollars' worth of gold had enriched the treasury of the United States. And the gold kept coming, year after year. During the Civil War, California gold poured into the financial center of New York at the rate of 5 to 6 million dollars' worth a month, and thereby prevented a total collapse of Lincoln's government. Without that gold to feed, clothe, and maintain the Northern armies, Lincoln's *Emancipation Proclamation* might not have been worth the paper it was written on. Heinrich Schliemann, a young German adventurer, made his fortune in the California goldfields and thus financed his childhood dream—to discover the site of ancient Troy. The list is endless. With California gold, dreams were possible. Without California gold, I wouldn't be writing this, and life would be much different for all of us....

When exactly Josefa arrives in the goldfields is unknown. Most likely she is from Sonora, one of 10,000 other Sonoran miners who worked and lived in the gold country. The Sonorans from northern Mexico, and other Latin Americans, had a long history of gold mining, and they brought with them the tools and techniques to extract the gold once the easy pickings were over. The Sonorans brought the wooden sluices called *bateas* for panning gold. And the Chileans introduced the *arrastra*, a heavy stone boulder that a mule drags over quartz to crush it and release the gold. They brought with them not just the culture of gold mining but the language as well; and as I'm driving down Highway 49, the Spanish names crop up like ghosts from the past—El Dorado, Placer, Campo Seco.

But the experience and success of the Sonoran miners were used against them. In 1849, the newcomers arriving from New England did not know the technique for panning or mining gold, and they felt envious of the Sonorans, who knew where to find the quartz veins. The United States had just taken California from Mexico, and the forty-niners believed they were the only ones who had a right to the gold—everyone else, especially nonwhites or those who spoke Spanish, was an interloper, a trespasser, an enemy. As it was, the camps were tense, tough, dirty places. Men survived the best they could, and the weak, those who couldn't protect their claims, didn't last long in the goldfields. Moreover, the laws were heavily stacked against foreigners, men and women. For instance, nonwhites could not testify in a court of law against whites. Then, adding further tension to the situation, California passed the Foreign Miners Tax of 1850, a monthly fee of twenty dollars levied on all nonwhite miners, with the explicit purpose of running the Sonorans, the Latinos, and the Chinese out of the goldfields.

The Sonorans were caught in an ironic situation. Many had been in California before the newly arrived forty-niners, and yet they were being taxed as foreigners. They were the founders of the town of Sonora, one of the richest in the gold country, and now they were being chased out. It wasn't lost on them that other foreigners, the Irish or the English, for example, were not taxed. And if the Sonorans refused to pay the taxes, the forty-niners encouraged each other to jump their claims. The Chinese turned to vegetable growing to survive, while many of the Sonorans left the goldfields disillusioned, or were run out by mobs of forty-niners. Towns they had founded, like Sonora, were abandoned; others, like Columbia, were left with but a handful of miners. But other Sonorans stayed, out of pride perhaps or out of stubbornness. Some were killed; some became outlaws. Out of such conditions arose Joaquín Murieta, the legendary Robin Hood of the Gold Rush era, the hero of a tale so twisted it will take a determined scholar to unravel it.

With a typical mix of the multiple nationalities in the goldfields, Downieville, originally a camp, was founded in 1850 by a Major Downie, with his crew of ten black sailors, one Irishman, one Indian, and one Kanaka, a native Hawaiian. Although the Foreign Miners Tax was repealed in March of 1851, mostly because of complaints by merchants that they were losing business, the damage had been done. By mid-1851, the once plentiful Sonorans were rare in the Sierra foothills. So for Josefa, or any Mexican woman, to have reached the gold country, she had to be resilient, brave, and determined. The last fifty miles of the road to Downieville deteriorated into a winding mule trail cut out of steep ravines along the Yuba River. The journey was not only hard; it was dangerous, whether on foot or on horseback. It was not uncommon for travelers to lose their footing and plunge into the ravine, mules and all. The living conditions along the fork of the river where the camp had sprouted were primitive at best: tents, lean-tos, shanties, and ankle-deep mud everywhere. But Downieville also had two-story wooden buildings, fifteen hotels and gambling houses, butcher shops and bakeries, a theater, and plenty of saloons.

An Argentine miner named Ramón Gil Navarro came to the Gold Rush in 1849 and spent the following three years living and working in the Sierras, alternating with travels to Stockton and San Francisco. [Navarro's account of vigilante justice meted out to Chilean miners appears in Chapter 2 of this anthology.] He kept a detailed diary that offers some interesting observations about the milieu in which Josefa lived. I quote Navarro because, as a Latin American, he gives a different perspective than the white-authored first-person narratives of that period, which tend to be prejudiced toward everyone of color....

Navarro also recounts the rumors that abounded of how Yankee bandits, called "The Forty," were planning to rally other miners to exterminate all Chileans, Mexicans, or Peruvians on July Fourth, 1849. He goes on to state that threats against foreigners are common on this day, causing many Mexicans to leave the towns and mines of the region. Considering the Foreign Miners Tax of 1850 and the open violence toward Mexicans and Latin Americans between 1849 and 1851, also detailed by Navarro, I'd suspect that the mood of the forty-niners two years later, on July 4, 1851, had become even more patriotically belligerent.

For Josefa to have lived in Downieville during this unsettled period was an accomplishment in itself. But her courage in the face of an angry mob of forty-niners is the stuff of legend, in the same league with Joan of Arc or whatever woman warrior you want to compare her to. A hundred years from now, all the names involved in this story, including that of the writer, will be forgotten, but Josefa's name will live on. In my eyes, Josefa is an amazing woman who, through great sacrifice and courage, claims her rights as a human being on the very edge of the goldfields, in a primitive camp twenty miles from the summit of the Sierra Nevada, a place where only the toughest arrived....

In the early morning darkness of July 5, 1851, while the streets of Downieville were littered with red-white-and-blue trash and the fervor of patriotic speeches still hung thick as Sierra fog, a white man was stabbed to death for abusing a Mexican woman. The day before, Downieville had celebrated the Fourth of July with a massive patriotic orgy. Hundreds of miners, would-be miners, merchants, travelers, gamblers, politicians, and even a few lawyers and other denizens of the Sierras had come together in a raucous party in honor of California joining the Union. There'd been patriotic speeches, shooting of guns, heavy drinking, several fights, even a stabbing and a flogging. Except for the speeches, it had been a typical day.

Shortly after the murder, a Mexican couple fled to Craycroft's Saloon, next to the Jersey Bridge. It is possible that the man worked there as a monte dealer, which may have been why they sought this as a place to hide. But the word had already spread like venom among the miners, many of whom now gathered in front of the saloon talking excitedly, many of them urging a quick hanging. When the accused Mexicans were brought out under guard, one of them was a quiet, timid man, the other, a woman named Josefa, whom many of the miners knew. She was small, about twenty-five years old, dark and attractive, with small white teeth and thick black hair that reached her shoulders.

The general attitude of the miners (and popular historians) toward women in the goldfields, unless they were married or merchants, was that they were morally suspect. But Mexican women were even more so. Antonia Castañeda, who has written extensively on gender in frontier California, points out that popular historians stereotyped Mexican women, casting them as "fandango dancing, monte dealing prostitutes, the consorts of Mexican bandits" and as "morally, sexually, and racially impure." It would be logical that the forty-niners, who were less educated than popular historians, held the same biases.

Now let's see how the broad generalities of race and gender, class and sexuality were brought to bear on a Mexican woman, alone, in the middle of nowhere.

Picture yourself as Josefa. You're trying to make a living in this town, scraping by as best you can and staying out of people's way. You live your life clean; you live with a man, therefore you're not naïve sexually, but you're not a prostitute. (It is important to note here that men who personally knew Josefa all state that she was not a prostitute, that her life—in the language of the time—was without the stain of moral turpitude.) Now picture your door being busted down in the middle of the night by a large intruder, a beefy man over six feet tall and weighing some 230 pounds. You yell at him, and he goes away. A few hours later there's a knock on your door. Perhaps you shouldn't answer, but you do. It's the same Americano and his friends. It's still dark outside, and the man who lives with you tells them to go away. The Americano insults you, calls you a whore. You tell him to repeat his insult inside your house. You believe he won't do it, but he does. The Americano steps inside; he is belligerent and aggressive, and shouts a demeaning slur in your face. The word whore, *puta*, is a highly charged epithet.

Now stop for a moment and think—what does the word *puta* imply at this juncture? It is both racially (because she's Mexican) and sexually (supposedly she's a whore) charged, but also infused with class prejudice (a whore works for a living by selling her body) and gender prejudice (Mexican women are whores). Furthermore, the white man says the word in Spanish (*puta*) to make the insult intimate and clearly understood, therefore metaphorically if not physically (the threat of which was obvious) violating Josefa, verbally and emotionally.

I don't believe Josefa thought in this way, nor did language exist then to describe violence of this sort, but I'm sure neither the implicit nor the explicit connotations of the word escaped her.

Josefa knew there was no man or law that would defend her if she was raped or even killed. It was just herself. Perhaps now you can explain why Josefa did what she did.

Before you judge Josefa, remember that in 1851, up and down California but especially in the gold country, a virtual war was being waged against Mexicans and Latin Americans. Josefa most certainly knew of the lynchings in Hangtown [Placerville's nickname even today], most certainly had heard of the violence against Mexicanos, and perhaps even knew some of the Sonorans who'd been run out of the gold country with only a few hours' warning, forced to leave everything behind. She'd maybe even seen a lynching or two, or known someone who'd been lynched. And the general ambience of the camp, with thousands of single men living in a lawless state, spewing lewd comments everywhere she went, surely generated the sense of injustice and fear that kept her door locked and a knife by her bed. Everything must have been building inside her, like a trip wire just waiting to set off an explosion.

Josefa's trial unfolded like a bloody finale to the Fourth of July. When Josefa and her male friend emerged from Craycroft's Saloon, a mob of some six hundred miners, fueled on patriotism and whisky, were ready to lynch them both right then and there. But others in the mob wanted more formality, so they named a judge and a prosecutor and selected a jury, all of them white males. When a lawyer who was present—one of the few times in history a lawyer appears in a favorable light—tried to talk the miners out of their rage, he was shouted down and pummeled by the mob. After these preliminaries, the trial commenced on the same platform where the day before the speakers had praised the United States for taking California from Mexico. The judge was seated, witnesses interrogated, and declarations duly noted. At least one reporter, from the *Pacific Star*, was present, and his is one of several eyewitness accounts of what happened at the so-called trial.

After several miners claimed the deceased was of good character and was just trying to make amends for earlier breaking down the couple's door, Josefa's companion testified. His version is somewhat different; he said the Americano was abusive, and that their door was knocked down with such force as to rip it from its hinges. He also stated that the Americano threatened him with violence, but since he was small, Josefa stepped in and told the Americano to strike her instead. Then the Americano heaped abuse on Josefa, first calling her a whore in English, then in Spanish. She told him to say that in her own house and left him in the street. When the Americano followed her and was about to enter, Josefa stabbed him.

Josefa, who'd laughed at some of the white men's testimony, appears as the final witness. What happened in private and in the dark, she now declaims in public and in daylight.

Here's her version of the incident: At about 4:00 a.m. on the morning of July 5, the Americano had arrived at the cabin that she shared with her man. The Americano was drunk and had no reason for disturbing them. He'd knocked down the door and, after an angry exchange of words, had gone away—only to return a few hours later. This time the Americano insulted her, calling her bad names.

Her own words have come down to us, describing that fateful moment: "I took the knife to defend myself. I had been told that some of the boys wanted to get into my room and sleep with me. A Mexican boy told me so and it frightened me so that I used to fasten the door and take a knife with me to bed. I told deceased that was no place to call me bad names, come in and call me so, and as he was coming in I stabbed him." It was that simple. Josefa hadn't gone out looking for trouble; trouble had come to her house. She felt threatened, sexually and otherwise, verbally abused, and her male companion wouldn't help her, so she defended herself as best she could.

Josefa told the truth, and it didn't go down well. After her testimony, the judge adjourned the trial till 1:30 p.m., and Josefa was taken away under guard to a log cabin behind the speaker's platform. During the break, the mob grew to well over two thousand angry miners, whose sense of justice, as it was later explained by apologists, demanded a hanging as some sort of revenge.

But more likely the miners were incensed to see a Mexican woman speak forcefully and openly, especially after having just taken the life of one of their own. In this sense, she speaks *sin pelos en la lengua*, holding nothing back, an attitude not unusual of Mexican women in pre- and post-1846 California, who, contrary to stereotypes, did act upon history, controlling their fate as much as possible within the confines of those times.

After the recess, a doctor came forth who stated that Josefa was *enciente*, pregnant, in other words, approximately three months along. By all moral standards, this should have prevented her hanging. Instead, what happens next is a symbolic rape of her by the miners via three white male doctors from Marysville who, in conjunction with the previous doctor, take Josefa into a makeshift shack and reexamine her for signs of pregnancy. Since it was pretty clear to everyone that the miners wanted revenge, from my point of view, this action was meant to humiliate her. How else to interpret this? Perhaps Josefa felt that if she submitted to this degrading body exam, her life might be saved. While the so-called doctors toyed with Josefa, the forty-niners grew more enraged and were about to storm the platform when the three doctors emerged and declared that, in their opinion, Josefa wasn't pregnant. The jury retired and within minutes announced its verdict: Josefa was guilty of murder, and she should suffer death in two hours. Her male companion was acquitted but advised to leave town within twenty-four hours. It was about two in the afternoon when Josefa was led off under guard to the cabin. During the next two hours, Josefa received visitors and perhaps prayed or made her peace with God.

But why, if women were so rare, cherished, and valuable, would a mob of womanless men condemn Josefa to the gallows? Only by looking at the context of those times can we perhaps understand the reasons. Antonia Castañeda provides the framework: "The woman who is defined out of social legitimacy because of the abrogation of her primary value to patriarchal society, that of producing heirs, is therefore without value, without honor." Josefa, as a Mexican woman living with a man, was outside the scope of patriarchal society, and as

Castañeda goes on to say, "A woman (women) thus *devalued* may not lay claim to the rights and protection the society affords to the woman who does have socio-political and sexual value" (emphasis mine).

It goes without saying that the men who clamored for Josefa's lynching were not thinking this way (if a mob can be said to think), but this is exactly how they behaved. A woman, Josefa (read valuable), who is Mexican (of no value) can be lynched, because without value (i.e., suitability for reproducing heirs), society (read men) would not grant her the rights and protection usually accorded women, thus they would not save her from the gallows.

Josefa is lynched because she is a Mexican and a woman considered "without value" to the white male patriarchal society. If all the doctors in the world had said she was pregnant, it would not have increased her value to white society, since she wasn't pregnant with a white man's child. The miners were not even obligated to follow a civilized code of moral conduct, since Josefa was considered outside "moral" society and therefore without any rights.

Around four o'clock, Josefa was escorted to the scaffold that had been slapped together over the river, an awkward affair of timbers strapped to the bridge with heavy rope. She was tastefully dressed, and her hair flowed freely over her neck and shoulders. She appeared calm and unrepentant. By then, two thousand miners had gathered around the Jersey Bridge and along the Yuba River, waiting impatiently for the finale, as if it was some patriotic celebration.

It's hard to imagine this tiny woman walking toward the scaffold through the mob of jeering miners. What was she thinking about as she took her last walk—her home in Sonora, or the dogwoods along the river, or, if she was pregnant, that her child would also die? Perhaps she recalled the day she arrived in the gold country, her head filled with wild dreams of fortune. She might also have considered the weird fate that had brought her to this town by the river. Perhaps she cursed all the Americanos, or forgave them. But somewhere along that final walk she made peace with herself, and she strode through the mob showing no fear. Like other California women of the time (I'm thinking of María de las Angustias de la Guerra at Monterey, California, during the war of 1846), when confronted by white male violence, Josefa showed cool-headed grace under life-or-death pressure.

Once on the platform, she turned to the few Mexicans who'd gathered by her side and told them that she'd killed the man and expected to pay for it. She shook hands with each of them and offered them a few words of good-bye and asked her friends to take her body so that she might be decently buried.

It was perhaps here that she decided on the act of bravery and defiance that has immortalized her. Unassisted, without fear or hesitation, she walked up the little ladder to the scaffold, where two vigilantes stood beside the noose, hoping to intimidate her. To the astonishment of the mob, she took the thick rope knotted into an awkward noose and slipped it around her neck, then arranged her hair so it would flow over her shoulders. It was more than an unmistakable gesture of courage, something every man that day would remember as long as they lived. It was Josefa's last defiant statement.

The two vigilantes pinioned her arms behind her back, which she protested. They ignored her. In their eyes, she had stopped being human the moment she stepped onto the scaffold—if indeed she'd ever been human in their eyes. They tied her dress down and slipped a hood over her head, then jumped free of the scaffold. At that point, two men axed the rope propping up the scaffold.

I reach Downieville at dusk and check into the Sierra Shangri-La Motel along the river's edge. The river cuts a deep ravine through the mountains that seem to rise up angrily out of the earth. There's nothing unique about the town; it consists merely of a few cheap motels and bars and the usual shops along the main drag. There's a bridge, and next to it a white brick building, which is the modern-day Craycroft's Saloon. Here, a small bronze plaque marks the occasion of Josefa's lynching with typical inaccuracy: "In memory of Juanita, the Spanish woman, lynched by mob from original bridge on this site, July 5, 1851." Thank god there are no souvenir stands offering little scaffolds with dolls in Mexican dresses hanging from them.

I've driven for nearly eight hours, but I'm not tired, so I wander around town. I know where I'm going, but I pretend it's an aimless walk. On Highway 49, the traffic is almost dead. There's a tense quiet in Downieville, as if I am disturbing something. I know Josefa was originally buried behind the theater, and that later her body was reinterred, but I don't know where. Tomorrow I will make inquiries, but I don't have much hope of finding her final resting place. The story goes that when she was reinterred, her skull was removed and used by a local secret society in an initiation ritual of some sort. Though hard to believe, it's not totally implausible, especially if one considers the fate of

Joaquín Murieta's own head. [A human head—billed by its promoters as Murieta's—was preserved in a jar and displayed throughout the region as a tourist attraction.] But I don't believe in ghosts, so I'm not sure what I expect to find here in this mean little town. By now I despise not just the forty-niners, but the Fourth of July, patriotic speeches, the American flag, and that cursed gold. I will never wear gold jewelry; I will never own so much as a grain of it.

I've read so many accounts of lynchings in which the victims were nameless Mexicans, or blacks, or Chinese, even Anglos, that perhaps I merely want to pay homage to all the nameless dead of the Gold Rush, to all those who perished here in the majestic foothills of the Sierra Nevada, yes, even to the Cornish miners who died in the bowels of this red earth so that others could become rich. Perhaps I just don't want Josefa to go into eternity so nameless, so insignificant, that not even her last name is recorded, because I despise the anonymity that is handed out to us like nooses with which to hang ourselves. Perhaps I just want to give one of these nameless dead a sense of closure. After all, every human being is worthy of at least that much. Every human life is more valuable than a mountain of gold.

In the quiet of the Sierra night, the Yuba River is rushing through the gorge. I come to the bridge, which looks dark, ominous. I know the original bridge where Josefa was lynched was washed away by the flood of 1852. I also know that this Craycroft's Saloon is not the original, since the whole town was destroyed by a conflagration less than a year after Josefa's lynching, as if the gods had brought down the divine hand of retribution on this place. It doesn't matter. I stand on the bridge and look over the railing, and I can almost see her face in the water, surrounded by her long hair. I want to do the natural thing and give her a last name, my last name, make her part of my clan, so her spirit will always have a home. But she deserves the honor of her single name, because she represents all the nameless ones who lived and died here and never made it rich, all the nameless faces in the photographs. In some way, perhaps, she is the Saint of the Mother Lode, martyr and inspiration to all Mexicas, symbol of our courage. No matter how hard they have tried to erase our names from history, our stories have endured.

There's no place on the bridge for a cross of flowers with her name on it, but the river is eternal. I toss a sprig of wildflowers that I've picked along the road into the frothy currents. It floats for a moment before it disappears beneath the roiling water. I am finished. I have told her story. I have returned her name to the dark mountains, buried it in La Veta Madre, like ancient gold returned to its matrix, undisturbed. I say her name one last time—Josefa. And I walk away from the bridge.

Sylvia Ross, "Tribal Identity Grade Three"

Sylvia Ross was born and raised in Los Angeles, separated from the culture of her Chukchansi heritage. A poet and artist, Ross worked for several years as an animation painter for Walt Disney Productions, after which she returned to school, graduated from Fresno State University, and became a teacher. Now retired, for many years she taught children from the Tule River Indian Reservation outside of Porterville, near the western flank of Sequoia National Park.

    Widely published in literary magazines, and a frequent contributor to the quarterly News from Native California, *Ross often produces work related to her Chukchansi heritage. The Chukchansi (which Ross calls the Chik Chancy here) are a tribal sub-unit of the Valley Yokuts, a native population located in the San Joaquin Valley and the southern Sierra Nevada foothills.*

The recess bell rings and we rush
for the hopscotch game
before the fourth grade is out.

Sister talked about the Plains Indians.
We saw a film on Navajos.
We colored a ditto of a pueblo.

Lisa brags, "I'm part Indian.
I'm Cherokee." She flips her blonde
curls and her feet own the ground.

"Me too," I say. "I'm part Indian too."
"Well, what are you then?" she says.
"I'm Chik Chancy," I answer.

"That's not a tribe," she tells the girls.
They turn away laughing.
"It is," I tell them. But they don't hear.

I take out my hair clip
to use as a lagger in the game
and dark wisps fall over my face.

The clip hits the sixth square
and then ricochets out past the line.
I pick it up and put it back.

Chik Chancy is a tribe.

David Beesley, from *Crow's Range*

David Beesley (b. 1938) is a professor of history, emeritus, at Sierra College. He received his Ph.D. from the University of Utah in 1968 and has published numerous articles on Sierra Nevada labor, ethnic, and environmental history. He is considered an expert on Basque culture in the Sierra and on the environmental effects of hydraulic mining. In 1995 and 1996 he was an associate with the Sierra Nevada Ecosystem Project and supplied a portion of its report to the United States Congress.

In this excerpt from Crow's Range: An Environmental History of the Sierra Nevada *(2004), Beesley considers the powerful natural forces at work in the range.*

An Ever-Changing Mountain Giant

The Sierra Nevada is always changing, making and remaking itself under the influence of powerful natural forces. Poet and Sierra Nevada resident Gary Snyder, referring to such mountain creating forces, put it this way:

> Erosion always wearing down;
> shearing, thrusting, deep plates crumpling,
> still uplifting—ice-carved cirques
> dendritic endless fractal streambed riffs on hillsides
> ...Streams and mountains never stay the same.

When humans first entered the Sierra, a long ice age was temporarily releasing the range from its frozen grip. But the ice would return later in what has been called a mini-ice age, a last gasp that produced some small glaciers that have managed to hold on into the historical present.

It is troubling to consider that what is referred to as "settlement" by European Americans began about 1850 to 1870, at the end of that mini–ice age. All the development and planning of the reservoirs that keep California and northern Nevada alive today occurred late in the last brief century and a half when the current warmer and wetter climate pattern emerged. For many of the years of the range's life before that time, very long cycles of drought or cooling produced very different climate patterns. How many years of drought could California's or Nevada's urban centers and commercial agriculturists survive if old patterns reemerge?

The shape-shifting nature of the range has affected its human inhabitants in different ways. Tectonic changes, often of interest only to geologists and geomorphologists, have also impinged upon the human history of the Sierra.

Consider an example from the eastern side of the range. Thousands of earthquakes have rattled the eastern Sierran community of Mammoth Lakes, California, since 1979. In that year a magnitude 5.8 quake occurred. It was followed the next year by four magnitude 6 temblors in one three-day period. In the fall of 1997, quakes came with such frequency that they attracted national attention. Eight thousand quakes above 1.2 magnitude occurred between October and December. Thirty small quakes occured in just four days the following April. Such periods of intense earthquake activity are called "quake swarms" by the United States Geological Survey scientists monitoring them, almost as if the tremors were a cloud of bothersome stinging insects.

But some of the quakes of this swarm were substantial, reaching magnitude 5. Responding to the increased activity, the USGS prepared a notice of possible volcanic hazard to heighten public awareness of potential risk. Merchants in the area promptly complained that the notice could frighten away fainthearted tourists and skiers, the lifeblood of the community. Clearly, this was a classic case of conflict between Mammon and science in a mountain enclave.

In March of 1990, the subsurface volcanic activity triggering these earthquakes nearly turned deadly. A United States Forest Service supervisor seeking shelter in a March snowstorm entered a snowbound cabin near Mammoth and nearly died from breathing carbon dioxide.

The odorless gas had been accumulating inside the structure, released from a volcano directly underneath. Both the cabin and Mammoth are located within the Long Valley Caldera. This valley was created 760,000 years ago in a previous eruption. Below the surface at Long Valley a new mass of molten magma was forming, pushing up a dome. One of the forces that created the Sierra Nevada was still very much at work.

For residents of the Mammoth area, the trembling in Long Valley was a troubling reminder. Natural forces have a way of disrupting everyday life for those who have chosen this mountain environment. The veneer of civilization that modern technologies have built there is no guarantee of security. Can you imagine how you would feel in an earthquake swarm? How many earthquakes would it take to make you concerned? The imposition of urban patterns on a natural landscape such as the Sierra Nevada brings potential risks. The geological forces that molded the Sierra Nevada—faulting, uplifting, earthquakes, erosion, volcanism, and glaciation—shouldn't be spoken of in the past tense. These influences have varied in intensity over the millions of years it has taken to shape the range, but they remain with us.

Mammoth stands as a useful metaphor for human contact with the Sierra Nevada. For over 10,000 years, people have had to cope with all the complex environmental and climatic variety that the range has imposed. This relationship of humans with the Sierra has been not only long, but dynamic. People have been involved in an intense and conscious shaping of the Sierran landscape and the use of its resources from the beginnings of human settlement. Collectively they have greatly altered the Sierra Nevada's "natural" systems. For thousands of years, waves of human occupation have left their imprint: native, Spanish Mexican, European American. But in the end, the Sierra Nevada still remains a force to be reckoned with in the lives of its occupants.

Similar geological forces create different responses and actions in different cultural contexts. Prehistoric Northern Paiute people and suburban Mammoth Lake residents alike have coped with Sierran geology in their own ways. Obsidian was a by-product of volcanism. In prehistoric times the Paiutes used it to fashion projectile points for hunting, and also traded it with other Sierran natives who lacked this valuable mineral resource. But because the Paiutes did not build permanent structures and lived there only seasonally, the effects of quake activity would have had limited physical significance to them. For example, Paoha Island rose in nearby Mono Lake from a huge volcanic eruption sometime in the 1700s. The Mono Paiute oral tradition was undoubtedly enriched with the explanations that the event inspired. But my guess is that volcanic activity is far more troublesome to current Mammoth residents and commercial interests than to their prehistoric predecessors, what with the millions of dollars invested in urban infrastructure in that recreation community today.

The Range That Crow Built

The Sierra is best seen as a whole—a single mountain range. But as with anything as huge and complex as the Sierra Nevada, it is hard to take it all in with a brief, though accurate, descriptive phrase. It would help to consider some of its aspects from several angles, especially its physical characteristics and life zones. Putting the two together will help in understanding how its human history has developed.

The Sierra Nevada that the Yokuts attribute to the master builder Crow is both majestic and unique. Most often recognized for its splendid peaks, it is also distinguished by its forest-covered ridges, river and glacial valleys, lake basins, deep midrange western canyons filled with magnificent mixed-conifer forests, and of course its alpine meadows. It rises from its base on its eastern side some 11,000 feet from the Owens Valley floor to the summit of Mount Whitney at 14,495 feet. This is a far greater rise in elevation than the Rocky Mountains, which lift up only 9,000 feet above the Great Plains. One of the elements that makes the Sierra Nevada so unique is its granitic core, pushed up as a single block. Because this great granite mass sparkled and shone in the sun, John Muir called the Sierra Nevada the "Range of Light."

The Sierra is massive, stretching some 430 miles along its north to south axis. It begins where the earliest rock formations of the range are overlaid by the Cascades' volcanic flows. From there it stretches far to the south to Tehachapi Pass. From the beginnings of its western foothills to the bottom edge of its steep eastern escarpment the range is around eighty miles wide. It is one of the three most dominant geomorphic features within California, along with the Central Valley and the Coast Range. And though mostly in California, the range flanks roughly a third of Nevada's long western border.

Its existence shapes climate and life forms on both of its flanks. Pity poor Nevada, because the Sierra cuts off most of the Pacific storms that water the range. The Sierra Nevada can generate massive amounts of snow and rain seasonally. This water, when trapped by dams, is distributed within a complex, modern hydraulic system. It provides the basis of life for the farms of the Central Valley in California and northern Nevada. The largest cities of California and northern Nevada could not exist without it.

David Gilligan, from *The Secret Sierra*

David Gilligan (b. 1973) has dedicated his life to exploring and under-standing the "Secret Sierra"—the Sierra Nevada's alpine zone, the fasci-nating world above the treeline. A graduate of Arizona's Prescott College in natural history and ecology, today he teaches at Sterling College in Vermont and he lectures extensively and leads field studies throughout the American West on ecology and environmental awareness. A naturalist by training and temperament, Gilligan has rambled throughout the Sierra Nevada, sometimes on backcountry trips of one hundred days. He is an expert at living off the land and in wilderness survival techniques.

In this excerpt from the prologue to his book The Secret Sierra *(2000), Gilligan examines the majesty and the challenge of the High Sierra.*

It had been storming every afternoon in Humphreys Basin [in the southeastern corner of the John Muir Wilderness, west of Bishop] for the past four days. They were strange storms, blowing in from the east instead of the west where summer thunderstorms typically come from in the High Sierra. These suggested something bigger happening down south, perhaps off the coast of Baja. Every day I watched as the clouds brewed up, huge and magnificent, over the crest of the range. They might drop hints of a storm by early afternoon, but their true power was always revealed by sunset. The clouds blazed peach, scarlet, then crimson with the fading light. Opposite the setting sun, smoke had been smudging the evening sky for three days against the outline of the White Mountains. A fire burned below the mountain crest, somewhere down in the Owens Valley, seven thousand feet below. The smoke played with the evening light, turning it from pallid yellow-brown to brilliant tangerine. By nightfall, only a few cloud wisps remained in the indigo sky. Eventually, these too would dissipate, leaving the crystalline stars to sparkle through until dawn.

The fifth evening began just as the others had, but the air had an unusual quality. The darkening clouds enshrouded Mounts Humphreys and Emerson. As the entire eastern sky grew a deeper, darker charcoal hue, the steel gray of the Sierran granite was illuminated, washed over in the clear golden light of the setting sun. Then the clouds burst. The rain fell in wide streaks, like gold dust sprinkling down from a great trove enshrouded by the billowing thunderheads. In four separate places the rain came down like this, each shower equal in such tremendous quality. Then, as if a long-forgotten god had returned to prove his omniscience, a rainbow appeared. As the fullness of its arc came into view, it seemed a bridge, spanning the ineffable distance between darkness and light. I felt as if I were sitting at the center point around which different worlds revolved, touching each other in a kind of transient embrace. I was in the middle. If there was magic in the world, this was it.

It rained into the night. Thunder and lightning joined the ensemble periodically, as an extended aftermath of the evening. I lay awake, realizing my love for this place. I have been lucky, for I have never doubted this love. Something about these mountains draws me to them. The Sierra Nevada has bestowed upon me some of the greatest gifts of my life. Not all have been joyous and beautiful. At times I have been terrified, emptied, afraid for my life. Other lessons have been quiet in their telling, and soft in their teaching. Such nights serve as reminders that amidst a world that sometimes seems impossibly confusing, somewhere on earth the sun is sending rich, golden light across landscapes stark with primeval antiquity. I was seeking to experience such a land in that light, and if possible, to tell about it.

Sleep came without my noticing. I couldn't remember any dreams, and don't think they would have been possible after such an experience.

The clouds broke away in the morning to reveal the sun. I awoke to the rosy fingers of dawn and looked out across the wide glacial basin. The first sound was that of water trickling out from beneath a late-lying snowbank. September, and still the snows of El Niño's winter lingered at 11,000 feet. I looked for the Mountain Bluebirds. They came every morning with the sun, perching on huge erratic boulders to view the land before them, flitting out to catch insects for breakfast. It was only minutes before they arrived. Yesterday a female blackbird had joined their company. Today she did not return. I sat quietly and watched the birds, their blue matching that of the sky, shining in the long light of morning. And a thought came to mind how much I cherished this place, and the life I've made here. For me, no other life is imaginable.

As a naturalist, I am a practitioner of natural history. One of the ways I see the land is as a story. Learn the language, and we can read the story. Human civilization may also be seen as a story, but as Henry David Thoreau stated over a century ago, there have been enough champions of civilization, and my interest lies elsewhere. Human history indicates with reasonable certainty that such civilizations will at least be around tomorrow and the next day. No rush to tell those tales. Wild land, however, is in grave, immediate danger the world wide. We need to tell the stories of these places before they are gone. Perhaps, if we are lucky, we can even stay the danger for awhile.

"Sagebrush, alpine gold and / Ponderosa pine / As we emerge from /
The 2-mile tunnel / Under Mount Judah"

Ishmael Reed, "Holiday Train to Reno"

*Ishmael Reed (b. 1938) is one of the best known, and most controversial,
African American writers of his time. Born in Tennessee, Reed grew up in
New York and went to college at the University of Buffalo, where he hosted
a radio program that was cancelled after he conducted an interview with
Malcolm X. An essayist, poet, and novelist, Reed was a pioneer in establishing the modern Black Arts Movement, and as part of that effort, he helped
found the Before Columbus Foundation, which, since 1976, has presented
the American Book Awards and vigorously encouraged American writers of
every ethnicity and background.*

*Reed's work includes nine novels, four poetry collections, six plays,
numerous essays, a libretto, and frequent contributions to the nation's
leading newspapers. His books have been translated into seven languages
and he has been a finalist for the Pulitzer Prize. Reed lives in Oakland and
recently retired from teaching at the University of California, Berkeley.*

Weary of the patting down,
X-raying and having to
Remove our belts and shoes
We board the California Zephyr
A grand old queen of the tracks
Inside the Emeryville station
Cheers explode when Chicago
Is announced
Pony girl gets on at Davis

She's about 5-foot-1, 180 lbs.
She's wearing a ponytail
Glasses, jeans and a T-shirt
A pony's picture on the front
Beneath the words
"I want a pony"
She sits next to me and
For hours she
Names every
Shrub and tree enroute:
Catclaw, acacia, banana yucca
Sagebrush, alpine gold and
Ponderosa pine
As we emerge from
The 2-mile tunnel
Under Mount Judah
Donner Lake is on
The left side
"It's 328 feet deep
3 miles long
three-quarters-mile wide
And packed with
Kokanee salmon"
Volunteers
The Stetson-wearing man
In the seat in front of us
Interrupting his humming
And talking to God
He has cerebral palsy
And is traveling alone
"Being disabled isn't
The end of the line"
He says
"If they'd just stayed
At the foothills
The Donner Party would
Have survived—
Look! there's a palomino!"
She says
"That's not a hawk

It's a harrier," she
corrects Carla
What do you do? I ask
"I'm a glorified janitor
But I really want to
Work on a horse farm
At Colfax"
At the end of our
Line is Café Andreotti
For fresh-baked
Bread with tapenade
Tuscan bean soup
Tacchinella farcita
Alla Trevigiana
At the end of hers
is grandmother
It's been years since
She's seen her
Her hair? as white
As the Sierra.

Maria Melendez, "Clan Markings, Stanislaus National Forest, 1980s"

Maria Melendez (b. 1974) is a poet, essayist, and editor whose work is influenced by her deep feelings for the land, her Chicana heritage, and the women's movement. She led environmental writing workshops while a writer in residence at the UC Davis Arboretum, and she has also taught at Saint Mary's College in Notre Dame, Indiana, and at Utah State University. Melendez's poetry, essays, reviews, and fiction have appeared in a wide variety of publications, and her poetry collection How Long She'll Last in This World *was a finalist for the 2007 PEN Center USA Literary Awards. She is currently the editor/publisher of* Pilgrimage *magazine and she will release her third book of poetry,* Flexible Bones, *in 2010. Raised in the San Francisco Bay Area, Melendez now lives in Pueblo, Colorado.*

In "Clan Markings, Stanislaus National Forest, 1980s," written especially for this anthology, Melendez recalls her first camping trip in the Sierra Nevada as a young girl. Stanislaus National Forest is located in the southern half of the Sierra Nevada. "Selkie" is an old Scottish term for a magical seal that can shed its skin and turn into a human. "Matins" and "vespers" are, respectively, daybreak and evening Catholic prayers.

Three hundred and eight mosquito bites later,
stepping out of a mountain creek
after splashing hours away with best-
friend Jenny, I belonged to Sierra streams
the way Jenny's parents sometimes belonged
to beer, cocaine, barbecue, to each other.

Nobody had sprayed us with Cutters before
we set off in flip-flops to walk the cobbled reaches,
little bikini-clad Balboas
charting new coasts for the Crown,
or river-sylphs, Sierra selkies,
I forget what we pretended to be that day.

If it weren't for public lands, car camps,
and the geologic grace of mountain making,
I don't know where that family would've gone
to be their best selves. The therapeutic stew
of camping smells (pine-spiked air
and vomit-scented mold in beloved tents)

combined with camp life's liturgy
of soothing hours (mouth-watering matins
of instant oatmeal packets ripped open
to start the day, the Coleman stove
whispering vespers for the evening's
cup of cocoa) to make The Parents a pair

of mood-elevated sages, sated with
mountain air, dispensing jovial banter
from their folding chairs with woven
plastic strips for seat and back. Where else
but in the pine trees had they room to be
their loud, cuss-mouthed selves, with their beaner

jokes and "Honey" for every kid's name.
I might've been the only Maria
for miles around, and I might
as easily have never been invited.
When they first moved four doors down
from my East Bay, mixed-race nest, The Dad

told Jenny not to play with any dirty Spic.
But that dad talked so much shit, no one
listened to him much, lucky
for me. The forest trees kept
deep sentry, rose together as the first
day fell, and pointed out something

398

sharp-scented and starry about God,
which we, all of us, The Dad, The Mom,
the sister and brother, Jenny and me
took with us into our bags, turned
over in our hearts like dogs turning
their bodies around an invisible axis

before descending into dreams. Without
the frayed rope of that family to pull me
to the woods with snow-smelt river,
to the ages' patient uplift, how long
could it have been until I first
heard coyotes? Sounding like silver

spirits in the trees, ringing
cries that ricocheted around the sky.
"Coyotes," said Jenny, dropping the "e"
like any good White girl who owns
a dirt bike knows to say. And who cares
about the bites? I didn't notice til the next day,

although that night I dreamed a continuous
tone, high and thready, encasing me
like spiders' silk. Jenny had only
gotten a few, but my back was covered.
I'm sure they itched like crazy,
but in the haze of memory

all I find is the snap and hiss of the morning's
re-lit logs, Jenny's mother
crooning, "Oh, Honey," smoothing
calamine onto my bumpy skin
as I stand in front of the fire
with my palms out to the heat.

"The declining sun had emerged beneath the sheet of cloud, and in its orange light the track of a tear shone down Rachel Conlon's cheek"

Jordan Fisher Smith, "American Woman"

Jordan Fisher Smith worked for the United States Forest Service, the National Park Service, and the California State Parks for more than twenty years, serving in Idaho, Wyoming, Alaska, and on the American River in the central Sierra Nevada. Now retired, Smith is a professional writer living in the historic Sierra gold mining town of Nevada City. An excerpt from his Nature Noir *appears in Chapter 5 of this anthology.*

In the following essay, written especially for this book, Smith tells of a memorable encounter in the American River Canyon, shares his visualization of the region's future, and ruminates on how the remarkable Sierra Nevada landscape can transform an individual's perspective.

> *Questo posto è abbandonato da Dio…*
> This place is abandoned by God…
> —an Italian expression

Over two decades ago now, as a thirty-one-year-old park ranger pursuing a career in the protection of public land, I found myself working in fifty miles of Sierra Nevada river canyons condemned to be utterly destroyed by the very government that employed me. It was there that I met a woman I'll call Rachel Conlon (although this is nothing like her real name), and through her began to understand how a place can become hostage to our ideas about it, and even our previous behavior toward it.

By the time I first got to know them in May of 1986, the lower North and Middle Forks of the American River had been scheduled for more than twenty years to slip under the waters of the 690-foot-

400

high Auburn Dam. But the dam lay unfinished, a great hole in the ground into which had already been poured hundreds of millions of dollars, thousands of yards of concrete, freight train loads of rebar, miles of blueprints, and decades of engineering. All kinds of problems had beset the project. There were cost overruns, design problems, defects in the rocks underlying the dam, and there had been heated environmental opposition. The condemned portions of the North and Middle Forks were exceptionally beautiful: two great rents in the earth a thousand to three thousand feet deep, their precipitous walls covered in lush forests of oak, pine, and fir, and wildflower fields, at the bottom of which lay miles of spectacular rapids beloved by whitewater rafters and kayakers from all over the country. And yet the project had never been called off, and the canyons had survived for decades like some men on death row do: under a series of legal stays of execution but without a reprieve.

The effect of this condemnation was startling. All of us who worked there—Park Rangers Finch, O'Leary, McGaff, Bell, Reich, and others who came and went over the years—had worked in more conventional parks, parks that were actually protected and cherished by the public. We had all witnessed the hushed voices and upraised eyes common among visitors to groves of giant sequoias elsewhere in these mountains; it was the same behavior I'd seen in the great cathedrals of Europe. If, however, there were a public lands experience representing the diametrical opposite of that church-like reverence, it was available in our canyons. Standing outside our ranger station, it was common to hear gunfire—mostly random shooting, occasionally poaching, every once in a while murder and mayhem. Each weekend morning we'd find the smoldering remains of the previous night's apocalyptic parties along the river beaches. Once, next to the coals of one such massive bonfire and a few dozen beer cans, we found the burned-out hulk of the automobile that had brought the celebrants. On another occasion we found an empty but freshly dug grave out in the woods, and next to it the duct-tape bindings of the poor creature who—we surmised—having promised to make good on some rural drug deal gone bad, had been given another chance. Our clients were not backpackers in Volvos; they were armed drunks with arrest warrants in four-wheel-drives with expired registration tags. It seemed as if these condemned canyons attracted people whose prospects were as hopeless.

For us park rangers, working there had the potential to be something between disappointing and lethal. In my first eight years on condemned ground I saw a lot of dead people and confiscated 108 weapons in criminal cases. Our jobs could be stressful, and to lighten the mood we festooned the walls of our squad room with ephemera from the bizarre events we witnessed: a test printout from the drunk driver with the highest blood alcohol of anyone we had ever heard of, snapshots of various combinations of tragedy and high comedy, and diverse weapons we confiscated, including, in one case, a medieval mace.

True, the timbered steeps of the canyon walls, the meadows where the scented air sparkled with insects and iridescent hummingbirds, and the endless ovation of tumbling water were beautiful. But the bullet-riddled signs, the worn-out sofas, refrigerators, and old cars, the broken bottles and rifle casings littering the roadsides gave a clear message to anyone who entered there. I'd like to say I figured out on my own how our behavior toward a place leaves a stamp upon it, and how that mark of previous abuse can replicate our bad treatment of that landscape indefinitely, unless we do something about it. But it was Rachel Conlon who taught me this. And she did it in a way that was particularly memorable, because to this day I am not proud of my own part in the matter.

That April day in 1987, Ranger Doug Bell and I were sent out to work with the Highway Patrol at an impromptu check station on Ponderosa Way, a steep, winding dirt road descending the west wall of North Fork Canyon to the place where the whitewater rafting outfitters collected their guides, rafts, and boatloads of clients, having put them in earlier in the day at Mineral Bar, upstream. Our job that day was to inspect the brakes, steering gear, emergency exits, and logbooks of a procession of often overloaded and superannuated school busses and secondhand twelve-passenger vans the outfitters used in those days to get their clients to and from the river.

By that afternoon a high overcast had formed, softening the shadows and saturating the colors of spring. The air was moist and fragrant. We set up where the road crossed the saddle of a small knoll, the only wide, level spot in a precipitous series of switchbacks between the canyon rim and the river. Around us the steep meadows were lit by crimson Indian paintbrush, orange poppies, violet giraffe's head, sulfur-yellow Lomatium, and brilliant balls of blue dick floating on tall stems above the grass. And on the rocky cutbanks, my favorite of all plants in these canyons was in bloom: a succulent called cañon Dudleya. For most of its life Dudleya's not much to look at, a little clump of concentric rosettes of thick, waxy-looking leaves the color of a bad bruise. But Dudleya's dusty, blighted appearance for eleven months of the year fails to prepare you for the breathtaking confection of delicate red-orange and yellow flowers it produces each spring.

I was writing a traffic citation to a man who had driven into our check area with an open beer in his hand and a driver's license revoked for previous drunk driving convictions. Within the next couple of years he'd be dead in a gunfight with another of my rough customers in those canyons. Nearby, Doug Bell and a tall highway patrolman, Mert Hall, were checking the brakes and steering gear on a van full of happy city people fresh off the river who stood watching us in bathing suits.

Just then I heard a rattle and howl. Looking down the canyon wall toward the dirt switchback below us, I saw a red Toyota sedan headed uphill fast, trailing dust. The car was still picking up speed as it disappeared into the turn behind the little knoll on which we stood. A moment later it reappeared, skidding sideways out of the turn, engine whining and tires slinging gravel. I strode into the road with my left palm raised, signaling the driver to stop. The Toyota skidded to a halt in front of me. I closed the distance between me and the open driver's window.

There were three people inside: in the front passenger seat, a man in his late thirties, unshaven, wild and dirty-looking; behind him a little boy of two or three, standing on the rear seat, steadying himself with his grubby little hands on the front headrests; and at the wheel, a dark-haired young woman. Notwithstanding her driving, her eyes were intelligent. Her delicate face was framed in a well-kept mane of black hair worn long, below her shoulders. And her purple blouse was unbuttoned and her brassiere pulled down so as to form a sort of shelf, over which cascaded her naked breasts.

Her lips parted, tentatively.

"I, you see, um…Do you want me to—?" She forced a smile.

"I stopped you because I'm concerned about the way you're driving," I said. "Have you been drinking today?"

"I, um, well I had three beers, but I'm not drunk…and I, um—" she said.

From her right the man spoke up. "Is there a problem, officer? Look, we're just going home. We'll slow down if you—"

"Right," I cut him off and continued, addressing the woman: "May I have your driver's license, please?" I tried to look only at her face, but I was feeling that the day had somehow become fortunate in a way I was trying to memorize.

She was breathing quickly, shallowly.

"Oh please don't...Look I'll just...Let's see, it's in here—" She reached for a worn leather purse under the feet of the man next to her, and from it she removed a clutch bag. She fumbled with the clasp.

"Oh...it's...Just a moment—" she mumbled.

I stood waiting.

"I, um, oh, here it is." Hand visibly shaking, she passed the driver's license out the window to me. In the picture on it she looked friendly and hopeful.

"Would you please get out of the car for me?" I asked her.

"Oh, couldn't we just—" she pleaded, reaching for the door handle. The car door creaked open. A look of despair flickered across her face. She got out and stood up. A breeze rippled the meadows around us. Dark wisps of hair strayed across her nipples. She made no attempt to cover them.

"Please come over here," I said, and began walking to where my Jeep was parked along the roadside. She followed. When we got there, I opened the clipboard and forms case I had left lying on the hood and removed from within it a form on which we recorded the results of various tests we gave to people suspected of driving while under the influence of alcohol or drugs. I took out a ballpoint pen.

"Please stand facing me," I said, and as I did, I turned my back toward my companions, Bell and Hall. Now, to face me, the woman would have to face them. I hoped Bell would have the presence of mind to grab his camera and record me giving sobriety tests to a half-naked woman for our gallery of the bizarre back at the office.

"Now," I said, "I'm going to have you stand with your feet close together, your hands by your sides, your head tipped back, and your eyes closed for what you think is ten seconds." I made a show of looking at my wristwatch, but once her eyes were closed I stole a glance over my shoulder at Bell and Hall. They were looking.

But now the fun was rapidly aging. There she was, head tipped back, breasts thrust toward me, head weaving in an attempt to balance, the rapid pulse of her arteries on the taut, pale skin of her throat above her clavicles. My power over her and her obedience mortified me. A growing murmur of voices drifted over from the crowd of whitewater rafters at the open door of the van nearby. Across the road, an acorn woodpecker chuckled its high, ratcheting laugh. I had the distinct impression at that moment that it was I who was laughable, not the woman, in the way that those in control are often more suitable objects of satire than the valiantly defenseless.

"Uh…wait…Miss Conlon, would you please cover yourself up?" I said in my best professional voice.

She looked at me, then down at her breasts, and without saying anything she pulled up each of the cups of the bra and buttoned her shirt. It was then that I noticed the needle tracks on her forearm.

I gave her the rest of the tests. She'd had some alcohol, but hers was not the stumbling drunkenness of beer alone; it was the reckless-driving, fast-talking, scattered buzz of a stimulant like cocaine or methamphetamine. The needle marks, her condition, and her driving behavior dictated that I should take her in for a urine test. I asked her if the child was hers.

"No, it's his, uh…Do you like your job? It must be nice, being here in nature, I mean…Is it hard to get, this job? Can't you let me go? Oh, please?"

"Can he take your car so we don't have to tow it?" I asked her, pointing at her passenger.

"Uh…yeah, it's his car. Are you arresting me? I'll just go home, I promise. We won't ever come back. Please don't," she begged.

"I'm afraid I have to," I answered.

I stepped forward, contained her small hands in my bigger ones, and handcuffed her as the department required. Then I guided her gently by the elbow to the back door of the Jeep, opened it, and motioned for her to sit inside. Once she had, I fastened her seatbelt with an elaborate show of avoidance for her body. I closed and locked the door. Through the window, I saw her chin drop and start to quiver.

We set off up the dirt road toward the jail in Auburn. I glanced at her though the metal prisoner screen, in the rear view mirror. The declining sun had emerged beneath the sheet of cloud, and in its orange light the track of a tear shone down Rachel Conlon's cheek. I continued to steal glances backward, and as the road turned this way and that, the shadow of the edge of the rear window passed back and forth over her face like the line between day and night that traverses our earth, stroking us to sleep and then waking us again for all the days of our lives, no matter what we have become. We lurched and bumped over the rim of the canyon into the deep green shadow of Douglas fir and pines. I tried to turn the car to avoid the bigger rocks and potholes, but each thump from below was like a fist in the gut.

At the Placer County Jail, the female deputy emerged from a holding cell with Rachel and told me my prisoner had been unable to pee for a drug test as the law required. So I loaded her back into the Jeep and drove her a few blocks to Auburn Faith Hospital to get a blood test.

We arrived in the blue glow of dusk. I got her out. The hospital parking lot radiated heat as we passed the desiccated shrubs next to the wooden benches where the nurses took their cigarette breaks. I placed my hand lightly on the back of Rachel's shoulder and motioned toward the door into the ER. Her blouse was damp with sweat. The electric doors opened and we were enveloped in a gust of air conditioning. Inside, the hard-edged chief nurse showed us to an exam room. I motioned for Rachel to sit on the upholstered table.

"You want something to drink? Water?" I asked her.

"Yes, please." She seemed demure now.

I removed her handcuffs—her hands had been behind her back as our policy required—and refastened them in front so she could drink. I filled a paper cup from the dispenser above the sink and handed it to her. She sipped, eyes lowered. She looked wan in the stark fluorescent light.

"You know, I can't help but feel you're intelligent," I said, "but I found you in a pretty stupid situation. That little kid could get killed standing up with no seatbelt on that dirt road with you driving like that."

"I know," she said.

"And that guy," I went on, "who is he? Do you think he cares about you?"

"I don't really know him very well," she answered.

"It doesn't seem like you respect yourself very much, driving around ripped out of your mind with your tits hanging out."

She looked down and said nothing. Her thighs were pulled together on the crinkly tissue paper covering the exam table. A forest of downy hairs stood up on them in the air conditioning. I looked away, finding something interesting in the soap dispenser at the sink.

"Why don't you respect yourself more?" I said to the corner of the room.

"You don't want to know," she replied quietly.

I pressed on: "If I didn't, I wouldn't have asked."

"Something happened," she said, so quietly I almost couldn't hear her.

"What?" I asked, quietly.

"It was a long time ago."

"What happened?"

"My father, he…" and her voice strangled off into a squeak.

"He hit you?" I asked.

"No, he slept with me. Not slept. I mean he used to come to my room."

"How old were you?" I asked.

"It went on for years." Her chin began to quiver again.

"God, I'm sorry," I said, shaking my head. "Do you understand that doesn't make you bad?" And the minute I said them, these words sounded hopelessly trite.

"I know…but—" She dabbed at her nose with an index finger. "Can I have a Kleenex?"

I pulled a wad out of a dispenser on the counter and handed it to her. "You need to get into counseling," I said.

"It wouldn't do any good. Anyway, I don't have the money."

"That's just a bunch of excuses. Look at yourself," I pointed an index finger at her. "You are going to wind up dead or permanently sad. You gotta do this thing."

Outside our room the intercom was paging a doctor. Somewhere a child was screaming the fearful cry they make when someone produces a syringe or begins to pull off a field dressing.

"I'll tell you what I'll do." I was staring at her hard.

She turned away.

"Please look at me," I said. She looked up.

"If you promise me to give this a try, I will request in my report that you be put in a treatment program, in counseling, instead of jail. Will you do it?"

"Yeah," she answered.

"No. Don't just say that if it isn't true." I leaned toward her. "Will you really do it?"

"I'll do it," she said, slightly more convincingly.

I was being naïve and gullible, I thought. What she had done had worked on me. It was not I who was in charge; she was, and had been all along. She wasn't unaware that her breasts were exposed when she got out of that car; she just didn't care, or worse yet, she knew exactly what she was doing, and she had been doing it to guys all over her life. And who knew if the story she told me was even true? A nurse entered carrying a plastic tray of blood tubes, tape, prep pads, and needles.

"This is an evidence draw?" she asked, setting down the tray.

"Yup," I replied.

"Fill these out, please." She handed me an envelope and two adhesive labels for the blood tubes. She went over to Rachel and picked up one of her arms—the one with the tracks. The nurse frowned, dropped the arm. It fell to Rachel's lap. The nurse picked up the other, plumping the veins on the inside of the elbow with her thumb. Satisfied, she applied the tourniquet and began scrubbing with an alcohol pad.

Rachel winced as the needle went in. The blood surged up, wine dark and viscous. The nurse changed tubes, filled the second, pushed a wad of cotton onto Rachel's arm, and retracted the needle. She handed me the two rubber-topped tubes full of blood. They were intimately warm to the touch. I looked at my watch and wrote the time on the labels, put the labels on the tubes, put the tubes in the envelope, and sealed it.

"Okay," said the nurse, gathering her things.

Rachel smiled shyly, decently. "Thanks, I guess," she said to the nurse.

"You take care, honey," the nurse said and left.

I picked up my clipboard and the envelope with the blood samples and guided Rachel out of the exam room toward the doors to the parking lot. On the way we passed a trauma room. In the middle of it was a gurney, and on it, draped in waffle-weave cotton blankets and plastic tubing, lay a very old, tiny woman. Her white hair was splayed out on the pillow. On either side of her stood a doctor and a nurse in surgical scrubs. The doctor was speaking in a loud voice, saying something like: "Do you understand what we are going to do now, Mrs. Blake?" He had a hand on the old woman's frail shoulder. We passed the door and then we could see no more. In front of us the doors to the parking lot parted and we entered the warm, blue night. The air smelled like hay from the fields north of town. Crickets sang. I put Rachel in the Jeep and we drove in silence back to jail. There, I put her in a holding cage with a stainless steel toilet, then filled out the booking sheet and dropped the envelope full of blood tubes in an evidence repository to go to the lab.

* * *

About a week later the blood test results showed up in the mail at my office dirty; it was methamphetamine and alcohol. In the weeks that followed I got a disposition sheet from the court. In response to my recommendation, Rachel had been diverted into treatment. I measured the days until, like so many others, I'd encounter her again, drunk or loaded. But I never did, and for a while I heard nothing more about her.

A couple of summers later, I was standing between the sunbathers on the river beach at Upper Clementine. A young, good-looking, and clear-eyed man in a T-shirt and jeans walked up to me as if I meant something to him. In those days everyone in town recognized me as the young ranger who was trying to bring the law—and in my mind, peace, safety, and at least a temporary cessation to the gunfire—to the canyons. Within a certain segment of society, I had arrested and jailed some acquaintance of almost everyone. I looked at him searchingly, feeling as if I ought to know who he was.

"Rick Conlon," he announced, extending his hand.

"Right. Okay," I shook his hand and let go. "Do I know you, Rick?"

"Not really. But you knew my sister."

"Oh…right. How is she?" I had no idea who he was talking about, and I was stalling.

"You arrested her for drunk driving up the canyon, remember?"

"What did you say your last name was?" I asked him, still stalling.

"Conlon. Her name is Rachel."

"Oh…got it," I said, still stalling, but a moment later I remembered her.

"I just wanted to tell you that everything changed." He continued. "Rachel got off drugs. Got married. She's working. They got a house. They're real happy."

"That's great," I said, seizing his hand again and pumping it. "You tell her I said hello and I wish her the best. You made my day, Rick."

"Well, okay then," he said. "I just wanted to tell you everything changed after that. I mean after the arrest." He withdrew his hand.

For an awkward moment we just stood looking at each other in silence. I was studying his face for its resemblance to hers.

He cleared his throat. "Well, all right then," he said, and then turned and walked away.

* * *

409

Our system of justice is designed for the protection of the innocent, and out of a hundred or two scary, pathetic, or somnolently drunk men and women who threatened me, wept, or mostly sat impassively on the other side of the metal screen behind me as I drove them to jail, Rachel Conlon was the only one I can think of who was saved, at least temporarily, by my arrest. She is also one of a very few whose later life I still wonder about, years later. There are ways to find anybody, but I've never tried. To do so would have been a further invasion.

And what of the place where I met her? Remarkably, the canyons are still above water. Well-organized resistance by environmentalists and the immense cost of the dam have been a factor, but maybe something else, too. My fellow rangers and I tried to clean up the canyons, make them presentable, to treat them as if they were not meaningless. We dragged out the old cars, moved large boulders into the illegal trails where off-road vehicles had torn up the hillsides, and built hiking trails and little campgrounds where you could go to sleep at night with the sound of the river in your ears. We set up a display case in our office offering hiking guides, maps, and wildflower books. Our naturalist gave courses on the history, wild plants, and animals of the canyons. A docent group was started to lead tours. In short, even if we did not always believe it, we at least behaved as if the ground we walked on and the water that flowed past us had a future.

Still, to this day, the American River canyons are owned by the Bureau of Reclamation, a federal dam-building agency. And if forecasts of the effects of climate change are true, drought and a shorter runoff season—what was formerly a slow-melting, high-elevation winter snow now increasingly falls as warmer rain—will only add to the impetus to increase available water storage for a growing population in this dry-summer state. And so, when I try to imagine the future of that place in the North Fork where I met Rachel Conlon, I see two divergent scenes.

In one, the canyon wall, the dirt road, and the turnout where we stood that day are discernable only in shape, but not in texture or details. Below an abrupt, level line of brush and drought-killed trees at the dam's high-water line, the land is stripped to red mud, and beneath this lies a flat, reflective plane of murky, lukewarm water.

In another vision, there is no lake. The canyon is still there. It's a late April day like the one when I met Rachel Conlon. But the road looks different, paved and bounded so that the clouds of dust and errant wheels no longer transgress on the spring meadows strewn with wildflowers.

There's a man in a uniform something like mine. He's standing close to where I arrested Rachel Conlon, talking to a group of people standing in a semicircle around him. He begins walking up the road, and they follow. The man in uniform stops at the rocky cutbank uphill of the road, crouches, and points to a clump of cañon Dudleya growing on the rock, a little stack of purple-brown, fleshy leaves and an exuberant stalk of flowers the colors of candy corn.

The man in the uniform is saying how this plant stores in its fleshy leaves the moisture it gleans from this rocky bank during the rainy months, and after eleven months of looking like it would amount to nothing, in spring it bursts into bloom.

In my imagination I am standing a short distance away and behind the group. One of the listeners is a statuesque woman with green eyes and long, glossy hair, now gray. She has her hands on the shoulders of two well-kept teenagers, maybe grandchildren, who are standing on either side and just in front of her. The naturalist beckons the group to get down close to the plant for a better look at this miracle of long dry time and then ripeness. The woman stays, but she gives the girl and boy gentle shoves on their upper backs and they go tentatively as if embarrassed, as teenagers are, to be interested in this swelling tiny thing, which, like all earthly life, now waits to see what we will do, like the heart of a young girl fluttering in the night as the floor creaks under her father's steps down the hall.

"If God hadn't wanted all these critters to be around, including
rattlesnakes and cougars, he wouldn't have put them on the Ark....
Let's be sure it's an ark that stays afloat."

Gary Snyder, "The Ark of the Sierra"

*Gary Snyder (b. 1930) is most famous for his Pulitzer Prize–winning
poetry, but he is also a prolific essayist. His themes often touch on "our
place in space," the human impact on society and the environment. Snyder's
philosophy is holistic—that all elements that we encounter in our lives are
interlinked and dependent on each other for value and existence.*

In this essay, "The Ark of the Sierra," from his collection Back on the
Fire *(2007), Snyder examines our relationship with fire and urges us
toward responsible stewardship of this unique and irreplaceable region.*

I'm a longtime forest and mountain person of the West Coast. I grew
up on a farm outside Seattle, my father and uncles all worked at
various times in logging and fishing, and I started off helping my dad
on one end of a two-man saw when I was about eleven. I've worked
in the woods from the Canadian border down to Yosemite. I've fought
fire, built trails, planted trees, done seasons on lookouts, been a timber-
scaler and a choker-setter. And I've considered myself a conservationist
since I was seventeen—when I first wrote to Congress in regard to an
issue in the Olympic National Forest.

I'm concerned primarily with two things: our new understanding
of the ecological role of fire, and something bigger that goes with that,
the possibility of a truly sustainable forestry in the Sierra. When I was
a self-righteous youth in my twenties I thought that my jobs as fire
lookout and firefighter gave me a real moral advantage—I told my city
friends, "Look, when I do this kind of work I can really say I'm doing
no harm in the world, and am only doing good." Such ironies. Now
I get to join in the chorus that says it was all wrong-headed, even if

well-intentioned (almost as wrong as when I climbed to the summit of Mount Saint Helens up in Washington at age fifteen and announced "this beautiful mountain will long outlast the cities." Now the mountain is half gone, and the cities are doing fine).

This North Central Sierra area, especially here on the west side, is not quite as charismatic and scenic as the southern Sierra. We have no Yosemite Valley or Kings River Canyon, but we do have exquisite little high country lakes and many meadows rich in summer flowers, high white granite ridges and crisp, bright snowfields. In the mid-elevations we have some of the finest pine forest in the world. The lower foothills are manzanita fields with extensive oak grasslands that have been changing, during the last two decades, from cattle ranches to ranchettes.

In the watersheds of the American, Feather, and Yuba River systems are some of the loveliest streams in California, offering top quality trout fishing. The oak and brush lands are major migratory songbird nesting territory—I know because my wife, Carole, was out early at least one morning every week last spring mist-net-trapping, banding, and collecting sex and age data on the little things. Deer and wild turkeys grace the front yards of people all across the foothills. My wife and I and many of our friends are among those who welcome back the bears and cougars, even while recognizing the risk. We didn't move up here to live the soft, safe, and easy life, and we love having these hairy scary neighbors. We will try to figure out how to be safe and smart even though they're around. One can always buckle on a bear-attack pepper spray canister when going for a lone jaunt. And speaking of lone jaunts, John Muir's famous adventure—that he wrote about in *The Mountains of California* of climbing high up into a sugar pine during a severe windstorm—took place a few ridges over, probably near the town of Challenge. [Muir's piece is in Chapter 3 of this anthology.]

Our North Central Sierra shares its geological and biological history with the rest of the Greater Sierran ecosystem. There are paleo-Indian sites in this county that indicate human presence from eight thousand years ago. The "pre-contact" forest was apparently a mosaic of various different forest stages, from brush fields to many broad and open ancient-forest stands. Spring and fall, salmon ran up all the rivers. Deer, salmon, waterfowl from the valley, and black oak acorns were the basis of a large and economically comfortable native population, a people who made some of the most skillful and beautiful baskets in the world.

The Yankee newcomers initially came to look for gold. They needed lumber and thought, as newcomers did everywhere else in North America, that the forest was limitless. One can see early photographs taken around the foothill towns, and the hills are denuded. It's a tribute to the resilience of the local forest that, where allowed to, it has come back quite well.

So early on there was the vigorous mining industry and extensive logging. Later much of the mountain land was declared public domain, and it came to be the responsibility of the U.S. Forest Service (USFS) and the Bureau of Land Management. The USFS from the twenties up until the seventies was a confident and paternalistic organization that thought it always knew best, and for a while maybe it did. During those years it was generally trusted by both the conservation movement and the timber industry. In any case, from the 1950s on there was a lot of heavy industrial logging in the public and private lands of the Sierra.

With the seventies came a renewed rise of environmental concern. Part of that consciousness was connected maybe to better biology education in the schools and a general growth of interest in nature. Curious people got out in the mountains by pickup, on foot, or by bike, and sometimes studied the areas that had been logged. People could see that old-growth habitat was drastically shrinking. We all knew that some species were being lost or endangered (the wolf and grizzly already gone, probably the wolverine) and there were rumors that the national forest logging was sometimes subsidized at an actual financial loss to the taxpayers. The public became aware, as never before, of its stake in the Sierra Nevada.

So we entered an era of reevaluation and reconsideration of past policies. The USFS unfortunately lost much of the respect of the conservation community, and it also got hammered by the timber industry. For awhile it looked like the Forest Service couldn't win, *whatever* it did. There *have* been some highly contested issues. For conservationists, extensive clear-cutting became symbolic of how the federal land managers seemed to be hostage to the timber economy; and the spotted owl became symbolic to the timber industry of hated environmental regulations, and money-losing issues involving critters that almost nobody has ever seen. The owl itself is a hapless and innocent bird that never meant to cause so much trouble. The gold rush era left many worthy legacies in this land; it also left some people with a sort of "use it up" attitude. Those who arrived in the seventies and after may have been quick to love nature, but they seemed to have little concern for the economy.

During the hearings that led to the establishment of Redwood National Park on the north coast, a sawmill operator testified, "Why, nobody ever goes in those woods but hippies and their naked girlfriends." Well, some of those girls went on to college and became lawyers.

These wrangles have led some of us to try and figure out where the different parties, those able and willing to argue with sincerity and in good faith, might find areas of agreement. The fairly recent realization that the Sierra Nevada is a fire-adapted ecosystem, and that a certain amount of wildfire has historically been necessary to its health, has given everyone at least one area within which they can agree. Another area of potential agreement is the growing awareness that we will sooner or later have to manage long-range sustainable forestry. In fact, the two absolutely go together. If we don't reduce the fuel load, the really big fires that will inevitably come will make good forestry a moot point. But it will take a little more than new fire policies to achieve good forestry.

I was on a panel in San Francisco several years ago with Jerry Franklin, the eminent forest scientist now based at the University of Washington. So last month I took it on myself to write him the following question:

> Dear Jerry,
>
> I would like to be able to say that "Long range sustainable forestry practices—such as will support full biodiversity—and be relatively fire-resistant—and also be on some scale economically viable—lasting over centuries—is fully possible. And what we must now do is search out and implement the management program that will do that." Do you think I can say this & that the science will support it?

Jerry Franklin immediately wrote me back:

> What you propose is totally and absolutely feasible for the Sierra Nevada, i.e., long-term sustainability, full biological diversity, relative fire resistance (low probability of catastrophic crown fire), and economic viability. A system which provides for restoration and maintenance of a large diameter tree component (with its derived large snags and down logs) and which provides for moderate to high levels of harvest in the small and medium diameter classes (allowing escapement of enough trees into the large diameter class to provide replacements for mortality in the large diameter group) and prescribed burning in some locations can do this. Other considerations include riparian protection and, perhaps, shaded fuel breaks. Economic and sustainable in perpetuity!

So it's theoretically possible. But science can only suggest—such a marvelous sustainable forestry cannot actually happen unless the culture itself chooses that path. "The culture" means not only the national public but also the working people of the very region where the resource policy decisions are made. It will take local people working together with local land managers to make the serious changes in public lands policies that we need. Just a quarter of a century ago, the idea of active local engagement with public land decision-making would have been thought pretty utopian.

One of the reasons we might trust the people of the Sierra to provide valuable input has to do with how much the local people have learned on their own. In the twenty-five years I've lived in this part of the Sierra we have seen a growing contribution of knowledge from a multitude of fine amateur naturalists. Just here in Nevada County we have seen the formation of a California Native Plant Society chapter, the local production of a hiking guide to the region, a locally written and published bird species checklist, a fine botany of a high country lake region by a person of the area, a similar low-elevation wildflower guide, and detailed forest inventories done by volunteers on San Juan Ridge. There's a sophisticated, locally based research project on pileated woodpecker behavior, family life, and reproduction going on right now. Extensive research has been done on the stream systems and main rivers of the Yuba by another set of volunteers. And many of us are in personal debt to the esteemed Lillian Mott for her generous help in identifying mushrooms.

Also the forestry and biology experts of the Tahoe National Forest, the B.L.M., and our colleges and universities have been generous in sharing their time and expertise with ordinary citizens. Timber operators have visited at least one school I know of, Grizzly Hill, and allowed children to come and observe a logging show. There are a number of significant new organizations in the North Central Sierra. Many are focused on ecological issues, and some are concerned with access to resources. They all have a stake in the health of the Greater Sierran Ecosystem. This process of newcomers becoming a "people of the place," which started in 1849, has been progressing at variable speeds ever since, and has surged ahead in the last two decades.

For new fire and forestry practices to really become national public policy, they must be *local* public choices first.

We locals can help bring this to reality by getting involved with the Bureau of Land Management and USFS in further community forestry projects, in working toward innovative value-added wood-products industries, and in supporting cooperative fire management projects. If we can clarify and express our own choices, our congresspersons just might represent us, and federal policies might begin to reflect local desires. Agencies might facilitate this process by being a lot more willing to take risks with the public than they've been so far, putting more of their people out in the field where they can meet folks, and looking for opportunities to break out and try things with locals.

There has always been fire. The catfaces on the oaks, the multiple stems sprouting from certain old oak centers, and the black cedar stumps that seem to be timeless made it clear to me that there had been a sizeable fire through our land some years back. A neighbor, now passed on, told me of a big burn some sixty years ago. But our local forest has recovered well. This Sierra ecosystem has been fire-adapted for millions of years, and fire can be our ally. The growing recognition of this fact—with the public and with the fire agencies—has been a remarkable change to watch develop during the past ten years. In my own neighborhood a small prescribed burn was done this spring with considerable success. And we have also been trying out the mechanical crunching of brushfields—expensive, but it works.

One word of caution, however. As our enthusiasm for prescribed burns and more sophisticated fire management grows, we need to remember for a moment the fire ideologies and bureaucracies of the past. Steve Pyne, in his book *World Fire*, traces the history of the American wildfire-fighting establishment and the way it demonized fire as an enemy. He points out how the language of forest firefighting for years ran parallel to the language of the Cold War—clearly militaristic, and speaking of forest fires as though they were Godless Communist armies. Firefighting requires organization, courage, and tremendous energy and dedication, to be sure. But we are called now to a more complex moral attitude, where we see fire as an ally in the forest, even while recognizing its power to do damage.

The understanding of fire—its hazards, its use as a tool, and the way it shapes a fire-adapted forest—should help keep our different factions working together. We may disagree as to how important the survival of some species might be or how many acres of land should reasonably be converted to suburbs or what the annual allowed timber cut ought to be, but we surely will agree that we're against tall flames burning timber and houses, and that we should work together for a "fire management" that sees fire as a partner in the ecosystem, not an enemy. This may be a tentative step toward new and more amicable relations between the conservationists, who want to go slow and be careful, and the resource users, who have their businesses to run.

There's another hard fact here that I haven't yet mentioned. It may in the long run be the most important factor of all. The whole west side of the Sierra (the entire *West*) is experiencing an amazing rate of housing growth, which brings suburban homes right up against wildlife habitat, public forests or mineralized zones, a zoning term meaning "areas under which significant mineral resources are known to lie, hence zoned so that mining might still be permitted at some point." These developments may be in conflict with both loggers and environmentalists. Public lands will become all the more precious to us, as ranches and farms give way to development.

Our public lands are lands held in trust for all of us. A certain responsibility goes with that, for the government, for the public at large, and for the people of the region. As for stewardship, or trust, we can see that the whole world is in the trust of humans now, whether we want this responsibility or not. The air and waters, the rivers, the deer and owls, the genetic health of all life are in our trust. We are here discussing Biodiversity—a word that sends shivers of alarm through some hearts—but it only means variety of life, and it means "Right to Life for Nonhuman Others," a moral sentiment I religiously support. If God hadn't wanted all these critters to be around, including rattlesnakes and cougars, he wouldn't have put them on the Ark. The high country and the forests are the twenty-first-century Ark of the Sierra, an Ark even for all of California. Let's be sure it's an ark that stays afloat. Let's not try to second-guess God.

Joe Medeiros, "The Power of Trees"

Joe Medeiros (b. 1948) has hiked and studied in the Sierra Nevada for more than thirty-five years, led countless trips of students and mountain enthusiasts, served as a National Park Ranger at Devils Postpile National Monument in the southeastern Sierra Nevada, and loves to share photographs and stories about his favorite place in the world. Now a professor emeritus, Medeiros taught biology at Sierra College, was coordinator of the college's Interdisciplinary Program, and continues to be involved in many campus events, including Earth Day. He also taught for many years at Modesto Junior College and was director of that college's outstanding Great Valley Museum.

In the following essay, written especially for this anthology, Medeiros considers the power of four species of Sierra trees. It is a natural and philosophical reminder of the wonder and legacy of not only these extraordinary organisms but the entire Range of Light as well.

Giant Sequoia

For more than thirty years I've transported busloads of students to giant sequoia groves in the Sierra. Each time I'd have them hold hands, extend their arms, and encircle a designated tree to see how many of us it would take to complete a chain around the massive plant. It would normally require more than twenty of us, young and old, to embrace the world's largest living things (and become official tree-huggers). I also took this opportunity to pick up a few of Wawona's freshly fallen cones, shake out a few seeds, and launch into a story about the wonders of trees, and plants, and anything else that could photosynthesize—manufacturing complex sugars from plain water and air. "It would take more than two hundred of these tiny seeds to weigh a gram—the weight of a small paper clip," I would enthusiastically announce. "And now look up! How did it get from here (the minuscule propagule perched upon my fingertip) to there (I'd point upwards toward the tree's crown)?" I told this story, and many others like it, to my students, not simply for their knowledge but for my benefit as well.

I wanted to review for myself the marvelous processes that acted silently, and without apparent cost, within these and other forests of the world; processes that drew in thousands of gallons of water each day and transported them upwards hundreds of vertical feet; processes in the newest tender rootlets that exchanged hydrogen ions for precious atoms of magnesium, calcium, and other minerals; processes that took simple matter from air, soil, and water and deftly constructed goliath plants weighing a million pounds. And for what purpose? Each individual tree in the grove most likely acted for its own self-interests— to grow, produce needles, make sugars and starches for its metabolism and cellulose for wood—and to muscle its way upwards through nearby sugar pines and incense cedars with which it competed for precious light and other resources. Our chosen sequoia grew in order to produce seeds—to make more of its own kind—its only apparent (to us) mission. It was genetically programmed to do this each year, for thousands of years, to hedge its bets that its offspring would rise above the forest as well.

While these natural efforts seem selfish, our tree was also benefiting us—Lilliputian visitors to its personal montane haunt. It was providing us oxygen while also sequestering those troublemaking carbon dioxide molecules that escape and contribute to the warming of our troposphere. Wawona was purifying the air and the water right where we stood. It was stabilizing the soils wherever its constantly growing root system could reach—keeping the nearby streams pure for fishes and the aquatic invertebrate life upon which they depended. It was providing us shade and immeasurable beauty. San Jose State University biologists Richard Hartesveldt, Tom Harvey, Howard Shelhammer, and Ron Stecker clearly had to be *in love* with this tree when they assembled the first definitive summaries of its natural history. These were grownup men reveling in life and spending every available weekend and summer romping around like boys in one of the Sierra's grandest playgrounds— studying one of its most famous inhabitants.

"These giant sequoias are the *biggest* individual species in the world! More than 450 tons of biomass! Hell, if their boles were hollowed out, you could slide three blue whales into them—with room for a few orcas and whale sharks to spare! Seventy-five elephants could fit in there!"

Somehow these examples never went over very well—but I kept using them for years. At the end of the day, after my sermons in the grove, we'd (calculatedly) end up at some even larger colossus for some quiet time. If we were in the South Grove of the Calaveras Big Trees, we'd lay on our backs at the base of the Louie Agassiz Tree to gaze upwards at this silent giant. High in the canopy chickarees chattered with staccato shrill, scolding us for trespassing. (Without them, millions of sequoia seeds would remain within their cones. Preferring the meaty cone scales for nutrition, the voracious tree squirrels liberate the tiny seeds within.) In the warming sun high above the forest floor, red-breasted nuthatches called like toy trumpets—hunting tasty invertebrate treats in the cracks and fissures of sequoia bark. Laying still, gazing upwards, most of us felt the power of the trees, trickling into our bodies, mingling like the smokes of two campfires, like spirits reunited after being separated for much too long. It was always hard to leave the grove.

Sierra Juniper

Other trees of the Sierra have affected me like the giant sequoia. I could never simply walk by a Sierra juniper without stopping and taking a longer gaze. There's something about these handsome rock-dwelling relatives of cypress that give me pause at each and every encounter—I have never frowned at a juniper. Some of my favorite juniper groves are easily visited just a short stroll from the car at Carson and Sonora Passes. One can even follow a dirt track back to the Bennett Juniper, in the Stanislaus National Forest, purportedly the most massive of all Sierra junipers. (A well-intentioned plaque placed at its base by the Clampers—the red-shirted, beer-guzzling, males-only, Californian self-anointed historical society—tells [erroneously] of its extreme longevity.) Countless specimens of majestic junipers exist throughout the Sierra. Numerous stately sentinels guard the western entrance to Evolution Valley along the John Muir Trail where it follows the energetic South Fork of the San Joaquin River. They seem to enjoy positioning themselves in massive and fractured boulder fields, while still within view of roaring waterfalls and cascades like those plunging downward from Dusy Basin into the LeConte Canyon.

One juniper grove stands out in my mind—without doubt my very favorite grove. It hovers in Yosemite, overlooking Washburn Lake and the Lyell Fork of the Merced River. On a lofty perch of massive intrusive rock, this collection of robust monarchs seems to radiate an energy that has beckoned us each time we've wandered into that little-visited corner of the Yosemite backcountry. In the warm summer afternoons this grove basks in the setting sun, unobstructed by other kindred mountain dwellers, where it begins to glow in the low-angle light—transforming from the crisp silhouettes of the morning cold into softer and inviting arboreal spirits—a fire that draws one to it, but lacking the pain of flame. Their shaggy brown overcoats change color, warming and illuminating, glowing an orangey-cinnamon that appears different than any other rival tree, even the sequoia. Their radiance calls us closer and invites us to lean against them to share the sundown. I've often wondered if this time of day is as spiritual and as pleasurable for them as it is for us. Do they find any comfort in the presence of Man?

Nevertheless, we feel the grove's energy—unexplainable, but unmistakable. It feels *different* sitting there than when in camp. Something calls us to stay here longer—and saddens us when be bid farewell to the grove. It's more than simply a warming feeling; it's an almost indescribable sensation of strength, truth, acceptance, welcome, and understanding. It is the palpable presence of wildness that I think Thoreau was trying to explain. Memories of this grove are etched in our recollections, not only as three-dimensional "pictures," but with an added dimension of deep sensation—gratitude for our acquaintance—enriched by the knowledge that these spirits were here long before us—and will be here still long after us.

Limber Pine

No one in their right mind would hike westward over Taboose Pass in a single day—not with a full backpack on. But some do. If they aren't consumed by the time they've climbed up 6,000 feet in only eight miles from the dusty trailhead in the Big Pine volcanic field, they'll find themselves walking among one of the most spectacular forests of limber pine in the Sierra. Named for their flexible twigs that tolerate the heavy snow loads of the high country, these pines were once well known for being some serious old-timers. Edmond Schulman, who would go on to become one of the founding fathers of dendrochronology—tree dating—was studying limber pines out West when someone alerted him to the old bristlecones in California's White Mountains. Before long, the limber pines of the southern Sierra were forgotten in the frenzy to find the world's oldest living trees. Thousands of cores were bored into the ancient and contorted bodies of White Mountain bristlecones that lived across the Owens Valley—establishing that they were still alive more than four thousand years after they'd germinated from seed.

Meanwhile the Sierran limber pines continued their quiet struggle to retain their hard-earned title as niche specialists of the arboreal kind in the upper treeline. Found throughout the West, from the Canadian Rockies and throughout the mountains of the Great Basin, limber pine probably made it into California by traveling through the Basin and Range mountains, into the Inyos and Whites, and westward to the highest regions of the Sierra and southern California mountains. Today they're found as far north as Yosemite—we've found them while scrambling down the volcanic rubble on the south face of Mammoth Mountain, where they claim purchase among the stony flanks of the sleeping volcano. We've scrambled up steep granite slabs to find the limber pines in the Sawtooth Peak region of Mineral King—where they occupy lofty positions along high, sunny flanks of the Great Western Divide. Wherever they grow they reward us with impressive structure, artistic form, and the unspoken wisdom of thousand-year-old elders.

Convergent Evolution

Their telltale wispy and upturned branches tell a story of convergent evolution—where two different species converge in form or function when subjected to similar influential forces. Like the whitebark pine found in similar subalpine conditions farther north, the long and spindly upper branches of foxtail pine seem to reach eagerly towards the sky. The purpose of this seems simple: to offer large, stony, and wingless seeds to passing birds—in hopes to have them dispatched to nearby uncolonized ground, thereby expanding the territory of the species.

Ron Lanner—who for a lifetime has studied the relationship between pines and jays—eloquently describes this mutualistic symbiosis in his book *Made for Each Other*. In *Conifers of California* he proffers an explanation of why whitebark and limber pines, while distantly related (genetically), both exhibit open, wispy branching at their tops. Research shows that ancient ancestors of whitebarks entered the western cordillera from Asia via the Arctic land bridge while foxtail relatives forged their slow path northward from the mountains of Mexico. Whitebark pine brought its "Johnny Appleseed" counterpart, an Asian nutcracker, along with it while ancestral foxtails cooperated with southern jays in the Sierra Madre. Once the foxtails arrived in the southern Sierra, the nutcrackers (by now a new species) applied their avian handiwork to the morphology of both whitebark and foxtail pines. Choosing to excavate wingless seeds from the most highly advertised cones (attached to the tallest and most upswept branches), the Clark's nutcracker selected the form that is represented now by both pine species. Who won this struggle for survival? They all did! While limber pine stakes out a few sites where it can dominate the forest niche, it commonly gives way to the foxtail pine.

Foxtail Pine

I first became acquainted with foxtail pine on Alta Peak in Sequoia National Park. High above me on this Kaweah watershed spire a small forest of hardy trees seemed to crawl up the slope towards the 11,000-foot summit. After a long walk up to take a closer look, I became a true admirer and lifelong student of this wonderful species. Years later, after an arduous introduction to Kearsarge Pass from Onion Valley on the Sierra's eastern flank, I was reintroduced to this close relative of bristlecone pine. While whitebark pines and mountain hemlocks dominate the lofty tree-niches of the northern and central Sierra, the foxtail and limber pines occupy comparable treeline haunts in the south. The bottlebrush form of the foxtail's twigs made me think immediately of the bristlecone pines that I had admired in the neighboring White and Inyo Mountains to the east. Closer inspection of the foxtail's needles and cones left no doubt among professional botanists that this tree belonged in the pine subfamily Balfourianae, that of the oldest of the world's trees. Unlike the bristlecones of the White Mountains and the Great Basin, whose forms were mostly twisted, or *krummholz*, in response to high-speed winds and long, harsh winters, the foxtails of the Sierra form robust forests of stout-trunked individual trees. Widely separated but with massive bases, their leading tops are often dead and the trees taper up quickly to barren armatures of barkless branches— exposed wood lacking its protective cover. All variety of forms exist and no two are alike—from the stout and tall to the leaning and the asymmetrical (like flags indicating telltale winds). The needles of these California endemic pines are fascicled in bunches of five and their cones are slightly elongated, deep purple in color, with tiny prickles punctuating each imbricate cone-scale—relating them to the famous bristlecones. Their characteristically checkered bark is immediately recognizable once one has become acquainted with these old ones. Unique to California, the foxtail's geographic distribution is puzzling; separated by a gap of three hundred miles, two populations exist in the state. One disjunct population flourishes in the Klamath Ranges in the northwestern region of the state. The other, larger population flourishes in the southern Sierra high country. It was here where our fondness for foxtails flourished.

High Elevation Forest Zones along the John Muir Trail

Our treks along the John Muir Trail are subdivided (in our minds) in many ways—"sections between resupplys," "watersheds of Sierran rivers," "high country and low valleys," "before crossing-over and after" (another story yet to be told). But the composition of upper-elevation forests also exists as a categorical benchmark in our minds—the northern whitebark/hemlock forests, the central limber pine forests, and the southern foxtail forests. While we certainly have walked right past the northernmost foxtail of the Sierra, we first recall seeing them on the trail when traveling southward, after climbing over Pinchot Pass. On the south side of the divide, in the looming shadows west of Mount Cedric Wright, our first foxtails appear—initially as solitary individuals for miles along the trail until we find the first stands basking in the warm metamorphic soils east of the Baxter Creek junction. Tall but tortured individuals in the upper canyon give way to denser but open forests of foxtail families as we walk downriver. Their foothold increases below the Castle Domes, where they line both glacially scoured walls of the Baxter Creek canyon. For the Muir Trail hiker the land of foxtails begins here. Their forests grace the high country of Kings Canyon and Sequoia National Parks and even farther south into the upper reaches of the Inyo and Sequoia National Forests. On the way southward the mountain traveler is treated to luxuriant foxtail forests through the famous Rae Lakes and Sixty Lakes Basins, surrounding Kearsarge Pass, and all along Bubbs Creek from Vidette Meadow to every nearby treeline.

Even though the southern Sierra is replete with foxtail pines, we've never gotten enough of these luxuriant conifers. They provided our Sierra saunters with open but verdant treescapes—especially from the upper Kern River drainages below Mount Tyndall to the Whitney massif, part of a bold collection of 14,000-foot peaks. We walked, literally energized by their presence, through foxtail forests, one after another, around Tawny Point, the Bighorn Plateau, and all the way up from Crabtree Meadow to Timberline Lake—a common basecamp for a Mount Whitney ascent. Thousands of thousand-year-old trees embraced us all along our pathway. From lofty haunts, even older trees (some maybe even two or three thousand years old) must have observed us along our odyssey at the upper edges of the Sierra's treeline. Our already protracted pace was slowed even more by the desire to closely inspect one magnificent individual after another. We have truly connected with these ancient spirits and they have given us much.

Their Power and Ours

When spirits reunite there are powerful forces that converge. The past and even the future are *re*-presented at the same moment. While the history of each species lies, like a frozen record, in the tightly coiled archives of the nucleus, the ability to adapt to the future lies at the very same locus, quietly awaiting the stimulus that will awaken its purpose and potential for change. The power of trees beckons spirits upon which its life is dependent as well as those for whom its own body will provide nourishment—roots and fungi, trunks and beetles, twigs and caterpillars, needles and grouse. Ten thousand years of our star's powerful rays lie quiescent, fixed in the rigid strands of wood and flexible fibers of leaves—in the ever-so-slow dance of transformation—from burning light to sweet sugars—from sugars to fibers of cellulose—from fibers to the bodies of creatures—from bodies to motion—and from motion to the long infrared rays that will wander without direction or apparent purpose into chaos, to which all life is inevitably destined.

If one is willing—and receptive—locating forces such as these require only a walk in the woods or a stroll along the beach. With or without vision, eyes open or closed, such forces draw us to them like iron filings to a magnetic field. For some the calling comes from crashing waves on the coast. For others, it's the celebratory calls of sandhill cranes flying three miles above as they pass overhead to their wintering grounds. For me it's the aura of wisdom—and time—and tolerance—and patience I find in old trees. It's the power of these trees that anchors me firmly to my one and only worldly home—and my special place, the Sierra.

What lies in store for all of Earth's ancient tree-people? Will they survive another millennium? Will the changes that we, as a new species in their neighborhood, have wrought prove too much for their seemingly invulnerable longevity? Do they watch, or listen, as we annihilate their kin in "managed" forests, malls, and residential housing tracts? They have survived flood and drought. They have awaited the end of century-long dry spells, record snowfall winters, monsoonal episodes, beetle infestations, and even axes and chainsaws. But will they survive the exponential onslaught of human overpopulation? Overexploitation? Avarice? Will Lord Man, as Muir so aptly described us, overwhelm billions of years of nature's tinkering and fine-tuning? Will we ever be able to measure the value of trees and forests without thinking in board feet? Cancer-curing drugs? Watersheds? Campgrounds? Hunting areas? Dollars? Will we ever be able to conceive of the value of trees from any other perspective than that of our own utility?

We have never been so numerous before. We have never lived at such exorbitant levels of affluence. We have never wanted so much more than we need. We have never converted so much of Earth's life-giving habitat for our explicit use. We have, quite frankly, never played such a dangerous, dangerous game.

Will our grandchildren be able to hike along a high ridge in the Sierra and lean against an old juniper? Feel its energy? Mingle with its spirits? Will they be able to scramble up a sparkling granite slab to touch a limber pine? A foxtail? If not, then, what *will* they have? What *will* they have to connect themselves? To *reconnect* themselves? From where will *their* power come?

Sources and Permissions

Adams, Alice. "Favors," from *After You've Gone*. New York: Alfred A. Knopf, 1989. © 1989 by Alice Adams. Used by permission of Alfred A. Knopf, a division of Random House, Inc.

Adams, Ansel. Excerpt from *Sierra Club Bulletin*, February 1932, from *Ansel Adams: An Autobiography* by Ansel Adams Publishing Rights Trust. © 1985 by The Ansel Adams Publishing Rights Trust. By permission of Little, Brown and Company.

Allende, Isabel. Excerpt from *Daughter of Fortune* (pp. 337–342). Translated by Margaret Sayers Peden. New York: HarperCollins, 1999. © 1999 by Isabel Allende. Reprinted by permission of HarperCollins Publishers.

Austin, Mary. Excerpt from *The Land of Little Rain*. New York: Houghton Mifflin, 1903.

Ballou, Mary. Excerpt from *I Hear the Hogs in My Kitchen*. New Haven, CT: Frederick W. Beinecke, 1962. Originally published in 1852.

Bancroft, Hubert Howe. Excerpt from *California Inter Pocula*. San Francisco: The History Company, 1888.

Beesley, David. Excerpt from *Crow's Range: An Environmental History of the Sierra Nevada*. Reno: University of Nevada Press, 2004. © 2004 by University of Nevada Press. All rights reserved. Reproduced with the permission of the University of Nevada Press.

Bigler, John. Quote from *(California) Senate Journal*, 3rd session, 1852, p. 714, from *The Other Californians: Prejudice and Discrimination under Spain, Mexico, and the United States to 1920,* by Robert F. Heizer and Alan J. Almquist. Berkeley: University of California Press, 1971.

Boyle, T. Coraghessan. "Sitting on Top of the World." © 1991 by T. Coraghessan Boyle. From *Without a Hero*. New York: Viking, 1994. Used by permission of Viking Penguin, a division of Penguin Group (USA) Inc.

Brewer, William. Excerpt from *Up and Down California in 1860–1864*. Berkeley: University of California Press, 1966. Originally published in 1864.

Brower, David. Foreword to *Gentle Wilderness: The Sierra Nevada*, edited by David Brower. Sierra Club, 1967. © 1967 by The Sierra Club. Reprinted by permission of the Estate of David Brower.

Bryant, Edwin. Excerpt from *What I Saw in California*. New York: D. Appleton, 1848.

Bunnell, Lafayette. Excerpt from *Discovery of the Yosemite and the Indian War of 1851 Which Led to That Event*. Chicago: Fleming H. Revell Co., 1880.

Burnett, Peter H. Quote from the governor's annual message to the State of California, January 1851, from *The Other Californians: Prejudice and Discrimination under Spain, Mexico, and the United States to 1920*, by Robert F. Heizer and Alan J. Almquist. Berkeley: University of California Press, 1971.

Burt, Olive. Excerpt from *Jim Beckwourth, Crow Chief* (pp. 167–174). New York: Julian Messner, 1957. © 1957 by Olive Burt, renewed 1985 by Beverly B. Nichols. Reprinted by permission of Beverly B. Nichols.

Carrighar, Sally. Excerpt from *One Day on Beetle Rock*. New York: Curtis, 1943. © 1944 and renewed 1972 by Sally Carrighar. © 1943, 1944 by the Curtis Publishing Company. Used by permission of Alfred A. Knopf, a division of Random House, Inc.

Dame Shirley (Louise Amelia Knapp Smith Clappe). "Letter of January 27, 1852," from *The Pioneer* (January 1854 to December 1855). Reprinted in *The Shirley Letters: From the California Mines, 1850–1852*. Berkeley: Heyday Books, 1998, 2001.

Dane, G. Ezra. Excerpt from *Ghost Town* (pp. 1–4). New York: Alfred A. Knopf, 1941. © 1941 by G. Ezra Dane, renewed 1969 by Deborah Dane Baker and Diana Dane Dajani. Reprinted by permission of Diana Dane Dajani.

Duane, Daniel. Excerpt from *Lighting Out: A Vision of California and the Mountains*. St. Paul, MN: Graywolf Press, 1994. © 1994 by Daniel King Duane. Reprinted by permission of the author.

Everson, William. "Bride of the Bear," from *The Integral Years: Poems*

1966–1994. Santa Rosa, CA: Black Sparrow Press, 2000. Poem © 1977 by the Estate of William Everson. Reprinted by permission of the Estate of William Everson.

Font, Pedro. Excerpt from "Tuesday, April 2, 1776," from *The Expanded Diary of Pedro Font* (October 23, 1775–June 5, 1776), based on *Font's Complete Diary: A Chronicle of the Founding of San Francisco,* edited and translated by Herbert E. Bolton. *Anza's California Expeditions,* Volume IV, 1931. Berkeley: University of California Press, 1931. Translation © 1931 by Herbert Eugene Bolton. Reprinted by permission of the University of California Press.

Foote, Mary Hallock. Excerpt from *A Victorian Gentlewoman in the Far West.* San Marino, CA: Huntington Library and Art Gallery, 1972. Reproduced by permission of Huntington Library Press.

Frémont, Jessie Benton. "My Grizzly Bear," from *Mother Lode Narratives,* edited by Shirley Sargent. Ashland, OR: Lewis Osborne, 1970. Originally published in 1858.

Frémont, John C. Excerpt from *Report of the Exploring Expedition to the Rocky Mountains in the year 1842, and to Oregon and California in the years 1843–'44,* from *Narratives of Exploration and Adventure,* edited by Allan Nevins. New York: Longmans, Green and Co., 1956. Originally published as *The Life of Col. John Charles Fremont and His Narrative of Explorations and Adventures in Kansas, Nebraska, Oregon and California.* New York: Miller, Orton, and Mulligan, 1856.

Gilligan, David. Excerpt from "Prologue: Magic in the World," from *The Secret Sierra.* Bishop, CA: Spotted Dog Press, 2000. © 2000 by David Gilligan. Reprinted by permission of Spotted Dog Press.

Gould, Janice. "Late Summer in the Sierra," from *Weber Studies: Voices and Viewpoints of the Contemporary West.* Ogden, UT: Weber State University, Fall 1995. © 1995 by Janice Gould. Reprinted by permission of the author.

Greeley, Horace. Excerpt from *An Overland Journey from New York to San Francisco, in the Summer of 1859.* New York: Saxton, Barker, 1860.

Greenwood, Grace (Sara Jane Lippincott). "Eight Days in the Yosemite," *New York Times,* July 27, 1872.

Harte, Bret. "The Luck of Roaring Camp," from *The Luck of Roaring Camp, and Other Sketches.* Boston: Fields, Osgood, and Co., 1870. Reprinted in *Bret Harte's Gold Rush,* edited by Reuben Margolin. Berkeley: Heyday Books, 1996.

Hopkins, Sarah Winnemucca. Excerpt from *Life Among the Piutes: Their Wrongs and Claims.* New York: G.P. Putnam's Sons, 1883.

Hotchkiss, Bill. "Indian Summer," from *Climb to the High Country*. New York: W. W. Norton, 1978. © 1989 by Bill Hotchkiss. Reprinted by permission of the author.

Houston, James D. Excerpt from *Snow Mountain Passage*. New York: Harcourt, 2001. © 2001 by James D. Houston. Endpaper map © 2001 by David Lindroth, Inc. Used by permission of Alfred A. Knopf, a division of Random House, Inc.

Houston, Jeanne Wakatsuki, and James D. Houston. Excerpts from *Farewell to Manzanar.* New York: Houghton Mifflin, 1973. © 1973 by James D. Houston. Reprinted by permission of Houghton Mifflin Harcourt Publishing Company. All rights reserved.

Hutchings, James. Excerpt from *Scenes of Wonder and Curiosity in California.* San Francisco: Hutchings and Rosenfield, 1860.

Joseph, William. Excerpts from "Football Big-Time" and "Football Free-for-All," from *The Way We Lived: California Indian Stories, Songs, and Reminiscences,* edited by Malcolm Margolin. Berkeley: Heyday Books, 1981, 1993. Originally published in "Nisenan Texts and Dictionary," by Hans Uldall and William Shipley. *University of California Publications in Linguistics* 46 (1966).

Kerouac, Jack. Excerpt from *The Dharma Bums* by Jack Kerouac and display memory. New York: Penguin, 1958. © 1958 by Jack Kerouac, renewed 1986 by Stella Kerouac and Jan Kerouac. Used by permission of Penguin, a division of Penguin Group (USA) Inc.

King, Clarence. Excerpt from *Mountaineering in the Sierra Nevada.* Boston: James Osgood and Co., 1872. Revised and reprinted in 1902.

Kingston, Maxine Hong. Excerpt from *China Men.* New York: Alfred A. Knopf, 1980. © 1977, 1978, 1979, 1980 by Maxine Hong Kingston. Used by permission of Alfred A. Knopf, a division of Random House, Inc.

Knudson, Tom. Excerpts from *The Sierra in Peril*, from *The Sacramento Bee*, June 9–13, 1991. © 1991 by The Sacramento Bee. Reprinted by permission of The Sacramento Bee.

The Konkow. "Old Gambler's Song," from *The Way We Lived: California Indian Stories, Songs, and Reminiscences,* edited by Malcolm Margolin. Berkeley: Heyday Books, 1981, 1993. Originally published in *Tribes of California,* by Stephen Powers. Berkeley: University of California Press, 1976.

LeConte, Joseph. Excerpt from *A Journal of Ramblings through the High*

Sierra of California. Originally published in 1875. Reprinted by the Sierra Club in 1960.

London, Jack. "All Gold Cañon," *The Century Magazine* (November 1905).

The Maidu. "Mountain Lion and His Children," from *The Maidu Indian Myths and Stories of Hanc'ibyjim*, by William Shipley. Berkeley: Heyday Books, 1991. Translation © 1991 by William Shipley.

Medeiros, Joe. "The Power of Trees." Written especially for this anthology by Medeiros, 2008. © 2010 by Joe Medeiros. Reprinted by permission of the author.

Melendez, Maria. "Clan Markings, Stanislaus National Forest, 1980s." Written especially for this anthology by Melendez, 2008. © 2010 by Maria Melendez. Reprinted by permission of the author.

Mighels, Ella Sterling Cummins. "Portrait of a California Girl." San Francisco: Harr Wagner Publishing Co., 1918. Written in 1885 and originally published in *Literary California*.

Miller, Joaquin. "Yosemite," from *The Complete Poetical Works of Joaquin Miller*. San Francisco: Whitaker and Ray, 1902.

Muir, John. "A Wind Storm in the Forests of the Yuba." *Scribner's Monthly* (November 1878). Reprinted in *The Mountains of California*, by John Muir. New York: The Century Co., 1894. Excerpt from *The Yosemite*. New York: The Century Co., 1912.

Murguía, Alejandro. "Josefa of Downieville: The Obscure Life and Notable Death of a Chicana in Gold Rush California," from *The Medicine of Memory: A Mexica Clan in California*. Austin: University of Texas Press, 2002. © 2002 by Alejandro Murguía. By permission of the University of Texas Press.

Navarro, Ramón Gil. Excerpt from *Los Chilenos en California*, from *We Were 49ers!*, translated and edited by Edwin A. Beilharz and Carlos Lopez. Los Angeles: Ward Ritchie Press, 1976. Originally published in 1853.

Norris, Frank. Excerpt from *McTeague*. New York: Doubleday, Page and Co., 1899.

Obata, Chiura. Newspaper series, 1928. (In 1928, Chiura Obata published a series of five newspaper articles in an unidentified Japanese newspaper.) Selection reprinted by permission of Kimi Kodani Hill.

Ortiz, Bev. Excerpt from *It Will Live Forever: Traditional Yosemite Indian Acorn Preparation*. Berkeley: Heyday Books, 1991. © 2001 by Bev Ortiz.

Potts, Marie. Excerpt from *The Northern Maidu*. Happy Camp, CA: Naturegraph Publishers, Inc., 1977. © 1977 by Marie Potts. Reprinted by permission of Naturegraph Publishers, Inc.

Reed, Ishmael. "Holiday Train to Reno," from *New and Collected Poems, 1964–2006*. New York: Carroll and Graf, 2007. © 1988, 2000, 2006 by Ishmael Reed. Reprinted by permission of the author.

Reisner, Marc. Excerpt from *A Dangerous Place: California's Unsettling Fate*. New York: Pantheon, 2003. © 2003 by D. L. Mott and the Estate of Marc P. Reisner. Used by permission of Pantheon Books, a division of Random House, Inc.

Rexroth, Kenneth. "Blues," from *The Collected Shorter Poems*. New York: New Directions, 1949. © 1949 by Kenneth Rexroth. Reprinted by permission of New Directions Publishing Corp.

Ridge, John Rollin. Excerpt from *The Life and Adventures of Joaquín Murieta, the Celebrated California Bandit*. San Francisco: W. B. Cooke and Company, 1854.

Rose, Wendy. "Questions for a Miwok Uncle: Ahwahneechee Man," from *The Dirt Is Red Here: Art and Poetry from Native California,* edited by Margaret Dubin. Berkeley: Heyday Books, 2002. © 1993 by Wendy Rose. Reprinted by permission of the author.

Ross, Sylvia. "Tribal Identity Grade Three," from *The Dirt Is Red Here: Art and Poetry from Native California,* edited by Margaret Dubin. Berkeley: Heyday Books, 2002. Poem © 1998 by Sylvia Ross. Reprinted by permission of the author.

Royce, Sarah Eleanor. Excerpt from *A Frontier Lady*. New Haven, CT: Yale University Press, 1932. © 1932 by Yale University Press. Reprinted by permission of Yale University Press.

Smith, Jordan Fisher. "American Woman." Written especially for this anthology by Smith, 2008. © 2010 by Jordan Fisher Smith. Used by permission of the author and the Sandra Dijkstra Literary Agency. Excerpt from "It Never Rains in California," from *Nature Noir: A Park Ranger's Patrol in the Sierra*. New York: Houghton Mifflin, 2005. © 2005 by Jordan Fisher Smith. Reprinted by permission of Houghton Mifflin Company. All rights reserved.

Snyder, Gary. "The Ark of the Sierra," from *Back on the Fire: Essays*. Emeryville, CA: Shoemaker and Hoard, 2007. © 2008 by Gary Snyder. Reprinted by permission of Counterpoint. Excerpts from "The Porous World" and "Language Goes Two Ways," from *A Place in Space: Ethics, Aesthetics, and Watersheds*. Washington, D.C.: Counterpoint, 1995. © 2008 by Gary Snyder. Reprinted by permission of Counterpoint.

"What Happened Here Before," from *Turtle Island*. New York: New Directions, 1974. © 1974 by Gary Snyder. Reprinted by permission of New Directions Publishing Corp.

Starr, Kevin. Excerpt from *Americans and the California Dream, 1850–1915* (pp. 172–191). New York: Oxford, 1973. © 1973 by Oxford University Press, Inc. Reprinted by permission of Oxford University Press, Inc.

Stegner, Wallace. Excerpt from *Angle of Repose*. New York: Doubleday and Company, Inc., 1971. © 1971 by Wallace Stegner. Used by permission of Doubleday, a division of Random House, Inc.

Stevenson, Robert Louis. Excerpt from *Across the Plains*. New York: Charles Scribner's Sons, 1892.

Stewart, Jack. "My Mountain," from *The Way We Lived: California Indian Stories, Songs, and Reminiscences*, edited by Malcolm Margolin. Berkeley: Heyday Books, 1981, 1993. Originally published in "Two Paiute Autobiographies," by Julian Steward. *University of California Publications in American Archaeology and Ethnology* 33 (1934), p. 423.

Taylor, Bayard. Excerpt from *Eldorado: Adventures in the Path of Empire*. Berkeley: Heyday Books, 2000. Originally published in 1850, New York: G. P. Putnam.

Thoreau, Henry David. Excerpt from *The Journal of Henry David Thoreau*, Volume I, 1962, New York: Dover. Originally published in 1852. Reprinted in *Gold Rush: A Literary Exploration*, edited by Michael Kowalewski. Berkeley: Heyday Books, 1997.

Twain, Mark. "The Celebrated Jumping Frog of Calaveras County," from *The Celebrated Jumping Frog of Calaveras County, and Other Sketches*. New York: C. H. Webb, 1867. Originally published in 1865. Excerpt from *Roughing It*, from *Gold Rush: A Literary Exploration*, edited by Michael Kowalewski. Berkeley: Heyday Books, 1997. Originally published in 1872, Hartford, CT: American Publishing Company. Reprinted in 1906, New York: Harper and Brothers.

The Washo. "Weh Hai Ge Ge A," from *Wa She Shu: A Washo Tribal History*. Reno: Inter-Tribal Council of Nevada, 1976. © 1976 by the Inter-Tribal Council of Nevada, Inc. Reprinted by permission of the Inter-Tribal Council of Nevada, Inc.

Whitman, Walt. Excerpt from "Passage to India," from *Leaves of Grass*. Philadelphia: David McKay, 1888.

The Yokuts. "The Origin of the Sierra Nevadas and Coast Range" and "Prayer for Good Fortune" from *The Literature of California: Native American Beginnings to 1945*, edited by Jack Hicks, James D.

Houston, Maxine Hong Kingston, and Al Young. "The Origin of the Sierra Nevadas and Coast Range" was originally published in *Myths and Legends of California and the Old Southwest,* by Katharine Berry Judson. Chicago: A. C. McClurg, 1912. "Prayer for Good Fortune" was originally published in *Handbook of the Indians of California,* by Alfred L. Kroeber. Washington, D.C.: Bureau of American Ethnology, Bulletin 78, 1925.

Zwinger, Ann. Excerpt from *Yosemite: Valley of Thunder.* San Diego: Tehabi Books, 1996. © 1996 by Tehabi Books. Reprinted by permission of Dalmatian Press.

Author Index

Acknowledgments

Our deepest appreciation is extended to the Sierra College Friends of the Library, whose extremely generous donation and ongoing support was instrumental in establishing the new Sierra College Press. The Sierra College Natural History Museum and Rocklin Historical Society also provided indispensable financial support and treasured camaraderie. We are profoundly grateful to our good friends on the boards of directors of the Friends of the Library, the Natural History Museum, and the Rocklin Historical Society.

We offer our sincere gratitude to the Sierra College Press Board of Directors. We applaud their diligent efforts to develop what we believe is the first community college academic press in the United States. In addition to publishing books, the press produces three electronic journals: *Snowy Range Reflections: A Journal of Sierra Nevada History and Biography; The Journal of the Sierra College Natural History Museum;* and the *Sierra Journal*, a literary journal.

From Rick Heide

"It's impossible to fall off mountains you fool," Jack Kerouac writes in *The Dharma Bums*. Yet in 1968—young and reckless—this fool *was*, in fact, free-falling off Tresidder Peak in Yosemite's high country. Turning midair, clawing toward the face, about seventy-five feet into the fall I finally clutched granite. Grasping fingers left ten feet of bloody tracks but slowed my descent. I was clinging by my fingertips to a small outcropping over the abyss and certain death. My army buddy, Gary Stensen, and community college friends, "Big Al" Judson and Bob Lee—risking *their* lives—rapidly traversed narrow ledges to pull me from my precarious perch. This fool owes those friends over forty more years of a charmed life.

That charmed life has encompassed frequent visits to my favorite part of the world—the Sierra Nevada. In recent years, I have even lived in its foothills. A few who have shared Sierra magic with me include: Steve Heide, Fred Jones, Kurt Jensen, Eric Bjorndahl, the DuFlon family, the Bunkers, the Hallinans, the Petersen-McLeod-Rolley family, James Bailey, Chris Stallard, Anita Wolff, the Alvers, Beauchamps, Jameses, Smiths, and dear grandchildren—Lorenzo and Naomi Camero (and soon Jonah Lacey).

My daughter's first Sierra visit into the Hetch Hetchy backcountry came as an infant. Cedra DuFlon-Heide, now Cedra Luce, has been my beloved hiking buddy ever since. For nearly thirty years we have shared the Sierra with my cherished step-daughters, Rachel Camero and Heather Lacey. My constant companion in those decades has been my lovely wife and love-of-my-life, Debbie Pond-Heide. She now creates beautiful oil paintings of the range and has long shared with me favorite places, such as Mono Lake, Calaveras Big Trees, Hope Valley, Yosemite, and the dramatic eastern Sierra.

California community college courses, spread over ten years, and the G.I. Bill were indispensable to my finally getting a B.A. at age thirty-one, and so helping build the first full-fledged community college press in our nation holds deep personal meaning. As a relatively recent Sierra resident, getting to know Sierra stalwarts in the college's Friends of the Library and its Press's Board of Directors has enhanced the joy of helping edit this special book. I will always be grateful for the Sierra College community's enthusiasm and support for the Sierra College Press and for this anthology.

I am happy to work again with longtime friends Malcolm Margolin and Jeannine Gendar at Heyday Books and Terry Beers at Santa Clara University. All have made great contributions to California literature, through the California Legacy series and otherwise. Thanks also to Maria Melendez for her transcendent poem and her patience; to Joe Medeiros for his drawings, love of trees, stewardship of the amazing Devils Postpile, and oneness with the Sierra; and to Lorraine Rath for the splendid book cover design. Our thanks and deepest appreciation to our other friends at Heyday Books: Gayle Wattawa for her support and aiding our focus, Lisa K. Manwill for skillfully polishing the book, and Lillian Fleer, Susan Pi, and Julian Segal for their expertise and enthusiasm in outreach, marketing, publicity, and sales.

Gary Noy had the original idea for this book, informed by his encyclopedic knowledge and love of Sierra Nevada literature and history. Working with him has been a privilege and pleasure—and will be only the first of several co-editing projects. Along the "trail," he has also become a treasured friend.

From Joe Medeiros

It is not by coincidence that the word "inspiration" derives from the Latin *inspirare,* meaning "to breathe." Whether one is inspired by divine or supernatural forces or simply by the sheer magnificence or elegance of the landscape itself, the result is the same.

My first "breath" of the Sierra stemmed from an insatiable desire to escape the stifling summer heat of the San Joaquin Valley. As the young son of a dairy farmer, I begged to join the Boy Scouts. "They camp!" I told my puzzled parents. "They sleep in tents under tall trees in the mountains!" Mom and Dad were horrified by the thought of sleeping on the ground—the same ground they swore they would never allow their children to suffer. But they would eventually relent. My first camping experience was in the foothills along the Merced River, close to where John Muir herded sheep and gazed at the nearby mountain range. It wasn't long before I was working all summer as camp staff along the Stanislaus River. Backpacking was what we did on our days off, and the Sierra drew me in like a powerful magnet.

From summer camp to seasonal work as a National Park ranger-naturalist, I couldn't stay away from this glorious range. My daughters Melissa and Erin happily shared many mountain summers running barefoot and carrying packs filled with the day's essentials. They followed along behind my naturalist-guided walks helping visitors learn the names of the wildflowers and the types of rocks. I suppose I never tired of the sleeping bag, and I still spend dozens of nights each year on the same ground that my parents abhorred.

I wish I could claim more credit for this marvelous piece of literary work, but I can't. I have enjoyed riding this wave on the shoulders of my good friends; my colleague Gary Noy hatched this idea and sought the expert advice of Rick Heide. Gary accumulated a vast collection of Sierrana, and then the daunting task of sorting and choosing began. Rick's experience, eagle eye, and tireless enthusiasm kept us all headed in the right direction. A longstanding association with Malcolm Margolin led us all to Heyday Books, where we were met with openness, kindness, and especially patience.

A constant source of motivation and reinforcement came from an interdisciplinary course that Gary and I co-coordinated for many years at Sierra College. With John Muir's Range of Light at its focus, this course explored the range from its natural core to its economic resources, and to its countless examples as a source of human inspiration.

Finally, while hundreds of friends and associates are clearly part of my Sierran gestalt, there is no one other than my wife, Lynnette, who enables me to fully realize the inspiration of the Sierra. She is like the exotic spice that enhances the flavor of food so that its full and true value can be savored. Together we have sauntered countless Sierran miles, spent our evenings under starlit skies, and discovered the power of wildness. We have learned freedom in the Sierra. We have found peace in the Sierra. We have healed in the Sierra. I can't thank her enough.

From Gary Noy

I am very grateful to my father, the late Howard Noy, for introducing me to the Sierra Nevada backcountry on an unforgettable camping trip to the Emigrant Wilderness Area in 1962. I can still smell the sweet fragrance of the sage, hear the rattling chirp of thousands of grasshoppers, and feel the gentle breezes of that magical Sierra summer in the shadow of Leavitt Peak. At that moment, I began an endless love affair with the range.

This love has led to treasured moments—being marooned on a High Sierra granite knob during a massive hailstorm, leaving an indelible memory and many welts; fishing at Woods Lake near Carson Pass when an osprey dive-bombed a trout ten feet in front of me; observing a herd of hundreds of elk grazing at sunset near Big Pine in the Eastern Sierra; staring up at the great granite monolith of El Capitan one warm October evening and seeing dozens of twinkling lights, the lanterns of rock climbers suspended in their slings for a night high on the sheer wall; and many more—recollections forever etched in my mind.

My favorite Sierra Nevada memories are of two special young ladies from Sonora who entered my life and took up permanent residence in my heart: Brook Allen and Sooner Allen. This book is for them.

Many of these mountain adventures have been shared by my old buddy (and as good a friend as one could possibly have), "my identical twin brother," Tedmond Leung. Thanks, Murph.

I am very thankful for the guidance provided by Heyday Books, in particular the wisdom and counsel of Malcolm Margolin, publisher, who was especially influential in helping us define the Sierra College Press mission, and Gayle Wattawa, editor, who shepherded us through the development of this anthology with grace, good humor, and excellent advice.

I am forever indebted to Terry Beers, Professor of English and Director of Santa Clara University's California Legacy series, for his collegial spirit and hospitality. I look forward to a long and happy relationship with Terry and the university.

My thanks to our friend Robert Hanna, for his wholehearted encouragement and endless enthusiasm.

I would be remiss if I did not express my profound appreciation and gratitude to my friend and valued associate, Joe Medeiros. Not only did Joe contribute to this anthology the splendid illustrations and a powerful essay, but he remains the single best example of the "Sierra Spirit" that I have ever encountered. His passionate mixture of continuing wonderment at the range, deep knowledge of and respect for its natural processes, and concern about the Sierra's future is inspirational.

Lastly, my special thanks to my remarkable friend and colleague Rick Heide for an extremely pleasurable collaboration and many long conversations about life, literature, and basketball.

And, finally, we offer our deepest respect to the people of the Sierra Nevada, whose trials and triumphs were shaped by the range over thousands of years, and who, in return, continue to influence the splendid setting of today—the extraordinary illuminated landscape of the Range of Light.

About the Editors

Gary Noy is the director of the Center for Sierra Nevada Studies at Sierra Community College in Rocklin, California. A Sierra Nevada native and the son of a hardrock gold miner, he is also the author of *Distant Horizon: Documents from the Nineteenth-Century American West.* Gary holds graduate degrees from U.C. Berkeley and Sacramento State University. The Oregon-California Trails Association, a national historical organization, named Gary the "Educator of the Year" in 2006.

A longtime hiker of the Sierra Nevada, Rick Heide now lives in its foothills. Although a mediocre basketball player in his fifty-year "career" of pickup games, he won two college All American awards…in journalism, that is. He was a founder of the underground press Berkeley Tribe before earning a B.A. from U.C. Berkeley and an M.A. from the University of London. As owner of a Berkeley typesetting firm, Rick helped produce thousands of publications as well as co-published six books with Heyday. His first anthology, *Under the Fifth Sun: Latino Literature from California*, won a 2003 American Book Award.

SIERRA COLLEGE PRESS

In 2002, the Sierra College Press was formed to publish *Standing Guard: Telling Our Stories* as part of the Standing Guard Project's examination of Japanese-American internment during World War II. Since then Sierra College Press has grown into the first complete academic press operated by a community college in the United States.

The mission of the Sierra College Press is to inform and inspire scholars, students, and general readers by disseminating ideas, knowledge, and academic scholarship of value concerning the Sierra Nevada region. The Sierra College Press endeavors to reach beyond the library, laboratory, and classroom to promote and examine this unique geography.

For more information, please visit www.sierracollege.edu/press.

Editor-in-Chief: Gary Noy

Board of Directors: Bright Rope, Rebecca Bocchicchio, Julie Bruno, Keely Carroll, Kerrie Cassidy, Charles Dailey, Frank DeCourten, Daniel DeFoe, Danielle DeFoe, Tom Fillebrown, Brian Haley, Robert Hanna, Rick Heide, Jay Hester, Joe Medeiros, Lynn Medeiros, Sue Michaels, Mike Price, Randy Snook, Barbara Vineyard

Editorial Advisory Board: Terry Beers, David Beesley, Patrick Ettinger, Janice Forbes, Tom Killion, Tom Knudson, Gary Kurutz, John Muir Laws, Beverly Lewis, Roger Lokey, Malcolm Margolin, Mark McLaughlin, jesikah maria ross, Michael Sanford, Lee Stetson, Catherine Stifter

Special thanks to our major financial supporters: Sierra College Friends of the Library, Rocklin Historical Society, Sierra College Natural History Museum

A California Legacy Book

Santa Clara University and Heyday Books are pleased to publish the California Legacy series, vibrant and relevant writings drawn from California's past and present.

Santa Clara University—founded in 1851 on the site of the eighth of California's original twenty-one missions—is the oldest institution of higher learning in the state. A Jesuit institution, it is particularly aware of its contribution to California's cultural heritage and its responsibility to preserve and celebrate that heritage.

Heyday Books, founded in 1974, specializes in critically acclaimed books on California literature, history, natural history, and ethnic studies.

Books in the California Legacy series appear as anthologies, single author collections, reprints of important books, and original works. Taken together, these volumes bring readers a new perspective on California's cultural life, a perspective that honors diversity and finds great pleasure in the eloquence of human expression.

Series Editor: Terry Beers
Publisher: Malcolm Margolin

Advisory Committee: Stephen Becker, William Deverell, Charles Faulhaber, David Fine, Steven Gilbar, Ron Hansen, Gerald Haslam, Robert Hass, Jack Hicks, Timothy Hodson, Jeanne Wakatsuki Houston, Maxine Hong Kingston, Frank LaPena, Ursula K. Le Guin, Jeff Lustig, Ishmael Reed, Alan Rosenus, Robert Senkewicz, Gary Snyder, Kevin Starr, Richard Walker, Alice Waters, Jennifer Watts, Al Young

Thanks to the English Department at Santa Clara University and to Regis McKenna for their support of the California Legacy series.

For more on California Legacy titles, events, or other information, please visit www.californialegacy.org.

Other California Legacy Books

Califauna: A Literary Field Guide
Edited by Terry Beers and Emily Elrod

California Poetry: From the Gold Rush to the Present
Edited by Dana Gioia, Chryss Yost, and Jack Hicks

Eldorado: Adventures in the Path of Empire
Bayard Taylor

Essential Muir
Edited with an Introduction by Fred D. White

Inlandia: A Literary Journey through California's Inland Empire
Edited by Gayle Wattawa with an Introduction by Susan Straight

Mark Twain's San Francisco
Edited with a New Introduction by Bernard Taper

No Place for a Puritan: The Literature of California's Deserts
Edited by Ruth Nolan

One Day on Beetle Rock
Sally Carrighar

The Shirley Letters: From the California Mines, 1851-1852
Louise Amelia Knapp Smith Clappe

Under the Fifth Sun: Latino Literature in California
Edited by Rick Heide

Unfolding Beauty: Celebrating California's Landscapes
Edited with an Introduction by Terry Beers

Unsettling the West: Eliza Farnham and Georgiana Bruce Kirby
in Frontier California
JoAnn Levy

HEYDAY INSTITUTE

Since its founding in 1974, Heyday Books has occupied a unique niche in the publishing world, specializing in books that foster an understanding of the history, literature, art, environment, social issues, and culture of California and the West. We are a 501(c)(3) nonprofit organization based in Berkeley, California, serving a wide range of people and audiences.

We are grateful for the generous funding we've received for our publications and programs during the past year from foundations and more than three hundred and fifty individual donors. Major supporters include:

Anonymous; Audubon California; Judith and Phillip Auth; Barona Band of Mission Indians; B.C.W. Trust III; S. D. Bechtel, Jr. Foundation; Barbara and Fred Berensmeier; Berkeley Civic Arts Program and Civic Arts Commission; Joan Berman; Peter and Mimi Buckley; Lewis and Sheana Butler; Butler Koshland Fund; California State Coastal Conservancy; California State Library; Joanne Campbell; Keith Campbell Foundation; Candelaria Fund; John and Nancy Cassidy Family Foundation, through Silicon Valley Community Foundation; Christensen Fund;; Community Futures Collective; Compton Foundation, Inc.; Creative Work Fund; Lawrence Crooks; Ida Rae Egli; Donald and Janice Elliott, in honor of David Elliott, through Silicon Valley Community Foundation; Evergreen Foundation; Federated Indians of Graton Rancheria; Mark and Tracy Ferron; Furthur Foundation; George Gamble; Wallace Alexander Gerbode Foundation; Richard & Rhoda Goldman Fund; Ben Graber, in honor of Sandy Graber; Evelyn & Walter Haas, Jr. Fund; Walter & Elise Haas Fund; James and Coke Hallowell; Sandra and Chuck Hobson; James Irvine Foundation; Marty and Pamela Krasney; Robert and Karen Kustel, in honor of Bruce Kelley; Guy Lampard and Suzanne Badenhoop; LEF Foundation; Michael McCone; Moore Family Fund; National Endowment for the Arts; National Park Service; Organize Training Center; David and Lucile Packard Foundation; Patagonia; Pease Family Fund, in honor of Bruce Kelley; Resources Legacy Fund; Alan Rosenus; San Francisco Foundation; San Manuel Band of Mission Indians; Deborah Sanchez; Contee and Maggie Seely; James B. Swinerton; Swinerton Family Fund; Taproot Foundation; Thendara Foundation; Lisa Van Cleef and Mark Gunson; Marion Weber; Albert and Susan Wells; Peter Booth Wiley; and Yocha Dehe Wintun Nation.

Heyday Institute Board of Directors:
Michael McCone (chair), Barbara Boucke, Peter Dunckel, Karyn Y. Flynn, Theresa Harlan, Leanne Hinton, Nancy Hom, Susan Ives, Bruce Kelley, Marty Krasney, Guy Lampard, Katharine Livingston, R. Jeffrey Lustig, Lee Swenson, Jim Swinerton, Lisa Van Cleef, Lynne Withey.

For more information about Heyday Institute, our publications and programs, please visit our website at www.heydaybooks.com.